D1473574

Encyclopaedia of the
MODERN
ROYAL NAVY
Including The Fleet Air Arm & Royal Marines

Encyclopaedia of the
MODERN
ROYAL NAVY
Including The Fleet Air Arm & Royal Marines

Paul Beaver

NAVAL INSTITUTE PRESS

Title pages Superb, *also known as 'Super Bee', in quiet waters* (RN).

Published and distributed in the United States of America and
Canada by the Naval Institute Press, Annapolis, Maryland 21402

Designed by Tim McPhee

Library of Congress Catalog Card No: 82–62890 ●

ISBN 0–87021–830–1

Printed in Great Britain

This edition is authorized for sale only in the United States and
its territories and possessions, and Canada.

Contents

Introduction

There could not have been a more interesting and yet challenging period in which to have been writing a book devoted to the Royal Navy since 1945. Not only have we seen the publication of two White Papers which have drastically altered thinking on the role of the modern RN, but the Falklands Operation to regain the British islands in the South Atlantic has led to the first operational use of so many naval systems, weapons and techniques that it is not possible to list them all here. A full appraisal will have to await a second edition.

As a result of the Government's decision to lead the RN away from the more traditional roles in surface warfare and as a result of the several lessons learned in the South Atlantic, the reader will find a much different Navy to that of, say, ten years ago. Yet, the professionalism has probably never been better and the standards never higher. One only has to recall the moving and poignant newsreel films from San Carlos Water and Falkland Sound.

However the modern Royal Navy is not just warships, support vessels, aircraft even, it is a combination of all the essential elements needed to safeguard British (and world) interests at sea or near the sea. The modern RN would not be complete without the Royal Marines, the WRNS, the QARNNS, the Royal Fleet Auxiliary Service and the Royal Maritime Auxiliary Service. In this book, I have tried to bring together all the elements 'under one roof'. There have been problems—the Falklands came just as the final pages were being typed, so there were many corrections; it is not easy to compile a work of this type at the best of times!

The work has nevertheless been rewarding and most interesting. The Royal Navy as a whole has been most helpful in providing the facilities necessary to see the Service operating, functioning and living, at home and in the final overseas bases, like Hong Kong and Gibraltar. To get the feel of the modern RN, I did several things which I would not normally have considered in the line of duty: sleeping in a ditch with a Company of RM Commandos in the middle of winter; speeding through Hong Kong harbour in a hovercraft; flying a high speed sortie in a Lynx or doing 'rounds' with Matron in a Naval Hospital.

The co-operation which I received from all to whom I talked is most gratefully acknowledged. I have been assisted through all the possible traps posed by security, ignorance and enthusiasm by a charming group of people. All the errors in the text must, of course, remain my responsibility but I would like to thank all those who have helped me, particularly Peter Hicks, Michael Hill and Tim Hunt of DPR(RN)'s staff, Lieutenant Commander Jan Larcombe and Chief Petty Officer Gorman of the FAA, Captain David Tong and Sergeants Haynes and Jones of the RM, Second Officer Georgette Purches of the WRNS and Cyril Quayle of Marine Services. To the many others around the world—thanks.

During the preparation of this encyclopaedia I have drawn on a number of published sources, of which several have been outstanding: *Jane's Fighting Ships* and *Jane's Weapons Systems; NAVY international* and *Ships Monthly*. In addition, various commercial concerns have assisted greatly, and the aid given by British Aerospace, British Shipbuilders, Ferranti, Westland and Richard Dunston has been especially welcome.

The Royal Navy has a long and glorious history and I have no doubt that it is in such capable hands today, that there should be no problems which it will not be able to overcome. Rule Britannia!

Paul Beaver
Sevenoaks
June 1982

Left *The first landing of a Sea Harrier on* Fearless, *during operations in San Carlos Water, Falkland Islands* (RN).

The Royal Navy since 1945

Like most sections of British society, the Royal Navy (RN) has not been quite the same since the end of the Second World War. That great conflict saw such widespread changes in the Navy, its ideas, its equipment, its ships but most of all in its men, that it can be truly said to be have been changed out of all recognition from the inter-war period.

The greatest single factor was the sheer increase of manpower, the influx of the Royal Naval Volunteer Reserve (RNVR)—the temporary gentlemen of the *Cruel Sea* saga. Mainly seconded to small ships and the Air Branch—the Fleet Air Arm, as it was popularly if a little inaccurately known—RNVR officers and ratings had provided the backbone of the world's second largest fleet when the war ended in 1945. That year saw many, the vast majority in fact, demobbed* and many of the warships in which they had served so gallantly, paid-off. Most arms of the RN were pared down to the bare minimum, from Coastal Forces to battleships, and even the new capital ships, the aircraft carriers, were rapidly taken out of service.

The war had seen the eclipse of the battleship and the rise of the carrier and, by August 1945, the RN could boast over 50 of the latter; sadly postwar austerity and a general rush, 'hell for leather', into peace saw the rapid decline of the 'flat top'. By 1947, only three remained active—*Implacable*, *Ocean* and *Triumph*.

The naval scene world-wide was changing rapidly although it would be only half a decade before the Cold War would begin in earnest leading to a rapid rebuilding plan by the seafaring nations of the West, or Free World as it was becoming known. Before this could take place, there were changes in the everyday life of the Navy. Despite the demobilisation of RNVR and other temporary personnel, the minority who stayed were quickly commissioned into the regular RN—the 'Rodney'. This led to an

* Demobilised or returned to civilian life.

Left Repulse *off the Scottish coast in 1981* (RN).

amazingly self-defeating idea to segregate officers into a 'wet' and 'dry' list so that those on the former were assured, all things being equal, of gaining command at sea; their counterparts on the 'dry' list, however, were destined never to command a ship. This came as a savage blow to many war-experienced naval officers. Their ability to command men and organise fighting units could not have been questioned judging by wartime records.

So, as the Empire gave way to Commonwealth, the RN began to adopt a new role, that of obligations under the large number of treaties drawn up postwar and the covering of the numerous guerrilla wars in colonies seeking independence. The foremost of the treaty obligations was the North Atlantic Alliance or NATO (North Atlantic Treaty Organisation). The growing tension in South-East Asia following the assistance given by the Allies to the Communist-led 'popular' resistance movements led to growing discontent in former colonial territories. The RN played a major part in the liberation from Japanese hands of many areas, particularly Hong Kong, Indo-China and Dutch East India. Many thousands of British and Commonwealth prisoners of war (POWs) were evacuated in various warships, including aircraft carriers, of the British Pacific Fleet. Besides POWs, there were a large number of internees from the prewar civilian populations to be released but the jubilation of liberation did not stay long in the Far East. Not only did pirates find a new freedom to operate on the civilian sea traffic which suddenly multiplied, but many former resistance fighters became 'Freedom' fighters.

By far the most serious area of tension was China where there was all-out civil war. Although the country was in theory one of the big five allies, the internal problems which followed the Japanese surrender led to a Communist take-over. Britain, like many western nations, had considerable commercial interests in China prewar and when the situation became too risky for UK citizens to remain in the towns and cities being caught between the

The RN frigate Amethyst *arrives in Hong Kong with shell damage bearing witness to her ordeal in Chinese waters* (courtesy Rear Admiral Bolt).

warring factions, the Navy went in to assist evacuation. In 1949, the frigate *Amethyst* was moving along the Yangtse River to take regular supplies to the British Embassy at Nanking. On April 20 the warship was fired upon by Communist artillery and forced aground. There then followed three months of protracted negotiations with the Communist authorities who were just a few months away from total victory and the formation of the People's Republic of China. Despite the fact that the initial Chinese assault had cost the lives of 17 of the ship's company, the Commanding Officer, Lieutenant Commander John Kerans, RN, decided to try and break for the high seas, 140 nm (259 km) away. The escape was both daring and hazardous, not only because of the hostile fire, but also because the Admiralty was not keen on an attempt being made. The *Amethyst* reached open water on July 8; her signal on the occasion has gone down in history as a proud moment for Britain's Senior Service: 'Have rejoined the Fleet. No damages or casualties. God save the King.'

Without doubt this action boosted morale at an important time because, within 12 months, the RN was again in action in that troubled area with a Communist government. On June 24 1950, the North Koreans crossed the 1945 frontier line into South Korea, taking almost everyone by surprise. Within 24 hours, British naval forces in the Far East were put at the disposal of the United Nations, or rather for practical reasons, the United States government. The RN's largest warship in the area was the light fleet carrier *Triumph* which had just begun passage from Japan to the UK. In addition there were cruisers and destroyers at several

locations, including Hong Kong.

This was to be the beginning of a sustained RN presence off Korea for the next three years during which the naval blockade of the Korean coast was maintained in all weathers by various navies, including those of Australia, Canada and the United States. Britain's main contribution was a light fleet carrier permanently offshore, apart from re-storing, to operate air strikes against ground and sea targets. The carriers involved were *Theseus*, *Ocean*, *Glory* and *Sydney* (RAN). The main task of naval blockade, to prevent coastal shipping moving men and materials for the other side, worked well and, following the peace treaty in 1953, the RN maintained warships in the area to monitor the peace for several years.

On the technological side, the Korean War did not hamper the developing Fleet, but rather accelerated certain aspects of it. Nowhere were the innovations more obvious than in the naval aviation field. The advent of the jet aircraft in carriers following the successful trials flown by Lieutenant Commander Eric Brown in December 1945, paved the way for jet air squadrons. The progress was slow at first until two amazing inventions made the whole concept of carrier flying a thousand times safer. The angled-deck principle invented by Captain (later Rear Admiral) Dennis Cambell and Mr Lewis Boddington of Farnborough was the first of these. It allowed the free take-off and landing of aircraft without the need to protect parked aircraft with a crash barrier. To assist the actual landing, Commander (later Rear Admiral) Nick Goodhart invented the mirror deck landing sight which allowed an incoming pilot to line himself up on the flight deck and then execute a safe landing without need of outside assistance.

The first operational jet squadron was No 800 (commanded by Lieutenant Commander George Baldwin) which commissioned the Supermarine Attacker aircraft into service in 1951. The first helicopter, a Sikorsky R-4B, had already been successfully landed on the frigate *Helmsdale* in 1946 by Lieutenant Alan Bristow, RN; the turbo-prop aircraft joined the Fleet in 1953 as slowly the carrier fleet and naval aviation was built up again. The RNVR Air Branch was reactivated until 1957 when the government of the day thought that manned aircraft would soon be totally replaced by missiles. It was during this period that the two most famous postwar carriers were launched and commissioned—*Eagle* (1952) and *Ark Royal* (1955).

At sea, the last of the cruisers were still on station in the Far East, Mediterranean and Caribbean. With no major rivals afloat except in the USN, the RN decided that most of the cruiser force could be discarded. By 1950, there were only about ten left in commission and although three new hulls were under construction their completion had been suspended in 1946. Off Korea cruisers, like the *Belfast*, had been used most successfully as flagships and to provide bombardment of shore areas. Their traditional scouting role had, of course, been taken over by radar and naval aircraft. The last of the conventional cruisers were the 6-in (15.2-cm) *Tiger* Class, of which two were converted into anti-submarine warfare helicopter cruisers during 1965–73 and the third scrapped in 1975. Although the RN has continued to build and commission cruiser-size warships, they have long been reclassified as destroyers.

Destroyers themselves continued to evolve, the most outstanding in the early postwar years being the *Darings*. Originally, because of their size, they were classified as fleet escorts but later the term destroyer was applied. They were truly beautiful 2,800-ton warships which first appeared with the fleet in 1952, designed as leaders but quite capable of independent operations, especially in the Far East. By 1954 there were eight of them and they were sovereigns of the seas. Their main armament was the then-new 4.5-in (114-mm) dual-purpose gun which, being 'radar controlled', put them in a different class compared to their wartime forbears. The *Darings* were tasked primarily with cruiser-type reconnaissance and anti-submarine warfare defence of a task group or convoy; their impressive gun armament was also a useful ASV weapon. Destroyers were in action during Korea, but before that in October 1946 *Saumarez* and *Volage* were severely damaged by Albanian offensive mines placed in international waters off Corfu—this was the period of the Greek civil war following liberation from the Nazis.

The anti-air warfare (AAW) side of naval operations was still the province of the small calibre gun in the immediate postwar years, but the increasing use of aircraft led to a number of destroyers being converted into radar pickets, and was an idea originally developed by the USN in the Pacific at the end of 1945 to combat the Japanese 'kamikaze' raiders. The main feature of these conversions was the conspicuous Type 965 (*qv*) air warning radar on the main mast—the 'bedstead' radar scanner. The first conversions were to *Weapons* Class warships originally completed in 1947–8 and converted 1958–9. The earlier *Battle* Class destroyers—beautiful ships which clearly represented the peak of traditional destroyer design—were also converted into radar pickets in 1962. The latter carried the double-bedstead Type 965 radars but, unlike the *Weapons*, they were positioned on the foremast.

The scene at the 1953 Spithead Review for the Coronation with the first appearance of helicopters, Westland/Sikorsky Dragonflies (courtesy Admiral O'Brien).

The last true destroyer in the RN is still afloat and acts as a museum ship for the whole concept of RN destroyers, being berthed at Southampton. *Cavalier*, one of the numerous *C* Class of war emergency construction, was not converted nor sold after the war and her only allowance to modern warfare is the Seacat surface-to-air missile (SAM) launcher and director installed aft. Built in 1944 and eventually paid-off at Chatham in 1972, she represents the last British warship to see action in World War 2.

On June 15 1953, the newly crowned Queen Elizabeth II reviewed her combined Fleet at Spithead. It was indeed an 'armada' with 197 RN warships being present, including the last British battleship *Vanguard* and eight aircraft carriers. For the first time, the flypast included jets and helicopters (led by the late Rear Admiral Walter Couchman). On the warship side, this review was remarkable because specialist landing craft were present for the first time. The most numerous of the surface combat ships were the smaller warships, including 62 *Ocean* Minesweepers and 47 frigates. It is these latter types which were the mainstay of the fleet in the postwar period in numerical terms, at least.

Just as the destroyer had migrated postwar into the cruiser tonnages, so the frigate continued to increase its size. Initially, the type had been revitalised during the war with the need to provide ASW escorts for the Atlantic convoys. In the late 1940s, the Admiralty reclassified most of its escorts as frigates. Most suited to work in the majority of theatres from 1945, the frigate made its own the role of peacekeeper and flag shower in the Far East, Mediterranean and West Indies. In warmer climes, such as the Gulf, the *Loch* and *Bay* Classes were well employed dealing with British interests, including the suppression of pirates. Displacing about 1,575 tons, both classes were very similar although the *Bays* retained four 102 mm guns whilst the armament of the *Lochs* was generally paired down to two. By the late 1950s, these two classes had been down graded into the Reserve or transferred into the embryo navies of the emerging Commonwealth.

Some destroyers, notably the War Emergency R–Z Classes and the famous *Hunts*, were fully converted to fast anti-submarine frigates. Mainly used for training and experimental purposes, these warships provided the RN with a much needed ASW capability in a time of gathering threat from the new classes of Soviet submarine. The first specialist frigates designed for the RN were initiated during the major western rearmament programmes caused by the Korean conflict. These were the *Whitby* Class, completed 1956–58, with their characteristic forecastle allowing better seakeeping than their predecessors. A further nine which followed were known as the *Rothesay* Class, 1960–1, under the 1954–55 programme; in 1966–68, *Rothesay*, the name ship of the class, was converted to operate ASW helicopters and the Seacat SAM. Remnants of the class are still in service and are described in Chapter Four.

Specialist frigates were also designed and built for anti-aircraft (AA) duties and for aircraft direction (AD) as well. The former were used with the Fleet and known as the 'Big Cats' or *Leopard* Class (1953–9), being equipped with 114 mm Mk 6 guns (*qv*) and Type 965 radar. The latter purpose-built radar pickets were ordered during the same period and the last, *Lincoln*, was completed in 1960. Their radar fit was far more extensive as they were designed primarily for the direction of carrier-based aircraft such as the *Scimitar* and the *Sea Vixen*, or their shore-based counterparts. More utilitarian but still worthy of a place in British postwar naval history is the *Blackwood* Class of second rate ASW frigates, built 1955–8.

By the middle of the 1950s, the need to have specialised frigates in the RN had been rethought by the Admiralty planners and this led to the most famous class of all postwar frigates—the *Leanders*. They are outside the scope of this chapter and are covered in detail in Chapter Four, but it will suffice to record that they were orginally considered in the 1955–56 Naval Estimates.

The Submarine Service, like the Fleet Air Arm, an élite group within an élite organisation, began postwar operations with a large number of diesel-powered patrol submarines of the *A*, *S*, and *T* Classes. For several years, four midget submarines of the *XE* Class were retained for training duties,

together with a new postwar 'improved' midget design. By 1950, there were 61 submarines of all types in commission, under refit or being used for experimental work with propulsion or sonar gear for the new era. The *A* Class continued in service until 1974, when *Andrew*, completed in 1948, retired. One of her claims to fame was the first submerged crossing of the Atlantic, in 1953. Some years later the whole class was reconstructed with streamlined conning tower and deck guns removed. With the capture of so many former German U-boats in 1945, it was possible for the RN to carry out trials with hydrogen peroxide-powered Walter-type submarines (eg, *Meteorite*, ex-*U-1407*). Later, two Vickers-built submarines tested the propulsion system in the late 1950s. Although amongst the fastest submarines in the world, they were overshadowed by the development of nuclear power.

Postwar conventional types have been confined to two classes—the *Porpoise* and *Oberon* Classes. It is undoubtedly in the Submarine Service that the RN has seen one of its greatest changes; for not only is the submarine in its Fleet role the capital ship of the 1980s and 1990s (succeeding the carriers in the 1970s), but it also represents the independent deterrent to aggression from unfriendly powers. The revolution which has caused this change is, of course, nuclear power.

The birth of the nuclear submarine fleet was planned during the days of the Cold War (in the 1950s) but the technology was not available to allow the RN to build a nuclear-powered submarine for some time. The first such boat, although British-constructed, relied on an American reactor and was commissioned on April 1963 as *Dreadnought*; an apt name for the first of a new generation of warships, like the *Dreadnought* of the battleship era. She cost a staggering £18.5 million which, although it compares well with the £177 million for a modern SSN, was a great deal of taxpayers' money at the time. Unaffected by the Defence Cuts of the 1960s, the submarine force has grown over the last two decades. There are two types of nuclear boat—the hunter-killer Fleet type or SSN and the nuclear-powered ballistic missile-carrying SSBM. The first all-British SSN was *Valiant* (*qv*), launched in 1965. The new submarines heralded, with their modern technology, a new era in crew comfort and amenity and for the first time provided submariners with unlimited fresh water, air and power. Morale was boosted by the provision of separate messes for junior and senior rates whose meals can be provided at cafeterias, such is the internal space available. All but one of the nuclear submarines which have been built remain in service and are covered in detail in Chapter Four.

The Anglo-American accord known as the Nassau Agreement led to the replacement of the nuclear strike V-Bombers of the Royal Air Force (RAF) with a small, yet powerful, fleet of submarines. Developing the technology used in the early SSNs, Vickers Armstrong and Cammell Laird produced four large (7,500-ton) submarines in the period 1966–68. These craft each carry 16 American-built Polaris (*qv*) medium-range ballistic missiles. The first nuclear-armed boat, *Resolution* (*qv*), left on her first top secret deterrence patrol in 1967; she had cost £52 million to build and equip. Such is the price of freedom.

In other branches of the Navy afloat, there were also changes during the 1960s. The converted aircraft carrier or Commando Carrier equipped only to fly helicopters but with a full Royal Marines (RM) Commando aboard had been developed. Its origins can be traced directly to the Suez police action or intervention in November 1956, when an Anglo-French fleet attempted to mediate between Israel and Egypt and thus secure the future of the recently nationalised Suez Canal. The political wheeler-dealing of America effectively hamstrung the RN's effort yet a very good use was made of carrier-based aircraft including helicopters. Several assaults and casualty evacuations (casevacs) were flown by the latter, manned by aircrew from the Joint Services Trials Unit based in *Ocean* and *Theseus*. It was these operations, coinciding with more powerful aircraft, such as the Wessex helicopter, being available, which opened the way for Commando Carrier operations. Thus the RN was given the flexible response to minor, brushfire wars. In addition, the smaller carriers were becoming too small for big jet operations. Ironically, it was Suez veterans *Bulwark* and *Albion* which were converted, followed in 1971–3 by the last conventional aircraft carrier to enter service, *Hermes*. The first test of the idea came in 1961 when the Kingdom of Kuwait was threatened by its larger neighbour Iraq; *Bulwark* was already in the Gulf of Oman and steamed at top speed into the Gulf, arriving off Kuwait within hours of the Ruler's plea for assistance. Britain had at that time a defence agreement with the Kingdom and so disembarked 42 Commando (Cdo) in Whirlwind HAS 7 helicopters of 848 Naval Air Squadron (NAS). Despite unfavourable flying conditions, a full Commando was deployed in position and the situation stabilised.

With the withdrawal from Empire, the Commando Carrier also looked to new horizons and concentrated on the NATO flanks, specifically Norway. By the mid-1970s, the need was more pressing in the ASW role and so the LPHs (NATO parlance for Commando Carriers) became joint LPH/CVS (anti-submarine warfare carrier) ships. 1966 saw the beginning of the end of the conventional aircraft carrier with its ASW helicopters and so it was important that they should still be afloat whether in a CVS or CCH role (like *Tiger* and *Blake*). This time the Defence Cuts axed the new generation of aircraft carrier, *CVA-01* and her class, rather than postponing the programme and thus, when *Ark Royal* decommissioned in 1978, she was the last fixed-wing conventional aircraft carrier.

In more peaceful waters, the RN began to turn its attention more and more to specialist surveying and hydrography. The ocean sciences not only benefit the navies of the world, but the merchant fleets as well. Britain, under the Hydrographer to the Navy, has always led the world in chart making and recording; now there was the new horizon of Antarctica as well. In addition, the new generation of deep-diving SSNs and SSBMs need more detailed oceanographic data to fight and survive in the modern undersea environment. In 1950, the RN laid down a specialist survey ship at Chatham; named the *Vidal* on launching in 1951, she was the first of her type to be equipped with a flight deck and helicopter. This enables independent survey parties to operate away from the ship and thus cover a greater area. She also has a place in the heart of all sailors of that era because she was the first warship to be designed to operate cafeteria messing.* Several *Bay* Class frigates were modified for survey duties but it was not until 1964 that the next new class of hydro-oceanographic survey ship was ordered. The *Cook* Class survey ships of the immediate postwar period carried out much initial survey work off the coast of the frozen southern continent. In the mid-1950s, the Ice Patrol Ship *Protector* spent some time in the South Atlantic and Antarctic following rather anti-social claims by Argentina. Designed to operate as Falkland Islands' guardship, survey vessel and transport for RM detachments, she remained in service until replaced by *Endurance* (*qv*) in 1968.

The serious problems created in World War 2, and to a certain extent during the Korean Conflict, led the RN to build a sizeable fleet of 54 minesweepers (later known as mines counter-measures vessels or MCMVs). These vessels of the *Ton* Class displace 360 tons and are still in service with the RN and several other Commonwealth navies. At the same time, a class of specially designed and built shallow water MCMVs were ordered; they were known as the *Ham* Class and very

---

* Hammocks went out with the introduction of *Ark Royal* in 1955; these improvements to the lot of the average sailor were greatly appreciated.

few are still in service, mainly in fringe roles such as tenders and torpedo recovery vessels. Both types used composite construction of non-magnetic signature aluminium alloys and wood.

The Coastal Forces, traditionally the forté of the RNVR, were to see the development of the Fast Patrol Boat (FPB) in Britain with the *Dark* and *Brave* Classes, which are both now sadly out of service, several being expended as targets. In the RN's NATO role, the use of the FPB has completely diminished although several overseas navies buy British designs from British shipbuilders. The three FTBs of the 1st Training Squadron based at Portland are now for disposal.

Specialist vessels for the Royal Fleet Auxiliary Service (RFA) and the Royal Maritime Auxiliary Service (RMAS)—which includes the Port Auxiliary Service—have abounded since the war. Both organisations have modern and large fleets of craft designed for many tasks. The latter did possess many wartime-constructed craft through until a building boom in the 1965–1980 period, and today most of the steam-powered craft have disappeared. Provisioning and refuelling at sea was learned the hard way during the Pacific campaign in 1944–5, but since then the RFA has perfected the art to such a degree that it now leads the world in replenishment at sea (RAS). Four Fleet Oilers were completed 1945–6 to form the *Wave* Class and these vessels bore the brunt of early 'RASing' exercises and operations; in 1954–8, the Class was augmented by the *Tides*, and later in 1965–6 by the *01* Class; Both *Wave* and *Tide* Classes are no longer in service. With the new range of weapons and aircraft carried by ships of the RN, the RFA ordered and manned a new type of ammunition, food, explosives and stores (AFES) carrier of several classes. Many are still in service and are detailed in Chapter Seven.

The non-naval manned supplies and transportation facets of the RN were run as almost separate organisations until the appointment of then Vice Admiral Lord Louis Mountbatten as Fourth Sea Lord in 1950. With a special responsibility for this part of the navy, Mountbatten set about reorganising the stores, victualling and armament supplies of the Fleet. A decade later Mountbatten, by then Chief of the Defence Staff, began to put his ideas into action and began the creation of the unified defence command—the Ministry of Defence. The scheme was much opposed at first, but with the backing of Prime Minister Macmillan and later Wilson, the Admiralty was merged with the other two Services. The merger was not as complete as in Canada in the same period, and thus none of their unfortunate problems have occurred in Britain. Mountbatten will be remembered with

great affection by the RN for his tireless efforts on its behalf during the postwar era.

The postwar years have seen a dramatic change in the Navy's overseas commitments and of the traditional RN Dockyards abroad, only Gibraltar remains and her future is limited. There are still facilities at Hong Kong and Bermuda but Ceylon was given up in 1956; Singapore in 1971 and finally Malta in 1979. Jolly Jack is now rarely to be seen in whites and this is somewhat ironic considering just how efficient the laundry service aboard a modern warship has become! The largest single factor in the RN's new role in the Eastlant (Eastern Atlantic) is the individual sailor, now a professional, a volunteer with a higher educational standard than ever before.

Vast changes have occurred in naval weaponry and, although the wartime sailor would be able to recognise the smaller calibre general purpose guns still fitted to destroyers, frigates, patrol vessels and the like, he would be completely bowled over by the guided weapons and their computerised directors. Both Oerlikon 20 mm and Bofors 40 mm guns are still carried in the same mountings as wartime users, but the guided missile has all but replaced the larger calibre gun in most warships. The missile has been the major weapons system of the last two decades after initial seaborne trials aboard *Girdle Ness*, the former Fleet Maintenance Ship, in October 1963 and July 1956. At first, missiles were designed in the AA role—Short Seacat and Seaslug—to combat high-speed aircraft at both close and medium ranges. Both these first generation weapons are still in service.

In the torpedo field, the World War 2 role for this weapon has gone as have the tubes aboard destroyers and the motor torpedo boat. The submarine still uses the weapon as its primary armament but since 1945 the guidance, either by wire or internally, has meant that success is almost guaranteed. The Mk 8 wartime design is still in service aboard SSKs. Submarine sonar, both passive and active, is now computer assisted and can classify the sound of another ship's screws, a facet of naval design in which the RN has led the world in the postwar era. In the late 1960s the SLAM (submarine launched air missile) was experimented with and operationally fired under trials condition in *Aeneas* but the programme was cancelled in late 1972.

In the modern naval environment, the radar array of modern warships could be more of a hindrance than a help, particularly in the opening gambits of conflict. So, although much effort has been put into the development of better and better radar in the period since 1945, the Mark One Eyeball still has a place in the modern RN. Aircraft are now equipped

Above left *Mainstay of the Fleet in the Mediterranean for very many years was the island fortress of Malta, seen here in 1955. The warship leaving Grand Harbour is the Light Fleet Carrier* Centaur (courtesy Rear Admiral Rolfe). **Above right** *The RN pioneered the use of helicopters for re-supply and jungle support operations, as here in Malaysia with Wessex HAR 1s from the Commando Carrier* Albion (RN).

with far better radar and other sensors than in the past, especially in the ASW role. The introduction of helicopters in this role in 1957 (Westland Whirlwind HAS 7) and the improved range and weapons delivery of the Wessex (in 1961) has been important. Small ships' flights were established in the early 1960s for operation, initially aboard the *Tribal* Class general purpose frigates which served in the West Indies, Far East and Gulf as independent units, showing the flag and being available to support the local friendly powers in time of national emergency.

Not only has the Navy's organisation afloat changed with the only sea-going Commander-in-Chief (CINCFLEET) residing in a 'stone frigate' at Northwood, and thereby contracting the warships of the RN into one Fleet, as opposed to the Atlantic, Home, Far East and Mediterranean Fleets of a couple of decades ago, but there is now a unified command organisation at home (CINCNAVHOME). Ashore, the number and purpose of RN establishments has changed since World War 2 with the FFA suffering the most as the number of air stations has decreased with the loss of fixed-wing flying in all but vertical take-off (VTO) and communications roles, to the RAF. The disbandment of the RNVR Air Branch in 1957 continued the shrinkage.

Between 1950 and 1980, nine overseas bases were closed: Bahrain, Bermuda (a small presence is retained), Colombo, Hong Kong (no dockyard facilities), Malta, Mauritius, Simonstown, Singapore and Trincomalee, as well at Sheerness at home. The WRNS, now under the Naval Discipline Act, have no longer the luxury of their own training establishment (*Dauntless* closed in 1981, transferring

recruit training to *Raleigh*) and several other naval branches now have shared accommodation and resources with the other services. The Navy's nursing service, the QUARNNS (*qv*) have now also been brought under the Naval Discipline Act.

After the war, it was decided that Commandos were needed for tasks demanding special skill in amphibious operations and the Royal Marines were given the task of providing these troops. Since 1945, the Commandos of the RM (all RMs are now Commando-trained except the Band Service, the RM sea service men coming ashore in the early postwar period) have taken part in operations in the following countries: Palestine, Egypt, Malaya, Korea, Cyprus, Kuwait, Aden, Tanganyika, Brunei, Borneo and Northern Ireland. Warships still carry detachments of RMs, although this was reduced in 1978, and they have carried out numerous landings abroad to assist the civil power in a number of ways, including disaster relief.

The most important series of operations undertaken since World War 2 were those of the South Atlantic Task Group under Rear Admiral 'Sandy' Woodward, First Officer First Flotilla during April, May and June 1982. On April 2, a strong force of Argentine commandos and regular troops invaded the British Crown Colony of the Falkland Islands and the British dependency of South Georgia, in the South Atlantic. British defence forces were limited to Naval Party 1009 (about Company strength) and the Ice Patrol Ship *Endurance* (on her last patrol before disposal). The result of the invasion was a foregone conclusion.

Although politically caught 'on the hop', the British were to assemble a Task Force, led by the carrier *Hermes*, within five days and warships, RFAs and requisitioned merchant ships sailed from Portsmouth, Rosyth and Plymouth. The immediate result was the postponement of the rundown of Portsmouth and Chatham, and also at Gibraltar where much work was carried out on vessels 'going south'. Using Ascension Island as a base, the task group of warships, Royal Marines (with Army support) and aircraft of the Fleet Air Arm, deployed to war stations. The initial operations were concerned with the re-taking of South Georgia, which was accomplished by the weekend of April 24–25. Prominent in the attack were the DLG *Antrim* (and her Wessex HAS 3 helicopter), the frigates *Plymouth* and *Brilliant*, plus associated landing ships and craft.

The main purpose of the powerful Task Force was the blockade by sea and air of the Falkland Islands. British nuclear-powered Fleet submarines were operational in the areas closest to Argentina because of the latter's powerful air force and fleet air arm. On May 2, one submarine, *Conqueror*, torpedoed the Argentine cruiser *Belgrano* but the RN suffered a major loss two days later when the Type 42 DLG *Sheffield* was hit and sunk by a single air-launched AM39 Exocet missile in its sea-skimming mode. Perhaps the greatest lesson learned by the RN during the 11-week operation was the power of the Exocet and vulnerability of warships without fleet airborne early warning. Later that month, *Sheffield*'s sister-ship *Coventry*, and the requisitioned container ship, turned mini aircraft/stores carrier, *Atlantic Conveyor* were sunk, the latter by the same means during a re-supply operation to the Task Force's

Broadsword *escorts* Hermes *in the South Atlantic during the battle for the Falklands* (Popperfoto).

operating base at Port San Carlos on East Falkland. In addition, the Type 21 frigates *Antelope* and *Ardent* were lost to aerial bombing whilst covering the ground forces in San Carlos Water and Falkland Sound. The lesson learned here was that neither were equipped with a viable point defence missile system, such as Seawolf, and this meant that, despite the superb performance of the Fleet air defence of Sea Harriers on Combat Air Patrol (CAP), the area missile defence of Sea Dart-equipped warships, plus the older Seacat and Seaslug systems, a single wave of attackers getting through only had 20 mm and 40 mm guns to contend with in the target area. In addition to the losses, the following warships were damaged by air and land attacks: *Broadsword*, *Argonaut*, *Glasgow*, *Glamorgan*, *Alacrity* and *Plymouth*.

Of the Royal Fleet Auxiliaries with the Task Force, *Sir Galahad* and *Sir Tristam* were caught in an unprepared situation on the south coast of East Falkland and hit by attacking Argentine aircraft. Like all the other attacks, the courage of those on board and that of the helicopter pilots involved in rescue operations was magnificent. Undoubtedly, but for the cool of the British Servicemen, there would have been more fatalities.

The intense air and sea and land pressure on the

Argentine forces (which outnumbered the British RM and Army units) led to a steady series of successes on the road to Port Stanley, the Islands' capital. On June 15, the Argentine forces surrendered and the Union Flag was restored to the Colony. But the lessons learned are still being analysed in the corridors of the Ministry of Defence and will undoubtedly shape the Fleet in years to come.

With the end of Naval National Service, the 'bull' of the RN has decreased and in recent years it has been possible for ratings to buy their way out of the Service with ease. Dress regulations have been relaxed and several of the old uniform patterns have gone. New material and fabrics have helped here. The Rum Ration—the Tot—was dispensed with in 1971, although on very special occasions it is still possible to 'splice the mainbrace' at the sovereign's command.

Naval rig, although superficially the same since the end of the last world war, has changed with the invention of modern materials and the needs of modern warships with automatic washing facilities. 'Square rig' has been maintained but modernised with the retention of essential features. In 1971, a new idea in dress was put to trials and competition and in 1975 the Queen approved a new jumper and a new suit of worsted serge, with velcro fastenings for the collar, while separate black silk, lanyard and tapes were dispensed with in favour of an integral trimming. WRNS uniforms also changed in the mid-1970s when the rough serge rig began to be phased out. The whole naval kit went through transformation, including the issue of slimmer-fit raincoats, new shirts to replace the existing No 8 and easy care white drill items. At the same time an orange working jacket had been introduced for greater safety, but this was found to be unworkable as it quickly picked up the dirt and the waterproof/windproof jacket was changed to navy blue in colour, which has proved far more serviceable.

Despite a continuous reduction in the number of combat ships and of personnel numbers, the RN continues to be the third most powerful navy in the world, after the United States and the Soviet Union. It has performed well since the end of the Second World War, changed with the times and needs of the nation, but it is still recognisable as a fine navy.

Major events in the Royal Navy since 1945

1945	First jet landing aboard a carrier; demobilisation	1963	ASW helicopters embark in frigates; *Leander* Class enter service, VTOL trials in *Ark Royal*
1946	RN operations off Palestine	1964	Ministry of Defence created
1947	Palestine operations cease	1965	Beira patrol
1948	RAN's first carrier commissioned; Walter-powered submarines	1966	Confrontation ends; drastic Defence Cuts; *CVA-01* cancelled
1949	Yangtze Incident; Britain joins NATO	1967	*Torrey Canyon* affair; first SSBM patrol
1950	Korean War begins; first RN helicopter squadron formed; cafeteria messing	1968	First supersonic jets for FAA (Phantoms); last warship built at Devonport launched
1951	First jet fighter squadron formed; 'wavy Navy' stripes abolished	1969	Torbay Fleet review; last *T*-Class SSK paid off
1952	*Darings* enter service	1970	*Hermes* begins LPH conversion
1953	Coronation Fleet Review; Korean War ends	1971	Withdrawal from Far East; rum ration finished
1954	Withdrawal from Canal Zone (Egypt)	1972	Last wartime destroyer paid off; SLAM trials
1955	*Ark Royal* commissioned; Mountbatten appointed First Sea Lord	1973	Cod War with Iceland; Exocet missile refits
1956	Suez landings, RN leaves Ceylon; guided missile trials begin	1974	First Group Deployment out of NATO area; RNR/RNVR review
1957	First RN operational ASW helicopter squadron	1975	Cod War with Iceland
1958	Nuclear strike aircraft for RN	1976	First Type 42 destroyer commissions
1959	Mountbatten appointed Chief of Defence Staff; Commando Carriers	1977	QARNNS put under Naval Discipline Act; Silver Jubilee Review; Devonport Frigate complex opened
1960	First nuclear-powered submarine launched; Sheerness closed	1978	First WRNS course at Dartmouth; *Ark Royal* decommissions
1961	Last cruiser commissions (*Blake*); last midget submarine paid off; Kuwait Crisis; Nore Command ceased to exist	1979	Last aircraft carrier and last cruiser paid off
1962	Indonesia Confrontation; first guided missile destroyer (*Devonshire*)	1980	First *Invincible* Class carrier accepted; Sea Harrier enters service
		1982	Falkland Islands confrontation

Organisation and role

Without doubt one of the finest maritime forces in the world, the Royal Navy, with traditions dating back to the Restoration, is a major contributor to the defence of peace in a modern context. It provides both a nuclear and a conventional deterrent to aggression, with a most valuable spin-off in terms of aid to the civil power in times of disaster or civil emergency.

A Navy is, however, only as good as the men and women who serve in it, and today, more than ever, the RN relies on the sailor as the single biggest factor in this effective service.

The capabilities of the RN are world-wide, yet it is mainly concentrated in the Eastern Atlantic (*Eastlant* to NATO) area where, as the largest navy in Western Europe (and the third largest in the world), it has a major role to play in protecting the freedom of the seas. Western Europe, like so many of the other so-called 'free' areas of the world, depends totally on a free flow of raw materials, notably for trade, but also to sustain ever-growing populations.

Since the end of World War 2, the UK Government (of whichever colour) has relied on the mutual assistance form of defence and this has meant a large commitment to and by NATO—the North Atlantic Treaty Organisation. For 35 years there has been stability in Europe and some satisfaction can be drawn from this fact although, sadly, the RN has been involved in many brushfire conflicts since. So, in effect, it is not possible to discuss RN policy and strategy without considering, at every juncture, the NATO connection.

1981 Defence Review

Entitled *The United Kingdom Defence Programme: The Way Forward*, the Conservative Government's Defence Review of June 1981 involved some really startling changes for the Royal Navy, especially the surface ship force. Whilst Britain remains a full and important partner in the NATO alliance, and while her Navy remains the largest in Western Europe (as well as the most efficient in the whole alliance), the emphasis has been changed. During the years 1981–84 there is scheduled to be an annual growth in the percentage of Gross National Product (GNP) devoted to the Armed Forces and the RN will receive its share, but mainly within the nuclear deterrent budget which is effectively separate from the Naval vote.

The new policy has been formulated by a new Secretary of State and is based on cash terms which have been shaped by the technological changes and resource constraints which have made major weapons platforms, like destroyers and frigates, more vulnerable. The new role for the RN is basically devoted to the ASW threat mentioned in detail elsewhere, and maintained under the umbrella of the Polaris and later the Trident

The RN of the future will be based on the SSN – Valiant *at sea (MoD).*

programme. At last, it does seem that the RN will receive more up-to-date MCMVs and the RNR is scheduled to receive a new type of deep-sweeper. The Government feels that it is not cost-effective to maintain a large surface fleet and try to keep pace with weapons and sensor development in all fields. Nevertheless, the RN is assured that there will be a wide range of special tasks and uses for the surface fleet, although only 50 (instead of 59) will be dedicated to NATO at any one time. The policy is to rid the fleet of the manpower-intensive designs such as the *Rothesays* and *Leanders*, plus the larger vessels like *Intrepid* and *Fearless*. Refits for the more modern, yet still expensive warships, such as the Type 42s, will not be carried and Batch Is of this type will not receive the Batch II mods at half-life as originally planned. An interesting fact which seems to have emerged from the Review is that a *Leander* costs about £70 million to refit, yet a more modern (but perhaps less effective) Type 23 would not cost that figure to build as new. Type 22 FFHs are reportedly costing £125 million to build and SSNs about £177 million.

The future in terms of new weapons looks good, yet most are devoted to ASW, especially for submarines. There seems to be no successor planned for the Sea Dart missile system and this again reflects the anti-surface attitude. Thankfully, the Royal Marines will remain much as they are, but the platforms to take them into action—the Assault Ships—may have gone by 1986. Naval Air Commando helicopter squadrons are already worked up in the non-embarked roles. What is not mentioned in the programme is how the Marines will arrive at the Northern Flank disembarkation points after the demise of the assault ships.

Another serious effect of the review is the closure of Chatham Dockyard and the partial closure of the Navy's home at Portsmouth. There also appears to be an inference that Gibraltar will not be maintained in the refit streaming programme after 1985, but this could well be linked to the political settlement of the Gibraltar Question with Spain.*

The numbers in the RN will be reduced by about 8,000 to 10,000 in 1986, partly through the surface fleet contraction, says the review, and partly by cutting out training billets ashore. What is certain, and this has been welcomed, is that more time will be spent at sea. Let us hope that the RN will be the effective force by the end of the present decade that the Government says it will be.

---

* It is now known that Gibraltar will be run down over the period 1983–5 and that the normalisation of the Gibraltar/Spain border in 1983 will pave the way for the establishment of a possible NATO base at Gibraltar.

Ajax entering Gibraltar: the Leander *Class is considered to be too manpower-intensive for the modern RN.*

Role of the Navy

The basis of the philosophy behind the present Royal Navy's operational role is linked to four elements: (1) the nuclear deterrent of the SSBN squadron*; (2) the re-supply of the NATO Central Front; (3) the protection of the UK and naval bases; and (4) the protection of maritime trade. Within this framework, the present political direction of HM Government calls for the dedication of circa 95 per cent of the Fleet to NATO needs.

In time of war, the RN would be operating almost exclusively in the North Atlantic, particularly in the Greenland-Iceland-United Kingdom (GIUK) Gap and the Norwegian Sea. In these areas, its role would be to prevent Soviet maritime forces, whether air, surface or sub-surface, from entering the re-supply convoy routes. The direction of the expected thrust is from the Arctic Ocean and hence the great importance of the GIUK area. Whether there are sufficient units to maintain defence against prolonged Soviet pressure is open to debate, but at the very least RN officers are confident, given the current Fleet, that they could make it very difficult for 'Ivan' to stop the re-supply operations to NATO ground forces in Europe completely.

Although the RN has a large commitment to NATO, the overriding importance of UK interests would not be forgotten in times of war or tension. It must be said, however, that most NATO

---

* The various abbreviations and specialist terms which occur throughout this book are explained in the relevant sections of the text, or in the glossary/index at the back.

The lynchpin of present naval policy is the SSBN, the vehicle of the strategic deterrence force. This is an R-boat at sea (RN).

Commanders (some of whom are serving RN Flag Officers, i.e., Rear Admirals or above) are independent from national considerations.

Tension

In this time between open hostility and normal détente, the RN would have a multi-choice role and it would be particularly important for the conventional and nuclear deterrent force to be displayed to counter aggressive 'sabre rattling' by any potential enemy. The Fleet would project its influence in particular sea areas, especially the choke-points like the Straits of Gibraltar and the Norwegian Sea. This projection of power would hopefully have the affect of deterring the aggressor from carrying on his aims to a state of war. It must be remembered, and this is important in the 1980s, that Britain is a member of a defensive alliance, and would not seek direct confrontation except in defence of its, or a fellow member's, interests. Britain cannot afford, as no country can now, to fulfil all the obligations of sovereignty alone.

The major dilemma would occur in the areas outside the alliance's boundaries. What aid such a Fleet could give to friendly nations south of the Tropic of Cancer or east of Suez is doubtful. In any one year, however, it is normal for an eighth of the RN's strength to be so deployed, but the doubt occurs when one considers the special problems that the Navy could face in the Gulf of Oman, the Arabian Sea or the Straits of Malacca to name just three. Would the Navy continue a presence in times of tension?

With war imminent, there would be a great need to protect the main sea trade routes to Britain and Western Europe. If one pauses a moment to consider that the average super-tanker carries the equivalent of a whole World War 2 convoy's freight tonnage in a single ship, the problem becomes somewhat nightmarish. The Cape of Good Hope, around which the UK annually imports a high percentage of its crude oil and a good proportion of its mineral raw materials, is a particularly vulnerable area. The Indian Ocean has seen, in recent years, an increased presence of warships of both super-powers—much, it should be said, to the annoyance of the Third World countries which surround its vast expanse. So for the RN to just be there in the sea lanes could do much in a time of tension to deter the potential aggressor.

Nuclear deterrence and Trident

Without doubt the most emotive issues in the current Defence debate and the Government's position is summed up in the following extract from the 1981 Defence White Paper (Cmnd 8212–1), entitled *Nuclear Weapons and Preventing War*:

'1. Nuclear weapons have transformed our view of war. Though they have been used only twice, half a lifetime ago, the terrible experience of Hiroshima and Nagasaki must be always in our minds. But the scale of that horror makes it all the more necessary that revulsion be partnered by clear thinking. If it is not, we may find ourselves having to learn again, in the appalling school of practical experience, that abhorrence of war is no substitute for realistic plans to prevent it.

'2. There can be opposing views about whether the world would be safer and more peaceful if nuclear weapons had never been invented. But that is academic; they cannot be disinvented. Our task now is to devise a system for living in peace and freedom while ensuring that nuclear weapons are never used, either to destroy or to blackmail.

'3. Nuclear weapons are the dominant aspect of modern war potential. But they are not the only aspect we should fear. Save at the very end, World War II was fought entirely with what are comfortably called "conventional" weapons, yet during its six years something like fifty million people were killed. Since 1945 "conventional" war has killed up to ten million more. The "conventional" weapons with which any East-West war would be fought today are much more powerful than those of 1939–1945; and chemical weapons are far more lethal than when they were last used widely, over sixty years ago. Action about nuclear weapons which left, or seemed to leave, the field free for non-nuclear war could be calamitous.

'4. Moreover, whatever promises might have been

given in peace, no alliance possessing nuclear weapons could be counted on to accept major non-nuclear defeat and conquest without using its nuclear power. Non-nuclear war between East and West is by far the likeliest road to nuclear war.

'5. We must therefore seek to prevent any war, not just nuclear war, between East and West. And the part nuclear weapons have to play in this is made all the greater by the facts of military power. The combination of geography and totalitarian direction of resources gives the Soviet Union a massive preponderance in Europe. The Western democracies have enough economic strength to match the East, if their peoples so chose. But the cost to social and other aims would be huge, and the resulting forces would still not make our nuclear weapons unnecessary. No Western non-nuclear effort could keep us safe against one-sided Eastern nuclear power.

'6. An enormous literature has sprung up around the concepts of deterrence in the nuclear age. Much of it seems remote and abstruse, and its apparent detachment often sounds repugnant. But though the idea of deterrence is old and looks simple, making it work effectively in today's world needs clear thought on complex issues. The central aim is to influence the calculations of anyone who might consider aggression; to influence them decisively; and, crucially, to influence them before aggression is ever launched. It is not certain that any East-West conflict would rise to all-out nuclear war: escalation is a matter of human decision, not an inexorable scientific process. It is perfectly sensible—indeed essential—to make plans which could increase and exploit whatever chance there might be of ending war short of global catastrophe. But that chance will always be precarious, whether at the conventional or the nuclear level; amid the confusion, passions and irrationalities of war, escalation must always be a grave danger. The only safe course is outright prevention.

'7. Planning deterrence means thinking through the possible reasoning of an adversary and the way in which alternative courses of action might appear to him in advance. It also means doing this in his terms, not in ours; and allowing for how he might think in future circumstances, not just in today's. In essence we seek to ensure that whatever military aggression or political bullying a future Soviet leader might contemplate, he could not foresee any likely situation in which the West would be left with no realistic alternative to surrender.

'8. Failure to recognise this complicated but crucial fact about deterrence—that it rests, like a chess master's strategy, on blocking off in advance a variety of possible moves in an opponent's mind—

underlies many of the criticisms made of Western security policy. To make provision for having practical courses of action available in nuclear war (or for reducing its devastation in some degree by modest civil defence precautions) is not in the least to have a "war-fighting strategy", or to plan for nuclear war as something expected or probable. It is, on the contrary, a necessary path to deterrence, to rendering nuclear war as improbable as we humanly can. The further evolution last year of United States nuclear planning illustrates the point. The reason for having available a wider range of "non-city" target options was not in order to fight a limited nuclear war—the United States repeatedly stressed that it did not believe in any such notion—but to help ensure that even if an adversary believed in limited nuclear war (as Soviet writings sometimes suggest) he could not expect actually to win one.

'9. The United Kingdom helped to develop NATO's deterrent strategy, and we are involved in its nuclear aspects at three main levels. First, we endorse it fully as helping to guarantee our security, and we share in the protection it gives all Alliance members. Second, we cooperate directly, like several other members, in the United States power which is the main component of the nuclear armoury, by making bases available and providing certain delivery systems to carry United States warheads. Third, we commit to the Alliance nuclear forces of various kinds—strategic and theatre—under our independent control.'

The main rationale behind the continued use of nuclear-powered ballistic missile-carrying submarines (SSBMs) is their invulnerability and, as the Tornado aircraft which is currently replacing the nuclear-capable Vulcans of the RAF (the former nuclear deterrent force), has less range than the older V-bomber, the SSBN is still vital if Britain is to maintain a nuclear umbrella without relying on the United States. Such a deterrence force is reasonably cost-effective since, with port and starboard crews manning each submarine, the hardware can be turned round and put back to sea in no time. The expertise is expensive, however, the basic annual cycle after refit being: work-up—9 months; assisted maintenance—1 month; on patrol—2 months. So having only four vessels creates a fairly tight operational cycle, especially when trade unions try to disrupt the schedule by 'blacking' what are already black-coloured warships!

The Trident submarines, probably similar to the USN designs currently under construction, will be able to operate with only four units because they will be second-generation boats and there will be no back-to-back turn-arounds necessary. The USN already extends commissioning times because of improved design and maintenance facilities, and the latter are currently being improved at *Neptune*, the Clyde submarine base.

In addition, the boats will be able to carry more warheads and thus be more effective as a deterrent. The areas of operation will be vastly increased, but even though transit time will increase in proportion, it is better to hide a SSBN in a larger area where it can remain undetected for long periods, yet still pose a risk to an aggressor. The advantages over Polaris are enormous, but so is the cost. Mind you, the bigger, more accurate and larger number of missiles per submarine (124 warheads in each Trident-type SSBN) has an appeal.

The arguments against Trident come from two sides: those against nuclear weapons in general, who believe that any system is morally wrong; and those who believe that it would be better to build up conventional forces to deter aggression. However, the United kingdom would only use a SLBM (submarine launched ballistic missile) if the nation was directly attacked; self-defence only. It is true that neither Trident nor Polaris can be classed as true first strike weapons, but the final firing decision lies with the Prime Minister of the day. The cost— about £6,000 million. Peace can be expensive.

The Navy and Northern Ireland

Without doubt, the RN has an important and continued role to play in the 'Troubles' which have beset the province of Northern Ireland for some years. There are two roles which the Service specifically operates, although both are less prominent than those of the RAF or the Army.

The RN operates in support of the General Officer Commanding (GOC) Northern Ireland in counter-terrorist missions, but it has its own more independent functions as well. Basically, the Navy has the somewhat arduous responsibility of preventing gun-running and the movement of arms within the Province's borders, by water. To carry out these duties at sea, *Bird* Class patrol craft have recently replaced the ubiquitous *Ton* Class MCMVs. These warships have a boarding role which is somewhat distant and unpublicised as it takes place beyond the gaze of the public eye, but the RN has been successful in keeping illegal seaborne traffic at bay.

On the Northern Irish loughs, such as Carlingford and Neagh, the Navy maintains regular patrols in conjunction with the Royal Marines—whose role is covered separately. On Carlingford Lough use is made of *Loyal* Class tenders, *Alert* (ex-*Loyal Governor*) and *Vigilant* (ex-*Loyal Factor*), and again their operations are in conjunction with the RMs.

In terms of organisation, the Senior Naval Officer

Northern Ireland (SNONI) is responsible to FOSNI for the efficient operation of the RN, although many of the missions are tasked by GOC with advice from SNONI.

The Navy very wisely plays down its role in the problems of Ulster, but it can be recorded here that the contribution is worthwhile and successful whether it be in foot patrols by Commandos in South Armagh, general helicopter support by Wessex HU 5s of the Naval Air Commando Squadrons, or by the prevention of smuggling on water.

The Navy and NATO

Since the cessation of hostilities in 1945, Britain's defence role has shifted from that of Imperial power to that of a European power. The withdrawal from Empire became rather rushed in the 1950s and 1960s, hastened by political rather than sound defence thinking. In 1971–2 the UK Armed Forces were withdrawn from East of Suez and only the passage of time will tell if this has been a prudent philosophy.

The NATO Military Command structure was set up in 1949 as an alliance of the 'free' western nations who were concerned about possible Soviet expansionism following that country's territorial gains after World War 2. The nations involved are: Canada, Belgium, Denmark, Norway, Greece, Turkey, Iceland, Italy, Portugal, the Netherlands, Great Britain, The United States, Luxembourg and West Germany. Although France would only become integrated in time of tension or war, nevertheless the French Navy is often to be found exercising with the other NATO partners. In the next few years it is envisaged that Spain will join NATO, bringing her not inconsiderable naval forces under the white NATO star.

NATO is a defensive organisation whose main aim is to deter war and to contain acts of aggression. At present, the threat is seen as coming from the Soviet Bloc and NATO strategy is deterrent in outlook, although the use of both tactical and strategic nuclear weapons would be possible in the last resort. The UK contributes a balanced range of forces to NATO, from all three Services and it is the maritime forces which perhaps face the greatest challenge from Soviet naval and naval air forces in the Arctic, Atlantic, Mediterranean, Black Sea and Baltic areas.

The RN also plays a significant part with other NATO naval units in the supply and re-supply of the Land Forces on the Central Front. In Northern Norway, known as the Northern Flank, there are contingency plans for the deployment of at least one Royal Marines Commando, complete with its equipment. Unfortunately, by 1986, the two specialist Commando Forces landing ships (LPAs) may have been phased out of service, with no alternative other than commercial vehicle ferries seemingly available.

The reinforcement and resupply of forces in Europe is completely dependent on the sea lanes across the Atlantic Ocean being kept open. In addition, the Channel ports and airfields of Britain will be vitally important to this effort. This is why, in recent years, the risk of mines and mining along the UK coasts has been, at last, taken seriously.

NATO naval forces in the Atlantic—mainly US, Canadian and Dutch, besides the now lessened RN contribution—must be able to respond to the threat at all levels. Firstly, in time of war, the enemy's submarine forces will need to be cleared from the area and the NATO Striking Fleet Atlantic (based on a US Naval Carrier Task Force) will need to be supported. Troops will have to be ferried to Norway and other vulnerable areas and then the seaward defence of Europe prepared. Unfortunately, nowhere in this strategy does there *appear* to be any concern shown for the raw material trade routes in the South Atlantic or Indian Ocean.

Some of the submarine forces will be deployed protecting the British, French and American SSBNs which may provide the West's last hope in time of war. At last, NATO has realised that the battle on the Central Front can only be won by the steady resupply of a million men and 11 million tonnes of equipment—nearly all of which will come by sea.

The old convoy commanders' maxim of ensuring the safe and timely arrival of his charges will never have a more apt situation.

The general context: Britain within NATO
(Reprinted in full from the *Statement on the Defence Estimates 1981*, Cmnd. 8212–1.)

'1. As a sovereign nation we must in the end decide for ourselves what tasks our armed forces should be ready to perform, and how they should be designed to meet them. But we cannot decide in a vacuum; many hard realities bear upon our choices. We have to consider what adversary we may face, and what his capability is and may become. We have to consider what level of resources to set for defence (and also—the other side of the coin—what security risks any such setting implies). And, in an Alliance, we have to consider how our contributions interact with those of our partners.

'2. NATO is not a supra-national authority assigning tasks to individual members as though to subordinates. Its international commanders and staffs seek to influence national choices in the common interest; but the pattern of roles has for the most part evolved gradually among the member nations themselves, by accommodation and adjustment which usually owes more to the interplay of historical, geographical, economic and political factors than to specific negotiations or bargains. The result (of which paragraph 309 gives

The RN exercises regularly with NATO and friendly navies: Juno *with the RNethN's* Friesland *and the Nigerian* Otobo (RN).

some features) is the defence posture of the Alliance. It is rarely what pure strategic theory might suggest; but it reflects a complex structure of inter-dependence and confidence which needs subtle understanding.

'3. Britain's own present pattern of force commitment to the Alliance illustrates this. Of our four principal roles the nuclear contribution (the least costly) derives from special factors which make us in practice the only possible European provider. Direct defence of the United Kingdom is a role where we must clearly shoulder the main burden ourselves, though others may help. We make the main European contribution to Alliance maritime effort and are well fitted to do so. In purely historical terms our stationing of major land and air forces on the Continent is the least obviously natural of our roles; yet this very fact gives it special significance. Beyond its direct military importance in protecting a key sector of front covering the Alliance's heartland, it expresses and guarantees the full commitment of our national effort (including our nuclear capability) to the collective security of our key European allies as inseparable from our own.

'4. It is unreal to suppose that the United Kingdom could safely or sensibly abandon any of these roles. Talk of choosing in some simple or exclusive way between, say, a "maritime" and a "Continental" effort is misconceived. We must, however, shape our future contribution to the four roles in a world of shifting military, political, economic and techno-logical pressures.

'5. The pace of technological advance, with the rising cost of exploiting it, puts inescapable financial pressure on our defence budget. It does not follow that we must be forced out of major areas of our defence effort, especially as the scale of that effort is ultimately a matter of free political choice, not of economic determinism. But we must take especial care, within each of our main roles, to concentrate our expenditure where it will be most truly effective for the Alliance, and this may sometimes mean hard decisions about the content of our programme.

'6. The resource pressures we face are common to all members of the Alliance. This, and the fact of interdependence, suggests that programme choices should so far as possible be made consciously within an Alliance framework. NATO's Long Term Defence Programme launched in 1978 was an important step in this direction. But as both the external threat from new challenges and the economic pressures sharpen, there will be a growing need to ensure that the contributions made by each ally individually fit into a sensible pattern of defence effort by the Alliance as a whole and that the Alliance obtains full value for the resources it spends

on defence. Even now, the Alliance appears to spend in total more than the Warsaw Pact on defence; and while much of the Pact's cost-effectiveness springs from features such as massive conscription and enforced uniformity which we should not wish to emulate, we cannot be complacent about the results. A willingness to look at new patterns of joint effort— more far-reaching interdependence, for example, or greater use of the Alliance's highly developed civilian resources for logistic support in emergency—may be worthwhile. The Government would welcome, and will seek to encourage, renewed effort by the Alliance in this general direction.'

Almost the entire RN would be assigned to NATO in time of war and, up until 1981, this would have included 59 destroyers and frigates declared to NATO plus the bulk of Submarine Command (*qv*) and the operational Fleet Air Arm squadrons. In the Defence Review entitled *The Way Forward*, which is dealt with in detail elsewhere, the Government decided to reduce the figure to 50 surface vessels, part of which could be made up of largely unmodernised warships, at present serving in the Standly Squadron (*qv*) at Chatham—a naval port itself under the shadow of axe. A further reduction in RFAs was announced to coincide with the reduction of warships and this programme is currently being carried out.

The RN forces which could be committed to NATO would be: 50 frigates and destroyers; Polaris SSBNs; about 25 SSNs and SSKs; large warships, such as *Invincible*; and some 25 RFAs. In addition, the RN's Mines Countermeasures (MCM) Squadrons are dedicated to NATO.

NATO in action To give an indication of the possible uses of RN warships in the NATO context, the following example is as good as any which can be contrived at the present time. The scenario is an Underway Replenishment Group (URG) consisting of nine supply ships and tankers which is escorted by a screening force of British, American, Dutch and Canadian surface warships with long-range maritime reconnaissance support by a Canadian CP-140 Aurora aircraft from Novia Scotia.

The RN screening forces are: *Invincible* Class (flagship), with nine Sea King HAS 5s; *County* Class, with one Wessex HAS 3; *Amazon* with one Lynx HAS 2. In addition, the Dutch frigate is equipped with a SH-14A Lynx, the American destroyer escort with a new Seahawk LAMPS III helicopter and a Canadian destroyer with a CH-124 Sea King aboard.

In the event of intervention by an enemy submarine, it is most likely that the Aurora's Tandem sonobuoy system would detect the target

STANAVFORLANT: steaming in Norwegian waters are Oslo *(Norway)*, Margaree *(Canada)*, Augsbourg *(FGN)*, Miller *(USN)*, Van Galen *(Dutch) and right*, Ambuscade (RN photo by PO Jones).

and by datalink this information would be passed on to the Flagship and hence to the rest of the escort group. It would be normal in all but the most severe weather conditions for an ASW helicopter screen to be deployed ahead of the URG with dipping active sonar. The helicopters would be Sea King HAS 5s (*qv*) from the flagship and they would be deployed to investigate the Aurora's contact, whilst two more Sea Kings would be scrambled to take up the screen position in case there is more than one hostile about in the area. Once active sonar contact is gained by the Sea Kings, the torpedo-armed Lynx from *Amazon* and the Dutch frigate would be scrambled to attack, being controlled by the Senior Observer in the Sea Kings who is designated 'Scene of Action Commander'. The American and Dutch warships detach from the screen and form a Surface Attack Unit (SAU), whilst the URG zigzags away from the contact. The helicopters, supported by Aurora, would attack the contact in coordination with the SAU. The result would hopefully be the destruction of the hostile submarine or, at the very least, it would be forced away to run deep out of the area.

STANAVFORCHAN On the other end of the scale is the Standing Naval Force Channel, a NATO permanent international naval force deployed in the MCM role. The Force provides a continuous MCM capability in peacetime and ensures that NATO common purpose and inter-ship/inter-nation operability could be rapidly reinforced in time of tension or war, not least by MCM 2, a *Ton* Class

squadron based at *Vernon* (*qv*), Portsmouth. STANAVFORCHAN is primarily formed from nations with an interest in the Channel and southern North Sea although other nationals, such as Germany, Denmark and the US, have contributed warships in the past. The French Navy is also known to have exercised with the Force on occasions.

Both minesweepers and mine hunters are deployed, each warship remaining with the Force for a minimum of six months and then returning to its normal duties with its own Navy. Only the RN, Belgium and the Netherlands provide the Force Commander, which allows for important experience in command of a multi-national warship group. This latter situation is most important to the well-being of NATO in time of tension or war. The fact that such a Force exists is not related to any escalation in normal NATO maritime strengths or purposes but it provides a base on which to build international co-operation and provides an added deterrence to war.

For operational purposes, command of the Force is the responsibility of CinC Fleet, in his NATO role as Commander-in-Chief Channel (CINCHAN). A typical complement of the Force is: *Truffaut*, Royal Belgium Navy (leader); *Abconde* and *Giethoorn*, Royal Netherlands Navy; *Konstanz*, Federal German Navy; and *Bossington*, Royal Navy.

STANAVFORLANT This is another NATO international naval force which was formed at Portland in 1968 'to threaten no-one, but to help keep the peace and to dissuade any potential

Backbone of the Fleet Air Arm's contribution to NATO—the Sea King (820 NAS illustrated).

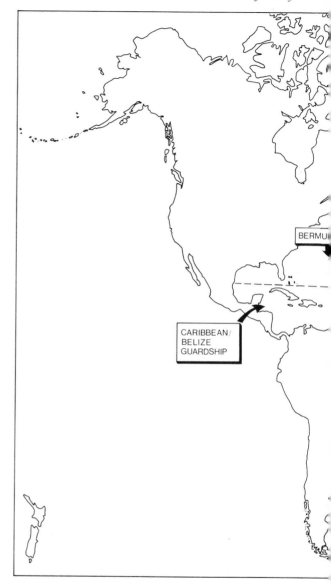

troublemaker in the vital area of the Atlantic'. Standing Naval Force Atlantic comprises up to eight frigates and destroyers, usually drawn from the navies of Norway, Canada, Federal Germany, Britain, the Netherlands and the United States, with command rotating amongst the different navies. Its role in wartime is to provide the nucleus for the defence of the shipping lanes which are controlled by SACLANT (Supreme Allied Commander Atlantic) from Norfolk, Virginia. The Force spends at least 60 per cent of the time at sea in the Atlantic area. A typical composition is: *Luce*, United States Navy; *Bacchante*, Royal Navy; *Nipigon*, Canadian Forces; *Isaac Sweers*, Royal Netherlands Navy; *Karlsruhe*, Federal German Navy; and *Stavanger*, Royal Norwegian Navy.

The Mediterranean In this area, there is no permanent naval force organised by NATO, but there is an On-Call Force to which Britain, the United States, Italy, Greece and Turkey contribute frigates or destroyers, as and when required. The RN is pledged to keep one (preferably two) surface vessels available in the Mediterranean and it usually doubles as Gibraltar Guardship; it could also be a frigate which has recently completed refit at the dockyard on the Rock.

Anti-Submarine Group Two This is the NATO force responsible for a major part of the anti-submarine defence of the NATO Strike Fleet Atlantic and is of key importance to NATO's Northern Flank. It is now under the Command of Flag Officer Third Flotilla (FOF3) (*qv*), whose NATO hat is a Commander of ASGRUTWO (COMASGRUTWO).

In wartime, the Group would comprise one, or two, of the *Invincible* Class anti-submarine carriers (or one of them plus *Hermes*) which would deploy a squadron of Sea Harrier FRS 1s and one of Sea King HAS 2/5s. In addition, there would be up to a squadron of Type 42 Destroyers in the anti-aircraft/anti-missile role, plus a number of Type 22 anti-submarine frigates and other warships, which may

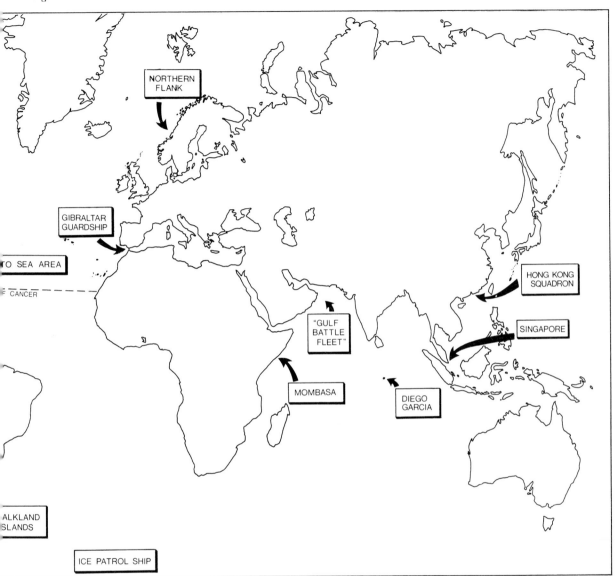

NORTHERN
FLANK

GIBRALTAR
GUARDSHIP

TO SEA AREA

CANCER

"GULF
BATTLE
FLEET"

HONG KONG
SQUADRON

SINGAPORE

MOMBASA

DIEGO
GARCIA

FALKLAND
ISLANDS

ICE PATROL SHIP

include one or more SSNs. Long-range maritime air patrol can no longer be provided by the RN since the cessation of fixed-wing naval aviation and so this role is left to Nimrod MR 2 aircraft based in Cornwall and Scotland.

UK/NL Amphibious Force Again the wartime role of FOF3, this Force provides Commando/ Marine units for Norway and Denmark, and also for the Atlantic Islands. In essence, the UK/Dutch Amphibious Force would arrive long before US and Canadian forces could be deployed and it is scheduled for protection in tension and war by the

RN/RNethN and possibly ASGRUTWO.

NATO sea training A great deal of expertise has been built up since World War 2 by the RN in the sea training role. Today, Portland Sea Training Area provide facilities for joint exercises where valuable experience can be gained by NATO navies. This is an important part of the NATO concept and it is not unusual to see German, Belgian or Dutch vessels alongside at the naval base. The RN also provides aircraft (FRADU) and 'targets', both surface and sub-surface, for warships to use in trials or work-up.

Fleet Air Arm contribution In recent years,

Squadron	Type	Deployment	Remarks
814	Sea King HAS 2	*Illustrious/Seahawk*	Assigned
819	Sea King HAS 2	*Gannet*	Assigned
820	Sea King HAS 5	*Invincible/Seahawk*	Assigned
824	Sea King HAS 2	RFAs/*Seahawk*	Assigned
826	Sea King HAS 2/5	*Hermes/Seahawk*	Assigned
706	Sea King HAS 2/5	*Seahawk*	Earmarked
737	Wessex HAS 3	*County* Class/*Osprey**	Assigned/earmarked
829	Wasp HAS 1	Frigates/*Osprey*	Assigned/earmarked
815	Lynx HAS 2	Frigates/Destroyers/	Assigned/earmarked
702	Lynx HAS 2	*Heron*	Earmarked
845	Wessex HU 5	*Hermes/Heron*	Assigned
846	Sea King HC 4	*Hermes/Heron*	Assigned
847	Wessex HU 5	*Heron*	Earmarked
848	Wessex HU 5	*Heron*	Earmarked
771	Wessex HU 5	*Seahawk*	Earmarked
772	Wessex HU 5	RFAs/*Osprey*	Assigned/earmarked

* 737 is scheduled to re-equip with Sea King in 1982/83.

the British Government has declared the above helicopter elements of Naval Air Command available to NATO in 1982.

Task Groups and out-of-area deployments For over a decade now the RN has been, for all intents and most purposes, withdrawn into the NATO area—from the Caribbean to the Mediterranean and from the Tropic of Cancer to the North Pole. This is, however, a very generalised view as not only has there been during this time a presence at Hong Kong (*qv*), but also since 1974–75, there has been a distinct and determined policy of 'showing the flag' by means of Task Groups working out of area. Just as significant was the Beira Patrol (*qv*) and the present 'Gulf Battle Fleet' operations.

The philosophy behind these forays into the South Atlantic, Indian and Pacific Oceans is not only one of publicity, because being away from the relatively cramped waters around the United Kingdom and North America allows a Group, usually 10–12 strong, to act independently in a continuous training and exercising role without the continued presence of Soviet snoopers. Further, although such organisations as CENTO and SEATO no longer function, the RN can take the opportunity of being in the waters of friendly nations to hold bilateral or even multi-lateral Fleet exercises. Notwithstanding the purely naval input, the Task Group Deployments provide a significant boost for sailors' morale, an opportunity to show our friends some of the latest naval hardware available (for example, the 1980 visit to the People's Republic of China was of benefit to the Defence Sales Organisation as well as increasing international understanding). Finally, in conjunction with MOD(N), the Foreign and

Commonwealth Office is able to put a British presence into areas where at other times this could not be done. For example, having a British naval force in the Indian Ocean goes some way to countering otherwise almost total Soviet domination at sea here.

It is a well-known fact that Britain and her other European allies rely on the use of merchant seapower to provide a means of bringing vital raw materials and other trade goods to our shores. British merchant ships work four million tonnes of cargo each day, with 97 per cent of our imports and exports being seaborne. In 1979, the UK imported about 59 million tonnes of crude oil by sea, without taking into account our own North Sea supplies. As a contrast, Department of Trade figures show that the Warsaw Pact countries rely on ships for only one per cent of their import-export trade; the bulk of their mercantile fleets being employed in carrying other peoples' goods and so earning valuable hard foreign currency. It is, therefore, vital that the RN is able to exercise world-wide Naval Control of Shipping (NCS). This long dormant relic of World War 2 has been recently resurrected to provide what would in wartime be a most valuable service to the Merchant Navy. NSC is discussed below.

In general, since 1974–75 there have been annually either one large deployment or two smaller ones, these having a duration of between five and nine months. For example, in May 1978 seven warships and three RFAs left the UK for a seven-month deployment to the Caribbean and the West Coast of North America, taking part in several exercises, including 'Suvoit' (French), 'Comptuex' (US) and 'Marcot' (Canadian). The warships were

Blake (flagship of Rear Admiral D.J. Halifax, Flag Office First Flotilla) together with *Birmingham*, *Hermione*, *Leander*, *Juno*, *Ambuscade* and *Conqueror*. Travelling in the other direction two years later another Task Group, this time led by *Antrim* (Rear Admiral D.C. Jenkin, Flag Office First Flotilla), went to the Indian Ocean and the Far East; a visit to Shanghai was made, being the first such visit to China since 1949. The contingent was somewhat smaller because the needs of the Fleet in other areas, notably the Atlantic, had to be satisfied; however *Coventry*, *Galatea*, *Naiad* and *Alacrity* were spared for this historic voyage.

'Gulf Battle Fleet'

Towards the end of 1980 in a Group Deployment to the Far East—coded Task Group 318.0—the guided missile destroyer *Coventry* was sent post-haste from Hong Kong to the Gulf of Oman where the Iraq-Iran war was threatening to cause an interruption to the free flow of merchant shipping of all nations, particularly crude-oil tankers from the Gulf States to the rest of the world. *Antrim* and *Naiad* later joined their deployment 'mate', to be relieved by *Birmingham* and *Avenger* in November 1980. These warships, now sporting Union Flags on their bridge tops for easy recognition, were destined to patrol the Gulf of Oman, backed up initially by *Olmeda* and *Fort Austin* until the arrival of *Apollo* and *Ardent*, which eventually meant that, through the use of Mombasa*, a former British naval port in Kenya, two frigates could be on patrol and two undergoing an AMP turn and turn about.

By Christmas 1980 there was definite talk of an RN presence for several years, especially as the 'Gulf War' was smouldering on. The problem facing the Royal Navy was without doubt one of economics, with perhaps a small amount of concern about cutting other permanent commitments. Talk in 1981 of a Western Quick-Reaction Force for the Gulf gave an added dimension to the RN presence.

The Caribbean

The continued problems, mainly consisting of threats from neighbouring nations on Belize (formerly British Honduras), has led to the continued deployment of a Caribbean Guardship. Until the end of the last decade, it was almost a permanent billet for *Tribal* Class frigates, but since their demise the RN has allocated DLGs and FFNs to the area. Besides showing the flag around former British colonies and providing nautical assistance to Belize, the Guardship has, in recent years, proved its

* Mombasa Liaison Office: a Lieutenant Commander (RNLO) plus a senior rating.

worth on humanitarian grounds. One especial example is the role played by *Fife* in the Dominican hurricane relief operations in August 1979. By some herculean effort, *Fife*'s ship's flight under Lieutenant Commander J. Passmore, stripped the Wessex HAS 3 (called 'Humphrey') of all its anti-submarine warfare gear and proceeded to fly aid into the island. A total of 530 flying hours saved an otherwise desperate situation. The ship's flight received a well deserved CinC Fleet's Commendation and the Flight Commander an MBE. Besides disaster relief, several RN warships on the Caribbean station have provided venues for important Summit meetings, for example Heath-Nixon in 1974.

Diego Garcia

In the Indian Ocean, the British island of Diego Garcia has been host to a substantial American presence for some years, mainly for use as a mid-Ocean staging post. The RN maintains a small naval party on the island led by a Commander and consisting of 26 other men.

The threat

'Our maritime forces are primarily designed for ASW (anti-submarine warfare) as the most dangerous threat is from Soviet Submarines'
Defence White Paper 1981

It is a regrettable fact of the modern world that there is in real terms a threat to the peaceful existence of the United Kingdom and other nations in the so-called Free World. 'The threat' is a convenient term which avoids all the problems of 'capabilities' and 'intentions'. The Ministry of Defence assesses the capability of the UK's potential enemy, the Warsaw Pact, to wage war on us and our allies, although it should be remembered that the final intentions of any Government are a complex mass of political feelings and events. The main justification for the West feeling 'threatened' is the current trend of the Soviet Union to build up her forces, both conventional and nuclear, to a position far in excess of her old, immediate postwar defensive role. This build-up has apparently been conducted in a climate of non-budgetary constraints, and over the past ten years Soviet military expenditure has risen at an average rate of four per cent per annum in real terms. This means that the Soviet Union is now allocating about 12–14 per cent of its Gross National Produce (GNP) to defence and weapons procurement amounts to 40 per cent of the defence budget. The UK figure is around five per cent of the GNP.

In peacetime, the role of the Soviet Navy would seem to be: maintenance of the deterrent;

Left *The threat?—the Soviet carrier* Kiev *is shadowed down the English Channel by a Sea Harrier of 800 NAS, on the Prince of Wales' wedding day* (HMS Heron).

Right *The major threat is judged to be that of Soviet/Warsaw Pact submarines as illustrated here by an* Echo II *Class cruise-missile type* (MoD).

surveillance and intelligence gathering; providing a naval presence to support foreign policy, and providing a naval counter-presence to foreign nations. The roles in wartime are different: nuclear strategic strike and nuclear defence; defence of the Soviet Union from seaborne attack; support of Soviet and allied ground forces, and ocean maritime warfare, both conventional and nuclear.

The Soviet strategic strike force is divided amongst the Russian armed services, but great emphasis is placed on the naval role with a priority being given to the submarine launched ballistic missile (SLBM). The second assumption is that the Soviets have concentrated a great deal of effort, know-how and cash into the anti-submarine forces of its navy which would 'deal' with NATO and Western SLBM forces in time of war. These forces are both surface and sub-surface, and could easily deal with Allied carrier task groups or any other type of warship which the Soviets themselves see as a threat.

Submarines
The SALT (Strategic Arms Limitation Talks) II arrangements have imposed a limit of 62 missile-firing submarines (SSBNs) and 950 accountable missiles on Russia. The leading classes are the Northern Fleet-based *Delta* and *Delta II* Classes, and the older *Yankee* Class. There is a new class of super-SSBN on the stocks in several shipyards in the USSR. The *Deltas* have the newer SSN-8 intercontinental ballistic missile which has an estimated range of 4,800 nm (8,890 km) and this

puts most of the supposed targets in the USA and Europe within range of a submarine operating within Soviet 'waters'. The older *Yankees* do, however, have to cross the Atlantic or Pacific to come into range of their supposed targets.

Besides the strategic intercontinental types, the Soviets have a fleet of tactical missile firing submarines, part nuclear and part conventional, with which they can support ground forces or attack likely targets at sea.

The hunter-killer submarine is also prominent in the Russian armoury and there are about 200 available to their C-in-C Northern Fleet. Again the forces are both conventional and nuclear. The SSNs in the Soviet Fleet are likely to be reserved for distant areas where lack of air coverage could restrict Soviet surface involvement. There are about 40 SSNs of which about half are *Victor* Class, with a speed of over 30 knots and estimated to be the best Soviet anti-submarine platform currently operational. The diesel-powered SSKs of the *Foxtrot* and *Tango* Classes are likely to operate at choke points, such as the Baltic approaches and North Cape.

The *Charlie* Class cruise missile, nuclear-powered, submarines (SSGN) which are operated in the Soviet Fleet pose a threat to the NATO strike carriers and anti-submarine warfare carrier task groups. Their missiles are only capable of a range of about 30 nm (56 km) but this means that, unlike some of the surface ships, they would not need the over-the-horizon guidance of aircraft or picket ships and are therefore more difficult to detect in the engagement area. The longer-range cruise missile-carrying submarines mentioned above are the *Echo*

II and *Juliet* Classes which have the over-the-horizon type of missile.

The major threat to the North Atlantic area is the Soviet Northern Red Banner Fleet which built up its submarine force from 194 submarines in 1968 to 195 in 1979; however, in 1968 only 44 of these were nuclear-powered, whereas by 1979 there were 104. It is the latter figure which is important because of the sheer overwhelming improvement of the nuclear boats over their conventional counterparts. The threat of the 'Bear' should not be over-emphasised but we should not ignore it either.

Surface ships

In recent years, the Soviets have begun to build larger warships, including battlecruisers and aircraft carriers; the latter being rather ironic as the RN has been forced to phase out conventional strike carriers because their political masters feel that they are outmoded weapons systems. The Russian Navy now has some of the most heavily armed ships in the world, and undoubtedly they are geared towards the anti-submarine role and against NATO strike carriers. ASW helicopters, such as the Ka-25 *Hormone*, have been in service for many years providing a screen similar to that of the earlier ASW helicopters in the RN, such as the Wessex HAS 3. Now, the Soviet Naval Air Arm is being equipped with the Yak *Forger* VSTOL fighter/strike aircraft which, although quite primitive by RN (Sea Harrier) standards, is probably the forerunner for a new generation of aircraft for the *Kiev* Class carriers, of which four appear to be planned.

The most formidable additions to the Soviet Fleet in the medium range in recent years have been the *Kara* Class cruisers which, with the *Moskva* Class anti-submarine carriers (CVS) and the *Kresta II* cruisers, are the backbone of the units which are seen deployed into the Atlantic and beyond. In terms of lower units, the Russians have large numbers of destroyers, frigates, corvettes and even hovercraft assault vehicles. One wonders why the Soviet Government feels it needs such weapons—could it really be that they feel threatened by the West?

Considerable alarm has been raised in recent years about the presumed stockpile of offensive, highly developed mines, which the Soviets are thought to have available to sow around NATO coasts—Britain like most NATO navies has tended to neglect the importance of mines counter measures, but the new *Hunt* Class (*qv*) will redress the balance a little.

In this decade, it is the new world-wide ability of the Soviet Navy which will concern Western observers, especially with the launching of the nuclear-powered *Kirov* and the two new *Kiev* Class carriers. Already large squadrons regularly deploy from their Atlantic, Black Sea and Pacific bases to the Indian Ocean and the Mediterranean. Together with the fixed-wing air support available to their Fleet, and improved support and amphibious assault capability, the Russian Government has the capability to project naval power in peacetime almost anywhere it chooses around the world. It is vitally important to the whole world that efforts are continued to find a reasonable path to disarmament, and that Peaceful Co-existence becomes a true phrase not just one of propaganda. Whatever happens NATO must always be watchful.

The offshore tapestry

With a major world-wide interest in undersea minerals and food supplies, every nation which has coastal areas is concerned with the problems which go with its littoral position. The United Kingdom has problems mainly involved with fisheries' protection and the surveillance of offshore hydrocarbon production. The 'offshore tapestry' can therefore be defined as a programme of overall control of Britain's continental shelf resources.

Fisheries' protection

In 1977 the UK, along with the other nations in the European Economic Community (EEC), extended her fishing limits to 200 nm (370 km), thus increasing the area of supervision from 30,000 square miles (77,700 sq km) to 270,000 square miles

(699,300 sq km). The tasks thus imposed on the RN for the fisheries' protection and offshore installation surveillance are undertaken by the Fisheries' Protection Squadron based at Rosyth.

Obviously, the decision on fishing limits was not taken lightly and the RN was prepared for its implementation. For several years, the ubiquitous *Ton* Class MCMVs had been used by the Offshore Division in English, Welsh and Irish waters for patrol, whilst in Scottish areas, the Department of Agriculture and Fisheries supplied civilian-manned vessels specially built on trawler lines for the comparatively bad sea conditions. The RN adopted the design and modified it for naval purposes; thus was born the *Island* Class OPV (Offshore Patrol Vessel) which entered service in 1976 and has now been followed by the improved *Castle* Class OPV-2s.

The RN undertakes fisheries' protection on behalf of the Ministry of Agriculture, Fisheries and Food, the Department of Agriculture and Fisheries (Scotland) and the Department of Agriculture (Northern Ireland). The offshore installation surveillance role is carried out for the Department of Energy and is undertaken by the Offshore Division only.

*Together for the first time are the three types of warship used for Fisheries Protection work—*Castle, Island *and* Ton *Classes (FOSNI).*

Aerial cover was provided in the southern North Sea, Channel and South-Western Approaches until 1981 by 781 NAS's Sea Devon aircraft. With the disbandment of the squadron, the sea areas are now covered for the time being by a longer-range Sea Heron from Culdrose Station Flight. In addition, the complete 270,000 square mile Economic Zone is constantly patrolled by RAF Nimrod aircraft tasked from the Maritime Headquarters at Mountbatten and Pitreavie as appropriate. This is perhaps the least cost-effective use of these magnificent aircraft yet devised! These operations have been undertaken since 1977 on the basis of 180 flying hours per month, and many arrests have been enabled through the swift action and co-ordination of Nimrod and OPV crews. A more cost-effective aircraft for these duties is currently being sought, and the British Aerospace Coastguarder is being considered for civilian-manned operations under the auspices of the Coastguard Service.

Every year some one million tonnes of fish are landed in Britain, having been taken from our waters, and this tonnage has a market value of £250 million. It is therefore of special importance to the fishing industry that all illegalities, particularly foreign interference, are prevented. The legislation required to control fishing is both extensive and complicated for it is derived from England and Wales, Northern Ireland, Scotland and the EEC. Legislation is notified to the 'Fish Squadron' by various Government Departments, but all other aspects of the role are under normal RN procedures. Every year, there is the Annual Fishery Protection Conference which is attended by all interested parties and this is when the following year's requirements are discussed. Frequently, fishing vessels are boarded* to have their catches and equipment checked by RN officers, all of whom have had to undergo a specialist course to fit them for their task. Trials are continuing to find a suitable tender for boarding to replace and augment the Gemini and the Avon Searider. Today, conservation is an important facet of fisheries' protection.

Current warship assets available to the Captain, Fisheries' Protection are: five *Island* Class (civilian-manned), by arrangement with the Department of Agriculture and Fisheries; nine *Ton* Class MCMVs (current deployments of this Class are given in Chapter Four); five *Island* Class OPVs (Offshore Division), and two *Island* Class OPVs (occasional use, dependent on refits, etc). Certain units of the Rosyth-based Eighth Frigate Squadron are also available, as are other units of the Fleet which can be

---

* In 1980, 1,508 British, foreign and EEC fishing vessels were boarded by RN parties and 16 convictions were later confirmed.

recognised by their black and yellow quartered flags; Fisheries' Protection aircraft also carry these pennants. In 1982, the first of the *Castle* Class began to replace the *Tons*, and the former are helicopter-capable, making rotary wing action far easier to operate. The Department of Energy pays for all Offshore Division's work on a day-to-day basis, plus contributing to the capital cost of hardware. As political developments are constant, the above balance of forces may be altered during the coming decade.

One aspect of the 'Fish Patrol' which does not usually receive attention is the seasonal salmon patrols carried out well inshore off the east coast of Scotland. These operations involve dawn and dusk patrols by ships' Gemini craft to deter salmon poachers who abound in these areas with illegal nets.

Natural resources

With so much of the world's natural resources on land having been exploited during the last hundred years, the reserve potential under the seas, especially on and under the relatively shallow Continental Shelf areas, are being examined in great detail. In the North Sea, Irish Sea and Celtic Sea areas, there are several major oil and natural gas operations underway which are of increasing economic importance to the United Kingdom. It has recently been estimated that the North Sea's contribution to the UK Gross National Product could be as high as £17.5 billion per annum by 1985 and it is a fact of life already that a production platform is worth in excess of £100 million, whilst a drilling platform costs about £15 million. In addition, there are pipelines to Scotland, East Anglia and the Shetlands, supply ships, pipe-laying barges, spare buoy storage points, diving systems and safety boats, etc, also in the area. By 1980, there were about 100 fixed platforms alone in the North Sea. All of these need protection in one form or another.

Deterrence of terrorism RN offshore patrol forces, both the seaborne Offshore Division and aerial reconnaissance operations, provide a useful deterrence to terrorism, although the forces are too thinly stretched. Should an incident occur there are now special units available in the form of a Quick Reaction Force (QRF). The backbone of the QRF is Commachio Company, RM which is based at RM Condor, Arbroath. These men are available to aid the civil power in an anti-terrorist or counter-terrorist role. They would approach possible targets by whatever means is necessary, including Sea Kings (819 NAS at Prestwick), Gazelles from Montfortebeek Flight at Arbroath, *Island* Class OPVs and SSKs. Commachio Company was

Royal Marines provide part of the offshore installation protection—elements of 45 Commando on a Shell/Esso rig (MoD).

formed on May 1 1980 and is under the control of HQ Commando Forces, Plymouth, and contains SBS elements (see Chapter Six).

Ocean safety Measures have also been taken to ensure the safety of production and other platforms from collision damage, by establishing a 1,604-ft (500-m) no-entry safety zone around the base of the installation. Included are the special tanker loading buoys. Offenders can be apprehended by patrol vessels or LRMP aircraft. The Department of Energy's backing of these patrols has already been discussed above.

Pollution control The RN, particularly the *Island* Class OPVs and the *Ton* Class MCMVs, act in co-operation with the Department of Trade's Marine Pollution Unit in the event of an oil or similar spillage at sea. In addition, very effective work has been carried out by Royal Maritime Auxiliary Service (RMAS) craft in spillage containment in such incidents as the *Amoco Cadiz* disaster. Specialist assistance is available to the civil power at most RN naval bases and port facilities, and includes firefighting and oil dispersant capabilities. The RN has no real, direct role in these operations, but it does have the facility to re-charge the costs of any involvement to the appropriate Government or civilian agency if called out.

Search And Rescue

RN Search and Rescue (SAR) helicopters play an important part in the 'offshore tapestry', in co-ordination with the RAF, HM Coastguards and the Royal National Lifeboat Institution. Life-saving operations are undertaken on behalf of the Department of Trade and are dealt with in detail in Chapter Five. It should not be forgotten that all

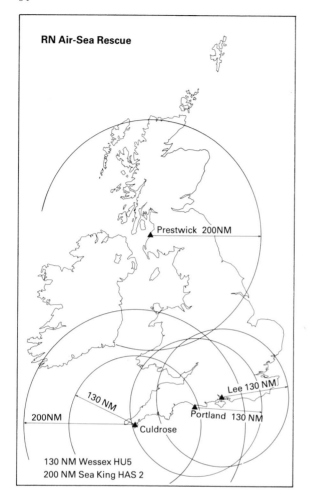

RN Air-Sea Rescue

Prestwick 200NM

Lee 130 NM

130 NM

Portland 130 NM

200NM

Culdrose

130 NM Wessex HU5
200 NM Sea King HAS 2

HM Survey Ship Bulldog—*an important element in the Offshore Tapestry.*

warships are SAR-capable and many now carry helicopter flights. The RN usually takes on a co-ordinating role in the event of a major disaster or rescue.

The survey task

RN ocean and coastal survey ships are designed for the dual role of hydrographic and oceanographic surveys on a world-wide basis. The task of keeping the international series of Admiralty charts up to date is carried out by these ships and at the Hydrographer to the Navy's department at Taunton, Somerset; it is never-ending.* The problems of shifting sandbanks and channels continually faces the surveyor but it is the great

* In 1980, the Admiralty's Hydrographic Department at Taunton produced 575,000 books and 2,772 million charts for sale to customers world-wide.

increase in the tonnage, draught and number of merchant ships in the last decade which has caused a major re-survey programme at home and abroad. In addition, the search for oil and natural gas, and now undersea minerals, means that charts and maps have to be that much better than before. Surveys in remote parts of the world were adequate when the only shipping in the area was passing far off-shore. Now, with new ports and harbours being developed in the Third World, especially to exploit natural resources, more detailed surveys and larger-scale charts are required and hence the amount of time spent by RN survey ships abroad.

Traditionally, the 'Drogie' has concentrated on recording depth and sea bed conditions against co-ordinated positions (or fixes) and the related activities of navigational, coastline and tidal reference work. Today, despite its formation in 1795, the RN's Hydrographic Department has managed to survey only a small fraction of the world's oceans (such is their size), but those mapped in the coastal areas especially are particularly well documented.

The two new facets which have made this work even more vital are deep draught merchant ships (VLCCs, etc) and deep-diving nuclear submarines, especially the SSBN type. To assist with this mammoth task, the traditional theodolite and depth plumbing lead have given way to the computer-enhanced sonar and satellite position fixing gear. In addition to pure surveying for good navigation, the needs of the modern RN include depth, salinity and other more oceanographic data. With the need for very accurate position fixing, the hydrographer also uses equipment to determine the earth's magnetic and gravitational fields at specific locations. In the coming decade, the RN will introduce a new class 15-m craft for inshore surveys, together with an

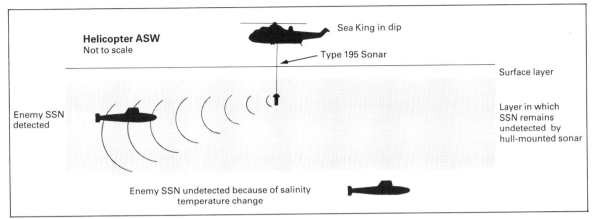

Helicopter ASW
Not to scale

Sea King in dip

Type 195 Sonar

Surface layer

Enemy SSN
detected

Layer in which
SSN remains
undetected by
hull-mounted sonar

Enemy SSN undetected because of salinity
temperature change

improved coastal survey ship for exposed sea areas and a surface effect ship (SES) in the sidewall hovercraft class for very shallow water work. Side-scan sonar for wreck location is already being procured.

Anti-submarine warfare operations

ASW is the major preoccupation of the modern Royal Navy. Ever since the Battle of the Atlantic during World War 2, when the German U-Boat fleets nearly crippled the UK economy, the RN has been keen to develop all aspects of ASW. Originally, the RN deployed large numbers of anti-submarine escorts which were developed into the anti-submarine frigate. With the development of the true submarine, a new era arrived with new styles and new tactics. Today, then, the nuclear-powered fleet submarine—the so called hunter-killer SSN—is the major weapon of the RN. This philosophy has been described as 'setting a thief to catch a thief'.

The underwater world of the North Atlantic is a vast battleground in which submarines can stalk each other, using the different layers of water caused by temperature or salinity, to hide their presence,

What could be the keystone of future ASW ops—the MAD-equipped Sea King helicopter.

but all the while to listen with passive sonar to any other vessel in the vicinity. For a submarine, that vicinity can be 2,500 square miles. The major threat is from Soviet submarines with a capability to launch anti-ship missiles whilst still submerged, so the primary mission of all ASW vessels is to detect and destroy those submarines whilst they are still many miles from potential targets, like URGs mentioned earlier. The threat to the RN and other NATO nations has been fully described above, but suffice to say here that a potential enemy would have no shortage of targets in the Continental Shelf area, where the sea trade routes meet, because Europe, unlike the Soviet Bloc for example, relies on imported raw materials and on exporting manufactured goods. UK merchant ships carry four million tonnes of cargo each day: 96 per cent of the UK's external trade goes by sea.*

Soviet submarines posing this threat to the European way of life would be probably based with the Soviet Northern Red Banner Fleet at Murmansk and other ports on the Kola Peninsula's military zone, and they are faced with the run down through the Greenland-Iceland-UK gap before arriving in the Allied shipping lanes and SSBM operating areas. NATO ASW efforts are therefore thought to be concentrated in this area. NATO obviously intends to make it as difficult as possible for the Soviets (or any other potential aggressor) to interfere with the re-supply convoys and other trade by blocking the GIUK gap with ASW Forces.

ASW is a team effort with an equal input of sub-surface, surface and air units to prevent submarine activity. No single element is sufficient to prevent penetration, so each one is equally important and the RN must be seen as one of the elements, not as the only one. Ashore, the RAF provides two

* Source: UK Defence Estimates, 1981.

squadrons of Phantom FG 1/FGR 2 aircraft for combat air interception within range of British bases; four squadrons of Nimrod MR 2 long-range maritime reconnaissance (LRMR) aircraft and two squadrons of Buccaneer S 2 anti-shipping strike aircraft. This formidable asset goes only part way to replacing the combined and readily available organic air complement presented by the fixed-wing carrier. The balance has been redressed to some extent by the introduction of the *Invincible* Class anti-submarine carrier (CVL) and by the refitting of *Hermes* (CVS) to operate Sea Harrier FRS 1 aircraft.

NATO's ASW effort is centred on the anti-submarine group of which the RN provides ASGRUTWO (see above and the role of FOF3). At the centre is a CVS or CVL with adequate escort of surface units capable of area ASW and AAW operations, such as the Types 22 and 42. Particularly important today is the anti-missile capability of the Sea Dart and, closer in, the Sea Wolf GWSs which can destroy sea-skimming or high flying, diving attacks simultaneously.

The helicopter has an important role to play in both hunting the submarine with passive sonobuoys or active dipping sonar, and then attacking it with depth bombs or lightweight air-launched torpedoes. The modern developments, such as LAPADS (Lightweight Acoustic Processing and Display System) linked to the mini-Jezebel sonobuoy, allows for the analysis and classification of submarine and other sub-surface noises. At present, the system is only operational with a few flights of several ASW squadrons equipped with Sea King HAS 5s, but it is envisaged that all Sea King units will operate with the equipment and the Magnetic Anomoly Detectors (MAD) currently under test with 826 NAS at Culdrose and aboard *Hermes*. The Sea King and the smaller Lynx are very stable platforms from which to fight the modern ASW battle out to a range of about 150 nm (278 km), thus providing the Task Group's first ring of defence. Should an enemy submarine penetrate the screen, the ships themselves are armed with various ASW systems such as Ikara (which is a vehicle designed to carry a homing torpedo out to a medium-range launch point) and the Mk 32 STWS (a ship-borne torpedo launching system). As a last resort, some of the older ships, such as *Leanders* and *Rothesays*, still carry the Mk 10 Limbo mortar.

Although ASW efforts are co-ordinated, the SSN operating with the Task Group would probably fight a battle in the extremities of the screen where it would have freedom of action and could operate at a speed which would not interfere with the surface elements; the SSN is the chief ASW asset available to the Task Group commander.

Many observers believe that NATO not only has a string of listening posts in the GIUK gap, along the coast of the Eastern USA and perhaps also in the Straits of Gibraltar, but that the alliance may have available plans to implement at short notice special anti-submarine minefields. Such a system is thought to exist in the Baltic and Mediterranean choke points. These fields could be remotely controlled but would only be viable in shallow waters and on a small scale could be used to protect important harbour installations, such as the Clyde Submarine Base.

In peacetime, ASW is not forgotten and the RN's maritime forces are constantly engaged in tracking and shadowing Soviet warships, particularly submarines which pass through the Eastlant area. This surveillance activity allows NATO to gauge the intentions of the Soviet Navy and to be forewarned of an increase which could lead to tension and war. Hydrography is also important in the peacetime ASW effort, because Admiralty charts of the ocean floor, salinity levels and possible hydrothermal zones, allow submarine commanders, especially of RN SSBNs, to navigate the ocean without being detected. In wartime, this would be vital. The towed array sonar currently being tested aboard *Phoebe* and *Sirius* (and due to be fitted in at least two other *Leanders*) will enable the ASW commander to penetrate the so-called 'surface duct' and listen for submarine in a different layer of the sea.

British maritime strategy calls for a continued upgrading of the ASW effort and the Government has indicated seven areas of special attention: **SSNs**—to continue the building programme to a minimum of 15 to be in service at any one time; **ASW ships**—to reassess the need for complex ships and to develop the Type 23 frigate with deep acoustic towed array sets; improved sonar and re-equipping of all frigates/destroyers with Lynx; **SSKs**—to issue a Staff Requirement for ten SSKs with a programme to allow the completion of the first by 1985; £300 million is already committed to development of systems and sonar; **Torpedoes**—to continue the development of heavyweight and lightweight torpedoes; **ASW technology**—to continue to improve the effectiveness of the submarine force, to improve passive and active sonar discrimination and to reduce detectability of RN forces; **ASW aircraft**—to introduce Nimrod MR 2s (each update costs £6.5 million) to all squadrons and to re-equip the Sea King units with Mk 5 variants with LAPADS capability; **Seabed**—to introduce the new SOV *Challenger* and to improve hydrographical facilities with the replacement of the inshore craft and the continuation of defence-orientated survey work.

Anti-air warfare operations

The defence of the Fleet against enemy aircraft and missiles has now taken second place to ASW, but nevertheless, with an estimated 200 combat aircraft, including 150 supersonic Tupolev Tu-26 *Backfires*, attached to the Soviet Northern Fleet, AAW is still important. There has, however, been a major change in technology and emphasis from the immediate post war era, the most important being that the fixed-wing aircraft carrier's potential is no longer available to the RN.

Today, the AAW environment extends from the surface of the sea, up through the high altitude haunts of the Myasishchev M-4 *Bison C* and the Tupolev Tu-20 *Bear C*, to the new space zones of the Soviet sky/maritime reconnaissance satellites. All nations fly as many surveillance missions as they can, paying particular attention to radar and communications transmissions from the other side's warships and aircraft. The threat in wartime is likely to come from anti-ship missiles launched by submarines and other warships and probably given mid-course correction by high-flying *Bear* aircraft. Aircraft themselves also pose a risk with the conventional bomb, rocket or stand-off missile. It is, therefore, essential that RN maritime forces are equipped to deal with the AAW threat, and as with ASW, it is better to engage the threat as far away from the target as possible.

The AAW combat zone has a radius of about 200 nm (370 km) from the ship or group of ships which are a threat. Because ship-borne radar is limited by physical constraints due to the curvature of the earth, airborne early warning (AEW) is most important. Today, the RN is devoid of its AEW aircraft (the Gannet went out of service in 1978) and has to rely on the aging Shackleton AEW 2 and its new successor, the Nimrod AEW 3. The former idea of radar picket warships has fallen into disfavour, but data-linking does allow all warships so equipped in a Task Group to see the best available radar coverage. Low-flying aircraft and missiles provide the greatest threat, and it is the use of fighters which forms the first ring of defence. The lack of AEW (airborne early warning) coverage was a major disadvantage during the Falklands crisis and has led many observers to predict that either an AEW helicopter conversion (thought by some to be the Sea King AEW 6) or a specialist aircraft, such as Bell XV–15 tilt-wing, may be ordered.

As the RN no longer has Phantoms for combat air patrols (CAPs), and because shore-based aircraft may be occupied elsewhere or take rather long to transit to a mid-ocean position, the RN can now deploy Sea Harrier FRS 1s at sea in *Invincible* Class carriers and aboard *Hermes*. The aircraft's roles are to provide long-range maritime patrol and CAP with a radius of action of 400 nm (741 km) at altitude. In this situation, the Sea Harrier, which has a multi-role purpose, would be armed with the American AIM-9L Sidewinder AAM and 30 mm Aden cannon, no doubt looking for such targets as a *Bear C*. The optimum patrol time at 100 nm (185 km) from the carrier is 90 minutes, allowing three minutes for full throttle combat manoeuvring and allowing sufficient fuel for a vertical landing back in the carrier. If, however, the embarked squadron, which only comprises five aircraft, came up against a saturation attack by, say, a squadron of *Backfires*, some of the latter would be certain to break through the air defence cordon. The Falklands operations did see the operational use of war-strengthened Sea Harrier squadrons deploying as many as 12 aircraft in *Invincible* or 18 in *Hermes* for air defence. This beefing-up of the air squadrons proved to be only just adequate to keep pace with the saturation air attacks of the Argentinian Air Force. The combat air patrols did, however, account for 75 per cent of the attacking aircraft before they reached the Fleet anchorages in San Carlos Water and Falkland Sound. They would then enter the missile engagement zone (MEZ).

This second round of defence is provided by the older Sea Slug SAMs of the *County* Class DLGs and the Sea Dart GWS aboard the newer destroyers. Both these systems have downed targets during the Falklands conflict and the Sea Dart is particularly successful because it has a quick-action capability. Sea Slug is considered to be a medium-range missile which rides a beam transmitted by its own shipborne radar of the Type 901M. Targets are identified and the co-ordinates fed into a computer which automatically tracks the target to a point where a launch is possible, at about 25 nm (46 km). The warhead is high explosive and one hit or near miss is sufficient to bring down an aircraft. The Sea Dart is more sophisticated, using radar guidance (from the Type 909 radar) and semi-active homing to targets at about 20 nm (37 km), but it is capable of simultaneous engagement of targets at sea level and at high altitude.

Should a target still penetrate the screen of missiles, then the Point Defence Missile Systems (PDMS) would be activated, linked to decoys and ECM (Electronic Counter-Measures). Some warships retain the Short Seacat SAM, whilst others are receiving, or being completed with, the Sea Wolf GWS. The former is a manually-loaded, optical-guided and command-linked system, but it has a fast response so that it can deal with high-speed, low-level attacks; it has a range of about 3 nm (5.6 km).

The Type 21 frigates provide ASV defence with Exocet SSM and 114 mm gun armament, plus the Sea Skua-equipped Lynx helicopter. This is Alacrity.

Without doubt, Sea Wolf, known as GWS 25 in the RN, is a very effective weapon which can even destroy 114 mm shells. It uses an automatic canard, line-of-sight guidance system linked to the Type 910 radar. It is the main shipborne weapon system of the Type 22 *Broadsward* Class frigates and is being fitted to selected *Leander* Class warships during the next few years.

A last-ditch defence is provided by Oerlikon 20 mm and Bofors 40 mm guns, which may be replaced by the Rarden 30 mm weapon in due course. Even the 114 mm gun can be used in an AA role. Some more important warships are now being equipped with the Vulcan Phalanx CIWS as a result of the RN's experiences in the South Atlantic.

AAW is therefore a large-scale operation calling for complex technology by way of IFF (Identification, Friend or Foe), computer-assisted action information systems (CAAIS), and, of course, skilled use of manpower. Future developments may include the introduction of an improved Sea Harrier—the AV-8B has been suggested although the RN would very much like a true supersonic V/STOL aircraft—and the Tornado F 2 for RAF air defence duties over the Fleet. The RN will not, however, receive the full quota of complex AAW destroyers and frigates which were expected. The Type 42s will have no successor type. Of all naval operations, the future of AAW looks the bleakest, even after the Falklands.

Anti-surface vessel warfare

ASVW has been the backbone of naval operations since the RN was formed back in the days of Alfred the Great. Since World War 1, however, the balance has moved away from the surface ship to the aircraft and now the submarine. The threat in this theatre of operations is to the unarmed merchant ships of which the UK has 700 at sea on any one day of the year. The manifestation of the threat is the large cruiser, destroyer and frigate units of which the Soviet Northern Fleet has about 60 in commission. These vessels carry guns and missiles, some of which can be given mid-course guidance from aircraft, thus demonstrating the fact that all naval operations are inter-connected. Small fast combat ships in the Baltic and Mediterranean areas could also be a threat, especially as many also carry sea-skimming missiles.

The missile in its turn is also the primary anti-shipping weapon of the RN and the initial system has been the French Exocet SSM with a range of over 25 nm (46 km). These missiles in non-reloadable canisters are fitted to Batch II *County* Class DLGs, *Amazon* Class FFHs and some eight, raising to 12, *Leanders*. Many of the AAMs have ASV potential, from the limited effect of the Seaslug and Seacat to the very effective Sea Dart.

The gun still has its role in the ASVW scenario and, today, many of the 114 mm systems aboard modern warships have automatic loading and firing with target tracking linked to computer-assisted radar. The small calibre weapons would be used against small craft which came within range or against sub-sonic missiles like the *Styx*.

The RN uses the Surface Action Group (SAG) of destroyer and frigates to challenge enemy warships in the ASVW scenario, usually using a radar-blind approach until within missile range. In addition, the RN has the use of modern air-launched missiles such as the Sea Skua (carried by Lynx HAS 2) and the Sea Eagle (to be carried by Sea Harriers). The RAF also provides maritime strike facilities if the targets are close enough to the UK bases.

In the next few years, it is envisaged that RN SSNs will be equipped with the Sub-Harpoon USGW which has completed successful firing trials in *Churchill*. Mines and mining have generally been neglected by the RN but there is still a sizeable MCM flotilla with new equipment in sight to replace the venerable *Ton* Class MSCs and MHs.

Technology and communications

The technological back-up to the Fleet has changed so dramatically in every department during the last three decades that it would undoubtedly make sailors from World War 2 blanch at the thought of operating it. Although ships still look like ships, they have gas turbine propulsion, submarines can be kept submerged for very long periods and targets can be acquired, evaluated, identified and destroyed automatically.

It is in the realms of electronic warfare (EW) and missile defence that the so-called 'Quiet Revolution' has been felt the most. There is still a pressing need for investment in EW, particularly in electronic countermeasures (ECM) and electronic counter-countermeasures (ECCM), the latter helping to prevent interference from friendly transmissions of radio and radar. Electronic support measures (ESM) are being fitted to most units to give the ability to intercept and analyse enemy electronic transmissions. These are then disrupted by ECM.

EW is playing an increasing role in the Fleet and according to the Defence Estimates (1981), substantial improvements in this area are planned for ships, submarines and aircraft. These include Sea Gnat, a new shipborne system for decoying enemy anti-ship missiles and new jammers and receivers to give early warning of enemy radar emissions. The Defence document goes on to confirm that if the RN is not adequately equipped with EW systems, the attrition rates would be

The new technology of the modern RN is exhibited in the Hunt Class MCMVs.

unacceptably high, as well as leading to the diminution of command control abilities. It is therefore true to say that EW systems in general are cost-effective weapons, provided they are developed in pace with, or faster than, the threat.

In the communications field, it is important to use all means available for effective command control to redress the balance between Soviet and NATO forces. In the modern RN, the use of all forms of communications is being studied, especially satellites, and it is possible that a new system will be evolved by 1985–6.

Personnel

It has been said many times before, but the single most important element in the Royal Navy of today is the sailor—in all his guises. The sailors' lot has gradually improved since the end of the last war, with bunks and in some cases individual cabins, the food is far better, discipline, where it can be, relaxed and the average sailor is able to leave the Service if he feels that he does not fit. The actual numbers have decreased during the last half of the decade and it seems that they will continue to do so as the surface fleet is reduced and as warships become more manpower-efficient.

	1977	**1979**	**1981**	**1982**
RN Officers	9,200	9,000	9,300	9,300
RN Ratings	55,400	52,200	53,100	53,200
Total	64,600	61,200	62,300	62,500
WRNS (all ranks)	4,000	3,800	3,900	3,900
RM Officers	600	600	700	700
RM Men	7,100	6,800	7,200	7,200
Total	7,700	7,400	7,900	7,900
RNR	27,800	28,300	26,600	n/a
WRNR	100	100	100	n/a
RMR	2,400	2,400	2,400	n/a
RMR (Auxiliary)	900	900	800	n/a
LEPs (Hong Kong)	287	261	338	n/a
Cadets	25,200	23,900	24,900	n/a

It is interesting to note that the 1981 Defence White Paper, from which the above figures were obtained, shows that in 1980, 1,998 RN and RM personnel were serving in Gibraltar, 334 in Hong Kong and 1,614 elsewhere in the Far East. All told, RN, WRNS and RM personnel overseas were 5,878. What is sad, is the number of trained and experienced personnel, especially aircrew and divers, who are leaving the Service ahead of normal time, although no official figures are available to quantify this problem.

RN tomorrow

The current trends are obviously towards submarines and the Trident programme in particular. Over the next 20 years or so, the RN can expect to have four or five Trident-type SSBNs in service replacing the older *R*-Class boats which now carry Polaris. This is, however, dependent on Government policy. In addition, there is a presumption to continue production of SSNs so that there are 20 in service at all times; the older *Valiant*

Class will be phased out by 1990 and replaced by the new *Trafalgar* Class already building.

There is a staff requirement for the replacement of the older SSKs with a new boat, probably the Type 2400 designed by Vickers, and it is expected that ten will ordered by 1985. The requirement is for a quiet boat with long range and the ability to operate in shallow water shunned by SSN skippers. The hull form would be optimised for underwater performance (unlike most current diesel designs) with six forward torpedo tubes for the standard range of weapons, including the new Marconi heavyweight torpedo. It is possible that Sub-Harpoon could be chosen as a weapon if funds permit. The Type 2400 has a complement of 44 and would be fitted with an unusually wide range of sensors, including long-range passive sonar, sonar intercept, classification and analysis gear, sound speed measuring equipment and a bathy-thermograph. Powered by Paxman Valenta diesels and General Electric motors, the new 70.25 m long design seems to be particularly important and will no doubt attract export orders.

Following successful firings from *Churchill* during 1979–80, the American Sub-Harpoon system for submarine strike against surface targets would seem to be the weapon of the late '80s for the 'Silent Service'. Details can be found in Chapter Ten.

Because submarines have a zero impact on affairs in peacetime, the need for a cheap yet effective surface escort is paramount. It is expected that orders for a new class, the Type 23, will be announced in 1983, and that they will cost half the present £122 million for a Type 22. The problem and the reason for the delay in this order would appear to be the choice of weapons systems, the most singly expensive piece of kit fitted to a new class.

In the aircraft world, the future procurement of Sea Harriers seems doubtful following the decision to operate only two CVLs in the 1980s, but there is a need for a replacement for the Sea King and an uprating of the present Lynx force, if the number of Sea King-capable platforms is to drastically reduce. It is possible that MAD and dipping sonar will be ordered for Lynx and then ships capable of operating two of these nimble helicopters—Type 22s and stretched Type 42s—will carry an attack-capable and a hunter-capable variant. The 1990 Sea King replacement problem is discussed in Chapter Five. Whatever happens, organic air is vital to the RN's surface forces.

In the missile field, developments with lightweight Seawolf and Sea Dart are likely to be important towards the end of the decade. Seawolf and Seacat are being improved and the latter is having a special fin-mounted height guidance

Modern warships like Birmingham *(D86) are equipped with the latest EW/ECM gear and are manpower-saving in their systems.*

system fitted to produce a better anti-ship capability. Sea Eagle, the Sea Harrier anti-shipping missile, has survived the 1981 cuts and is likely to see service in 1985/6, while various NATO projects are reportedly underway.

Because of RN commitments, it is unlikely that any further Light Forces will be ordered for the Fleet, although the work with hovercraft is continuing, especially in the MCM role as a support for the Hunt Class and the possible new cheap deep sweepers. The RNR is likely to be re-equipped in the late 1980s with a new type of single-role MCMV.

Manpower will reduce slightly in the later years of this decade but the need to recruit the better-educated will continue. All in all, the future for the RN is not as bleak as some readers of the 1981 Defence Review may have imagined.

Command

The RN's command structure has been evolved and developed over many years, especially since the withdrawal from Empire—from east of Suez—into the NATO Atlantic area of operations. Today, the watchword is flexibility, because gone, never to return, are the days of the flotilla strength operations, even though that system of command is still used. The operational plans for the various alert states are updated frequently as circumstances and political situations change. Throughout the draughting of such plans (by the Whitehall-based Director of Plans) this flexible approach is maintained. After all, with only 50 surface ships and 30 submarines available, any response has to be that way inclined.

The Admiralty Board

The Board is the major policy-making body in the RN and through its Chairman, the Secretary of State for Defence, it can advise the Government and hence the Monarch (the Lord High Admiral) on maritime affairs and policy. The Secretary of State for Defence is also a member of the Board, whose naval members are: First Sea Lord (1SL); Chief of the Naval Staff (CNS); the Second Sea Lord (2SL); Chief of Naval Personnel (CNP); the Controller of the Navy; the Chief of Fleet Support (CFS) and the Vice Chief of the Naval Staff (VCNS). Additional civilian members are the Second Permanent Under-Secretary of State, the Controller Research and Development Establishments and the Deputy Under Secretary of State (Navy). (NB: The political membership of the Admiralty Board was reviewed following the 1981 Defence White Paper and Review, and there is no longer an Under-Secretary of State for Defence for the Royal Navy.) The First Sea Lord is also represented on the Defence Council which is chaired by the Secretary of State too. On rotation, the retiring 1SL can become Chief of the Defence Staff (CDS).

The RN and the Royal Family

The British Royal Family has had a naval tradition for many, many years, but since the days of Queen Victoria, it has been a 'must' for Princes of the Blood Royal to train as officers in the Royal Navy. Probably the most famous sailor of the 20th century was Queen Elizabeth's cousin, Admiral of the Fleet Lord Louis Mountbatten of Burma, who followed his distinguished father into the RN in 1913, aged 12 years. He rose through the hierarchy, becoming known as an inventor and leader of men until he became initially First Sea Lord and then an Admiral of the Fleet (as his father had done before him). In 1965, he became Life Colonel Commandant of the Corps of Royal Marines.

His nephew, HRH Prince Philip, had also been a serving naval officer and it was at Dartmouth, the naval college, that he first met the then Princess Elizabeth. Prince Philip had command of a frigate in the Mediterranean before his naval career was ended with his marriage to the present Queen. In 1953 he was appointed Admiral of the Fleet and Captain General of the Royal Marines; he is also Admiral of the Fleet of the Royal Australian Navy (RAN) and the Royal New Zealand Navy (RNZN).

When Prince Charles joined BRNC Dartmouth as graduate entrant in September 1971, he was also destined to command at sea. In February 1976 he

The First Sea Lord is the most senior serving officer—Admiral Sir Henry Leach, GCB, ADC, who held the post in 1980–82.

assumed command of the coastal minehunter *Bronington* (*M1115*) (*qv*), but left the active list later that year to become deeply involved with the organisation of the Queen's Silver Jubilee celebrations; he was promoted Commander RN on January 1 1977. In September 1979 his younger brother, Prince Andrew, became a Midshipman at Dartmouth and followed Prince Charles into a career with the Fleet Air Arm, being posted to 820 NAS (*qv*) flying Westland Sea King HAS 5 anti-submarine helicopters from *Invincible* (*qv*), including war service in the South Atlantic.

The Women's Royal Naval Service (WRNS) have not been without their representation at Buckingham Palace for, as long ago as 1939, Queen Elizabeth, now the Queen Mother, was appointed Commander-in-Chief of the WRNS and, in July 1974, her granddaughter, the Princess Anne, became Chief Commandant, WRNS. The Queen Alexandra's Royal Naval Nursing Service (QARNNS) have a famous Patron in Princess Alexandra whose namesake transformed the Service in 1902.

Lord High Admiral

Her Majesty Queen Elizabeth II, the Commander in Chief of the British Armed Forces, is Lord High Admiral of the United Kingdom, in which position she is supported by a Vice Admiral of the United Kingdom (also known as Lieutenant of the Admiralty) and a Rear Admiral of the United Kingdom. The Queen has a Principal and a Flag Aide-de-Camp, plus 13 ADCs of Captain or Commodore rank. Two Colonels of the RM, four RNR ADCs and the WRNS Director are included in the accreditation. Their duties, once so important to the Monarch in time of war, are now ceremonial. The nine extra naval Equerries to the Queen carry out a similar function.

It is interesting to note that two foreign Monarchs, the Kings of Norway and Sweden, are Honorary Officers in Her Majesty's Fleet, with the rank of Admiral. The Princes of Belgium and Spain are Honorary Lieutenants and HRH the Crown Prince Harald of Norway, GCVO, is an Honorary Colonel of the Royal Marines.

Flag Officers

The Flag Officers of the Royal Navy, so-called because their rank entitles them to a flag rather than a pennant, range from Rear Admiral to Admiral of the Fleet. Excluding HRH Prince Philip, there are six Admirals of the Fleet, who are still technically serving officers in the RN irrespective of age. Only one can ordinarily expect to really inhabit the hub of the Command structure, being Chief of the Defence

Staff (CDS), a post which alternates between the three Services. There are six full Admirals currently in the Navy List, mainly in CINC or other important associated and important roles, including First Sea Lord (1SL). Below them are 12 Vice Admirals and 30 or so serving Rear Admirals.

Senior appointments Besides the Admiralty Board (*qv*), there are two Commanders-in-Chief: CINCFLEET, who is responsible for the 'teeth' of the RN, and has the NATO posts of Allied Commander in Chief Channel and Commander in Chief Eastern Atlantic; his Fleet Headquarters is at Northwood, Middlesex, near London; and CINCNAVHOME, who is responsible for all naval establishments; he wears no NATO 'hats' and is based at Admiralty House, Portsmouth.

The Commandant General of the Royal Marines (CGRM) is the most senior RM officer and quasi-CINC, but with no seat on the board. The rank held by CGRM is usually that of Lieutenant General. In addition, there are three Major Generals: Head of Commando Forces; Head of Training & Reserve Forces; and Chief of Staff to CGRM. Other details relating to the RM will be found in Chapter Six.

Senior allied appointments NATO appointments change in rotation with other friendly navies, but in 1981 the RN appointed Vice Admirals to the roles of: Commandant NATO Defence College; Deputy Supreme Allied Commander Atlantic; and Chief of Staff to COMNAVSOUTH at Naples.

Flag officer appointments

In 1980, there were three appointments which were filled by Vice Admirals and the remaining 14 by Rear Admirals; these appointments change about every 18 months to two years:

RN appointments	NATO appointments
FO Plymouth and Port Admiral, Devonport	Commander Central Sub-Area Eastern Channel; Commander Plymouth Sub-Area Channel
FO Scotland and Northern Ireland	Commander Northern Sub-Area Eastern Atlantic; Commander Nore Sub-Area Channel
FO Submarines	Commander Submarines Eastern Atlantic
FO Portsmouth and Port Admiral, Portsmouth	None
FO Medway and Port Admiral, Chatham	None
FO Gibraltar and Port Admiral, Gibraltar	Commander Gibraltar Mediterranean Area
FO Royal Yachts	None
FO Naval Air Command	None
FO Sea Training	None
FO First Flotilla	None
FO Second Flotilla	None
FO Third Flotilla	Commander Anti-Submarine Group Two
Hydrographer of the Navy	None
Port Admiral Rosyth	None
Chief of Fleet Support	None

As a result of the 1981 Defence Review it is very likely that three of the above posts will disappear from the list in their present form. The roles and responsibilities of FONAC (Flag Officer Naval Air Command) and of FOF3 (Flag Officer Third Flotilla) are similar and in several respects they overlap; it is more than possible that one FO rule will emerge from this Review. In addition, the closure of the Chatham Naval Base in 1984 may well mean that the appointment of Flag Officer Medway and Port Admiral Chatham will disappear in that year.

Flag Officer Plymouth (Port Admiral Devonport) Flag Officer Plymouth (FOP) is responsible for the operational control of HM ships in the Plymouth Sea Area (which includes the Irish Sea,

Left *Part of the domain of Flag Officer Plymouth—Devonport dockyard.*

Right *FOSN provides sea training facilities for the RN, NATO and friendly navies—Norfolk leading a squadron of frigates (RN).*

English Channel, southern North Sea and the Atlantic Ocean down to the coast of Mauritania), for a NATO sea area as Commander Central Atlantic and as Commander of the Plymouth Sub-Area in the Channel Command. At Mount Batten on the shores of Plymouth Sound, near the city, is the Maritime HQ which provides the necessary co-ordination for SAR, aircraft (NAC) and other emergency services. In national terms, FOP controls six major shore establishments in his land area and wears the hat of Port Admiral Devonport (PAD). Also within the Flag Officer's area are two RM Commando units (HQ 3 Commando Brigade, Commando Logistic Regiment and HQ Major General Commando Forces (MGCF)). The following diagram gives an

indication of the organisational structure of the Plymouth Command:

Flag Officer Scotland and Northern Ireland
This is a senior post within the naval command structure and is based on the joint RN/RAF Maritime Headquarters at Pitreavie in Fife on the north banks of the Forth. Flag Officer Scotland and Northern Ireland (FOSNI) has four separate but inter-related commands: Sea Area Commander— Morecambe Bay to the Wash; Land Area Commander—Solway Firth to Whitby (including Northern Ireland); Commander Northern Sub-Area Eastern Atlantic (NATO); and Commander Nore Sub-Area Channel (NATO).

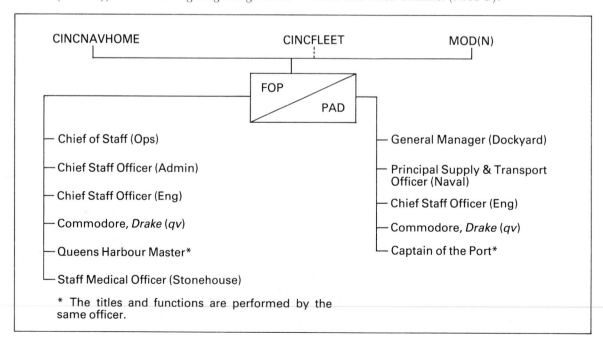

As Sea-Area Commander, FOSNI reports to CINCFLEET and is responsible for all naval operations taking place in the waters around the northern half of Britain, including oil rig and fisheries' protection. The main task is the defence of the area in times of tension or war, but equally today there is a role in the security of the facilities within the UK's European Economic Zone (EEZ) and territorial limits. Security of rigs and production platforms is vested in the owning or operating companies and so to the Chief Constable of Police for the appropriate areas. The Royal Navy and Royal Marines act in support of the civil power and have become highly proficient in the protection of offshore installations. The Fisheries' Protection Squadron, which is based at the Rosyth Naval Base, operates within the complete UK EEZ, but for ease of operations, the operational control always lies with FOSNI although there will be courtesy communication with FO Plymouth when vessels are operating in the southern sectors.

Within his land boundaries, FOSNI reports to CINCNAVHOME for the efficient operation of all naval establishments, personnel and locations, including RNR and RMR units. There are specific exceptions such as 45 Commando Group, RM, at Arbroath, who are responsible to CGRM (Commandant General Royal Marines), yet FOSNI can have a large say in their tasking when they are on Scottish soil. Security, a role in which 45 Commando has much experience, is, after all, FOSNI's concern. The naval base at Rosyth is directly controlled by the Port Admiral (usually a Rear Admiral, whereas FOSNI is commonly a Vice Admiral), but he is subordinate to FOSNI, especially for policy and operational effectiveness. On the other side of Scotland, the British Independent Deterrent Force is based at the Clyde Submarine Base (*Neptune*) giving FOSNI a significant responsibility, although neither he (nor FOSM) is actually responsible for the boats during their operational cycles.

FOSNI's two NATO hats are worn in time of tension, war or exercise and here again he is subordinate to CINCFLEET in his NATO roles of CINCCHAN and CINCEASTLANT. The exact tasks in this role are constantly being updated, but remain classified. Suffice to say that a NATO Commander acts rather in the same way as a Flag Officer but has control over all other NATO nations' warships operating in his chunk of the sea.

Flag Officer Portsmouth (Port Admiral Portsmouth) One officer, normally a Rear Admiral, holds the two appointments of Flag Officer Portsmouth and Port Admiral Portsmouth; in the former appointment he has two roles, as a

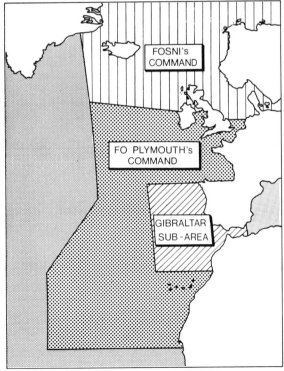

subordinate sea area commander and as a land area commander. His primary task as sea area commander is control of naval operations in the Portsmouth area on behalf of CINCFLEET and to support RN ships based in Portsmouth or undergoing maintenance there. His secondary roles include such matters as the clearance of oil pollution in his sea area and support of the civil power. He is also responsible for ensuring that the naval base's support facilities are utilised to meet the operational requirements and priorities of the Fleet.

As land area commander he is responsible to CINCNAVHOME for ensuring that shore establishments in his area fulfil their training role and their commitments to support the Fleet and, when required, to aid the civil and military authorities. He exercises functional authority in matters of administration over establishments in the Portsmouth area.

As Port Admiral, he is responsible to the Chief of Fleet Support (*qv*) for the co-ordination of the naval base's facilities and support resources. These comprise five main support groups: the ship repair organisation of the dockyard; the Royal Navy supply and transport organisation; the Fleet Maintenance Base; the Port and Fleet Operational Base; and the Fleet Accommodation Centre in *Nelson*. The Port Admiral chairs the Port Board which consists of the heads of these five groups, some of whom are civilians.

Flag Officer Medway This is a subordinate command and currently FO Medway is responsible to CINCNAVHOME for the land-based establishments from Chichester, West Sussex, to North Yorkshire, and for the Thames Estuary area to CINCFLEET. Although the sea areas which correspond to the land area in FO Medway's care are in the province of FO Plymouth, the former is not responsible to the latter. There is therefore the somewhat anomalous position of one Area Flag Officer looking after the shore side and another FO looking after the sea. FO Medway, in common with all Area Flag Officers, is responsible for the RNR and RNXS divisions and units within his shore-based responsibility if their headquarters are so located. For example, London and Sussex RNR Divisions and the RNXS unit at Chatham.

Flag Officer Gibraltar Unlike the Area Flag Officers in the United Kingdom, FOGIB has not had his responsibilities delegated by CINCFLEET although there is a functional link between them. In actual fact FOGIB reports to the Ministry of Defence (Navy) and hence to the Admiralty Board. His is also a NATO commander, being known as COMGIBMED with reporting responsibilities to

COMIBERLANT at Lisbon and hence to SACLANT. COMGIBMED reports to COMN-AVSOUTH in times of peace and tension, but in time of war the French return to the NATO fold and he reports to a French Admiral at Toulon. In a civil role, FOGIB is the Deputy Governor of the Rock of Gibraltar, and is responsible for the Maritime Headquarters set deep in the Rock.

In summary, FOGIB is the last independent Flag Officer, being only 'controlled' in relation to ship's programmes for refit and exercise in the Gibraltar area. Details of the Gibraltar complex of dockyard, MHQ and establishments can be found elsewhere in the chapter.

Flag Officer Royal Yachts This appointment carries with it a tremendous responsibility and represents the only remaining regular seagoing appointment for a Flag Officer. FORY is the master of the Royal Yacht *Britannia* and as such commands her on every important voyage. The Royal Yacht is based at Portsmouth and so there is a link between him and FO Portsmouth and for programming to CINCFLEET. The tasking of the Royal Yacht is usually a matter for the Government and Buckingham Palace and so the relationship is somewhat ambivalent. For obvious reasons much of the Flag Officer's role is considered highly secret.

Flag Officer Naval Air Command This officer's role is dealt with in detail in the Fleet Air Arm section of this book, so suffice to say that FONAC is responsible to CINFLEET for the training and operational readiness of the flying elements of the Fleet and to CINCNAVHOME for the Naval Air Stations and other FAA establishments. In some ways, he can be likened to a C-in-C because he does 'run' the training of the important elements of many ships and in this capacity he is totally responsible. The main operational side of FONAC's role is devoted to the ASW helicopters which are provided for FOF3 (*qv*).

Flag Officer Sea Training FOST is based, for the time being at least, at the Portland naval base and from here he organises, with a special staff of 'experts', the basic operational and continued operational sea training of all elements of the Fleet and of some friendly navies. A regular feature of FOST's role is that of the 'Thursday War' when warships take part with aircraft from nearby *Osprey* and *Heron* in mock wartime exercises and training. Warships which have recently been commissioned are sent to work-up at Portland and at the end of the eight-week or so period, FOST and his staff carry out an important inspection which will confirm that the warship (or RFA) is fit for operational duties. The role of this Flag Officer is thus most important, but as there is a question mark hanging over Portland's future, the FOST role may well go elsewhere.

Flag Officers First and Second Flotillas The RN's small surface warships of the frigate and destroyer types are allocated to squadrons and these form two flotillas for deployment around the world. At the 1977 Jubilee Fleet Review both FOFs were in attendance using DLGs and CCHs (the now defunct *Tiger* Class cruisers) as flagships. At that time squadron distribution was as follows: **First Flotilla**—First Frigate Squadron (F1); Second Frigate Squadron (F2); Fifth Frigate Squadron (F5); Sixth Frigate Squadron (F6); **Second Flotilla**—Third Frigate Squadron (F3); Fourth Frigate Squadron (F4); Seventh Frigate Squadron (F7); Eighth Frigate Squadron (F8). For Out-of-Area Deployments and major exercises, the FOF will go to sea in his flagship, but he is not as regularly there as FORY.

Flag Officer Third Flotilla This Flag Officer (FOF3) is concerned with the naval air element and in his NATO role with the ASW warships and assets such as helicopters. He controls the larger warships such as *Invincible*, *Hermes*, *Fearless* and *Bristol*. One naval air squadron, 815 with Lynx HAS 2 helicopters, is directly tasked by FOF3, through the FONAC network, and these aircraft deploy to units of both the other flotillas. In addition, FOF3 is the NATO Anti-Submarine Warfare Commander for Group Two and would presumably fly his flag in *Invincible* in the event of going to sea in time of tension or war. The FOF3 position is understood to be under review.

Hydrographer to the Navy With a headquarters at Taunton in Somerset, this officer, usually a career Rear Admiral surveyor/oceanographer specialist, tasks and controls the RN's survey vessels in oceanic, coastal and inshore areas via the controls of CINCFLEET and the Area Flag Officers. For example, the Inshore Survey Squadron (*qv*) operates from Chatham Naval Base. The Hydrographer is responsible for the preparation and continuous updating of all the Admiralty Charts world-wide. Details of the RN's Surveying Service can be found elsewhere.

Port Admiral Rosyth Whilst several of the Area Flag Officers are also Port Admirals, the role at the northern naval base of Rosyth is undertaken by a specific Port Admiral because the higher authority, the Flag Officer Scotland and Northern Ireland (*qv*) is a major element in the command structure. The Port Admiral's task is the smooth and efficient running of the naval base and the dockyard.

Chief of Fleet Support This officer has an important role to play in the running of the modern Royal Navy. The role of CFS is unique in that he is the only Admiralty Board member with a major accounting function. Through the office of the CFS, a number of major support operations are controlled by various naval and civilian Director Generals. Perhaps the most important function is that of the Royal Dockyards (of which, see later) with their responsibility for maintaining the warships of the RN. In addition, the various armament, stores and vitualling depots under the Director General Supplies and Transport (Navy) are controlled by CFS, as are the naval air repair yards at Perth and Fleetlands, through DGA(N). The policy, maintenance and general upkeep of the nation's strategic deterrent forces (the SSBNs) are under CFS's control, but not the operational cycle. On the land side, the Port Admirals have a reporting responsibility to him and, following the 1981 Defence Review, the closure phasing of the Royal Dockyards will be administered by the assistant to CFS, usually a senior Captain.

In terms of bricks and mortar, the Property Services Agency, which controls all Government property maintenance and building, liaises directly with CFS and the associated Directorate of Quartering reports to him. Such miscellaneous, but associated items as Naval Fire Prevention, the Bureau West computer facility and Engineering Support Policy comes within the CFS's gambit. Through Director of Engineering Services (Navy)—DES(N)—the refit cycles are drawn up and this is another facet which has been affected by the 1981 Review.

An important asset to the RN has always been the Marine Services which include the RMAS (see Chapter Eight) whose 'fleet' is larger than the actual combat vessels of the modern RN.

Food is important to the RN and CFS controls Fleet Supply, or in other words, naval catering policy. Although never really in the public limelight, the CFS's role is vital to the everyday operation of the RN.

Royal Naval Supply and Transport Service

The Director of this Service is a civilian but its importance to the smooth operation of the RN is considerable. There are a number of establishments and offices throughout the United Kingdom, although several are due to be closed under the 1981 Defence Review, and are marked thus(*). RNSTS comes under the heading of Fleet Support and under its care are a large number of vehicles which are driven and maintained by civil servants and thus are outside the scope of this Encyclopaedia.

RN Torpedo Range	Arrochar, Strathclyde
RN Armament Depot	Beith, Strathclyde
RN Victualling/Depot	Botley, Hampshire
RN Armament Depot	Broughton Moor, Cumbria
NATO POL Depot	Campbelltown,/ Strathclyde
RN Store Depot	Copenacre
RN Armament Depot	Coulport, Strathclyde
RN Armament Depot	Dean Hill, Wiltshire
RN Store Depot* Spare Parts/	Deptford, London
Distribution Centre	Eaglescliffe, Cleveland
RN Store Depot	Exeter, Devon
NATO Ammunition Depot	Glen Douglas,/ Strathclyde
HM Oil Fuel Depot*	Invergordon, Highlands
RN Store Depot*	Llangennech, Dyfed
NATO POL Depot	Loch Ewe, Highlands
NATO POL Depot	Loch Striven, Highlands
RN Armament Depot	Milford Haven, Dyfed
HM Oil Fuel Depot	Old Kilpatrick,/ Strathclyde
Admiralty Compass/ Observatory	Slough, Buckinghamshire
RN Armament Depot	Trecwn, Dyfed
RN Store Depot*	Woolston, Hampshire
RN Base Facility*	Pembroke Docks, Dyfed
RN Base Facility	Greenock, Strathclyde

The Naval Staff

Chief of the Naval Staff is the First Sea Lord and his aspect of the RN caters for the administration and policy implementation of the Service. Each department has its own Director, usually of Captain RN rank (but it can be an appointment above or below) and deals with a specific specialist subject, as follows.

Directorate of Naval Plans (DNP)
The future of the RN

Directorate of Naval Assistance Overseas (DNAO)
The aid given to friendly navies

Directorate of Naval Operations and Trade (DNOT)
Where the Fleet will go and the protection of merchantmen

Directorate of Naval Oceanography and Meteorology (DNOM)
Scientific research

Directorate of Naval Operational Requirements (DNOR)
What's needed, where and when

Directorate of Naval Warfare (DNW)
Underwater, surface and air threats

Directorate of Naval Air Warfare (DNAW)
Fleet Air Arm operational needs

Directorate of Naval Management and Organisation (DNMO)
Business management of the RN

Directorate of Naval Officer Appointments (DNOA)
Four sections: Seaman; Engineers; Supply and Secretariat plus WRNS; Instructor Officers

Directorate of Naval Service Conditions (DNSC)*
'Industrial relations'

Directorate of Naval Physical Training and Sport (DNPTS)
Self-explanatory

Directorate of Naval Manpower Requirements (DNMR)
Planning naval manning

Directorate of Naval Manning and Training (DNMT)
A separate Directorate for each section: Seaman; Engineers; Supply and Secretariat plus WRNS; Instructors

Directorate of Naval Education and Training Support (DNETS)
Instruction and 'Schoolie'

Directorate of Naval Foreign and Commonwealth Training (DNFCT)
Training friendly navies.

In addition to the examples quoted above, there are departments dealing with other Staff requirements, but which have not, for a variety of reasons, been formed into Directorates. For example:
Defence Operations Staff, led by the Assistant Chief of the Defence Staff (Operations), usually a Rear Admiral. Defence Policy Staff, led by the Director of Defence Policy, usually a Commodore.
Hydrographer to the Navy, whose team is repsonsible for producing world-renown Admiralty charts and plans.
Chief Naval Signal Officer (CNSO), is usually a Captain RN and his responsibility includes all matters dealing with communications.
There is also a Naval Secretary's Department which probably traces its ancestry to Samuel Pepys, and beyond, under the control of the Naval Secretary, a Rear Admiral in the modern RN.

The Chief Naval Engineer is a Vice Admiral, as is the Chief Naval Supply and Secretariat Officer, whilst the Chief Naval Instructor Officer is a Rear

---

* Naval personnel matters come directly under the Second Sea Lord who is also Chief of Naval Personnel.

Admiral. Naval Personnel Services are also led by a Rear Admiral, who is designated Director of Naval Personnel Services (DGNPS).

Naval Weapons Department

Within the Navy Department, and still part of the Naval Staff, is the Weapons Department (Naval) under the control of the Director General Weapons (DGW(N)), a Rear Admiral. Basically, the technology which now goes into each and every gun, missile and torpedo is so complex that separate Directorates have been formed to administer Underwater Weapons (DUWP(N)), Surface Weapons (DSWP(N)), Weapons Resources and Programmes (DWRP(N)) and Ship Weapon Systems (DSWS).

There are a number of sub-sections devoted to specific aspects of the naval weapons field, under the following titles: Captain Surface Weapons Acceptance (CSWA); Captain Naval Operational Command Systems (CNOCS); Captain Polaris Weapons Acceptance (CPWA); Captain Underwater Weapons Acceptance (CUWA); Captain Weapons Trials (CWT); Weapons Systems Timing Group (Naval); Admiralty Degaussing Service, Fort Rowner; Directorate of Weapons Production and Quality (Naval); Directorate of Weapons Production (Naval); and Directorate of Naval Weapons Quality.

These examples, together with others not mentioned, go to make up one of the most efficient naval systems in the world, especially so since the amalgamation of the three Services under the Ministry of Defence in the 1960s.

The Navy and the law

One of the Courts within the High Court of Justice, Queen's Bench Division is the Admiralty Court (which also comprises the Prize Court). Other sections are specifically for legal advice to the Admiralty Board and the Admiralty Marshall's Office. The Chief Naval Judge Advocate is a Captain RN in the Supply and Secretariat Branch. The Admiralty has legal agents at each major port and there is provision under the Supreme Court of Judicature Act, 1925, for Admiralty Appeals in the Court of Appeal; the Elder Brethren of Trinity House are *ex-officio* assessors here.

The officer and rating alike are bound by the Naval Discipline Act, which recently has been widened to incorporate the WRNS and the QARNNS (1977). Both of the latter services are exempt from the Sex Discrimination Act, but the Admiralty has been keen to comply with the spirit of the Act although females are still not allowed to go to sea on a regular basis. It may well be that in due

course the male barrier will be broken and women may be allowed to go to sea as communications and navigation numbers in the Royal Fleet Auxiliary Service (RFA).

The Naval Prize Courts have been established for many, many years and during the 17th, 18th and 19th centuries much valuable tonnage was captured by the RN, on the high seas, on one pretext or another. Today, the procedures originate in the Naval Prize Act, 1864, through to the Prize Salvage Act, 1944. There is more salvage pay than prize reward in the modern RN!

The RN is empowered to appoint assessors to attend formal investigations into shipping casualties under the Merchant Shipping Act, 1894. There are also Fisheries' Assessors.

Submarine Command

'Our most powerful vessels for maritime war are our nuclear-propelled attack submarines . . .'
The United Kingdom Defence Programme: The Way Forward (Cmnd 8288, 1981)

Throughout history, seapower has proved a deciding factor in the ambitions of one country over another and the most decisive element in modern seapower is the submarine. A submarine can dive deep and stay deep—away from the highly dangerous ocean surface where every vessel can be easily located by aircraft, surface surveillance, or satellites and where it is increasingly vulnerable to long-range air- or surface-launched missile attack.

Submarine Command's role

The RN's Submarine Service is unique, effective, well organised and steeped in a fine heritage. Today, it is a carefully balanced force of SSNs, SSKs and powerful SSBNs which, together with surface and air units of the RN and the RAF (in combination with other NATO forces), provides a complete mix to counter a variety of maritime threats. In peacetime, the tactical units—the SSNs and SSKs—are employed on training, exercise and goodwill tasks, whilst the strategically important SSBNs are constantly on patrol to keep the British independent nuclear deterrent of the Polaris missile completely credible. With the threat of war, the submarines of the RN would be deployed to tactically important positions and it is probable that their main stamping grounds would be the chokepoints of the GIUK gap, the Faroes-Shetland area in particular, where they would wait for their prey. This would be an enemy submarine. It is repeatedly said that the best counter to a hostile submarine is another submarine, and the UK has some of the best vessels and undoubtedly some of the best crews in the world. New weapons are constantly being developed for the submarine to make it more effective. The helicopter and the LRMP aircraft are its main threats above the surface but new knowledge of temperature and salinity layers in the oceans make detection difficult. In fact, the oceans are the new jungles, where the different layers can conceal a submarine from the probing sensors of various threats leaving the initiative on the side of the submarine commander.

The tasks given to Flag Officer Submarines (FOSM) can be described as follows: to provide the nation's nuclear deterrent force; to maintain that force at all times; to provide attack submarines for tactical and strategic purposes; to provide assistance for training surface vessels and aircraft; to provide a means of transportation for special commando forces; to safeguard the coastal waters and Continental Shelf areas, and to detect, hunt and destroy enemy submarines in time of war.

Flag Officer Submarines FOSM is the administrative authority and head of the RN's Submarine Command and as such reports to CINCFLEET. In this capacity, FOSM is now based at the Northwood Headquarters complex in Middlesex, where he is in easy reach of CINCFLEET and the Air Officer in charge of Maritime Patrol aircraft of the Royal Air Force. In addition, he is responsible for submarine bases and squadrons, being the submarine type commander.

In essence, CINCFLEET retains full command and control of all RN submarines but operational command and control is passed to FOSM. The one exception is the command and control of Polaris boats during their operational cycles. Although part of FOSM's staff is still located at the traditional haven of the submariner, Fort Blockhouse, Gosport, in Hampshire, most of the engineering, administrative, operational, training and warfare staffs are at Northwood, forming part of the Fleet Headquarters.

Like most RN commanders, FOSM has a NATO responsibility, being COMSUBEASTLANT (Commander Submarines Eastern Atlantic) in the event of hostilities.

Role of the submarine

Today, the submarine has a joint anti-surface vessel (ASV) and an anti-submarine (AS) role in the modern Royal Navy. In the 1970s, this type of vessel replaced the fixed-wing aircraft carrier as the Navy's premier capital ship. By 1981, the RN had 13 nuclear-powered Fleet submarines (SSNs) in service, plus 16 conventional patrol-type boats (SSKs) of the *Oberon* and *Porpoise* Classes. The 1981

Dolphin, *alma mater of submarines, seen here on a very busy day with ten SSKs alongside* (MoD/LA Delvis).

Defence Review has pointed the way forward to further SSNs of the *Trafalgar* Class (each costing an amazing £177 million) with additional potential provided by a new class of SSK from 1985/6 onwards.

The main weapon of the submarine is still the heavyweight torpedo of homing and/or salvo types, plus the new generation of sub-surface launched anti-shipping missiles for the SSNs. In the late 1980s, the Government is pledged to introduce a new heavyweight torpedo of British design and manufacture.

The submarine of today has the ability to operate at great sustained speeds and at great depths compared to the semi-submersibles of the immediate postwar era. The four British Polaris-armed submarines have the deterrent role and as such contribute towards NATO's current strategic deterrent as well.

Submarine bases

There are three submarine bases from which any boat can operate, although each type is now assigned to a specific one for ease of operation and economic maintenance. They are; *Dolphin* (Gosport), for *Oberon* and *Porpoise* Classes of SSK; *Neptune* (FASLANE), for *Valiant* Class SSNs, SSBNs and SSKs; and *Defiance* (DEVONPORT), for *Swiftsure* Class SSNs and some SSKs.

Dolphin The RN's first submarine boat station was established at Gosport in 1905 and the name is derived from an old sailing training ship which provided headquarters facilities to the early boats, 1906–23. The base served as the headquarters of the Service for many years and, in 1977, was the site developed for the RN's world-renowned Submarine School which will provide submariner training for the next 30 years, at least. *Dolphin* is home of the First Submarine Squadron (SM1), which is the only completely conventional squadron in the RN, being made up of the three *P*-boats and about ten *O*-boats at any one time. Nuclear boats cannot be permanently based at *Dolphin* for several reasons, including the restricted entrance to Portsmouth Harbour/Haslar Creek and the nearby conurbations. There are special nuclear facilities available at Portsmouth for docking and essential defects (DED). The base also houses the Submarine Museum and the Submarine Escape School. FOSM moved his headquarters from *Dolphin*'s Fort Blockhouse in the late 1970s and now resides at *Warrior* with CINCFLEET.

The Clyde Submarine Base: Neptune This base plays such an important part in the role of the modern Royal Navy that it deserves specific attention. The base comprises the Faslane Complex (including *Neptune*) on Gare Loch, the RNAD at Coulport on Loch Long and several supporting outstations. Within the Faslane Complex there are three distinct parts: the dockyard, the barracks and the logisitic support/training area. The dockyard area contains the usual jetties plus a floating dock, all of which are necessary to maintain submarines,

particularly SSBMs. The barracks (officially named *Neptune* and to which all personnel are appointed) have accommodation for 250 officers and 1,500 men. The training function is also very important and the facilities include the Royal Naval Polaris School, the Submarine Attack Teacher and the Propulsion Plant Control Trainer (FASMAT).

All SSBNs must acquire their warloads at Coulport and this task is carried out by civilians whose unpatriotic behaviour made the headlines in 1981 during the Civil Servants' Strike. Missile transfers take place in the open at the deep water jetty, the ICBMs being transported from underground storage areas by AEC Lowloader and winched aboard by dockside crane so that each is presented vertically to its own launch tube aboard the SSBN.

Neptune is home for the Third and the Tenth Submarine Squadrons, being SSK and *Valiant* Class SSNs, and *R*-Boats respectively. In addition, the *Neptune* complex supports visiting warships, including those of the US Navy based elsewhere in Scotland. The establishment was commissioned in August 1967, following the Nassau Agreement on the Polaris programme for the RN.

Defiance* Devonport is one of three dockyards which specialises in the maintenance and refit of

---

* Battle Honours: Orfordness 1666; Barfleur 1692; Finisterre 1747; Ushant 1747; Louisberg 1758; Quiberon Bay 1759; Havana 1762; Copenhagen 1801; Trafalgar 1805.

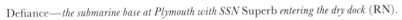

Defiance—*the submarine base at Plymouth with SSN* Superb *entering the dry dock* (RN).

nuclear-powered submarines, being mainly concerned with the *Swiftsure* and *Trafalgar* Classes (whilst Chatham and Rosyth deal with the older *Valiant* Class and the *R*-boats respectively). These operations at Devonport are carried out at *Defiance*. The name was formally used between 1972 and 1978 by the Depot Ship *Forth*. Today, *Defiance* is part of the Fleet Maintenance Complex at Devonport, as well as being home to Captain Second Submarine Squadron (SM2).

SSKs are still dealt with in the Devonport system, and in the future the work from Portsmouth and Chatham may be passed on with the closures proposed for these bases and dockyards. Portsmouth still retains the floating dock facilities. SM2 at Devonport is a mixture of *Oberon* and *Swiftsure* Class and without doubt *Defiance*'s place in the submarine refit stream is secure.

Warship squadrons

For many hundreds of years the RN has divided up its forces into squadrons flotillas. Today there are three major surface vessel flotillas which are made up of eight warship squadrons of frigates and destroyers with additional units of submarines, Mines Counter Measures (MCM) vessels, Patrol Boats at Hong Kong and the famous Fisheries' Protection Squadron.

The following warships are deployed in the flotillas: First Flotilla (Flag Officer First Flotilla—FOF1)—two *County* Class DLGs leading First, Second and Sixth Frigate Squadrons plus Third Destroyer Squadron; Second Flotilla (Flag Officer Second Flotilla—FOF2)—two *County* Class DLGs leading Fourth, Seventh and Eighth Frigate Squadrons plus Fifth Destroyer Squadron; and

Third Flotilla (Flag Officer Third Flotilla—FOF3)—major surface warships—see separate entry.

Today, each major surface warship squadron is devoted to a particular type or sub-type of warship and these are based at a particular base port: Chatham, Portsmouth, Plymouth or Rosyth. This grouping together of like warships does not mean that every vessel is either in commission or will operate together at the same time. In 1981, the frigates and destroyers of the RN were organised as follows: First Frigate Squadron—*Ikara Leander* Class (Plymouth); Second Frigate Squadron—Type 22 *Broadsword* Class (Portsmouth); Fourth Frigate Squadron—Type 21 *Amazon* Class (Plymouth); Fifth Destroyer Squadron—Type 42 Batch II Sheffield Class (Portsmouth); Sixth Frigate Squadron—Type 12 *Rothesay* Class (Rosyth); Seventh Frigate Squadron—*Exocet Leander* Class (Plymouth); and Eighth Frigate Squadron—*Gun Leander* Class (later to be all Broad Beam *Leanders*) (Portsmouth).

The leader of each squadron is a Captain's command and his warship, such as *Avenger* with F4, carries the Squadron Staff Officers, such as Aviation—SQUAVO—and Science. Each of the leaders can be distinguished by the broad black band around the top of its funnel, whilst the half leader (a senior Commander) can be identified by a thin black band near the top of the funnel. All warships in a particular squadron carry the number of their squadron in black on the side of the funnel. Some of the larger warships, such as the DLGs, carry only the warship's crest on the funnel.

The demise of the *Tribal* Class frigates with the operational Fleet, meant that for several years, Rosyth had no frigates base-porting there. In June

Left Newcastle *pictured in 1978 as Half-Leader of F6, is now leader of D3; changes of command necessitate changes of leader on a fairly frequent basis* (CINCFLEET).

Above right *The Inshore Survey Squadron at Chatham, their home until 1983/4.*

Right Gibraltar—*the last filling station before the world—seen from part of the Rock.*

1981, the refitted FFH *Plymouth*, leader of F6, arrived at Rosyth to begin a new era of frigate work from the naval base. With her are *Rothesay* and *Yarmouth*, whilst the other warships of the squadron are based at Portsmouth and Chatham.

Submarines are also organised into squadrons, but are dealt with elsewhere in this account. The Mines Counter Measures Vessels (MCMVs) of the Fleet, whether Minehunter (MH) or Coastal Mine Sweeper (CMS) are divided into squadrons, but the current reorganisation of the RN's MCM flotilla means that accurate identification of these vessels is not possible. As a general guide there are four squadrons—MCM1, MCM2 (at *Vernon*), MCM3 and the RNR-manned MCM10.

The Fisheries' Protection Squadron is dealt with separately in this chapter, as is the Hong Kong Patrol Squadron. In 1980, the First Fast Training Boat Squadron (1FTB) was disbanded and the three FTBs laid up at Portland pending a decision on their future.

The small but important Inshore Survey Squadron is based at Chatham until 1984 and charts the shallow, estaurine waters along the East Coast of England and parts of Scotland. Particular attention is paid to regular surveys of the constantly changing sea bed in the outer approaches to the River Thames, the Straits of Dover (including the Goodwin Sands) and the approaches to the East Anglian ports. Three specialist craft currently serve with the squadron: *Egeria*, *Echo* and *Enterprise*.

RN Overseas
Gibraltar

The naval presence at Gibraltar goes back many years to the 18th century when the RN was captialising on the gains made in the Imperial wars with Spain and France. Naval works were first projected in the shadow of the Rock during the period 1739–1750. It was not, however, until 1900 that the dry dock and the Detached Mole were constructed to give the harbour its characteristic shape. Throughout two World Wars the harbour paid an important part in the deployment of the RN and the safeguarding of British interests in the area. It is the nearest thing to a UK port there can be abroad, but with a touch of glamour that the proximity of the North African coast brings. The primary role of Gibraltar Dockyard and Naval Base depends on the situation prevailing—peace, tension or war.

There are good defence reasons for maintaining a presence at Gibraltar in peacetime for the colony with its docks (to be run down from late 1982) and airfield (to be de-militarised in 1984) provides an ideal location from which to monitor shipping passing through the Straits of Gibraltar. Surveillance is not only by visual means but also by aerial reconnaissance, radar and underwater detection devices. Gibraltar provides the usual naval base facilities for the Fleet—technical, logistical and general support, as well as Provost, dental, medical and communications facilities. Major maritime exercises are held regularly (eg, 'Spring Train' and 'Test Gate') and the surrounding sea areas have deep water for ASW training and warship work-up. The good weather conditions often mean that warships transit from the UK to work-up in the fine weather of the Gibraltar area.

NATO Maritime Forces have a significant role to play in a time of tension in a 'counter sabre-rattling' guise. Both SACLANT and SACEUR have an operational capability to establish a definite presence in the Straits.

With a commanding position and a very important strategic location at the gateway to the Mediterranean, Gibraltar sits on the southern reinforcement route to NATO's Southern Flank (Italy, Greece and Turkey) in time of war. This is especially important as a monitoring base as well as a port of command and control for the local area. In wartime, it is envisaged that the Straits would not be blocked but movement would be controlled to NATO's advantage, especially now that it is clear Spain will become a fully fledged member of the Alliance. The airfield is also designed as a forward operating base for maritime reconnaissance aircraft.

Gibraltar guard ship At one time in the more recent past, a guardship (usually a frigate) was permanently deployed at Gibraltar; today it is officially stated that the guardship is 'on call' but a rather longer notice than was usual in the past is in force. Quite often, the guardship is the frigate working up after refit at Gibraltar or the frigate awaiting refit and crew change.

Flag Officer Gibraltar's HQ The Naval Administrative Building also houses the staff for FOGIB's NATO role of COMGIBMED and of the Port Admiral Gibraltar. The port provides a maritime headquarters (MHQ), facilities for naval control of shipping (NCS) and general dockyard support (ceasing by about 1984). It is possible that Gibraltar will become a special NATO base with the Spanish application to join NATO. Since 1960, the Spanish work force in the naval set-up has been replaced by Moroccans.

Rooke The naval establishment at Gibraltar takes its name from the British Admiral who defeated the Spanish in 1704 and raised the Union Flag over what is now Britain's major overseas base. The 'stone frigate' was rebuilt between 1969–78 and presents the visitor with local architectural design in modern materials. It was inaugurated by the Governor of Gibraltar in 1978.

Today, *Rooke* has no operational role but exists to provide support and accommodation for visiting warships, the Gibraltar Refit Group (GRG), FOGIB and exercises. The Commanding Officer is a senior Commander RN whose roles are: to carry out the personnel administration and services for naval personnel at Gibraltar, their families and dependants; to provide base support facilities for visiting warships; to provide for the upkeep and maintenance of installations, etc, and for the craft attached to *Rooke* (the fleet tenders *Alness*, *Ashcott*, *Elsing* and *Ettrick*, some of which are naval manned); and to provide a trained naval contingent to meet the requirements of FOGIB. Despite its small size, *Rooke* is now the RN's largest single overseas facility.

Calpe Although there is no Gibraltar Navy as such, there is the competent and well-organised RNR HQ Unit on the Rock called *Calpe*. Perhaps not quite on a par with MHQ in the United Kingdom, the facility is gradually coming up to strength. Regular RN and WRNS staff assist the unit in its functions dealing with communications and the present RNR complement is 21 officers (NCS) and 118 ratings for plotting and communicating. There is a Gibraltarian Commander RNR and occasionally RNR personnel from the UK are drafted in for exercises.

WRNS at Gibraltar No naval shore establishment is really complete without its complement of WRNS. Gibraltar, and *Rooke* in particular, is no exception. Commanded by a Second Officer WRNS, the Wren Unit Officer, there are two officers and 54 Wrens with a variety of tasks. They mainly man posts in the Communications Centre but there are also stewards, writers and physical training instructors. FOGIB has four WRNS personnel on his staff but for administration and discipline they are carried on the books of *Rooke*.

Hong Kong

The five 425-ton *Ton* Class Patrol Craft which make up the Hong Kong Squadron (formerly the sixth Patrol Craft Squadron/Far East Fleet Inshore Squadron) come under the operational control of Captain-in-Charge Hong Kong (CAPICHK). The squadron has a leader, *Wasperton* (commanded by the Senior Officer, a Commander, SOHKS). The half leader is *Monkton* and the other ships are *Beachampton*, *Wolverton* and *Yarnton*. The squadron's role is to maintain the RN presence in Colony and neighbouring waters, but at the moment it is actively engaged, with other units of the British Forces on Hong Kong, in the anti-Illegal Immigrant (anti-II) duties in support of the Police. Operational training and flag-showing visits are made to friendly nations in South-East Asia, including Korea, Japan, Brunei and Singapore. The squadron's base is at *Tamar*, the headquarters of British Forces Hong Kong.

Tamar This is the resident command of CAPICHK and is situated on the waterfront of Hong Kong Island overlooking the Star Ferry crossing to Kowloon. The establishment itself is tri-Service and the main accommodation is a modern 27-storey block of futuristic design. Maintenance for Hong Kong-based ships, which currently include the converted Improved *Girl* Class tug *Clare*, is undertaken at the Hong Kong Shipyard Limited where syncrolift facilities are available; the RN Dockyard closed in 1957. Normal berthing is carried out in the basin, where there is a 50-ton crane, and there are typhoon buoys available in Victoria Harbour. Permanent strength is approximately 600 (250 British, 270 locally enlisted personnel [LEPs] and 60 civilians).

Naval Party 1009 The anti-II situation has now passed its peak, but during 1979 and 1980 considerable RN effort was put into countering the movement of fast speed boats, known locally as *snake* boats. Two SRN-6 *Winchester* Class hovercraft were transported by sea to Hong Kong to provide the RN with fast and mobile vessels. Naval Party 1009 is based at Stonecutters' Island, which lies to the west of the Kowloon Peninsula and is also home to several specialist Army maritime units. The headquarters building is a converted former colonial-style married quarter, but sleeping and living accommodation is usually to be found at *Tamar*.

Naval presence at Singapore Although the RN has had no permanent facilities at Singapore for the last decade or more, the need for a liaison officer has not ceased. The RN has two berths available under the terms of the Five Power Defence Agreement (Australia, Britain, Malaysia, New Zealand and Singapore) and the Assistant Defence Advisor at the British High Commission acts as RN Liaison Officer, Singapore. He has no staff. This officer, usually a Lieutenant Commander, comes under CAPICHK for administrative functions.

Hong Kong Clearance Diving Team CAPICHK has responsibility for ordnance disposal in Hong Kong below the high water mark and maintains a team of specialist divers to deal with bottom searches and the usual run of routine naval diving problems. The CO of one of the Patrol Craft is always a Clearance Diver. The Navy also runs a

Much of the RN's work in Hong Kong is in checking for smugglers and illegal immigrants—Beachampton's boarding party aboard a Taiwanese vessel.

decompression chamber for all military and civilian casualties.

Search and Rescue CAPICHK has a responsibility for SAR in the Hong Kong Flight Information Region (FIR) to latitude 15°N. RN vessels are always available in this role and the hovercraft have been very successfully used in casualty evacuation roles.

Hong Kong Defence Cost Agreement In 1980, a new Defence Cost Agreement was concluded between Whitehall and the Colony's Government. It will run for seven years from April 1 1981 and provides for 75 per cent of the cost of maintaining British Forces in Hong Kong to be funded by the Colony. Linked to this is the new *Peacock* Class of OPVs being built to replace the aging *Ton* Class vessels, and these vessels are described in Chapter Four.

The Royal Dockyards

The earliest mention of Royal Dockyards is to be found in records dating back to 1212 when King John required the Sheriff of Southampton to fortify the docks at Portsmouth. It was not until Nelson's day that the Royal Dockyards, as they became known, took on the shape we know today. By this time, installations had been provided for His Britannic Majesty's Fleet at Port Royal, Jamaica; Halifax, Nova Scotia; English Harbour, Antigua; Bermuda and Trincomalee, Ceylon (now Sri Lanka). Today, there are four Royal Dockyards in the British Isles and one at Gibraltar; together they constitute the largest industrial enterprise within central Government. Figures released in early 1981

Half leader of the Hong Kong Squadron in 1981/2 was Monkton, *seen here anchored offshore on radar picket duties.*

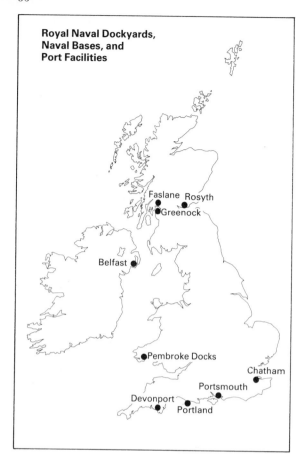

Royal Naval Dockyards, Naval Bases, and Port Facilities

The tasks

The modern warship is an increasingly complex piece of hardware and refit work takes an increasingly long time. Today, it is refitting which provides the mainstay of work for the dockyards, which no longer build warships themselves. The last warship to be built at Devonport, for example, was *Leander* Class frigate *Scylla*, launched in 1968. The tasks of every dockyard are as follows: to refit, modernise and repair British (and at times other nations') warships and supporting auxiliary craft; to manufacture and overhaul equipment associated with the repair and refitting task; to provide assistance and services to the associated naval base, particularly to warships and auxiliaries docked or anchored there; to install and repair plant and machinery in the dockyard; and to install and maintain equipment in Fleet Establishments in the Command area.

In recent years, there have been so many technical changes that the complexity and the cost of refitting and maintaining warships has grown considerably. In 1981, the Defence Review suggested that a major half-life refit on a *Leander* Class FFH amounted to about £70 million if a new weapons system was to be fitted; a brand new Type 23 frigate would cost between £40 and £50 million by comparison.

There have been rapid developments in the fields of sensors, computers and communications equipment, which now have added satellite facilities, such as SCOT. The modern Fleet relies heavily on guided weapons and many surface combat ships carry a helicopter, usually of the advanced Lynx design. All this, plus the increase in gas turbine propulsion units, has led to a recruitment of highly skilled manpower in an ever-increasing range of skills and crafts.

With about half of the submarine fleet being powered by nuclear reactor/steam turbines, the need has also been to recruit highly technical personnel to Chatham, Rosyth and Devonport for maintenance and refit work. At Rosyth, for example, it takes an incredible 2.6 million man-hours of industrial effort to refit an SSBN of the *R* Class; an event which cannot take longer than 20 months because of the need to maintain the independent nuclear deterrent with only four submarines. Dockyard General Managers fight a continual battle to prepare for refits and modernisation programmes of the future; what new equipment will the Type 22s need in five years time?

Portsmouth The Dockyard at 'Pompey' has been in existence for over 700 years and was the venue for the first British dry dock in 1496. Shipbuilding was a facet of the yard until relatively recently, and during

state that in the home dockyards there are 7,800 non-industrial employees and 23,000 industrial Civil Servants, whilst at Gibraltar there are a further 1,400 employees (being split 300 and 1,100 respectively). It is interesting to note that 50 per cent of the industrial employees are craftsmen, serving about 30 trades.

Organisation

A Royal Dockyard forms part of a naval base, which is under the general supervision of a Port Admiral; eg, Flag Officer Medway is also Port Admiral Chatham—until 1984 anyway. Whilst each HM Dockyard is under the immediate control of a General Manager, who reports to the Chief Executive Royal Dockyards, the naval base has four major departments: PSTO—Principal Supply and Transport Office; Captain of the Port; Captain, Fleet Maintenance; and Commodore, Royal Naval Barracks.

World War 2 many of the warships used for Operation 'Overlord'—the D-Day landings—were built or extensively refitted at Portsmouth. In 1981, a total of 7,100 men and women were employed in the yard, but unfortunately the 1981 Defence Review has indicated a rundown in the dockyard. This is mainly due to the lack of warships which will base-port at Portsmouth, because each dockyard (including Gibraltar) specialises in specific types or even classes of warship. 'Pompey' is base port for the CVL aircraft carriers, assault ships, *County* Class DLGs and some smaller types. It is anticipated, however, that the first three groups will have been placed in reserve, Preservation by Operation (PbyO) or sold by 1984.

There are three basins within the 300-acre site, of which No 3 is the largest, and all have several docks leading off them. All these are capable of being dried down as are the basin enter locks. Portsmouth also has a floating dry dock, usually to be found on the northern side and being occupied by an SSK from *Dolphin* (which is just across the harbour).

Devonport Plymouth's naval dockyard is sited on the Hamoaze, overlooking Cornwall. Plymouth Sound is a good natural harbour and this led to a port being established from earliest times. In the reign of William III, a dry dock was built and

Devonport, complete with its detached breakwater, was established at the beginning of the 19th century. The yard was extensively reorganised in 1967, and in 1969 it was allocated part of the responsibility for maintaining SSNs. It is now the largest ship repair yard in the British Isles and employs 12,100 men and women, 9,200 of whom are industrial employees. Besides the work carried out on the *Swiftsure* and *Trafalgar* Classes, it is the lead yard for frigates (especially the modernised *Leanders*, *Amazons* and *Broadswords*) and SSKs.

In pursuance of the new policy of specialised repair, the Admiralty announced in 1969 that a new Frigate Refit Complex would be constructed at Devonport. In order to maintain good progress and because modern equipment does not like being exposed to the elements when its covers are off, the whole complex was designed to be under cover. It includes offices and general amenities, and has the ability to be self-contained within the dockyard itself. The site chosen was the old Keysham Steam Yard and some reclamation work was put in hand. Along each side of the docks there are 20-tonne cranes, and a total of four tower cranes carry out the heavy work at the open berths. One useful feature is that warships entering or leaving the complex can do so under their power and this is the first such installation at a Royal Naval dockyard. Each dock

*Portsmouth Dockyard—*Cardiff *entering,* Juno *(F52) and* Kent *alongside (RN).*

Devonport Dockyard—the new 'garage' refit facility with Naiad (F39) *docked down, two Rothesay Class under maintenance and two type 21's (including* Antelope (F170)) *alongside (HMS Drake).*

under cover is protected by sliding doors and the roof is specially constructed to provide as much natural light as possible.

Associated with this surface ship facility is the new Submarine Refit Facility which was opened by Commander, The Prince of Wales in May 1980. The role of the facility is to enable Devonport to refit and refuel SSNs of the modern *Swiftsure* Class, and later the *Trafalgars* coming into service. It has two dry docks, a wet berth and all the necessary workshop facilities. Of course, the facility has the ability to maintain or refit surface warships as well. With the development of the RN's sub-surface fleet as predicted in the 1981 Defence Review, there is a distinct possibility that a third dry dock will be built. The dominating feature of the complex is an 80-tonne tower crane which is 138 ft (42 m) high and used in the submarine refit programme, presumably for dealing with such items as nuclear power plants. There are five other cranes alongside the berths.

Chatham Originally called Gillingham Dockyard, Chatham has been associated with the RN since 1547. It was used primarily for graving work until the reign of James I. In 1667, Chatham, and the Medway on which it is sited, was the scene of

a great naval disaster when the Dutch Fleet under De Ruyter attacked and virtually wiped it out. During the wars with France, a large number of 'wooden walls' were constructed here; especially of note was *Victory*, Nelson's flagship, launched in 1765. At the beginning of the 20th century considerable effort was put into the updating of Chatham to meet the threat of the expanding Kaiserliche Marine. In 1966, Chatham was selected as the second dockyard for servicing nuclear submarines, its special responsibility being the *Valiant* and *Churchill* classes of SSN.

As SSNs require special facilities, work was put in hand to create a Submarine Refit Complex with docking and refuelling facilities, although not under cover. An important feature of any refit is the maintenance of quality and this is especially so with a submarine. The refuelling process requires highly developed tradesman's skills and imaginative, often creative, thinking by the personnel employed on the task.

Chatham, as a naval base, has always experienced problems related to tidal and restrictive entry, and to some extent poor facilities for warships alongside. In the late 1970s, a naval base development plan was announced to improve all facets of the base and to ensure that No 3 basin has space for operational warships and auxiliaries to carry out AMP and SMP programmes. In 1981, Chatham employed 1,600 non-industrial and 4,300 industrial civil servants, but their future has been overshadowed by the 1981 Defence Review which foresees the closure of the dockyard in 1984.

Based at Chatham is the Reserve Ships Unit (RSU) where warships are held to provide additional hulls for the RN's operational Fleet at relatively short notice. Warships can be brought forward at any time, so the RSU has to keep them in good order. There are two methods used in this connection:

Preservation by Operation (PbyO): the majority of the machinery and equipment is kept in full working order and operated regularly. The upper decks of the warship are covered except when the ship is taken to sea, which happens regularly, but not often. There is about a 30-day lead time to make such warships fit for service;

Massive dehumidification: the larger ships are kept sealed and isolated from the weather. The ship is maintained dry in order to prevent active corrosion and all machinery is put into a state of preservation.

Warships of the Standby Squadron are kept in PbyO, being maintained by a special crew.

Rosyth This dockyard is on the northern shore of the Firth of Forth and was first operational in 1916, when it played a major part in the repair of warships

Rosyth Dockyard—part of the new syncrolift facility for maintenance/refitting of OPVs (Orkney illustrated) and MCMVs (British Steel/RDL photo).

damaged at the Battle of Jutland. Between the wars, it was placed in Care and Maintenance, only to be reopened in 1938. Today, Rosyth is mainly concerned with Fisheries' Protection and the RN's nuclear submarine fleet. In 1963, the dockyard was chosen as the first refitting base for nuclear submarines, the first of which arrived in 1970. It is particularly important for SSBNs, and this operation has now become nose-to-tail. At any one time, a number of other vessels can be found in refit, including *Rothesay* Class FFNs, OPVs, *Ton* Class MCMVs and SSKs.

A new feature of the Rosyth skyline is the Syncrolift which replaced the three 1,000-tonne floating docks used for the refitting of small ships. The main advantages of the new system are quicker and more economical docking operations with a greater versatility by the separation of the docking operation from the berthing facilities. A feature very necessary in Scotland is the under-cover operations which allow the maximum benefit to be made of the facilities. Small ship work is centralised so as to be close to the main workshops, thus allowing work to be carried out with a minimum of fuss and bother.

The Rosyth Syncrolift is the first of any significance in the UK, but the concept, an American idea, has been proved in many countries. In fact, *Ton* Class OPVs of the Hong Kong Squadron are refitted in the Colony using a similar system. Its main elements are: a ship lift located in a non-tidal basin, which ensures reasonably consistent water levels (this lift is rated at 1,646 tonnes by Lloyds of London; it could take 2,500 tonnes evenly distributed); a rail system of 656 ft (200 m) length which incorporates a Side Transfer System; and a Refit Shed 315 ft × 250 ft × 108 ft (96 m × 76 m × 33 m) high with five bays each 50 ft (15 m) wide. The ten-acre site also includes an external refit bay and the work, commenced in August 1977, was completed in August 1980.

Women and the Royal Dockyards

As the Government is an equal opportunities employer, it follows that almost all trades, crafts and other jobs, both industrial and non-industrial, are open to women as well as men. Today there are a large number of female apprentices at the training schools of the Home Dockyards, especially Rosyth.

Fleet Maintenance Groups

The Fleet Maintenance Groups (FMGs) at the Royal Dockyards were first conceived in the 1950s to render technical and diagnostic assistance to warships in commission anywhere in the world. Most dockyards have a Mobile Team to work overseas, a Craft Support Unit and a Static Unit to give shore service support. The skills involved cover the complete spectrum of maintenance tasks: marine propulsion domestic services; weapons systems; radar and communications. They can 'beef-up' a ship's company during AMP as well as provide a rapid 'service'.

Gibraltar

Over the years, the foreign dockyards of the Royal Navy have been thinned down to only one, at Gibraltar. Described as 'the motorway service area for the RN on deployment', Gibraltar has a history going back to 1900, when the dry dock facilities were commenced and the Detached Mole built to enclose the harbour. Though its capacity is limited by size, the dockyard still contributes to the Naval refitting programme. The refit facility available at Gibraltar which, incidentally, was included as one of the five Royal Dockyards for the first time in the 1981 Defence White Paper, has enabled frigates (mainly *Leander* Class) and MCMVs to be placed in the refit stream. Besides refitting and half-life conversion, RN warships can undertake AMPs at Gibraltar. Like its cousins in the UK, the dockyard has normal oil and material storage facilities, plus the usual PSTO(N) set up. NATO warships are able to use the dockyard facilities on request and very often do; the real need would comes in times of tension or war.

The harbour itself is 440 acres of protected water with three moles: New (South) Mole; the Detached Mole; and the North (Commercial) Mole. There are also 11 acres of slipways, stores and workshops with three dry docks: No 1, Prince of Wales'; No 2, Queen Alexandra's; and No 3, King Edward VII's. The General Manager of the Gibraltar Dockyard provides repair facilities for ships; refits, under the direction of the CED; remedies defects, mainly for warships on passage; provides operational services required by the Fleet, base development co-ordination, repair and manufacturing back-up and services to other users.

The No 1 dry dock is capable of taking the largest warships in the RN, including *Hermes*, whilst No 2 is FFH size. The system employed is called 'Garage Refitting' whereby one crew transfers to the refitted frigate whilst the GRG (*qv*) provides a crew for the vessel going into refit.

The Dockyard labour force is mixed Gibraltarian and ex-patriot British, of whom 25 per cent are skilled. Additionally, unskilled tasks, previously undertaken by the Spanish, are now done by Moroccans who have labour permits granted by the Governor of Gibraltar. MOD(N) has about 3,000 civilian at Gib. Without doubt, these are the best dockyard facilities in the Western Mediterranean and, in recent years, warships from Canada, Eire, the Netherlands and the United States have made use of the facilities. There is a fully integrated design staff who can produce, with the assistance of the machine shops, etc, the vast majority of the bits and pieces necessary for refits. The foundry is unusual because it can make castings in almost any metal specified.

A normal refit for a *Ton* Class MCMV takes 40–50 weeks but the older the warship, the longer it generally takes. A *Leander* refit, such as that for *Ajax* completed in April 1981, takes about 32–40 weeks, plus two weeks' trials, before work-up at Portland under FOST (*qv*). In November 1981, it was announced that Gibraltar Dockyard will begin to run down in early 1983; the base facilities will remain.

Gibraltar Refit Group The GRG provides a permanent refit group for the 'Garage Refit' system and is commanded by a senior Commander (E). The Group provides all Naval services in association with the Dockyard GM, and there are about 150 specialist personnel. *Rooke* is used for accommodation, administration and, perhaps most importantly, pay.

In 1981, the main effort had begun to be devoted to Batch 1 *Leander* Class (Ikara Conversion) frigates, but the GRG has been evolved over ten years since *Leanders* began half-life refits. The *Ton* Class warships take less time, effort and manpower because of their small size and relatively uncomplicated equipment. The maintenance requirements of the average warship are as follows: SMP—Self Maintenance Period; AMP—Assisted Maintenance Period; DED—Docking and Essential Defects; Refit—Every five years or so; and Half-life—Extended refit or modernisation. The 1981 Defence Review confirmed the present Government's view that no half-life modernisations will be carried out on the remaining Batch 3 *Leanders*, the Type 21s nor 42s. The policy would appear to be that surface warships will be replaced one for two with simpler types in the middle to late 1980s.

Naval shore establishments

The 'Stone Frigates' under the command of CINCNAVHOME in the United Kingdom are mainly devoted to training and accommodation for the Fleet. Other establishments with specific purposes within Naval Air Command and Submarine Command are dealt with in their respective sections. Similarly, overseas establishments are described together with the other naval involvements in Gibraltar and Hong Kong.

Medway Command *Pembroke*.

Portsmouth Command *Excellent* (including Phoenix); *Vernon*; *Centurion*; *Mercury*; *Nelson*; *Sultan*; *Collingwood*; INM Alverstoke; *Dryad* and *Temeraire*.

Plymouth Command *Drake*; *Cambridge*; *Fisgard*; *Inskip*; *Royal Arthur* and *Raleigh*.

Scotland & Northern Ireland Command *Caledonia*; *Cochrane* and *Vulcan*.

London *President* (RNR) and *Warrior* (CINC-FLEET).

Submarine Command *Dolphin* (Portsmouth); *Defiance* (Plymouth) and *Neptune* (Scotland & NI).

Naval Air Command *Heron*; *Seahawk*; *Osprey*; *Daedalus* and *Gannet*.

In addition, there are naval hospitals at Plymouth (Stonehouse), Portsmouth (Haslar) and Gibraltar: these are described below. RN Colleges are Manadon, Greenwich and Dartmouth.

Pembroke Fleet Accommodation Centre and Royal Naval Supply School; Flagship of Flag Officer Medway (who is also Port Admiral of the Dockyard). This establishment within HM Naval Base at Chatham supports and accommodates some 2,000 personnel who make up the 'ship's companies' of the RN Supply School, the Fleet Maintenance Group, the Submarine Refit Group, Reserve Ships Unit and those of warships in refit. Within the complex is St Mary's Island where there is a School of Naval Firefighting for ratings pre-embarkation. On the mainland is the Leading Rate's Leadership School, designed to pick out those POs and CPOs who have self-confidence and power of command. The establishment has full medical and dental facilities.

The Royal Naval Supply School was established in 1958, having moved from the now closed *Ceres*, Yorkshire. The School is divided into five separate sub-branch professional schools: Writers; Stores Accounting; Catering Accounting; Cookery, and Stewards. Except for Catering Accounting, all the schools have WRNS on their complement of training personnel who number about 2,700 annually. The RN Catering and Cookery Department will be remembered for producing the wedding cake for Commander, The Prince of Wales, and Lady Diana in July 1981; at the time the style of the cake was one of the closest guarded secrets in the Navy!

The Writers School handles all clerical work taught, including Pay and Accounting. The Stores Accounting School deals with all logistics support techniques taught. The Catering Accounting School teaches stock control and menu planning. In the Cookery School, trainee cooks are taught their trade and profession, and in the Stewards School trainee stewards learn their trade. In addition there is the Officers Training School, where officers of the Supply and Secretariat Branch are taught in all five disciplines and junior officers complete courses pre-embarkation in a secretarial appointment. Senior officers attend the Supply Charge Course to fit them for Head of Department appointments afloat and ashore.

The future of *Pembroke* is now short following the decision to close the Chatham complex in 1984; Pembroke will close in 1983 and the Supply School will be transferred to *Raleigh* (the catering training of all three services may well be standardised, perhaps at Aldershot).

Excellent This establishment has a famous name and one which can strike a chill note in many former matelots' breasts. Today, *Excellent* is the Naval Leadership Centre and is situated at Whale Island in Portsmouth Harbour. Units lodging at Excellent include the Fleet Photographic Unit; the Portsmouth Command Field Gun Team; RN Display Team; Technical Training Group (TTG), linked to nearby Collingwood (*qv*); Naval Weapons Trials under Captain Weapons Trials; RN Regulating School; Leading Rates Leadership School; Tipner Rifle Range; Phoenix NBCD and Ship Firefighting Schools; RN Divisional and Management School and HMY *Britannia*. The RN Regulating School deals with the training of

Excellent—an aerial view showing some of the historic buildings and the Royal Yacht facilities (HMS Excellent).

Regulating Branch ratings (from Leading Rate to Sub Lieutenant (X) (Reg)) and the Captain of *Excellent* is the head of the branch. The Fleet Photographic Unit includes the Joint School of Applied Photography and is responsible for training and covering all important aspects of RN operations and life. *Phoenix* is where the RN learns damage control, firefighting, NBC defence and first aid. The School is an integral part of *Excellent* although it is situated some way across the northern suburbs of Portsmouth. The Ship Firefighting School is situated on Horsea Island and this is where firefighting techniques are learned in a replica of a ship's interior. Also at *Excellent* are the Harbour Accommodation and Training Ships *Rame Head* and *Kent*, moored on the south side of the island.

Excellent is most famous for its role in the Ceremonial Training of the Fleet and the establishment is now considered the leading authority for such activity in the RN. When performing in public, at home or abroad, the RN demands the peak of smartness and high standards of drill. The establishment also runs a small Internal Security (IS) training cadre which also deals with the Fleet's small arms training for landings and boarding parties.

Under the terms of the 1982 RN Establishments' Review, the various schools at *Excellent* are due to be transferred in 1984–5: Naval Weapons Trials (to the Naval Base); Technical Training (*Collingwood*); LR Leadership (*Royal Arthur*); Regulating and Divisional (*Drake*); Weapons Systems (*Daedalus*); IS (*Cambridge*); Photographics (Tipnor and RAF Cosford). *Phoenix* will close in 1984, the Fraser Gunnery Range and *Excellent* in 1986.

Temeraire The establishment bears a most famous name in the annals of the RN and since 1971 has been the name given to the Royal Naval School of Physical Training (RNSPT) at Portsmouth. The establishment cannot boast an integrated complex and facilities, but it is an independent command under a Captain RN.

Temeraire is mainly concerned with training RN and WRNS Physical Training Instructors—the 'clubswingers'. The Branch is today tasked with organising recreational activities for men and women in the RN to keep personnel mentally and physically fit for duty. Adventurous training, such as expeditions, round-the-world sailing and mountaineering, is also the province of the Branch and *Temeraire* is the *alma mater*. The PT instructors are all volunteers with leadership potential, and are therefore experienced Able rates. Promotions are possible to PO Physical Trainer, CPO Physical Trainer and Fleet Chief Physical Trainer, the latter being the head of the Physical Training and Recreation Staff and certain shore establishments. Promotion to officer is also possible by selection.

Sultan This establishment, built on the site of a former World War 1 airfield near Gosport, has been so-named since 1956. Today, it is home to the Marine Engineering Branch of the RN. It is one of the major establishments of Naval Home Command.

Sultan's Captain is tasked with: training RN personnel in the Marine Engineering discipline; providing craft training for MEM and Mechanician rates; training elements of MoD, civilian contractors, RNR, CCF and SCC, as well as Foreign and Commonwealth navies, in Marine Engineering; advising on all matters, including advancement, in the Branch; providing facilities for Fleet Examination Boards; supporting with accommodation, etc, the neighbouring establishments of *Centurion* and the *Admiralty Interview Board*; and providing, as necessary, men and equipment for CINCNAVHOME.

The establishment's former moored training vessel, the destroyer *Diamond*, was disposed of to the breaker's yard in early 1982, but the School of Marine Engineering still has use of the former frigate *Russell*, moored at Priddy's Hard in Portsmouth Harbour.

Dryad Commissioned as the RN's Navigation School in 1906, *Dryad* now lies to the north of Portsmouth Harbour in the South Downs. The Navigation Branch of the RN has developed in the 20th century from the plotting board to the Action Information Organisation (AIO) and the establishment has developed in parallel. In 1970, the Maritime Tactical School moved to *Dryad*, now formally established at Southwick House. Today, the establishment is involved in all aspects of command training, including the famous

Organisation and role

Right Vernon—*The MCMVs' berths and the Portsmouth area heliport show up well in this view* (HMS Vernon).

Below left Temeraire—*PT instruction underway in one of the many locations which go to make up the establishment* (RN).

Submarine Command 'pershers' course' and is used for Principal Warfare Officer (PWO) training with tactical simulation in the *Leander*, Type 21, Type 42 and lately the Type 22 Operations Room trainers. The Navigation section is now established at *Mercury*, with other sections of the School of Maritime Operations, using *Vernon* and the Fraser Gunnery Range. The establishment shares the title 'School of Maritime Operations' with *Mercury*. The Fraser Gunnery Range's tasks will be transferred here in 1986.

Vernon This establishment has been involved in torpedo and other underwater weapons for about 110 years, since the commissioning of *Vernon*, the RN's Torpedo Instructional School in 1872. Later it included the Mining School and the establishment was commissioned at its present location in 1923. It is also responsible for seamanship training and boat handling. Today, diving, mining, countermeasures and anti-submarine warfare are all part of the *Vernon* brief. The Second Mine Counter Measures Squadron (*Ton* Class MCMVs) is also based at *Vernon*, and other lodger units are: support for *Speedy*'s trials; Base Supply Support; Underwater Warfare Faculty of Captain SMOPS; Maritime Trade Faculty of Captain SMOPS; UW Staff of Captain Weapon Trials (DGW(N)); Superintendent of Diving; Experimental Diving Unit; RN Saturation Diving; Fleet Clearance Diving Team (CINCFLEET); Portsmouth and Medway Clearance Diving Team (FO Portsmouth); Portsmouth Photographic Bureau; RNXS Ports-

mouth; Aircrew Underwater Escape Training Team (FONAC), and *Vernon* is also the base for UK elements of Standing Naval Force Channel and RNR operations.

Vernon's primary tasks are to provide full support and administrative facilities for ships and craft based at *Vernon* and visiting the establishment; and to support and administer the lodger units at *Vernon*. There are also secondary tasks: operating the Portsmouth area heliport; administering the UK Contingency Portable Radio Pool; planning continued development of facilities; providing certain facilities in the event of war; and providing resources for FO Portsmouth and FO Medway as required. Naval Party 1007 for *Seaforth Clansman* is based at *Vernon*.

Although some time away, it has been announced that *Vernon* will close in 1986 with a small part continuing until 1988. Most of the facilities and schools are being transferred to the Portsmouth Naval Base. Some elements will go to *Dryad* or *Sultan*.

Centurion This is an impressive and modern establishment which was re-commissioned at its present site at Gosport in October 1970. Its principal tasks are: to maintain the computer record; to account for pay and allowances to the Fleet; to 'man' the Fleet; to provide personnel and management information; to provide pay office services for 3,500 officers and men in the Portsmouth area; and to plan for future resources and systems.

Centurion is considered unique in the Fleet, being responsible directly to the Director General Naval

Manpower and Training in the Ministry of Defence (DNMT). Nearly two-thirds of the ship's company are civilians and yet there are 930 personnel all told, including RN and WRNS. The nearby *Sultan* is used for accommodation.

Mercury Today, *Mercury* is the School of Maritime Operations and the twelfth ship to bear the name in the RN, being a 'stone frigate' situated in the peaceful Hampshire countryside near Petersfield. The present role is to carry out both officer and rating training in the following tasks: all RN officer communications and navigation training ranging from day-long acquaint courses to three-month specialist courses of an advanced nature; pre-joining updates for COs about to assume command of RN ships; RFA, RNR, RNXS, etc, familiarisation courses in communications and navigation; NATO and Commonwealth officer training in both fields. The usual training complement is 30.

No less exacting are the courses run for ratings from Chief Yeoman to New Entry: New Entry Communications training (Parts II and III) (23-week basic course prior to going to sea for eventual advancement to Able, Leading and Petty Officer rates); Professional Advancement Training Course for Leading and PO rates; refresher training for all ratings who are joining or rejoining warships after a period ashore; NATO and Commonwealth communications and navigation courses for ratings; Navigator's Yeoman Courses for ratings of the Seaman Group; CCF and School acquaint courses; RNR Continuation and Advancement training; and WRNS radio operators training. The usual training complement is 300. *Mercury* has a staff of some 70 officers and 590 ratings and the establishment is headed by a Captain RN.

The Fleet Operational Exercise Pool, a group of competent sailors from the Communications Branch, is based at *Mercury*, but comes under the control of CINCFLEET. The task of the nine Senior and 41 Junior rates is to augment ships' companies and establish Communications Centres during major exercises.

Nelson Today, *Nelson*, situated in Portsmouth Naval Base, houses the RN School of Educational and Training Technology and the Dental Training School. It is also the major RN centre for vocational training prior to release and has a primary role as Fleet Accommodation Centre for the Portsmouth Area. (NB: Until 1853 there was no regular Navy and no need for a depot and/or barracks, but with continuous service the need for a barracks—a home establishment—was confirmed and, by 1903, the new *Nelson* had been fully completed. The establishment was, however, called *Victory* by order of HM King Edward VII as it was thought that

Nelson—*Admiralty House, Portsmouth, which is the HQ of CINCNAVHOME who administers all the UK establishments. The house is located adjacent to* Nelson *(RN).*

Nelson's flagship was about to decay. For many years after the wooden ship was saved there were two *Victory*s in the RN—the wooden ship (Flagship of CINCNAVHOME) and the establishment next door. In August 1974, the RN barracks was renamed *Nelson*.)

Collingwood This establishment is situated between Portsmouth and the Royal Naval Air Station at Lee-on-Solent. It is named for Admiral Lord Collingwood (1748–1820) who led the lee line Fleet at Trafalgar and took over command on the death of Lord Nelson. The present *Collingwood* is the fourth ship in the Royal Navy to bear the name and was built to train New Entry 'hostilities only' ratings of the Seaman Branch in 1939. In 1979, the Engineering Branch of the RN was restructured and the former Weapon and Electrical Engineering Branch which used *Collingwood* for officer and rating training was designated the Weapon Engineering Sub-branch, passing Electrical Generation and Distribution to the Marine Engineering Sub-branch and gaining Explosives from the Operations (formerly Seaman) Branch. *Sultan* has now taken over the training of electrical generation and distribution trades.

Collingwood is commanded by a Commodore RN and has a Commander RN in charge of each of the five specialist schools: Basic Training; Mechanic Training; Electrotechnology Training; Systems Training and Technician Training. All are part of the Weapon Engineering Sub-branch.

INM Alverstoke Conveniently near RNH

Haslar (*qv*) is the Institute of Naval Medicine Alverstoke which is involved in occupational and environmental medicine. Today INM's role is to act as a centre of expertise for the RN Medical Service with three main functions: Operational Medical Support, Applied Research and Specialist Medical Training. For example, work is carried out into nuclear problems and those of deep diving saturation personnel. The Institute was formed in 1969 although it can trace a history back to 1912. Alverstoke, then, is very much involved with the human factors of the RN, such as the problems associated with living under pressure for periods up to 30 days during saturation diving, or living for extended periods in a life raft, or decontaminating the upper decks of warships. In the event of a nuclear accident anywhere, the INM has a specialist Naval Emergency Monitoring Team ready to go at anytime. In the same vein is the Diving Accidents team which monitors accidents, survival and tests new equipment.

In June 1980, the redeveloped facilities were opened to provide a nationwide medical advisory service for diving and decompression illnesses. The new facilities consist of a laboratory complex with physiology, pathology and audiology areas, a lecture theatre, and the new Naval Radiological Protection and RN Mass Radiographic Services.

Drake* This famous West Country name is the fleet accommodation unit at Devonport naval base and the establishment is the 24th 'ship' to bear the name in the RN. The establishment was commissioned as a barracks in 1934 and has one of the finest wardrooms in the RN with wooden relief carved panels depicting famous British naval battles in the main dining room. After the war, *Drake* was reconstructed and the old training task of the barracks was transferred to the various training establishments which were now available.

Cambridge This is the RN's Gunnery School, set high on the cliffs overlooking the approaches to Plymouth Sound. It is the only establishment in the United Kingdom where officers and ratings can be trained in the control and live firing of conventional gunnery systems. The training courses include those for Principal Warfare Officers and, at the other end of the scale, Junior Seaman. At *Cambridge*, internal security (IS) is also taught to naval personnel for the occasion when a naval party would have to be landed to restore order or to assist the civil power. Small-arms, as well as the 114 mm gun mountings, are in evidence at the establishment.

Cambridge has five primary tasks: above water

* Battle Honours: Lowestoft 1665; Baltic 1855; Pei-Ho Forts 1859.

warfare and weapons training for Electrical Engineers; pre-joining training for Electrical Engineers; Ships' Gunnery Team training pre-BOST (Basic Operational Sea Training); continuation training for Ships' Gunnery Teams; and Seamen (Missile)—S(M)—Part III training. In addition, the Captain of *Cambridge* is tasked with providing advice to Flag Officer Plymouth on gunnery matters. Secondary tasks include IS training for ships in the Plymouth area; the establishment has ample facilities in its 150-acre site; facilities for direction finding and radio/radar calibration; plus facilities for special trials by DGW(N).

Fisgard This is the Naval Artificer Training Establishment for New Entry training before personnel undertake specialist training at *Caledonia*, *Collingwood* or *Daedalus*. The apprenticeship covers technical education, craft training, naval general training and technical training on naval equipment and systems. The training brief is very thorough and includes many items not usually associated with artificers, such as firefighting, sea survival, personal finance and NBC training. *Fisgard* is situated on the Cornish side of Plymouth Sound, adjacent to *Raleigh*.

It was announced during the production of this book that *Fisgard* will close as a Naval training establishment in December 1983, with most of the courses going to *Raleigh*, and a few to *Collingwood* and *Daedalus*. The future of the establishment is unsure as it may be used for other defence purposes.

Inskip Away from the conglomeration of establishments around Plymouth, *Inskip* is situated in 600 acres on the Fylde Peninsula, Lancashire. The site was originally a naval air station under the name *Nightjar*, but in 1958 the establishment was turned over to communications and became a Transmitting Station, being commissioned as *Inskip* in March 1966. Today, *Inskip* plays a vital role in the constant communications role by providing LF (low frequency) and HF (high frequency) transmissions to the Fleet. The current naval complement is two officers and 50 ratings.

Royal Arthur During World War 2, *Royal Arthur* was the name of the New Entry induction centre at Corsham, later at Skegness (the former Butlins' Holiday Camp). Today, the establishment is the Petty Officers' Leadership School with the aim of training POs for future leadership responsibilities in the modern RN. These courses take five weeks and there are 45 annually. In addition, there are courses for WRNS, QARNNS and WRNR POs, RNR POs, Sub-Lieutenants and CCF officers. The training staff consists of 16 officers and CPO instructors drawn from all specialisations.

Raleigh Commissioned in 1940 as a shore training establishment for naval seamen, the establishment was later taken over by the US Navy for pre-invasion operations and accommodation. In 1971 the site, on Torpoint, Cornwall, but close to Plymouth, was redeveloped and now caters for all new entrants to the RN except Artificer Apprentices, who go to *Fisgard* which it adjoins. Young men are taken at *Raleigh* at about 16–17 and given basic (Part I) instruction to fit them for naval service. Part II training is taken at specialist schools: Marine Engineering Mechanic (MEM) at *Sultan* or *Collingwood*; Weapon Electrical Mechanic (WEM)—'greenies'—at *Collingwood*; Supply and Secretariat (eg, writers and stewards) at *Pembroke*; Naval Airman at *Culdrose*; Naval Air Mechanic at *Daedalus*; Radio Electrical Mechanic at *Daedalus*; Electrical Mechanic at *Daedalus*; Radio Operator at *Mercury* and Medic at RNH Haslar.

Members of the Seaman Operations Branch do, however, take their Part II training at *Raleigh*. Some young ratings who have successfully completed Part II go on to undertake sub-specialist training: Clearance Diver at *Vernon*; Radar and EW at *Dryad*, or Sonar and Mine Warfare at *Vernon*. From September 7 1981, *Raleigh* took over responsibility for the training of recruits to the Women's Royal Naval Service (WRNS).

Caledonia This establishment is situated on a hill overlooking Rosyth and the River Forth and is the centre for Part II Marine Engineer Artificer Apprentices' Training. Apprentices come to *Caledonia* having completed Part I at *Fisgard* and much time is spent afloat training as well as in the classroom/workshop. *Eastbourne*, a former Whitby Class anti-submarine frigate, serves as a Harbour Training Vessel and trainees are embarked in the Dartmouth Training Ship for short periods. *Caledonia* is the fifth ship in the RN to bear the name, but will close in 1985, transferring its training programme to *Sultan*.

Cochrane This is the Fleet Accommodation

RNC Greenwich—the Staff College seen from the air with a Lynx HAS 2 overflying (Westland).

Britannia Royal Naval College, Dartmouth, in its beautiful Devonshire setting. Here both male and female officers are trained (MoD).

Centre for FOSNI at Rosyth and was purpose-built in 1968. Today, the establishment houses 1,256 men and women and provides training in firefighting, leadership and certain academic subjects for Naval junior management. In addition, the Naval Provost and the Scotland and Northern Ireland Clearance Diving Team are based at *Cochrane*.

Vulcan Until recently housing the Naval Nuclear Power School (now at *Sultan*), *Vulcan* today is the RN Nuclear Propulsion Test and Training Establishment (RNPTE) at Dounreay, Caithness.

Warrior This is the Headquarters of CINCFLEET and is situated at Northwood in Middlesex. It is also home for Flag Officer Submarines, the Commanders-in-Chief Committee and liaison with the Royal Air Force's No 18 (Maritime) Group. CINCFLEET wears his NATO hats for Channel and Eastern Atlantic at Northwood.

Royal Naval Hospitals

RNH Stonehouse As long ago as 1744, the Navy Board proposed the construction of hospital facilities at Plymouth, Portsmouth and Chatham. After some delay, the hospital at Plymouth, named Stonehouse, was opened in 1762. Today, there are ten three-storey wards surrounding a central lawn, which doubles as a helicopter landing pad for critically ill patients. There are all the facilities of a modern hospital, including a rehabilitation gymnasium and two major plus one minor operating theatres. In the years following World War 2, casualties from Korea, Suez, Aden, Malaysia and, more recently, Northern Ireland have been treated at Stonehouse. This is one of the naval establishments which may be closed down in 1983/4.

RNH Haslar The foundations for Haslar were laid on the Gosport side of Portsmouth Harbour in 1746 and the first patients were admitted in 1753— the hospital has served the Royal Navy and Royal Marines ever since. Today, besides ordinary medical treatment for naval personnel, military civil servants and their families, Haslar is the teaching hospital for the RN, specialising in Naval Medical Officers, nurses, radiographers, physiotherapists and all Medical Branch staff.

RNH Gibraltar This is the only overseas Royal Naval Hospital and it is under the command of a Surgeon Captain, called the Medical Officer in Charge (MOIC). The establishment is of traditional colonial architecture yet inside is modern and fully equipped to contribute to the medical wellbeing of naval and military personnel as well as the civilian work force at Gibraltar. It comprises about 65 beds as well as a fully equipped 'disaster' ward, known as the 'Gib Cap Ward'. The hospital is staffed by RN medical and dental officers, QARNNS, C & Q personnel and locally recruited auxiliaries.

In addition, each establishment and ship has a sick bay and trained medical staff for first aid and emergency treatment.

Royal Naval Colleges

RNEC Manadon: HMS Thunderer This college is responsible for the education and training of Engineer Officers in the RN and certain friendly navies. It is situated midway between the Plymouth-Devonport dockyard and the Dartmoor National Park. The original college, established at Keyham in 1880, was re-established at Manadon in 1940. It offers first and second degree facilities to naval officers and provides practical and theoretical experience for all trainees. Officers undergo training in the Marine Engineering, Weapon Engineering, Air Engineering and Control and Computation Engineering fields.

RNC Greenwich Greenwich is the RN's staff college and houses three separate departments: the nuclear department for COs and Engineering Officers of SSNs and SSBNs; Special Duties (SD) courses for Sub-Lieutenants on promotion from CPO and the Staff courses; the Lieutenants' Course and the Staff Course. Staff training is intended to fit an officer for command of a ship, an appointment at MOD or appointment to a Flag Officer's staff. The main feature of Greenwich, situated in a beautiful building next to the Thames, is claimed to be that having selected the right man for the job, his course is so structured that he enjoys it.

BRNC Dartmouth The very best way to start a career as an officer in any navy. The Britannia Royal Naval College Dartmouth is a magnificent Edwardian building overlooking the mouth of the River Dart and the English Channel. Every naval officer, male or female, is now expected to pass out of Dartmouth having completed a course in technical, naval, liberal and physical activities. Entry can be as school leaver, graduate or 'Upper Yardman'—from the ranks. The college has a number of tenders, including two *Bird* Class PVs, a single helicopter (Westland Wasp) for helicopter experience, plus a Flight of Chipmunk trainers at Roborough (see Chapter Five). The Training Ship cruises, in *Fearless*, *Intrepid* or previously *Norfolk*, are the highlights of the course. The Passing Out Parade is one of the most impressive occasions in the Dartmouth calendar.

Royal Navy warships

This chapter deals with the surface and sub-surface combat units which make up the Royal Navy today. The last few years have seen a change in emphasis from large surface groups centred on a major warship, such as an aircraft carrier, to reliance on nuclear-powered ballistic missile submarines as capital ships of the modern fleet. The Royal Navy still commands a position in the top five navies of the world in terms of numbers of combat surface ships and is, despite recent Defence Cuts, a force of power and deterrence. The trend over the next few years will be towards cheaper and smaller ships, and more submarines. Technology is continually improving and hull design is following the same route, albeit more slowly.

Definitions

Net tonnage This is the measurement of the net cubic capacity of a ship, excluding engine, boiler, crew, stores and working compartments.

Sea Harriers and Sea Kings aboard Hermes *on April 4 1982 just before sailing to the South Atlantic* (Popperfoto).

Gross displacement This is the measurement of the total cubic capacity of a ship.
Standard displacement This is the total weight of the ship with everything aboard less the weight of fuel and reserve feed water for the boilers. This is the international 'standard' for quoting warship displacement.
Full displacement This is the total weight of the ship fully loaded and is particularly used for auxiliaries.
Light displacement This is the weight of the fabric of the ship.
hp horsepower.
bhp brake horsepower.
ihp indicated horsepower.
shp shaft horsepower.

Aircraft carriers (CVSs)

Class *Hermes*
Name *Hermes;* **Pennant number** R12; **Flight deck code** H; **Standard displacement:** 23,900 tons; **Full displacement** 28,700 tons; **Length** 226.9 m overall; **Beam** 27.4 m (at waterline); **Draught** 9.0 m; **Propulsion** Steam turbines; **Speed** 28 knots; **Complement** 143 officers and 1,207 ratings; **Armament** 2 × Seacat SAM launchers (one on each quarter); **Sensors** 965 (AKE-1); 993; 1006; 2 × GWS 22; HF/DF; MF/DF; SCOT; EW; IFF; 184; **Aircraft** 5 × Sea Harrier FRS 1 and 10 × Sea King HAS 5 with 1 × Wessex HU 5 (plane guard); **Small craft** Ship's launches plus 4 × LCVPs; **Vehicles** AWDs; Coles crane; Hyster lift and JCB 520; Land Rover; **Builders** Vickers (Barrow); **Laid down** June 21 1944; **Launched** February 16 1953; **Completed** 1959; **Commissioned** November 18 1959; **Refits** 1964–66; 1971–3; 1976–7; 1979–81; **Fuel capacity** 4,200 tons FFO, 320 tons diesel; **Armour** 0.02 m on flight deck, 0.03 m over magazines.

Hermes has had a long and distinguished career with the RN, starting life as a Light Fleet Aircraft

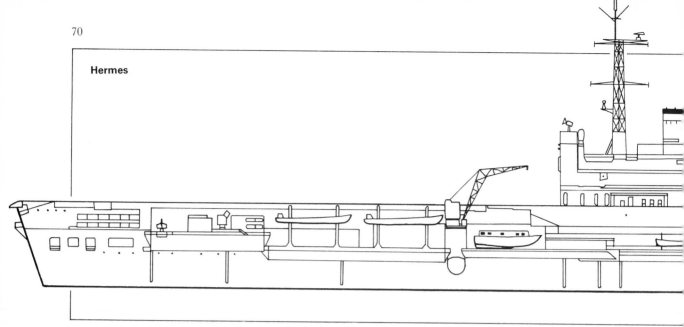

Hermes

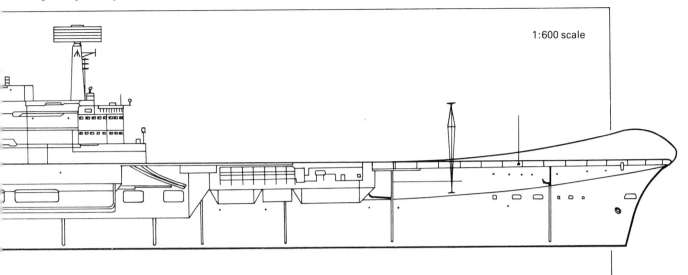

1:600 scale

Carrier under the wartime building programme. Her launching was delayed postwar and in 1959 she joined the Fleet as the last conventional fixed-wing carrier to be completed. She served in this role, mainly in the Far East and Indian Ocean, until 1971, when she was taken in hand for conversion into a Commando Carrier (LPH). When she emerged in 1973, the RN's role had changed and she concentrated on the NATO area but did take part in the dramatic rescue of civilians during the Cyprus Emergency of 1974. In this role she was equipped to operate a complete Commando Brigade and its vehicles using Wessex HU 5 helicopters. As the Soviet submarine menace grew, the ship was taken in hand, at Portsmouth, yet again for modernisation and conversion in 1976, this time her role being to operate ASW Sea King helicopters as well, for which she was prepared by 1977. The joint CVS/LPH was a compromise at the best of times and did not succeed too well. With the introduction of the Sea Harrier into front-line service and the delay in producing the new CVLs of the *Invincible* Class, *Hermes* was refitted at Portsmouth and given the distinctive 7° ski-jump for operating jets again. In the summer of 1981 she commenced work-up with Sea Harriers of 800 Squadron and Sea King HAS 2s of 826 Squadron.

Hermes retains her four Admiralty three-drum type boilers which produce steam for the Parsons geared turbines (rated at 76,000 shp) which in turn drive two shafts; the recent refit has apparently meant the removal of two shafts from the original four-shaft design.

Left Hermes *departs Portsmouth for the South Atlantic* (RN).

The recent refit has given the *Hermes* the most comprehensive sensor and electronics fit in the RN to date and really has made her a 'better' ship than the CVLs coming into service. Despite proving her value during the Falklands operation where she acted as flagship, her future is, at the time of writing, limited to the introduction of *Ark Royal* in 1985. A sad end to a magnificent warship.

Light aircraft carriers (CVLs)
Class *Invincible*
Name *Invincible*; **Pennant number** R05; **Flight deck code** N; **Standard displacement** 16,000 tons; **Full displacement** 19,810 tons; **Length** 206.6 m overall/192.9 m waterline; **Beam** 31.9 m flt deck/27.5 m waterline; **Draught** 7.3 m; **Propulsion** 4 × gas turbines; **Range** 5,000 nm at 18 knots; **Speed** 28 knots; **Complement** 131 officers and 869 ratings*; **Armament** 1 × Twin Sea Dart launcher (Exocet fitting planned not proceeded with due to cost); **Sensors** 2 × 1006; 2 × 909; 992R; 1022; 2016; IFF; SCOT; HF/DF; MF/DF; EW; ESM; **Aircraft** 5 × Sea Harrier FRS 1; 9 × Sea King HAS 5 and 1 × Wessex HU 5, or 10 × Sea King HAS 5; **Small craft** 4 × ship's launches;

* Figure excludes Air Group. NB: In an emergency, *Invincible* could be deployed to Norway with a Commando of RMs, their Sea King HC 4s plus vehicles in overload conditions, but it is doubtful that SACLANT would use such a valuable ASW asset in this way. Commando accommodation would be provided in camp beds, as during the deployment to Ascension Island in April 1982.

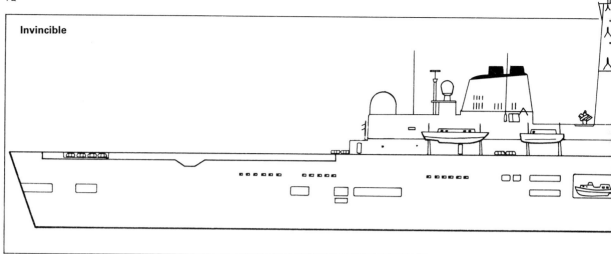

Invincible

1 × Gemini; 1 × Dory; **Vehicles** AWDs; Coles crane; Hyster lift and JCB 520; Land Rover; **Builders** Vickers (Barrow); **Laid down** July 20 1973; **Launched** May 3 1977; **Completed** March 19 1980; **Commissioned** June 11 1980; **Refits** 1982; Fuel capacity Classified; **Armour** Classified.

Although in early 1982, it was announced that *Invincible* would be sold for £175 millions to the Royal Australian Navy in late 1983, the decision was later revoked.

The *Invincible* Class are equipped with the MADGE microwave landing system manufactured in Sussex by MEL, a Division of Philips Industries. After trials in *Hermes* (which is now equipped with MADGE) during 1978–80, the system was adopted for RN use in 1979. The main 'client' is the BAe Sea Harrier FRS 1 which is unable to use its standard Blue Fox (*qv*) radar in a foul weather approach to the deck because of the frequency agility of the radar. The Sea King HAS 5 can use Type 1006 (*qv*) radar for talk-down assistance. There is, therefore, a requirement for a proper landing/talk-down system. The result is MADGE, which as well as dealing with six individual 'targets' can provide a data link between aircraft and ship. The system allows the ship to manoeuvre fully during a Sea Harrier's 20 nm (37 km) approach, giving Flyco the aircraft's position and status at all times. In addition, pilot interpretation is simplified because the system is fully integrated with the aircraft's avionics software, making full use of the Ferranti aircraft computer and the Smith's HUD (head-up display). On the ship, the installation is a ground unit together with a processor and both these devices have been tried operationally in offshore petro-chemical installations. Without doubt, this is a key element in the

operational techniques used for Sea Harrier sorties in the North Atlantic.

In fact, during exercises in the 1981 season, the *Invincible* Class proved that they could launch four Sea Harriers (out of a possible five) in about 50 seconds, which was as much time as the largest US carrier could launch one F-14A Tomcat. In addition, the aircraft from 801 NAS were able to maintain an adequate CAP for more than 80 hours during the exercise and keep away from the Task Group all intruders. It says much for the Fleet Air Arm personnel and for the facilities which a warship of this type can provide. The Ship's Air Department consists of ten officers and 73 ratings whilst the embarked squadrons (normally 800 and 820) bring 54 officers and 218 ratings with them.

In April 1973, *Invincible* was ordered from Vickers Shipbuilding Group Limited of Barrow-in-Furness, a company with a long reputation as naval builders. The keel was laid in July 1973 and HM The Queen launched the ship at Barrow on May 3 1977. She commenced Contractor's Sea Trials in April 1979 and was accepted into service at Portsmouth on March 19 1980. The ship is designed to operate the V/STOL British Aerospace Sea Harrier FRS 1 aircraft and Sea King HAS 5 anti-submarine warfare helicopters; it has the following roles as a flagship for FOF3 and as part of the British commitment to NATO in the event of war in the Atlantic: Command and Control; anti-submarine warfare; air and missile defence (Area basis); surface strike and Commando amphibious lift. It is envisaged that *Invincible* and her sister ship(s) would

Right Invincible *heads for the Falklands with Sea Harriers and Sea Kings embarked* (RN).

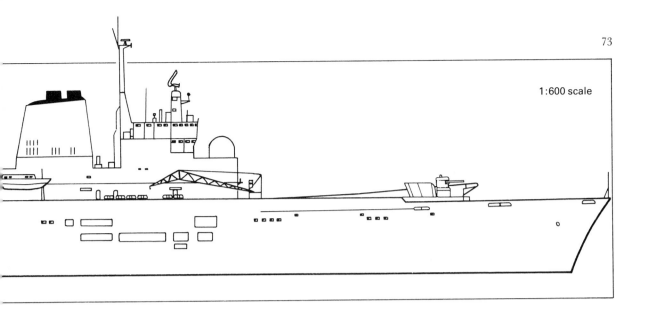

1:600 scale

lead an anti-submarine Task Group operating in the Greenland-Iceland-UK gap area to prevent penetration of the Atlantic re-supply routes by Soviet submarines. The cost of the warship rose from £66 million projected in 1977 to £175 million on completion (of which £19 million is accounted for by the design costs).

Refinements in the ship's design include the ski-jump at 7° which was incorporated during the ship's construction following successful trials with the design at RAE Bedford. Her sister-ship *Illustrious* has the same inclination of ramp, but *Ark Royal*, the third and last CVL will have a ramp of 12°. The ski-ramp allows for launches of Sea Harriers with a greater payload than would be possible with free take-off or vertical lift. It also allows complete tactical freedom in that the ship does not necessarily have to turn into wind to launch the Sea Harriers. Sea Acceptance Trials (Air) were completed in the winter of 1980 and, in 1981, the ship deployed Westlant for the first

Illustrious *on trials from the Tyne in November 1981* (Swan Hunter).

time. During the 1981 exercise season she represented the RN in the North Atlantic and in 1982, of course, she formed part of the Falklands Task Force.

Invincible has set the following records: first ship with V/STOL ramp; first ship with 'scissors' lift; largest warship powered by gas turbines; largest propellor shaft; largest propellors; largest electricial power; largest air conditioning system. The electrical generation is carried out by eight RP200 1.75 MWs whilst propulsion is via four RR Olympus TM3B marine gas turbines (112,000 shp) driving two shafts through a reversible gearbox.

Name *Illustrious;* **Pennant number** R06; **Flight deck code** L; **Armament:** 1 × Twin Sea Dart launcher; 2 × Vulcan Phalanx CIWS; **Builders** Swan Hunter; **Laid down** October 7 1976; **Launched** December 1 1978; **Completed** June 18 1982; **Accepted** June 21 1982.

Illustrious has now joined *Invincible* as the second of the RN's Sea Harrier-carriers, her first commission taking her to the South Atlantic. She has been constructed from the beginning with the ski-jump ramp at 7° and it was at her launching, just after the demise of the previous *Ark Royal*, that the then Secretary of State for Defence stated that the third unit would be named *Ark Royal*.

Name *Ark Royal;* **Pennant number** R09; **Flight deck code** R; **Armament:** 1 × Twin Sea Dart launcher; 2 × Vulcan Phalanx CIWS; **Builders** Swan Hunter; **Laid down** December 14 1978; **Launched** June 2 1981; **Completed** 1984/5; **Commissioned** 1985.

The ship was launched by HM The Queen Mother who had been patron of the previous *Ark Royal*, the last fixed-wing aircraft carrier. This ship was originally to be named *Indomitable* after another of the *Illustrious* Class carriers of World War 2 and in 1982 it was announced that she would replace *Hermes* in late 1985.

Submarines and the RN

There are several classes of submarine in the RN, falling into three distinct categories: SSBNs — Polaris missile-firing submarines; SSNs — Fleet-type hunter-killer submarines; and SSKs — Patrol Class submarines.

SSBNs The *R*-Class of SSBN is based at Faslane, Scotland, and always has one of its number on patrol carrying Polaris missiles which form the main British strategic deterrent force.

SSNs There are three classes of SSN in service: the older *Valiant* Class modelled on the *Dreadnought* but with British reactors; the deeper-diving and faster *Swiftsure* Class and the recently ordered *Trafalgar* Class of which the first have been ordered.

SSKs These are smaller diesel-powered boats for coastal work and for use in landing agents and SBS (*qv*) patrols on enemy coasts. Although conventional, the *O* and *P* Classes remain highly efficient and quiet boats. They are due to be replaced by 2,400-tonne displacement Vickers-built SSKs, known at present as the Type 2400. They will be capable of over 20 knots submerged, 12 knots on the surface, and have a complement of 46 (seven officers and 37 ratings). The future of the RN very much depends on the submarine, which is regarded as the best anti-submarine weapon available to the modern RN.

Trident Class Initial indications are that the new Class will displace 14,680 tons, have a diameter of 12.19 m and carry 16 Trident 2 missiles with 14 warheads each. It is anticipated that the first will be laid down at Barrow in 1986 and commissioned in 1993. There will be four boats in the Class.

Ballistic missile submarines (SSBNs)

Class *Resolution*

Name *Resolution*; **Pennant number** S22; **Surface displacement** 7,500 tons; **Full displacement** 8,400 tons (dived); **Length** 129.5 m overall; **Beam** 10.1 m; **Draught** 9.1 m; **Propulsion** Nuclear reactor; **Speed** 25 knots (dived); **Complement** 13 officers and 130 ratings (two crews); **Armament** 16 × Polaris SLBM; 6 × bow torpedo tubes (53 cm); **Builders** Vickers (Barrow); **Laid Down** February 26 1964; **Launched** September 15 1966; **Completed** 1967; **Commissioned** October 2 1967.

The first of the Royal Navy's nuclear-powered Polaris submarines to enter service was *Resolution*, built by Vickers at Barrow-in-Furness. She was laid down in 1964 and launched in September 1966 by HM The Queen Mother. Sea trials started in June 1967 and the boat was commissioned later that year. Early in 1968, *Resolution* sailed for American waters, making her first successful firing of the Polaris guided missile on February 15 1968 and beginning operational life four months later.

The *Resolution*, like American Polaris boats, has two crews, port and starboard, each of about 140 officers and ratings. By this means, the maximum operational time at sea is obtained with each crew taking the submarine to sea for a patrol lasting about three months. The patrol area is known only to key personnel aboard. When not aboard, the spare crew takes leave and works in the submarine base at *Neptune*.

The *R* Class are designed to carry and maintain in a state of readiness to fire, 16 Type A3 Polaris missiles in addition to conventional Mk 24 Tigerfish torpedoes. Sonars include the Type 2001 and 2007 sets. The missiles are fired beneath the water and the guidance requirements for each missile are calculated by two high speed computers. To ensure that these requirements are correct, the computers check calculations to see where the missile would fall if launched and, if all is correct, fire the missile on the Captain's command. All this is within 30 milliseconds.

Considerable effort has been made to make the long periods on patrol as comfortable as possible with messes designed to make living spacious and

there is a cinema with a plentiful supply of films, an excellent library and many opportunities to study.

Name *Repulse*; **Pennant number** S23; **Builders** Vickers (Barrow); **Laid down** March 12 1965; **Launched** November 4 1967; **Completed** 1968; **Commissioned** September 28 1968.

Repulse has been operating deterrent patrols since 1968, but has also taken part in submarine rescue trials off Scotland using commercial equipment made in the United States.

Name *Renown*; **Pennant number** S26; **Builders** Cammell Laird; **Laid down** June 25 1964; **Launched** February 25 1967; **Completed** 1968; **Commissioned** November 15 1968.

In early 1982, *Renown* became the first SSBM to become operational with the Polaris update system known as Chevaline. Tests were carried out off the coast of the Eastern USA in January 1982.

Name *Revenge*; **Pennant number** S27; **Builders** Cammell Laird; **Laid down** May 19 1965; **Launched** March 15 1968; **Completed** 1969; **Commissioned** December 4 1969.

Revenge fired her first test missile down the Eastern Atlantic test range, off the Florida coast, in June 1970 and began her first operational patrol in September 1970.

Resolution at sea, *showing her sleek lines* (RN).

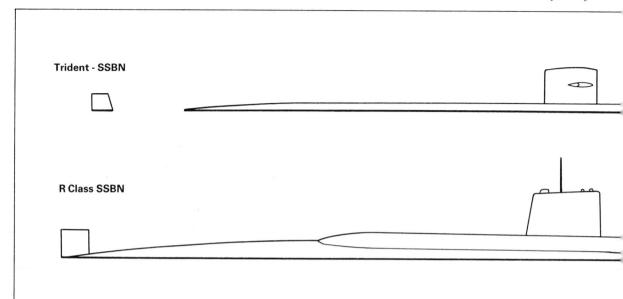

Trident - SSBN

R Class SSBN

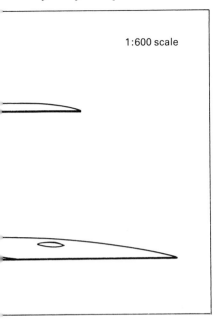

1:600 scale

Fleet submarines (SSNs)

Class *Trafalgar*

Name *Trafalgar*; **Pennant number** S107; **Full displacement** 4,500 tons dived; **Length** est 83 m; **Beam** 10 m; **Draught** est 8.5 m; **Propulsion** Nuclear reactor; **Speed** 30 knots+; **Armament** 5 × bow 53 cm torpedo tubes; Sub-Harpoon; **Builders** Vickers; **Laid down** 1978; **Launched** July 1 1981; **Completed** 1982/3; **Commissioned** 1983/4.

At the time of writing, at least four others of the Class are to be built, including *Turbulent* (laid down in 1979), *Tireless* (1981) and another, as yet unnamed by the Ministry of Defence. The Class is faster and quieter than the *Swiftsure* Class from which it is developed in general terms.

Above Renown *enters the Clyde Submarine base in January 1981* (RN). **Far left** Trafalgar, *first of a new class of SSNs, launched in 1981* (Vickers). **Left** Swiftsure, *nameship of the Class, with RMAS craft in background* (RN).

Class *Swiftsure*

Name *Swiftsure;* **Pennant number** S126; **Full displacement** 4,200 tons (4,500 tons dived); **Length** 82.9 m; **Beam** 9.8 m; **Draught** 8.2 m; **Propulsion** Nuclear reactor; **Speed** 30 knots (dived); **Complement** 12 officers and 85 ratings; **Armament** 5 × 53 cm torpedo tubes (bow); Sub-Harpoon; **Sensors** 183; 197; 1003; 2001; 2007; 1006. **Builders** Vickers (Barrow); **Laid down** April 15 1969; **Launched** September 7 1971; **Completed** 1972; **Commissioned** April 17 1973.

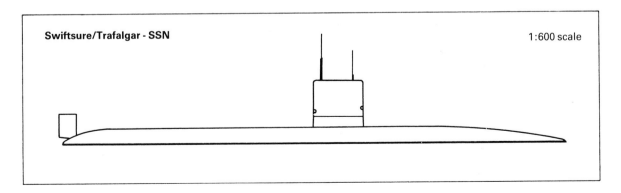

Swiftsure/Trafalgar - SSN   1:600 scale

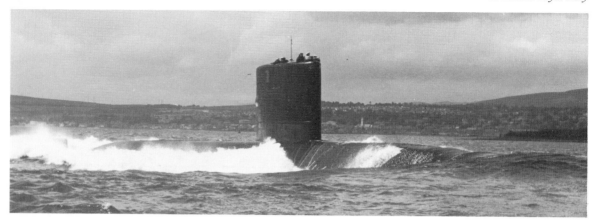

The first of the *Swiftsure* Class to be commissioned, the name-ship is designed to carry out long submerged patrols entirely independent of shore support. She is slightly larger than the previous Fleet-type 'nukes' and refuelling of her nuclear reactors is necessary only at long intervals; in fact *Swiftsure* underwent a long refit at Devonport in 1979–82, which included such work. Interior design is for comfort and safety during these long patrols. She has the latest air conditioning and purification equipment and an improved distilling plant for showers and a fully-fitted laundry. Senior and Junior rates have their own messes on either side of the modern galley.

The Class' main wartime role is to seek and destroy enemy submarines and surface ships. Ocean-wide covert surveillance can also be carried out. Armament is currently the Tigerfish torpedo and soon the Sub-Harpoon submarine-launched missile for engaging enemy vessels at long range.

Name *Sovereign*; **Builders** Vickers; **Laid down** September 17 1970; **Launched** February 17 1973; **Completed** 1974; **Commissioned** July 11 1974.

Launched by the wife of the former First Sea Lord, Lady Ashmore, *Sovereign* gained fame for being one of only a few submarines to have surfaced at the North Pole after operating for at least ten days under the ice cap in the Arctic Ocean.

Name *Superb*; **Builders** Vickers; **Laid down** March 16 1972; **Launched** November 30 1974; **Completed** 1976; **Commissioned** November 13 1976.

Known as 'Super B' to the Fleet, the submarine *Superb* is the ninth ship to bear the name in the RN. She was one of the four SSNs to be engaged in patrolling in the Exclusion Zone around the Falklands in April-July 1982.

Name *Sceptre*; **Builders** Vickers; **Laid down** October 25 1973; **Launched** November 20 1976; **Completed** 1977; **Commissioned** February 14 1978.

Name *Spartan*; **Builders** Vickers; **Laid down** April 24 1976; **Launched** December 7 1978; **Completed** 1979; **Commissioned** September 22 1979.

Name *Splendid*; **Complement** 12 officers, and 98 ratings; **Builders** Vickers; **Laid down** November 23 1977; **Launched** October 5 1979; **Completed** December 1980; **Commissioned** March 21 1981.

Class *Valiant*
Name *Valiant*; **Pennant number** S102; **Standard displacement** 3,500 tons; **Full displacement** 4,500 tons (dived); **Length** 86.9 m; **Beam** 10.1 m; **Draught** 8.2 m; **Propulsion** Nuclear reactor; **Speed** 28 knots (dived); **Complement** 14 officers and 96 ratings; **Armament** 6 × 53 cm torpedo

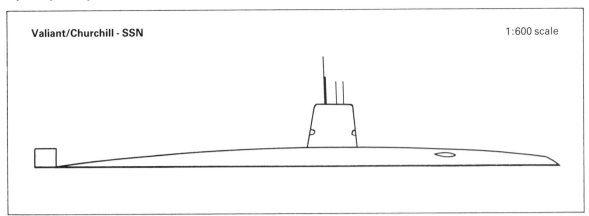

Valiant/Churchill - SSN   1:600 scale

tubes (bow); **Sensors** 183, 197, 1003, 2001, 2007, 1006; **Builders** Vickers (Barrow); **Laid down** January 22 1962; **Launched** December 3 1963; **Completed** 1966; **Commissioned** July 18 1966.

Valiant was the first of the all-British nuclear-powered Fleet-type submarines which followed the successful trials of the first British (but American-powered) nuclear submarine, *Dreadnought* which was only withdrawn from service in 1982. The ship is powered by a small pressurised water-cooled nuclear reactor which provides heat to produce steam to drive English Electric turbine machinery. Fresh water is distilled from seawater and a small amount of fresh water is electrolysed to produce oxygen and hydrogen, the former replenishing the boat's 'air'. The steam turbines also provide massive amounts of electrical power to drive the sensors, computers and navigational equipment. Using the different types of sonar, the submarine is able to identify possible targets and other ships by

identifying the noise signatures made, a process called classification. This can be done at a range outside any surface warship's own sonar range.

Submarine targets can be engaged by the Tigerfish wire-guided homing torpedo which has now been given an anti-ship capability as well. Most surface targets would, however, be engaged by salvo-type torpedoes of the unguided variety, such as Mk 8. The new Marconi Heavyweight torpedo which is due to enter service in 1985 will probably equip this boat.

In addition, the Fleet submarines of the *Valiant* and *Churchill* Classes are expected to be armed with Sub-Harpoon, an underwater launched, air-flight guided missile to attack surface ships. Development of the system has been completed but the first units to be fitted will be the *Swiftsure* Class.

Name *Warspite*; **Pennant number** S103; **Builder** Vickers (Barrow); **Complement** 14 officers and 92

Above left Sceptre *begins a patrol in May 1979* (HMS Neptune).

Left Valiant *in an Atlantic swell* (MoD).

Right Warspite *in January 1981* (HMS Neptune).

80

ratings; **Laid down** December 10 1963; **Launched** September 25 1965; **Completed** 1967; **Commissioned** April 18 1967.

The third British SSN, *Warspite* has been deployed to the Far East (November 1967—March 1968), to the Mediterranean (1969–70) and again East of Suez (1974–75). Like her sister ship *Valiant*, the boat is due to be paid off in the late 1980s, but in the meantime both submarines operate in support of the Fleet's requirements for exercises, training and deterrence.

Class *Churchill*
Name *Churchill;* **Pennant number** S46; **Standard displacement** 3,500 tons; **Full displacement** 4,500 tons (dived); **Length** 86.9 m; **Beam** 10.1 m; **Draught** 8.2 m; **Propulsion** Nuclear reactor; **Speed** 28 knots (dived); **Complement** 13 officers and 90 ratings; **Armament** 6 × 53 cm torpedo tubes; Sub-Harpoon; **Sensors** 183; 197; 1003; 1006; 2001; 2007; **Builders** Vickers (Barrow); **Laid down** June 30 1967; **Launched** December 20 1968; **Completed** 1970; **Commissioned** July 15 1970.

The *Churchill* Class represents some improvements in equipment and performance over the earlier *Valiant* boats. In 1979–81, trials were carried out with the new Sub-Harpoon system and *Churchill* acted as trials boat off the American East Coast for part of the work.

Name *Courageous*; **Pennant number** S50; **Complement** 13 officers and 96 ratings; **Builders** Vickers; **Laid down** May 15 1968; **Launched** March 7 1970; **Completed** 1971; **Commissioned** October 16 1971.

Name *Conqueror*; **Pennant number** S48; **Complement** 13 officers and 100 ratings; **Builders** Cammell Laird; **Laid down** December 5 1967; **Launched** August 18 1969; **Completed** 1971; **Commissioned** November 9 1971.

Churchill *in Scottish waters, November 1980* (HMS Neptune).

Conqueror underwent a major refit at Chatham, 1975–77 and a year later was used for the Mk 24 Tigerfish trials in the Bahamas. She is the vessel which torpedoed the Argentine cruiser *Belgrano* during the Falklands operation, as well as carrying out SBS/SAS operations.

Patrol submarines (SSKs)

Class *Oberon*
Name *Oberon;* **Pennant number** S09; **Standard displacement** 1,610 tons; **Full displacement** 2,030 tons/2,410 tons (dived); **Length** 90.0 m; **Beam** 8.1 m; **Draught** 5.5 m; **Propulsion** Diesel-electric; **Range** 5,000 nm; **Speed** 12 knots (surfaced); 17 knots (dived); **Complement** 6 officers and 62 ratings; **Armament** 6 × 53 cm torpedo tubes (bow); 2 × 53 cm torpedo tubes (stern); **Sensors** 187; 1002, 2007; **Builders** HM Dockyard, Chatham; **Laid down** November 28 1957;

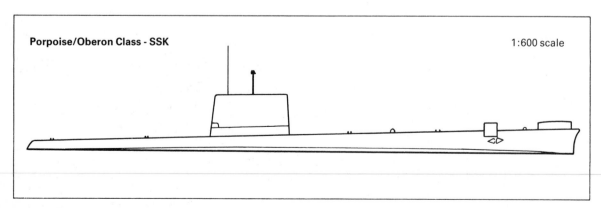

Porpoise/Oberon Class - SSK

1:600 scale

Above Courageous (HMS Neptune). **Below** Oberon (HMS Excellent).

Launched July 18 1959; **Completed** 1961; **Commissioned** February 24 1961.

Patrol submarines of the *Oberon* Class rely on batteries to drive main motors which give the boats an underwater speed of 17 knots. Two diesels (V16 generators) recharge the batteries periodically and to reduce the possibility of detection the air for the diesels can be drawn down through a snort (or snorkel) system while the submarine remains submerged. By this means, the submarine can remain dived for periods of more than six weeks.

The Class is regarded as the best of its type in the world and in spite of modern developments and underwater detection equipment, the sea itself affords the submarine excellent cover from which to strike. Patrol boats operate in coastal, continental shelf and inshore waters, on covert operations with swimmer-canoeists, laying mines, gathering intelligence or as hunter-killers. Today, their role within the RN includes a large element of training for the RN, RAF and allied Services.

Name *Orpheus*; **Pennant number** S11 **Builders** Vickers (Barrow); **Laid down** April 16 1959; **Launched** November 17 1959; **Completed** 1960; **Commissioned** November 25 1960.

Name *Odin*; **Pennant number** S10; **Builders** Cammell Laird; **Laid down** April 27 1959; **Launched** November 4 1960; **Completed** 1962; **Commissioned** May 3 1962.

Name *Olympus*; **Pennant number** S12; **Complement** 6 officers and 64 ratings; **Builders** Vickers; **Laid down** March 4 1960; **Launched** June 14 1961; **Completed** 1962; **Commissioned** July 7 1962.

Name *Onslaught*; **Pennant number** S14; **Builders** HM Dockyard, Chatham; **Laid down** April 8 1959; **Launched** September 24 1960; **Completed** 1962; **Commissioned** August 14 1962.

Name *Otter*; **Pennant number** S15; **Complement** 7 officers and 62 ratings; **Builders** Scotts; **Laid down** January 14 1960; **Launched** May 15 1961; **Completed** 1962; **Commissioned** August 20 1962.

Otter, formerly with SM 3 at Faslane, has been recently attached to SM 1 at Gosport for training duties. She has had her ballast tanks, twin shafts and main vents strengthened to enable unarmed underwater weapons to be used against her.

Name *Oracle*; **Pennant number** S16; **Complement** 7 officers and 58 ratings; **Builders** Cammell Laird; **Laid down** April 26 1960; **Launched** September 26 1961; **Completed** 1963; **Commissioned** February 14 1963.

Name *Otus*; **Pennant number** S18; **Complement** 7 officers and 61 ratings; **Builders** Scotts; **Laid down** May 31 1961; **Launched** October 17 1962; **Completed** 1963; **Commissioned** October 5 1963.

Name *Osiris*; **Pennant number** S13 **Complement** 6 officers and 64 ratings; **Builders** Vickers; **Laid down** January 26 1963; **Launched** November 29 1962; **Completed** 1963; **Commissioned** January 11 1964.

Name *Ocelot*; **Pennant number** S17; **Complement** 7 officers and 62 ratings; **Builders** HM Dockyard, Chatham; **Laid down** November 17 1960; **Launched** May 5 1962; **Completed** January 1964; **Commissioned** January 31 1964.

Name *Opossum*; **Pennant number** S19; **Builders** Cammell Laird; **Laid down** December 21 1961; **Launched** May 23 1963; **Completed** 1964; **Commissioned** June 5 1964.

Opossum has the distinction of being the last conventional submarine to be refitted at Chatham; such work now being carried out at Devonport.

Name *Opportune*; **Pennant number** S20; **Builders** Scotts; **Laid down** October 26 1962; **Launched** February 14 1964; **Completed** 1964; **Commissioned** December 29 1964.

Top left Olympus *heads out into the Atlantic* (RN). **Centre left** Otter *passes Flag Officer Portsmouth's semaphore tower* (RN). **Left** Onslaught *in the Channel, November 1980* (HMS Dolphin).

Name *Onyx*; **Pennant number** S21; **Builders** Cammell Laird; **Laid down** November 16 1964; **Launched** August 18 1966; **Completed** 1967; **Commissioned** November 20 1967.

Class *Porpoise*
Name *Porpoise*; **Pennant number** S01; **Standard displacement** 1,610 tons; **Full displacement** 2,030 tons/2410 tons (dived); **Length** 90.0 m overall; **Beam** 8.1 m; **Draught** 5.5 m; **Propulsion** Diesel-electric; **Range** 5,000 nm; **Speed** 17 knots (dived); **Complement** 6 officers and 65 ratings; **Armament** 6 × 53 cm torpedo tubes (bow); 2 × 53 cm torpedo tubes (stern); **Sensors** 187; 1002; 2007; **Builders** Vickers (Barrow); **Laid down** June 15 1954; **Launched** April 25 1956; **Completed** 1958; **Commissioned** April 17 1958.

The *Porpoise* Class patrol submarines of the RN are powered by diesel-electric motors of the Admiralty Standard Range 1, rated at 3,680 bhp with two electric motors of 6,000 shp driving two shafts. Their primary war role is the detection and destruction of enemy submarines and surface ships. In addition, they can be used for intelligence gathering, minelaying and landing agents and specialist troops, such as the Special Boat Squadron of the RM.

Name *Sealion*; **Pennant number** S07; **Complement** 6 officers and 66 ratings; **Builders** Cammell Laird; **Laid down** June 5 1958; **Launched** December 31 1959; **Completed** 1961; **Commissioned** July 25 1961.

Name *Walrus*; **Pennant number** S08; **Complement** 6 officers and 62 ratings; **Builders** Scotts; **Laid down** February 12 1958; **Launched** September 22 1959; **Completed** 1961; **Commissioned** February 10 1961.

Assault ships
Class *Fearless*
Name *Fearless*; **Pennant number** L10; **Flight deck code** FS; **Standard displacement** 11,060 tons; **Full displacement** 12,120 tons (16,950 tons when ballasted down for landings); **Length** 158.5 m overall; **Beam** 24.4 m; **Draught** 7.0 m forward/9.8 m aft; **Propulsion** 2 × steam turbines; **Range** 5,000 nm at 20 knots; **Speed** 21 knots;

Top right *Sealion, last of the existing P-boats to be commissioned* (RN). **Centre right** *Ocelot manoeuvres alongside the wall at* Dolphin (RN). **Right** *Porpoise at* Faslane (RN).

Fearless Class

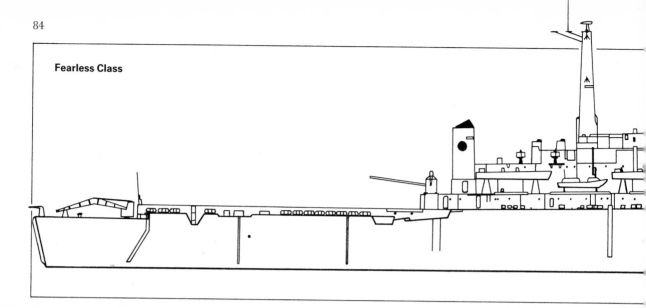

Complement 37 officers and 500 ratings, plus 80 RM for manning Landing Craft and the Amphibious Beach Unit. When acting as Dartmouth Training Ship, 150 Midshipmen and Cadets are carried; **Armament** 2 × 40 mm Bofors Mk 9 GP; 4 × Seacat SAM launchers; **Sensors** 978, 994, HF/DF, MF/DF, SCOT, IFF; **Aircraft** Up to 5 × Wessex HU 5 or 4 × Sea King HC 4 and/or up to 5 × Gazelle AH 1; **Small craft** 4 × LCVP (davits), 4 × LCU (docked); 2 × ship's boats; **Vehicles** 15 × tanks; 1 × BARV; 7 × 3t trucks,

20 × ½-ton trucks or similar combination; **Builders** Harland and Wolff; **Laid down** July 25 1962; **Launched** December 19 1963; **Completed** 1965; **Commissioned** November 25 1965.

The 1981 Defence Review forecast the ship's demise in 1984, but a Government statement in March 1982 confirmed that the ship will remain in service for the forseeable future in support of the RN's Northern Flank Commitment. Alternative periods under refit will be spent with sister-ship *Intrepid* taking over the role.

Fearless *moored on the Thames during a Harrier demonstration* (CINCFLEET/Russ Whalley).

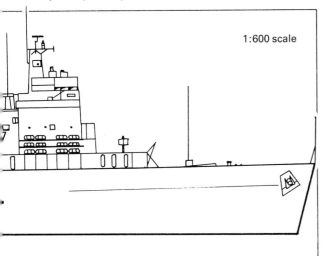

Intrepid enters Portsmouth in November 1981 (RN).

With her sister ship *Intrepid*, *Fearless* was designed to operate Commando forces or regular land forces in areas in which Britain has Defence Agreements or to reinforce NATO. Today, the latter is their sole role as Britain has withdrawn such forces from east of Suez. The ships were based on similar US Navy designs to provide amphibious capability and operational facilities, which include a docking area, flight deck for heli-borne assault and a fully equipped operations room for control of the operation. These are amongst the most versatile warships yet designed for amphibious warfare and are fitted with three vehicle spaces and accommodation for up to 700 RMs.

The docking area is flooded down by taking over 3,000 tons of ballast in to lower the stern area and thus allow the LCUs and LCVPs to move in and out of the dock. In addition, 'swimming' vehicles can use the dock to leave their spaces on board. Each ship has its own Beach Armoured Recovery Vehicle (BARV) for attending to stranded vehicles on the beach and its immediate environs.

The Amphibious Detachment is made up of an Assault Squadron (4 Assault Squadron normally resides in *Fearless* and 6 AS in *Intrepid*) which consists of RM and RN personnel under a Captain, RM. The squadron can be broken down again into the Landing Craft (LC) Squadron, Amphibious Beach Unit (ABU) and Vehicle Decks Party (VDP). The ABU usually has its own Land Rover and operates ashore whilst the VDP marshalls vehicles for embarkation into LCs.

The flight deck is capable of operating most types of helicopter and even Sea Harriers in an emergency; it measures 50.29 m × 22.86 m. There is a radar-

controlled approach facility for bad weather operations and the provision for fuel bowsers to be carried on jettisonable cradles. It is possible via vehicle ramps to stow smaller RM types in the vehicle spaces when they are not operating.

In the late 1970s and early 1980s, the *Fearless* and *Intrepid* were used as Dartmouth Training Ships to give RN Cadets and Midshipmen their first naval sea experience after initial training at BRNC. Up to 150 were embarked for nine-week courses and the LPDs provide an ideal base to teach all aspects of naval operations and life.

Both *Fearless* and *Intrepid* formed part of the Falklands Task Force in 1982.

Name *Intrepid*; **Pennant number** L11; **Flight deck code** IS; **Builders** John Brown; **Laid down** December 19 1962; **Launched** June 25 1964; **Completed** 1964; **Commissioned** March 11 1967.

Intrepid undertook the first seaborne trials of the SCOT system in 1969, but is currently under refit after service in the South Atlantic; her demise had been forecast by late 1982 following the end of a commission in 1981, but she will continue in service until circa 1985.

Guided missile destroyers (DLGs)

Class *Bristol* (Type 82)
Name *Bristol*; **Pennant number** D23; **Flight deck code** BS; **Standard displacement** 6,100 tons; **Full displacement** 7,100 tons; **Length** 154.5 m overall; **Beam** 16.8 m; **Draught** 5.2 m; **Propulsion**

COSAG; **Range** 5,000 nm at 18 knots; **Speed** 30 knots; **Complement** 29 officers and 378 ratings; **Armament** 1 × 114 mm Mk 8; 2 × 20 mm Oerlikon GP; 1 × Twin Sea Dart GWS 30; 1 × Ikara ASGWS; 1 × Limbo Mk 10; **Sensors** 965 (AKE-2); 909; 1006; 992Q; GWS 22; EW; HF/DF; MF/DF; SCOT; IFF; 184; 185; 189; **Aircraft** Landing platform only (Wasp capable); **Small craft** 4 × ship's launches; 2 × Gemini; **Builders** Swan Hunter; **Laid down** November 15 1967; **Launched** June 30 1969; **Completed** December 1972; **Commissioned** March 31 1973.

Bristol was the only Type 82 DLG (rated a destroyer yet the size of a light cruiser) to be built following the Defence Cuts of 1966 and the cancellation of the *CVA-01* aircraft carrier programme. The type was designed to escort these carriers worldwide. The ships were expensive to build (£27 million) and are still not very cost-effective in manpower terms. It is interesting to note that she is only helicopter capable and does not have hangar facilities but room only for a Wasp HAS 1 or similar small helicopter.

The ship was launched at Wallsend-on-Tyne by Lady Hogg. She is powered by the COSAG (combined steam and gas turbine) arrangement of two standard Range geared steam turbines (30,000 shp) and two RR/BS Olympus marine gas turbines (30,000 shp) linked into two shafts.

The ship's role today, following a period proving the Sea Dart GWS, is that of flagship for a force commander, such as FOF3, and the area defence of a Task Group. Her communications equipment is very comprehensive for such a relatively small warship. The ship's inertial navigation system

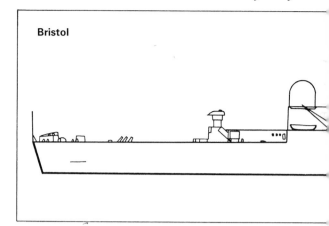

Bristol

(SINS) computes geographical position and the SCOT system allows worldwide communications at all times. In addition, she has good firepower, good seakeeping qualities and considerable range, which make her a worthwhile member of the Fleet in the Third Flotilla. She was also in the Falklands Task Force.

Class *Sheffield* (Type 42; Batch 1)
Name *Sheffield*; **Pennant number** D80; **Flight deck code** SD; **Standard displacement** 3,150 tons; **Full displacement** 4,100 tons; **Length** 125.0 m; **Beam** 14.3 m; **Draught** 6.7 m; **Propulsion** COGOG (gas turbine); **Range** 4,500 nm at 18 knots; **Speed** 30 knots; **Complement** 26 officers and 273 ratings; **Armament**: 1 × 114 mm Mk 8; 2 × 20 mm Oerlikon GP; 1 × Twin Sea Dart GWS 30; Corvus; **Sensors** 965 (AKE-2); 1006; 992 Q; 909; SCOT; HF/DF; MF/DF; IFF; EW; **Aircraft** 1 × Lynx

Bristol leaving Portsmouth for the South Atlantic with pennant number painted out.

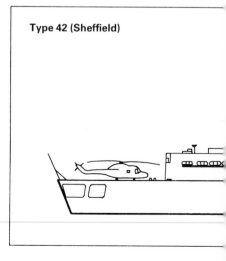

Type 42 (Sheffield)

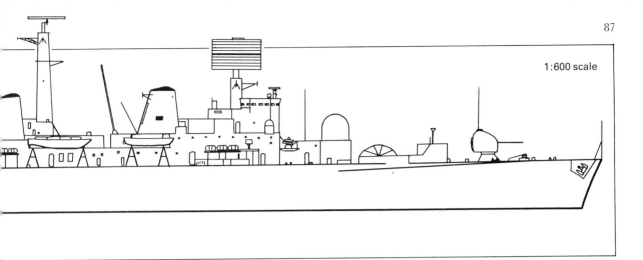

1:600 scale

HAS 2; **Small craft** 2 × ship's boats; 1 × Gemini; **Builders** Vickers (Barrow); **Laid down** January 15 1970; **Launched** June 10 1971; **Completed** 1974; **Commissioned** February 16 1975; **Lost** South Atlantic May 10 1982.

These are the first RN destroyers built to Staff Requirements with gas turbines as the main means of propulsion using the now standard Rolls-Royce Tynes (8,000 shp) for cruising and the Marine Olympus (50,000 shp) for maximum speed: these are 18 knots and 32 knots respectively. The COGOG arrangement is linked through David Brown reversible gear boxes to two shafts with controllable-pitch propellors. Using centralised and sophisticated engine room controls, the type needs only 75 per cent of the personnel in the engineering department that are necessary in conventional ships of this tonnage.

Perhaps the greatest disadvantage of the Type 42s

is their lack of adequate length to house two Westland Lynx HAS 2 helicopters. To a certain extent Batch 3 Type 42s will redress some of the balance with about 16 m being added in the 'middle' but it is not clear yet whether two helicopters will be embarked in these vessels.

Known to the Fleet as the 'Shiny Sheff', the first of the Type 42s was launched by HM The Queen and represented the Third Frigate Squadron at the Silver Jubilee Fleet Review; in the 1981 reorganisation this squadron was renamed the Third Destroyer Squadron (D3). The ship maintained close links with the City of Sheffield. *Sheffield* had two side vents on her funnel and thus could be told apart from other '42s. The destroyer was part of the Gulf Patrol, 1981–2, and, of course, the Falklands Task Force. She was hit by an Argentine Exocet missile on May 4 and sank on May 10 after strenuous efforts to keep her afloat failed.

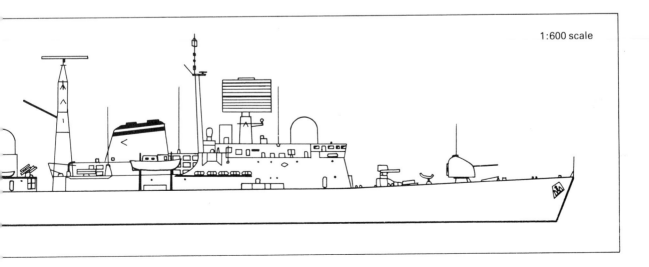

1:600 scale

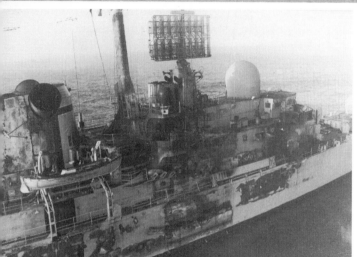

Name *Birmingham*; **Pennant number** D86; **Flight deck code** BM; **Complement** 20 officers and 280 ratings; **Armament** 4 × 20 mm Oerlikon GP; all Type 42s except *Sheffield* have 2 × 3 Mk 32 STWS in addition; **Builders** Cammell Laird; **Laid down** March 28 1972; **Launched** July 30 1973; **Completed** 1976; **Commissioned** December 3 1976.

Officially designated 'Admiralty Board Yacht' for the 1977 Silver Jubilee Review, *Birmingham* followed HMY *Britannia* during the actual review. At the time, the ship was half-leader of 5th Frigate Squadron, but today she is the half-leader of 3rd Destroyer Squadron. The second Type 42, *Birmingham* was launched by Lady Empson (wife of Admiral Sir Derek Empson) and is the third ship in the Fleet to bear the name. She has taken part in a number of major deployments, including the Gulf Patrol.

Name *Glasgow*; **Pennant number** D88; **Flight deck code** GW; **Complement** 21 officers and 249 ratings; **Builders** Swan Hunter; **Laid down** March 7 1974; **Launched** April 14 1976; **Completed** March 9 1977; **Commissioned** May 24 1977.

When commissioned *Glasgow* had cost £23 million, including the repair of serious damage caused by a fire during fitting out at Swan Hunter's yard. She served at first with F7 as half leader but is now with D3; a Portsmouth-based ship. In 1980, the ship greatly assisted the Caribbean island of St Lucia following a major hurricane disaster, and in 1982 she formed part of the Falklands Task Force, where she was damaged when a bomb passed right through her hull without exploding!

Name *Newcastle*; **Pennant number** D87; **Flight deck code** NC; **Complement** 21 officers and 278 ratings; **Armament** 2 × Vulcan CIWS; **Small**

craft None; **Builders** Swan Hunter; **Laid down** February 21 1973; **Launched** April 24 1975; **Completed** February 1978; **Commissioned** March 23 1978.

Currently the leader of D3, *Newcastle* was originally half leader of F6. Adopted by her namesake city (and with a Lynx helicopter called 'Wee Geordie'), *Newcastle* has been much travelled since she was commissioned in 1978; Brazil, St Helena, Gibraltar and Sierra Leone to name but a few countries. During an RAS operation, the ship flies a 'Newcastle Brown Ale' flag.

Name *Cardiff*; **Pennant number** D108; **Flight deck code** CF; **Complement** 20 officers and 260 ratings; **Builders** Vickers (Barrow); **Laid down** November 3 1972; **Launched** February 22 1974; **Completed** 1979; **Commissioned** September 24 1979.

Commissioned a half leader but now with D3 at Portsmouth, *Cardiff* is the sixth of the Type 42s in RN service. In 1979, the ship was in the headlines following a major sea search operation off the Isle of Wight for survivors from the MV *Pool Fisher*.

Name *Coventry*; **Pennant number** D118; **Flight deck code** CV; **Complement** 20 officers and 248 ratings; **Builders** Cammell Laird; **Laid down** March 22 1973; **Launched** June 21 1974; **Completed** 1978; **Commissioned** October 20 1978; **Lost** South Atlantic May 25 1982.

In 1979, *Coventry* carried out first of Class trials with the Lynx helicopter involving over 400 deck landings. The ship was launched by Lady Lewin, wife of the then CINCFLEET, and in 1980 was one of the RN Group Deployment to the Far East, including the famous trip to China. *Coventry*, like her Batch 1 sister-ships, also served with D3 before

being sunk during the major Argentine air attack on May 25 1982.

Class *Sheffield* (Type 42; Batch 2)
Name *Exeter*; **Pennant number** D89; **Flight deck code** EX; **Builders** Swan Hunter; **Laid down** July 22 1976; **Launched** April 25 1978; **Completed**

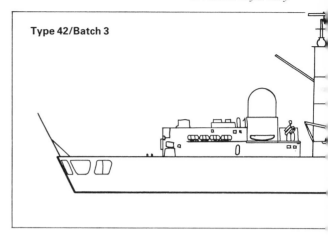

Type 42/Batch 3

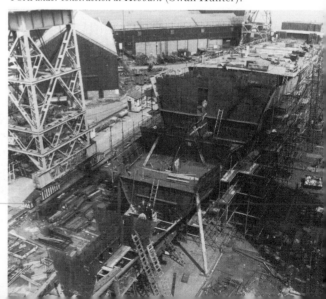

Exeter *in toned-down paint scheme in the Falkland Islands* (RN/HMS Exeter).

August 29 1980; **Commissioned** September 19 1980.

Although keeping the same hull shape and internal arrangements for air conditioning, accommodation, weaponry and propulsion, the Batch 2 Type 42s have a new and improved sensor system over the earlier ships of the *Sheffield* Class. The new Type 1022 long-range air search radar above the forward superstructure sets the four ships of the Batch—*Exeter*, *Southampton*, *Nottingham* and *Liverpool*—apart from the 965-equipped forerunners. The initial ships cost £60 million raising to an estimated £90 million for the latter one.

Exeter completed her Operational Readiness Inspection (ORI) for sea duties in early 1982 and joined the Fleet in the command of Captain 5th Destroyer Squadron (D5). Her Lynx helicopter flight commissioned in July 1981. All Batch 2 and 3 Type 42s will join D5 based at Portsmouth.

She, too, formed part of the Falklands Task Force, following Belize guardship duties.

Name *Southampton*; **Pennant number** D90; **Flight deck code** SD; **Armament** 4 × 20 mm Oerlikon GP; **Builders** Vosper Thornycroft; **Laid down** October 21 1976; **Launched** January 29 1979; **Completed** August 17 1981; **Commissioned** October 31 1981.

Southampton was launched from the Woolston yard of Vosper Thornycroft near midnight on January 29 1979 because the original launching would have been disrupted by industrial action. The ship was named by Lady Cameron (wife of the former Chief of Defence Staff (CDS)). She is the eighth Type 42 to enter service and the sixth ship to bear the name in the RN.

The following ships were due to Commission in late 1982:

Name *Nottingham*; **Pennant number** D91: **Flight deck code** NM; **Builders** Vosper Thornycroft **Laid down** February 6 1978; **Launched** February 18 1980; **Completed** 1981; **Commissioned** 1982.

Name *Liverpool*; **Pennant number** D92; **Flight deck code** LP; **Builders** Cammell Laird; **Laid down** July 5 1978; **Launched** September 25 1980; **Completed** 1982; **Commissioned** 1982.

The Falklands Crisis caused the delivery of this ship to be speeded up and, following sea trials in November 1981, January and April 1982, she was accepted at Devonport (her base port) about a year ahead of schedule.

Class *Sheffield* (Type 42; Batch 3)
Following the initial sea trials and the first months of

York *under construction at Hebburn* (Swan Hunter).

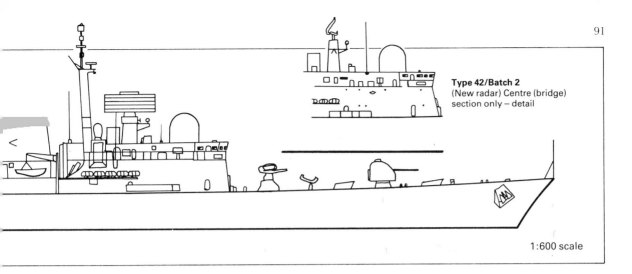

Type 42/Batch 2
(New radar) Centre (bridge)
section only – detail

1:600 scale

operation, the Batch 1 Type 42s, although adequate, were found to be lacking in length and beam. It is therefore not surprising that the RN sought an improved batch for service in the 1990s. The result is four units of 3,500 tons standard displacement/4,500 tons full displacement with a waterline length of 132.3 m (as compared with 119.5 m in earlier units), an overall length of 141.0 m (125.0 m) and a beam of 14.9 m (14.3 m), but the draught should remain the same at 5.8 m. The ships ordered are:

Name *Manchester*; **Pennant number** D95; **Builders** Vickers (Barrow); **Launched** November 24 1980.

Name *Gloucester*; **Pennant number** D96; **Builders** Vosper Thornycroft; **Launched** 1982.

Name *Edinburgh*; **Pennant number** D97; **Builders** Cammell Laird; **Launched** 1982.

Name *York*; **Pennant number** D98; **Builders** Swan Hunter; **Launched** June 21 1982.

It is possible that the ships will have two Lynx HAS 2 helicopters as complement but that only one will be carried in peacetime; additionally they may be fitted with Seawolf PDMS, although the cost will be high and in view of the 1981 Defence Review decision not to modernise the Class at half-life, Seawolf remains a remote possibility only. Many observers believe that the Class should have been constructed in the 'stretched' and 'broad-beam' form from the beginning. *Edinburgh* and *York* may have Type 996 radar fitted.

Class *County*
Name *Antrim*; **Pennant number** D18; **Flight deck code** An; **Standard displacement** 5,440 tons; **Full**

Antrim *at sea during pre-Deployment work-up.*

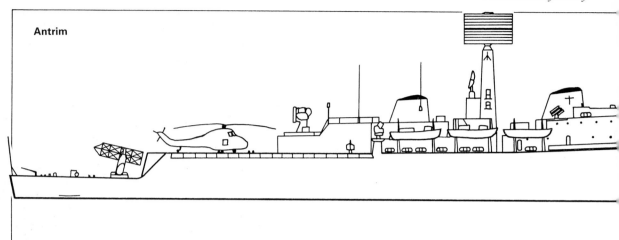

Antrim

displacement 6,200 tons; **Length** 158.7 m overall; **Beam** 16.5 m; **Draught** 6.3 m; **Propulsion** COSAG; **Speed** 30 knots; **Complement** 33 officers and 438 ratings; **Armament** 1 × 2 114 mm Mk 6; 2 × 20 mm Oerlikon GP; 2 × Seacat SAM; 1 × Seaslug II; 4 × Exocet SSM; Corvus; **Sensors** 278; 965 (AKE-2); 975; 992; MRS-3; GWS 22; HF/DF; MF/DF; SCOT; IFF; EW; **Aircraft** 1 × Wessex HAS 3; **Small craft** 4 × ship's launches; 1 × whaler; 1 × Dory; **Builders** Fairfield; **Laid down** January 20 1966; **Launched** October 19 1967; **Completed** 1970; **Commissioned** July 14 1970.

The *County* Class were envisaged as far back as the mid-1950s and represent the first postwar design of destroyer/fleet escort. They eventually became light cruisers in all but name being 6,200 tons displacement at full load. In addition they were the first warships built in the United Kingdom to operate guided missiles and the largest then designed to be propelled by COSAG. They were built in two batches: Batch 1—*Devonshire, Hampshire, Kent* and *London,* 1961–3; and Batch 2—*Antrim, Glamorgan, Fife* and *Norfolk,* 1966–70. The two batches differ in their armament (the later batch have been refitted with Exocet), radar (the later

Fife moored against the Accommodation Ship Rame Head. *Although the missile tubes are not fitted, the Exocet mountings are in the place previously occupied by 'B' turret* (Robin A. Walker).

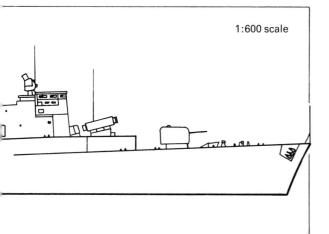

1:600 scale

Glamorgan *during anti-aircraft drill* (FPU).

batch have AKE-2 965) and mark of Seaslug SAM (the later batch have the improved Mk 2 from construction). Basically, the Mk 2 offers an anti-ship potential.

Since the mid-1970s, *Devonshire* (nearly sold to Egypt) and *Hampshire* have been withdrawn from service, *Kent* is now an accommodation ship at *Excellent* with a doubtful future and *London* completed her last commission, including the firing of the RN's last 'broadside' from four 114 mm Mk 6 mountings in the Atlantic training area, at the end of 1981. Both *Kent* and *London* had their mainmasts stepped aft during construction. Propulsion is via two Babcock & Wilcox boilers and two sets of geared turbines (30,000 shp) linked to two marine gas turbines per shaft (30,000 shp). The ships are steadily being replaced by Type 42 destroyers and by late 1984 only *Antrim* is destined to remain in service. *Norfolk*, was sold to Chile in 1981 and her sister-ship *London* to Pakistan in 1982.

Launched by Mrs Roy Mason (wife of the then Minister of Defence), *Antrim* was the last of the four DLGs to be converted to Exocet at Portsmouth. Used as a flagship on many occasions, including the Far East Deployments of 1976 and 1980, the ship was the first RN warship to visit the People's Republic of China for 30 years, when she arrived at Shanghai. On her return from the Far East, *Antrim* became the Flagship of STANAVFORLANT until replaced by *Norfolk* in 1981. She was in the Falklands Task Force.

Name *Fife*; **Pennant number** D20; **Flight deck code** FF; **Builders** Fairfields; **Laid down** June 1 1962; **Launched** July 9 1964; **Completed** 1966; **Commissioned** June 21 1966; **Exocet conversion** 1974–6; **Additional sensors** ADAWSI.

Fife was launched by the Duchess of that County in 1964 and is the first warship to be named after the ancient Scottish kingdom. Like other 'Counties', *Fife* has been a flagship on several occasions, including wearing the flag of FOF2. She was the first ship to be fitted with ADAWSI (automated weapons system) which is linked into the Seaslug II. The ship's future is unsure, even though she was refitted at Portsmouth 1979–81.

Name *Glamorgan*; **Pennant number** D19; **Flight deck code** GL; **Builders** Vickers (Tyne); **Laid down** September 13 1962; **Launched** July 9 1964; **Completed** 1966; **Commissioned** October 11 1966.

Glamorgan was launched by Lady Brecon as a guided missile destroyer, but several times in her career there have been plans to convert her: Dartmouth Training Ship and Fleet Minelayer, being two. She went into refit immediately after the 1977 Silver Jubilee Fleet Review and was fitted with the Mk 32 STWS and new communications equipment. In 1981/2 she was present with the Gulf Patrol before being sent to the South Atlantic as a unit in the Falklands Task Force, where she became the first warship to survive an attack and hit by an Exocet missile off Port Stanley. She is destined to be paid off in 1983.

Frigates
Class *Amazon* (Type 21)
Name *Amazon*; **Pennant number** F169; **Flight deck code** AZ; **Standard displacement** 2,750 tons; **Full displacement** 3,250 tons; **Length** 117.0 m

Type 21 (Amazon Class)

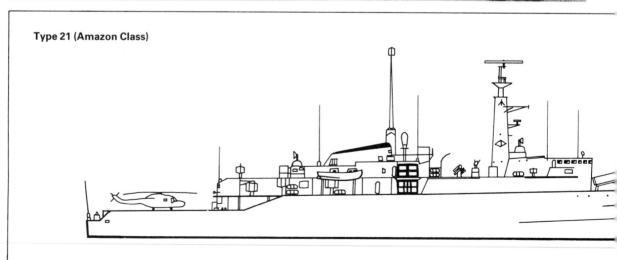

overall; **Beam** 12.7 m; **Draught** 6.8 m; **Propulsion** COGOG; **Range** 1,200 nm at 30 knots/4,500 nm at 18 knots; **Speed** 34 knots; **Complement** 11 officers and 159 ratings; **Armament** 1 × 114 mm Mk 8; 2 × 20 mm Oerlikon GP; 1 × Secat SAM; 4 × Exocet SSM; 2 × 3 STWS Mk 32; Corvus; **Sensors** 978; 992Q GWS 22; 184; IFF; EW; HF/DF; MF/DF; **Aircraft** 1 × Lynx HAS 2; **Small craft** 2 × ship's launches; 1 × Gemini; 1 × Dory; **Builders** Vosper Thornycroft; **Laid down** November 6 1969; **Launched** April 26 1971; **Completed** 1974; **Commissioned** May 11 1974.

Ships of this Class are probably the most exciting designs to come from British naval builders since the Second World War for not only are they the first frigates to be ordered from private designs since 1945, but they are also the first to be designed around all gas turbine propulsion. This is provided by a COGOG (Combined Gas and Gas) arrangement where the main engines are Rolls-Royce Marine Olympus TM3 turbines (56,000 bhp) and two Rolls-Royce Tyne gas turbines of 8,500 shp used for cruising at 18 knots. There are two shafts.

The initial design could be criticised for a lack of surface weaponry even with the automatic Vickers Mk 8 mounting, so in 1976 the MM38 Exocet SSM was chosen as the gap filler. The original concept of refitting the class of eight with Seawolf PDMS has now been abandoned leaving only the Seacat SAM (one quad launcher), the Mk 8 turret and two 20 mm Oerlikons for air defence. Not that powerful in today's anti-air environment.

The Staff Requirement was written in 1968 and the order with Vosper Thornycroft (for three warships) and Yarrow (for the remaining five) placed in the same year. The Royal Australian Navy did show an interest but this was later cancelled. The ships have even better seakeeping qualities than the redoubtable *Leanders* which they are replacing in the general purpose role. The Action Information Organisation (AIO), known as the Computer Assisted Action Information System (CAAIS), was specially developed by Ferranti for the Type 21s and like all similar systems in use with the RN provides the Command with all the data required to fight the ship. This is, of course, usually done from the Operations Room and overall the personnel required to handle the ship in action have been substantially reduced; approximately two-thirds of the complement needed for earlier ships of the type.

Originally only five of the Class were fitted with Exocet but the remaining three were re-fitted when commitments allowed. In addition, Mk 32 torpedo tubes (STWS) were fitted abeam of the hangar to all either from new or by retro-fitting. The re-equipment by Exocet meant that the earlier warships had their Corvus launchers repositioned after a few years in service.

All Type 21s are now collected in the Fourth Frigate Squadron, based at Devonport with *Avenger* (F185) as Squadron Leader, under the command of Captain F4.

Amazon was launched by HRH the Princess Anne and is nicknamed 'Silver Bird of the Ocean' because of her turn of speed; she is also capable of stopping dead in 55 seconds from 34 knots!

Left Amazon *uses the 'garage' at Plymouth;* Sirius *alongside* (RN). **Below right** *The Type 21 propulsion system compared to the DLG layout* (Rolls Royce).

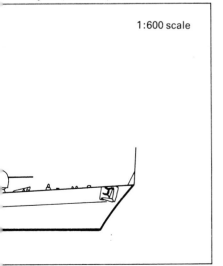

1:600 scale

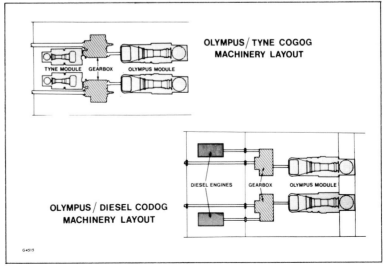

OLYMPUS/TYNE COGOG MACHINERY LAYOUT

TYNE MODULE   GEARBOX   OLYMPUS MODULE

OLYMPUS/DIESEL CODOG MACHINERY LAYOUT

DIESEL ENGINES   GEARBOX   OLYMPUS MODULE

Name *Antelope*; **Pennant number** F170; **Flight deck code** AO; **Complement** 13 officers and 164 ratings; **Builders** Vosper Thornycroft; **Laid down** March 23 1971; **Launched** March 16 1972; **Completed** June 30 1975; **Commissioned** July 19 1975; **Lost** South Atlantic May 1982.

Antelope was affiliated to the Royal Regiment of Fusiliers and was adopted by the city of Hereford in 1974. Originally serving with F7, the ship was with F4 at Plymouth before she sank in San Carlos Bay after a 500 lb bomb exploded in her engine room on May 24 1982 while being defuzed.

Name *Ambuscade*; **Pennant number** F172; **Flight deck code** AB; **Complement** 12 officers and 168 ratings; **Builders** Yarrow; **Laid down** September 1 1971; **Launched** January 18 1973; **Completed** 1975; **Commissioned** September 5 1975.

Ambuscade was the first of the Yarrow-built Type 21s to be commissioned and she serves with F4 at Plymouth, being affiliated to the Town of Crewe.

Name *Arrow*; **Pennant number** F173; **Flight deck code** AW; **Complement** 13 officers and 167 ratings; **Builders** Yarrow; **Laid down** September 28 1972; **Launched** February 5 1974; **Completed** 1976; **Commissioned** July 29 1976.

She was commissioned into F3 at Sunderland in 1976 and since has been active with STANAVFORLANT and on deployment, including the Gulf of Oman. In 1982 she formed part of the Falklands Task Force.

Name *Active*; **Pennant number** F171; **Flight deck code** AV; **Complement** 11 officers and 160 ratings; **Armament** As for *Amazon*, but no Mk 32 STWS fitted; **Builders** Vosper Thornycroft; **Laid down** July 23 1971; **Launched** November 23 1972; **Completed** 1977; **Commissioned** June 17 1977.

Although launched in 1972, *Active* was not completed until 1977, being alongside in Southampton docks for some months awaiting delivery of components, especially for the Exocet

Above left *HMS* Antelope *explodes in San Carlos Bay on May 24 1982* (Popperfoto). **Above** Ardent, *lost following an Argentine air strike, at sea with Lynx on flight deck in happier times.* **Left** Ambuscade *entering Portsmouth* (RN).

Above right Alacrity *lying off Portland during exercises.* **Right** Active *passes Southsea Pier* (HMS Dolphin).

SSM. She was eventually the fifth of the Type 21s to commission and joined F8 at Devonport, but like all her sister ships she is now part of F4.

Name *Alacrity*; **Pennant number** F174; **Flight deck code** AL; **Complement** 11 officers and 160 ratings; **Builders** Yarrow; **Laid down** March 5 1973; **Launched** September 18 1974; **Completed** 1977; **Commissioned** July 2 1977.

The frigate has served with the 'Gulf Battle Fleet' and was one of the first Type 21s to receive a Lynx helicopter; although sea trials were carried out at Malta and in the Mediterranean, she is nevertheless a Plymouth-ship, and also served in the Falklands operation.

Name *Ardent*; **Pennant number** F184; **Flight deck code** AD; **Complement** 12 officers and 163 ratings; **Builders** Yarrow; **Laid down** February 22 1974; **Launched** May 9 1975; **Completed** 1977; **Commissioned** October 14 1977; **Lost** South Atlantic May 1982.

Ardent was the first Type 21 to be fitted with Mk 32 STWS. Not long after commissioning the ship was in collision with a merchantman in the Solent and spent several weeks at Portsmouth under repair. She was the second British warship to be sunk during the Falklands operation when she was hit by 15 missiles.

Name *Avenger*; **Pennant number** F185; **Flight deck code** AG; **Complement** 13 officers and 160 ratings; **Builders** Yarrow; **Laid down** October 30 1974; **Launched** November 20 1975; **Completed** 1978; **Commissioned** May 4 1978.

The last Type 21 to commission under the command of Captain F4, *Avenger* carries the squadron staff (including a chaplain). She was launched by Mrs Christine Judd, wife of the then Secretary of State for the Royal Navy. She is the best equipped of the Class and is normally equipped with SCOT*. Like all Type 21s, *Avenger* will not, under

* All Type 21s are fitted for but not necessarily with SCOT.

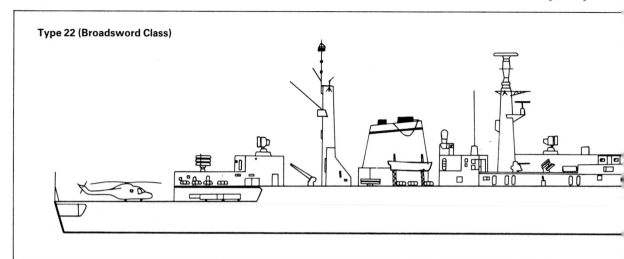

Type 22 (Broadsword Class)

current Government plans, be modernised at her mid-life point.

Class *Broadsword* (Type 22; Batch 1)
Name *Broadsword*; **Pennant number** F88; **Flight deck code** BW; **Standard displacement** 3,500 tons; **Full displacement** 4,000 tons; **Length** 131.2 m overall; **Beam** 14.75 m; **Draught** 4.3 m; **Propulsion** COGOG (gas turbines); **Range** 4,500 nm at 18 knots; **Speed** 30 knots+; **Complement** 25 officers and 225 ratings; **Armament** 2 × 40 mm Bofors GP; 2 × 6 Seawolf PDMS; 4 × Exocet SSM; 2 × 3 Mk 32 STWS; Corvus; **Sensors** 910; 967; 968; 1006; MF/DF; IFF; EW; 2016; **Aircraft** 1 × Lynx HAS 2 (two carried in war); **Small craft** 2 × ship's boats; 1 × Gemini (RM); **Builders** Yarrow; **Laid down** February 7 1975; **Launched** May 12 1976; **Completed** 1978; **Commissioned** May 4 1979.

These destroyer-size frigates have set records not only for their size (at 4,000 tons full displacement), but for being the first warships designed to metric dimensions, the first major warship design for the RN to be built without major gun armament (other than the Bofors 40 mm) and for being equipped from building with the Seawolf PDMS. They are primarily anti-submarine weapons and are capable of carrying two Westland Lynx HAS 2 helicopters (although normally only one is embarked in peacetime, except for exercise). They also can carry a Royal Marines detachment.

The main propulsion system utilises two Rolls-Royce Tyne gas turbines to enable the ships to cruise economically at about 18 knots, but for higher speeds the RR Marine Olympus turbines would be

cut in to give as much as 32 knots under some conditions. The turbines drive two controllable-pitch propellors through non-reversing main gearing and two shafts. The Tynes are rated at 8,500 bhp and the Olympus at 56,000 bhp.

The first four Type 22s—*Broadsword*, *Battleaxe*, *Brilliant* and *Brazen*—are already in commission and represent Batch 1 whilst the next four will be enlarged and thus form a Batch 2.

All units have modern facilities and air con-

Below Broadsword *during trials off Scotland* (Yarrow).
Above right Brilliant *at Portsmouth; the tall structure behind is* Dolphin*'s submarine escape training tower* (RN).

1:600 scale

ditioning, with accommodation for 24 officers, 69 senior rates and 155 junior rates, although the normal complement will be 18 officers and 205 ratings. The daily food allowance, which is considerable in terms of nutrition, is £1.18½ per day for all ranks (1981).

The heart of the ship is the Ferranti CAAIS which monitors all weapons, sensors and data link functions including those of its or associated helicopters. In general, many observers have concluded that these ships, although expensive, are balanced and well arranged for their role in the North Atlantic area. They may even be 'better' than the Type 42s. It is therefore unfortunate that Government policy would seem to indicate that they have limited lives, not being destined for a mid-life conversion/modernisation in the late 1980s.

Broadsword was launched by HRH Princess Alexandra and spent 18 months carrying out first of Class trials in the Western Isles and the Mediterranean before becoming the command of Captain 2nd Frigate Squadron, to which all Type 22s will belong. The ship's special mascot is a replica of a Crusader broadsword copied from the original in the Doge's Palace, Venice.

She was in the Falklands Task Force in 1982.

Name *Battleaxe*; **Pennant number** F89; **Flight deck code**: BX; **Complement** 20 officers and 203 ratings; **Small craft** 1 extra Gemini carried; **Builders** Yarrow; **Laid down** February 4 1976; **Launched** May 18 1977; **Completed** 1980; **Commissioned** March 28 1980.

Battleaxe has been undergoing trials and exercises with the Fleet and the USN since commissioning.

Name *Brilliant*; **Pennant number** F90; **Flight deck code** BT; **Complement** 18 officers and 205 ratings; **Builders** Yarrow; **Laid down** March 25 1977; **Launched** December 15 1978; **Completed** April 10 1981; **Commissioned** May 15 1981.

Formed part of the Falklands Task Force and is credited with the first operational use of the Seawolf missile by destroying hostile Argentine jets in Falklands Sound.

Name *Brazen*; **Pennant number** F91; **Flight deck code**: BN; **Complement** As for *Brilliant*; **Builders** Yarrow; **Laid down** August 18 1978; **Launched** March 4 1980; **Completed** June 15 1982; **Commissioned** 1982.

Class *Broadsword* (Type 22; Batch 2)

These frigates have been stretched and remodelled internally as a result of the trials carried out in earlier ships. Four have been ordered: *Boxer*, *Beaver*, *Brave* and *London* (ex-*Bloodhound*). Additional sensors will include Type 165 towed array sonar and it is thought that propulsion will be by means of the much quieter RR Marine Spey gas turbine, four of which will be fitted.

Name *Boxer*; **Pennant number** F92; **Length** 143.6 m overall; **Beam** 14.75 m; **Draught** 4.3 m; **Complement** 223; All other features as per four earlier frigates. **Laid down** November 1 1979; **Launched** June 17 1981; **Completed** 1982/3; **Commissioned** 1983.

Name *Beaver*; **Pennant number** F93; **Laid down** 1980; **Launched** May 8 1982; **Completed** 1983; **Commissioned** 1984.

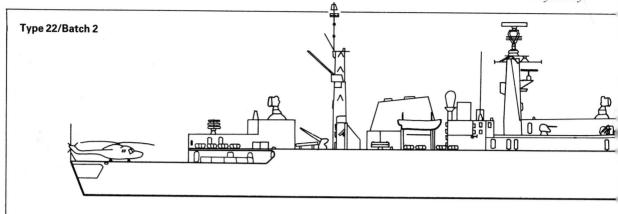

Type 22/Batch 2

Name *Brave*; **Laid down** 1981; **Launched** 1983.

Name *London* (ex-*Bloodhound*); **Pennant Number** F94; **Laid down** 1982.

Class *Leander* (Improved Type 12; Batch 1— Ikara *Leander*)

Name *Leander*; **Pennant number** F109; **Flight Deck code** LE; **Standard displacement** 2,450 tons; **Full displacement** 2,860 tons; **Length** 113.4 m overall; **Beam** 12.5 m; **Draught** 5.5 m; **Propulsion** 2 × steam turbines; **Range** 4,000 nm at 15 knots; **Speed** 28 knots; **Complement** 17 officers and 230 ratings; **Armament** 1 × Ikara ASGWS; 2 × 40 mm Bofors GP Mk 9; 2 × Seacat SAM; 1 × Limbo Mk 10; 2 × Corvus; **Sensors** 975; 992; 993; SCOT; MF/DF; HF/DF; IFF; EW; 199 (VDS); **Aircraft** 1 × Wasp HAS 1; **Small craft** 2 × ship's launches; 1 × Gemini; **Builders**

Harland and Wolff; **Laid down** April 10 1959; **Launched** June 28 1961; **Completed** 1963; **Commissioned** March 24 1963; **Ikara modernisation** 1971–3.

The *Leanders* are undoubtedly the outstanding frigates of the postwar period and have been built in greater numbers than any other major RN surface ship. Not only have they been highly successful in the RN, but there has been considerable foreign naval interest in the design. By the middle of 1983, however, the Class will be somewhat tired and several ships will have been in service for 20 years by that time. Hence the Class is being replaced by the Type 22 and to a certain extent by the Type 21 general purpose frigates.

The origin of the *Leanders* goes back to the Type 12 *Whitby* Class (now all off the active list) and the Modified Type 12s (*Rothesay* Class) which are still in

Below *Leander with Wasp HAS 1 on flight deck* (RN). **Above right** Dido (HMS Excellent).

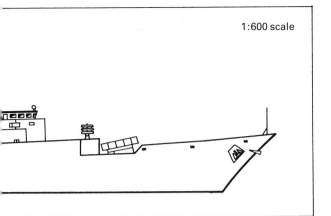

1:600 scale

service in limited numbers. The ships were designed to carry a first generation anti-submarine helicopter (Westland Wasp HAS 1), surface-to-air missiles and long-range search radar (Type 965). There were 16 Leanders initially (Batches 1 and 2), followed by ten 'Broad-Beamers'. Propulsion is via two Admiralty drum-type boilers and two double reduction geared turbines (30,000 shp) through two shafts. Although the machinery was uprated throughout the building period the speed and range of the original *Leander* as against *Ariadne* (the last Batch 3) was minimal. Over a dozen shipyards were involved in the construction programme including all the major pre-nationalisation greats of the British shipbuilding industry.

With various refits, the accommodation has been improved and today less men are required than before despite more complex equipment: complements are Batch 1—257; Batch 2—223; Batch 3—260.

It is impossible in this work to document all the changes which have taken place in the Class over the years, such as the removal of Variable Depth Sonar (VDS) and the plating over of the VDS well to provide accommodation for ships' detachments of Royal Marines. However, the current position can be documented in Batch order; Batch 1—Ikara refits; Batch 2—Exocet refits; Batch 3—Broad-Beamers.

When laid down at Harland & Wolff's Belfast yard, *Leander* was to be a unit in the *Rothesay* Class of anti-submarine frigates, named *Weymouth*. She was later completed as the first *Leander* Class general-purpose frigate and subsequently converted to carry the Ikara system. She has served as half-leader of F5 before joining F1.

Name *Dido*; **Pennant number** F104; **Flight deck code** DO; **Builders** Yarrow; **Laid down** April 10 1959; **Launched** June 28 1961; **Completed** 1963;

Leander Class (Ikara)

1:600 scale

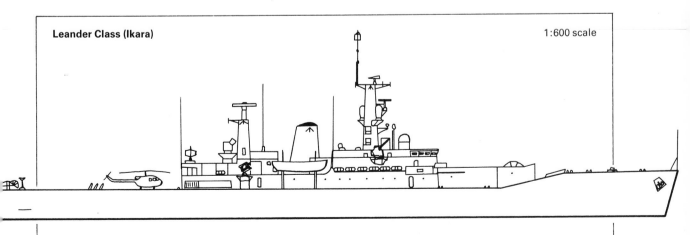

Commissioned September 18 1963; **Ikara modernisation** 1975–78.

This particular *Leander* started life as *Hastings*, an improved Type 12 ASW frigate. After completion she served as a general-purpose frigate (including a stint as *Hero* for BBC tv's *Warship* series). She was one of the last *Leanders* to be converted to carry Seacat SAM (replacing 40 mm guns for AA defence). Now a member of F1, *Dido* has been with F4 (until 1978) and then F3. She is due to transfer to the RNZN in 1983 after refit in the UK.

Name *Arethusa*; **Pennant number** F38; **Flight deck code** AR; **Builders** Whites; **Laid down** September 7 1962; **Launched** November 5 1963; **Completed** 1965; **Commissioned** November 24 1965; **Ikara modernisation** 1975–77.

Arethusa's Ikara refit was completed at Portsmouth in 1977 and she then joined F3, before being reassigned to F1 in 1981. She was launched in 1963 by Lady Hamilton (wife of Admiral Hamilton). Her nickname of 'Saucy *Arethusa*' originated from a ballad composed after an engagement in an 18th century war with France.

Name *Cleopatra*; **Pennant number** F28; **Flight deck code** CP; **Full displacement** 3,200 tons; **Complement** 20 officers and 230 ratings; **Armament** 4 × Exocet SSM; 3 × Seacat SAM; 2 × 3 Mk 32 STWS; 2 × Corvus; 2 × 40 mm Bofors GP Mk 9; **Sensors** 965 (AKE-1); 975; 993; GWS 22; SCOT; HF/DF; MF/DF; IFF; EW; 184; **Aircraft** 1 × Lynx HAS 2; **Builders** HM Dockyard, Devonport; **Laid down** June 19 1963; **Launched** March 25 1964; **Completed** December 1965; **Commissioned** March 1 1966; **Exocet modernisation** 1972–75.

Cleopatra is the only *Leander* not named after a Greek hero; her namesake being a former Queen of Upper Egypt. When commissioned from Exocet refit, *Cleo* was leader of F4 but after re-organisation, she is today with F7. After taking part in the Silver Jubilee Review she went east with a Group Deployment. She was the first of the Exocet *Leanders* and re-commissioned as such on March 1 1976.

Name *Phoebe*; **Pennant number** F42; **Flight deck code** PB (when worn); **Complement** 20 officers and 230 ratings; **Builders** Alex Stephen; **Laid down** June 3 1963; **Launched** July 8 1964; **Completed** 1966; **Commissioned** April 14 1966; **Exocet modernisation** 1974–77.

The eleventh *Leander*, *Phoebe* has served as a half-leader and with the NATO Standing Naval Force Atlantic. Her Lynx helicopter carried out the first of Class trials. The ship was launched by Lady Frewen

Cleopatra comes alongside a RFA during a RAS(S).

(wife of Admiral Frewen) in 1963 and in 1967 was part of the covering force for the withdrawal from Aden. She was guard ship for the 1971 Nixon-Heath talks and was guard ship for Belize on several occasions. Her pennant number 'F42' has been used continuously in the BBC tv series *Warship* for which *Phoebe* was the first prototype. Following refit at Portsmouth, *Phoebe* has lost her Type 965 radar and MRS3 director, these items being replaced by 2 × 20 mm Oerlikon guns (one on the bridge top and the other on the flight deck).

Name *Ajax*; **Pennant number** F114; **Flight deck code** AJ; **Complement** 20 officers and 237 ratings; **Builders** Cammell Laird; **Laid down** October 12 1959; **Launched** August 16 1962; **Completed** 1963; **Commissioned** December 10 1963; **Ikara modernisation** 1972–74.

Laid down as the *Fowey*, *Ajax* has been leader of F8 (after Ikara refit) and is presently the command of Captain F1. Her nickname in the Fleet is the 'White Tornado' and she has developed strong ties with Ajax, Ontario, after a Westlant deployment.

Name *Aurora*; **Pennant number** F10; **Flight deck code** AU; **Complement** 20 officers and 237 ratings; **Builders** John Brown; **Laid down** June 1 1961; **Launched** November 28 1962; **Completed** 1964; **Commissioned** April 9 1964; **Ikara modernisation** 1973–75.

One of the first *Leanders* to be refitted with the Anglo-Australian Ikara ASGWS, *Aurora* presently serves with F1, based at Plymouth.

Name *Galatea*; **Pennant number** F18; **Flight deck code** GA; **Builders** Swan Hunter; **Laid down** December 29 1961; **Launched** May 23 1963; **Completed** 1964; **Commissioned** April 24 1964; **Ikara modernisation** 1972–75.

At the 1977 Silver Jubilee Review at Spithead, *Galatea* was the command of Captain 1st Frigate Squadron; although she is currently still a member of F1 (along with other Batch 1s) she is no longer leader.

Name *Euryalus*; **Pennant number** F15; **Flight deck code** EU; **Builders** Scotts; **Laid down** November 2 1961; **Launched** June 6 1963; **Completed** 1964; **Commissioned** September 16 1964; **Ikara modernisation** 1974–76.

There are apparently 32 ways of spelling *'Euryalus'* and probably as many ways of pronouncing it. The ship was the sixth Ikara refit and this involved computerisation of the weapons control as well as a new system.

Name *Naiad*; **Pennant number** F39; **Flight deck code** NA; **Complement** 17 officers and 239 ratings; **Builders** Yarrow; **Laid down** October 30 1962; **Launched** November 4 1963; **Completed** 1965; **Commissioned** March 15 1965; **Ikara modernisation** 1972–5.

Naiad attended the 1977 Fleet Review as half-leader of the Sixth Frigate Squadron (F6), but by 1981, with the surface fleet reorganisation she had joined F1 at Devonport. She was the first of her class

to be completed with Seacat SAM already fitted. In early 1981 she completed a deployment with the 'Gulf Battle Fleet'.

Name *Sirius*; **Pennant number** F40; **Flight deck code** SS (when worn); **Complement** 20 officers and 203 ratings; **Builders** HM Dockyard, Portsmouth; **Laid down** August 9 1963; **Launched** September 22 1964; **Completed** May 1966; **Commissioned** June 15 1966.

The last *Sirius* was a cruiser of the 1940–56 vintage, and like the seventh to bear the name, all ships have had a close link with Portsmouth. *Sirius* has operated in Icelandic and Far Eastern waters, and in August 1970 she was the rescue ship for a ferry disaster in the Caribbean. Re-commissioned as leader of F6, she was involved in Lynx helicopter trials before joining F7, a Plymouth-based squadron. As the ship is fitted with towed array sonar, she is not able to operate helicopters and has no hangar.

Name *Argonaut*; **Pennant number** F56; **Flight deck code** AT; **Complement** 18 officers and 206 ratings; **Builders** Hawthorn Leslie; **Laid down** November 27 1964; **Launched** February 8 1966; **Completed** 1967; **Commissioned** August 17 1966; **Exocet modernisation** 1978–80.

Naiad (HMS Excellent).

The leader of F7, *Argonaut* was originally a gun-Leander equipped with a 114 mm Mk6 mounting and a Wasp HAS 1 helicopter. Following Exocet refit, she re-commissioned at Devonport as the command of Captain (F) Seventh Frigate Squadron in March 1980, but was Portland-based for a time undergoing Basic Operational Sea Training (BOST). She is the fourth ship in the RN to bear the name of the Greek heroes who sailed for the Golden Fleece. She was damaged by fire on May 27 1982 while a welding crew was repairing damage caused by two Argentinian bombs which, fortunately, failed to explode.

Name *Juno*; **Pennant number** F52; **Flight Deck Code** JO; **Complement** 18 officers and 210 ratings; **Builders** Thornycroft; **Laid down** November 27 1964; **Launched** February 8 1966; **Completed** 1967; **Commissioned** August 17 1967; **Exocet modernisation** 1981–82.

In September 1981, *Juno* departed Chatham under tow for Rosyth and conversion into the Fleet's new Trials ship, to replace *Torquay*. *Juno* was also one of the 'prototypes' for the 'HMS *Hero*' in the television programme.

Name *Minerva*; **Pennant number** F45; **Flight deck code** MV; **Complement** 18 officers and 210 ratings; **Builders** Vickers; **Laid down** July 25 1963; **Launched** December 19 1964; **Completed** 1967; **Commissioned** September 7 1967; **Exocet modernisation** 1976–79.

One of the warships in which HRH Prince Charles carried out seamanship training, *Minerva* was a gun-Leander before refitting with Exocet and becoming leader of F5. Today, she is a member of F7. She is the ninth ship to bear the name in the RN.

Name *Danae*; **Pennant number** F47; **Flight deck code** DN; **Complement** 18 officers and 205 ratings; **Builders** HM Dockyard, Devonport; **Laid down** December 16 1964; **Launched** October 31 1965; **Completed** September 1967; **Commissioned** September 7 1967; **Exocet modernisation** 1977–78.

Danae is a member of the Seventh Frigate Squadron (F7), a Plymouth-based ship and another of the 'HMS *Hero*' prototypes. *Danae*, like most frigates, has served in many corners of the world, including a spell on Icelandic Fish Patrol.

Name *Penelope*; **Pennant number** F127; **Flight deck code** PE; **Complement** 19 officers and 200 ratings; **Builders** Vickers; **Laid down** March 14 1961; **Launched** August 17 1962; **Completed** 1963; **Commissioned** October 31 1963; **Exocet modernisation** 1980–82; **Sea Wolf trials refit** 1971–73; **Exocet and modernisation refit** 1980–82.

Penelope has had an eventful career, being originally laid down as a *Salisbury* Class frigate (named *Coventry*—now a Type 42 destroyer bears the name). She later became a Gun *Leander*, then the Sea Wolf PDMS trials ship before undergoing refit for Exocet SSM and being re-allocated to Batch 2. She is probably the last *Leander* to be modernised with Exocet.

Below Minerva *leaves Portsmouth to begin a short refit at Devonport; her Lynx helicopter was then deployed to Gibraltar for Operation 'Springtrain' and later to NP 1222 for the Falklands deployment* (HMS Daedalus). **Above right** Argonaut. **Above right** Penelope *during Seawolf PDMS trials in 1973* (MoD).

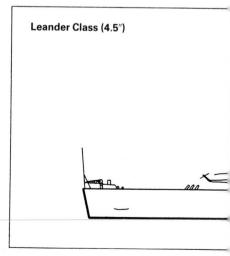

Leander Class (4.5″)

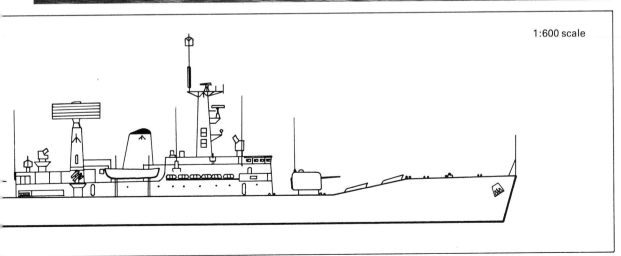

1:600 scale

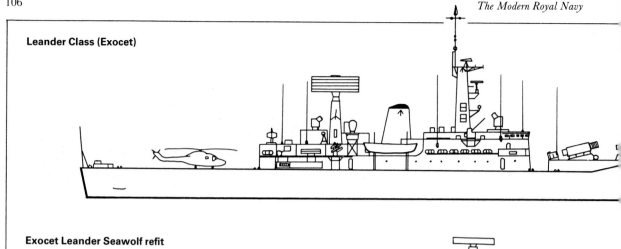

Leander Class (Exocet)

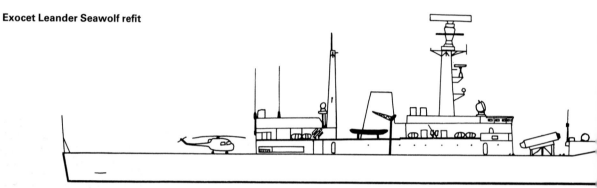

Exocet Leander Seawolf refit

Class *Leander* (Improved Type 12; Batch 3—
Broad-Beamers)
Name *Bacchante*; **Pennant number** F69; **Flight
deck code** BC; **Standard displacement** 2,500 tons;
Full displacement 2,962 tons; **Beam** 13.1 m;
Complement 18 officers and 240 ratings;
Armament 2 × 114 mm Mk 6; 2 × 20 mm
Oerlikon GP; 1 × Seacat SAM; 1 × Limbo Mk 10;
2 × Corvus; **Sensors** 965 (AKE-1); 975; 993; IFF;
MF/DF; HF/DF; EW; GWS 22; 2016; **Builders**
Vickers Armstrong; **Laid down** October 27 1966;
Launched February 19 1968; **Completed** 1969;
Commissioned October 17 1969.

Following service experience, it was decided to
broaden the beams of the last batch of *Leanders*;
length and draught were not affected. The gun-
armed Batch 3s retain the Wasp HAS 1, the Exocet-
equipped vessels the Lynx HAS 2.

Following the 1981 Defence Review, *Bacchante* will
be paid off from the RN in 1983 to refit in New
Zealand before joining the RNZN in 1984. She has
previously served with NATO Standing Force
Atlantic.

Name *Achilles*; **Pennant number** F12; **Flight deck
code** AC; **Complement** 17 officers and 243 ratings;
Builders Yarrow; **Laid down** December 1 1967;
Launched November 21 1968; **Completed** 1970;
Commissioned July 9 1970.

The present *Achilles* is the eighth ship to bear the
name in the RN; the last was a veteran of the River
Plate engagement. In 1975, she assisted the
evacuation of UK citizens from Vietnam and in 1976
served in the Cod War off Iceland in protection of
British fishing vessels. *Achilles* is scheduled to be paid
off in 1983–4.

Name *Diomede* **Pennant number** F16; **Flight deck
code** DM; **Complement** as *Bacchante*; **Small craft**
Also carries 1 × Dory 17; **Builders** Yarrow; **Laid
down** January 30 1968; **Launched** April 15 1969;
Completed 1971; **Commissioned** April 2 1971.

Like all *Leanders*, *Diomede* bears the name of a
Greek hero; this is the fourth *Diomede* in the RN. For
many years the ship has base-ported at Chatham
and played *Hero* in the BBC tv series *Warship*. In
1981–2, she was part of the RN Gulf of Oman patrol

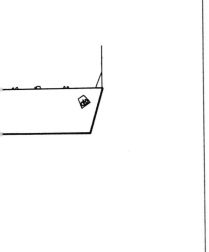

1:600 scale

based at Mombasa. *Diomede* is scheduled to be paid off in 1983. The ship's nickname is 'HMS Dimweed'.

Name *Apollo*; **Pennant number** F70; **Flight deck code** AP; **Complement** as for *Bacchante*; **Builders** Yarrow; **Laid down** May 1 1969; **Launched** October 15 1970; **Completed** May 1972; **Commissioned** May 28 1972.

Launched as the 25th *Leander*, *Apollo* spent several years with F2, the training squadron at Portsmouth before joining F8 in 1981; she was leader of the former in the mid-1970s.

Name *Ariadne*; **Pennant number** F72; **Flight deck code** AE; **Complement** 20 officers and 240 ratings; **Small craft** 2 × Gemini carried; **Builders** Yarrow; **Laid down** November 1 1969; **Launched** September 10 1971; **Completed** 1972; **Commissioned** February 10 1973.

The last of her Class to be completed, *Ariadne* is presently the command of Captain F8 and was present at the American celebrations to mark the end of British rule in her former colonies, at

Top *Bacchante* is destined for the RNZN in 1984 (RN). **Above** *Diomede* in traditional *Leander* guise (RN Portsmouth).

Yorktown in October 1981. Later she was guardship for the Independence celebrations at Belize.

Class *Leander* (Improved Type 12; Batch 3— Exocet-armed Broad-Beamers)
Name *Andromeda*; **Pennant number** F57; **Flight deck code** AM; **Full displacement** 3,200 tons; **Complement** 20 officers and 196 ratings; **Armament** 4 × Exocet SSM; 1 × 6 Seawolf PDMS; 2 × 3 Mk 32 STWS; 2 × 40 mm Bofors Mk 9; 2 × Corvus; **Sensors** 910; 967; 968; 1006; IFF; EW; 2016; **Aircraft** 1 × Lynx HAS 2; **Small craft** 2 × ship's launches; 2 × Gemini; **Builders** HM Dockyard, Portsmouth; **Laid down** May 25 1966; **Launched** May 24 1967; **Completed** 1968; **Commissioned** December 2 1968; **Exocet modernisation** 1977–81.

These Batch 3 *Leanders* have been retrofitted with

launchers, an enlarged hangar for a Lynx, a new mainmast, a flat-topped funnel and STWS tubes. Extensive computerisation has been included, leading to a reduction in manpower. Earlier in her career, *Andromeda* took part in the Beira Patrol, Icelandic patrols, Far East deployments and the evacuation of UK citizens from Cyprus in 1974. She joined the 8th Frigate Squadron in 1982.

Name *Charybdis*; **Pennant number** F75; **Flight deck code** CS; **Builders** Harland and Wolff; **Laid down** January 27 1967; **Launched** February 28 1968; **Completed** 1969; **Commissioned** June 2 1969; **Exocet modernisation** 1979–82.

The second of the Seawolf GWS 25 refits, *Charybdis* (known as 'Cherry B' to the Fleet) began trials in the Portland areas in late 1981 before joining F8.

Name *Hermione*; **Pennant number** F58; **Flight deck code** HM; **Complement** 18 officers and 196 ratings; **Builders** Alex Stephens; **Laid down** December 6 1965; **Launched** April 26 1967; **Completed** 1969; **Commissioned** July 11 1969; **Exocet modernisation** 1980–82.

Hermione joins F8 on completion of Portland Operational Sea Training in late 1983, following the major half-life refit at Chatham, where Type 165 towed array sonar was fitted at the expense of the ship's flight.

Name *Jupiter*; **Pennant number** F60; **Flight deck code** JP; **Complement** As for Hermione; **Builders** Yarrow; **Laid down** October 3 1966; **Launched** September 4 1967; **Completed** 1969; **Commis-**

Above Ariadne *in heavy weather off Scotland* (RN/LA (Phot) Ferguson). **Above right** Andromeda *in her refitted guise of Seawolf Batch 3* (RN). **Below** Charybdis (HMS Excellent). **Below right** Scylla (HMS Excellent).

the Exocet SSM. In addition to the sensors listed above, towed array may be fitted in a lightweight form later and some warships will undoubtedly be fitted for SCOT terminals.

Andromeda completed a major refit at Devonport in 1981 which has resulted in Seawolf PDMS

sioned August 9 1969; **Exocet modernisation** 1980–83.

Name *Scylla*; **Pennant number** F71; **Flight deck code** SC; **Complement** As for Hermione; **Builders** HM Dockyard, Devonport; **Laid down** May 17 1967; **Launched** August 8 1968; **Completed** February 12 1970; **Commissioned** February 14 1970; **Exocet modernisation** 1980–83.

Scylla has been a Portsmouth- and Chatham-based ship during her service, which has also seen her operating in the Far East, on Fisheries' Protection duties and as West Indies guardship (especially for the Independence celebrations on St Lucia).

Class *Rothesay* (Type 12 Modified)
Name *Rothesay*; **Pennant number** F107; **Flight deck code** RO; **Standard displacement** 2,380 tons; **Full displacement** 2,800 tons; **Length** 109.7 m; **Beam** 12.5 m; **Draught** 5.3 m; **Propulsion** 2 × steam turbines; **Range** 4,200 nm at 12 knots; **Speed** 30 knots; **Complement** 15 officers and 220 ratings; **Armament** 2 × 114 mm Mk 6; 2 × 20 mm Oerlikon GP; 1 × Seacat SAM; 1 × Limbo Mk 10; 2 × Corvus; **Sensors** 975; 994; GWS 22; IFF; EW; MF/DF; HF/DF; **Aircraft** 1 × Wasp HAS 1; **Small craft** 2 × ship's launches; 1 × Gemini; **Builders** Yarrow; **Laid down** November 6 1956; **Launched** December 9 1957; **Completed** 1959; **Commissioned** April 23 1960; **Seacat modernisation** 1966–68.

Designed as specialist anti-submarine warfare frigates, the *Rothesay* Class are important in the development of frigates and several of the original class are still on the active list, either as trials and

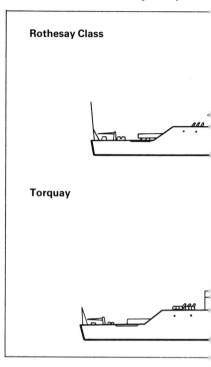

Rothesay Class

Torquay

Above Torquay *during a RAS(L) whilst training navigators from* Mercury. **Below right** Rothesay—*neo*-Leander *lines* (FPU).

training ships (*Lowestoft* and *Londonderry*) or as members of the Sixth Frigate Squadron (F6), usually based at Rosyth. Their future is, however, limited, especially because they are expensive to run and to man.

The Class is based on the earlier *Whitby* Class* (the original Type 12) but during the course of their early years, they were modified to take a Westland Wasp HAS 1 and this type of helicopter still operates from their decks. Inexorably, the fate of the Wasp and the *Rothesay* Class would seem to be linked— when one goes so will the other. After the introduction of the Wasp helicopter, the anti- aircraft defence was beefed up using the Shorts Seacat SAM in place of 40 mm Bofors guns; the Class had already lost one set of Limbo Mk 10 mortars to provide a flight deck and hangar.

The ships are powered by steam turbines via two

* The one remaining *Whitby* Class frigate is the navigational training ship *Torquay* which was commissioned in May 1956 and is now due for retirement in 1983. She has the distinction of the first CAAIS (Computer Assisted Action Information System) and carried a complement of 12 officers and 213 ratings. Dimensions are exactly similar to the *Rothesay* Class except that the draught is only 5.2 m. The former *Whitby* Class frigate *Eastbourne* is alongside at *Caledonia* as a training ship, stripped of armament.

Admiralty Standard Range turbines (15,000 shp each) from two Babcock and Wilcox boilers; the Class all have two shafts.

The last three ships of the class were laid down but their construction altered to make them Improved Type 12s—the *Leander* Class (*qv*).

The lead ship of the Class, *Rothesay* has been on Gulf Patrol in 1981 and was used for officer recruitment material by DNR (Director of Naval Recruiting) in 1981/2. The ship was launched by the Countess of Selkirk and is now based at Rosyth with F6.

Name *Yarmouth*; **Pennant number** F101; **Flight deck code** YM; **Builders** John Brown; **Laid down** November 29 1957; **Launched** March 23 1959; **Completed** 1960; **Commissioned** March 26 1960; **Seacat modernisation** 1968–70.

Yarmouth was the first of the *Rothesay* Class to be completeted and later underwent refit for the addition of a Wasp and the Seacat system. The ship has had a very active career and like so many of her class has operated in every corner of the globe. She has served on Icelandic guardship and Gibraltar guardship duties and was part of NAVOCFORMED (Naval On-Call Force) in the Mediterranean. In 1982 she was in the south Atlantic with the Task Force.

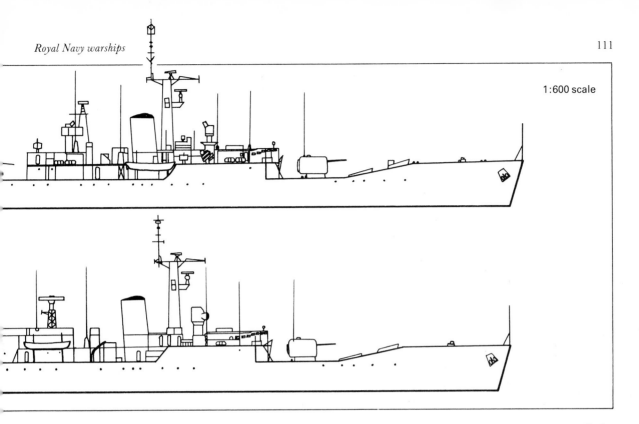

1:600 scale

Name *Rhyl*; **Pennant number** F129; **Flight deck code** RL; **Armament** 4 × 20 mm Oerlikon GP; **Builders** HM Dockyard, Portsmouth; **Laid down** January 29 1958; **Launched** April 23 1959; **Completed** 1960; **Commissioned** October 31 1960; **Seacat modernisation** 1969–72.

Another veteran of the Gulf Patrol, *Rhyl* is scheduled to pay off for the last time in late 1982/ early 1983. Between 1960 and 1969 she served with the Home, Far East and Mediterranean Fleets; later, in 1972–5, she was a member of a Group Deployment to the Far East. In 1975–6 she refitted at Gibraltar and then joined F2; today she is a member of F6.

Name *Plymouth*; **Pennant number** F126; **Flight deck code** PL; **Small craft** Includes dinghy; **Builders** HM Dockyard, Devonport; **Laid down** July 1 1958; **Launched** July 20 1959; **Completed** 1961; **Commissioned** May 11 1961; **Seacat modernisation** 1969–71.

One of nine warships to take part in the 1975 Round-the-World deployment, *Plymouth* is the command of Captain F6. She was the third Rothesay Class to undergo refit for helicopter and Seacat SAM. In 1982 she also formed part of the Falklands Task Force and was damaged during an air attack on June 8.

Name *Brighton*; **Pennant number** F106; **Flight deck code** BR; **Builders** Yarrow; **Laid down** July 23 1957; **Launched** October 30 1959; **Completed** 1961; **Commissioned** September 28 1961; **Seacat modernisation** 1970–71.

On recommissioning from refit, *Brighton* returned to the Sixth Frigate Squadron where, in 1980, the ship was involved in a major exercise with the Spanish Navy. It is thought that *Brighton* will be withdrawn from active service in 1983.

Class *Rothesay* (Trials)
Name *Londonderry*; **Pennant number** F108; **Flight deck code** LD (when worn); **Propulsion**

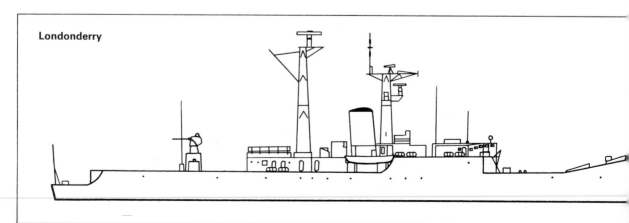

Londonderry

Left Brighton *on patrol during the 'Cod War' in December 1975* (RN). **Below left** Londonderry *enters Portsmouth to pay off; note her after mast has been replaced by a Rarden 30 mm Laurence-Scott mounting* (RN). **Right** Brecon, *the first of the GRP-made* Hunt *Class* (HMS Daedalus).

Experimental; **Complement** 17 officers and 220 ratings; **Armament** None; **Sensors** Various, but include 975; 994; MF/DF; **Builders** Samuel White; **Laid down** November 15 1956; **Launched** May 20 1958; **Completed** 1960; **Commissioned** July 22 1960; **Seacat modernisation** 1967–69; **Trials refit** 1975–79.

Formally a *Rothesay* Class frigate, *Londonderry* is now a trials ship for the Admiralty computer and communications work under ASWE (Admiralty Surface Weapons Establishment) control. In 'former life', she was part of the RN presence off Iceland during a Cod War before going to Gibraltar for limited refit. In 1974, with F3, she was deployment to the Indian Ocean but was back off Iceland again in 1975. She is now immediately recognisable from her ungainly masts and all her armament has been removed to save top weight. She paid off into reserve in 1982 after conducting gunnery trials. Later she was put into limited service to cover RN commitments to NATO whilst other warships were in the South Atlantic.

Name *Lowestoft*; **Pennant number** F103; **Flight deck code** LT; **Builders** Alex Stephens; **Laid down** June 9 1958; **Launched** June 23 1960; **Completed** 1961; **Commissioned** October 18 1960; **Seacat modernisation 1969–70.**

Lowestoft is now a trials ship for specialist sonar work and still carries her regular armament but does not regularly have a ship's flight embarked. Used extensively for training with F2 in the late 1970s, the ship is now a member of F6, but is seen often in the Portland area still.

Mines Counter Measures Vessels

Class *Hunt*

Name *Brecon*; **Pennant number** M29; **Standard displacement** 615 tons; **Full displacement** 725 tons; **Length** 60.0 m overall; **Beam** 9.9 m; **Draught** 2.2 m; **Propulsion** 2 × diesels; **Range** 1,500 nm at 12 knots; **Speed** 17 knots; **Complement** 6 officers and 39 ratings; **Armament** 2 × 40 mm Bofors GP (when carried); 2 × GPMG (for detonating floating mines); **Small craft** 2 × Gemini; minehunting submersibles (PAP104); **Builders** Vosper Thornycroft; **Laid down** September 15 1975; **Launched** June 21 1978; **Completed** 1979; **Commissioned** March 1980.

Hunt Class   1:600 scale

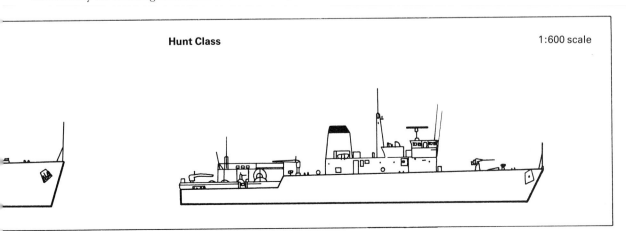

The first of the *Hunt* Class was launched by the Duchess of Kent and she is the second ship to bear the name in the RN. Most of her life to date has been carrying out trials and work ups, together with the first MCM exercises with NATO navies to prove the design.

The *Hunt* Class is a new generation of mine warfare vessels whose glass reinforced plastic (GRP) construction is revolutionary in design and technology. Originally estimated to cost £8 million, the latter members of the class will take about £25 million of the Defence vote apiece. Like the Type 21 frigates, the construction is a joint venture between Vosper Thornycroft and Yarrow. The ships are the largest to be made of GRP and the most expensive pound for tonne in the world.

The ships' role is to replace some of the older *Ton* Class MCMVs and to provide a comprehensive minehunting and minesweeping support for the older vessels in a particular area. It is possible that the ships will be used as flotilla leaders in this way. Although there were problems with the seakeeping ability of the Class in the early trials period, these problems now seem to have been corrected, and there is no doubt that the *Hunts* are magnificent ships.

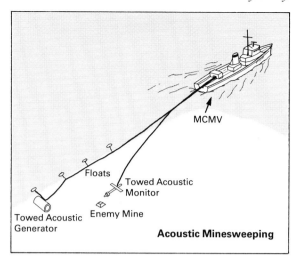

Acoustic Minesweeping

Ledbury *showing her sweep deck and minehunting gear* (RN).

In terms of magnetic signature, the type are well within NATO guidelines although the first of the Class, *Brecon*, did experiment with not having the 40 mm Bofors GP mounting at sea. It is not known whether any decision has yet been made about self-defence for these vessels if the Bofors is to remain on the dockside.

In June 1980, four more units were ordered from Vosper Thornycroft, making a total of nine at sea, under construction or ordered from a total ideal procurement of 12. The mine problem posed by the Warsaw Pact fleets and other potentially unfriendly nations will be by no means countered by the Hunts and experiments are currently underway to determine the best possible low-cost alternative to replacing the remaining *Tons*. Experiments with stern-towed gear from converted trawlers seem to be working well and the RNR is operating second-hand vessels already.

The *Hunt* Class are designed to dispose of mines in three ways: sweeping moored mines so that the mine comes to the surface to be destroyed by gunfire; using influence and acoustic sweeps to explode magnetic or other specialist bottom mines; hunting the mines with specialist sonar and using clearance divers to place charges so that the devices may be harmlessly exploded.

The prime reason for using GRP in the Class is that the material is non-magnetic and does not conduct electrical current which may cause magnetic fields to be generated which in turn could detonate mines. The experimental programme for the GRP construction was tested some years ago in *Wilton* (*qv*) using the existing *Ton* Class hull form and redundant equipment to fit the warship out. Clear resin is used in the manufacturing technique so that

Cattistock *during acceptance trials for the RN* (HMS Daedalus).

any faults may be detected immediately. A great deal of effort has gone into the research and development of the resin and the process and this must account for the high cost of each hull; hopefully in real terms the costs of the later vessels will be reduced by about 40 per cent.

The Class is powered by Deltic diesel main engines driving fixed-pitch propellers through ahead/astern clutches and reverse reduction gearboxes. A third Deltic engine provides power for slow-speed running and manoeuvring via hydraulic power transmission. There is also a bow thruster. The propulsion is rated at 3,540 bhp.

The RN was the first navy to use GRP mines

Bronington *(MH), pictured in 1976 dressed overall for HM The Queen's birthday; at that time she was the Command of HRH the Prince of Wales.*

countermeasures vessels and there are currently three in service—*Brecon*, *Ledbury* and *Cattistock*—with *Brocklesby*, launched January 12 1982; *Cottesmore*, launched February 9 1982; and *Middleton*, launched May 10 1982, nearing completion; and *Chiddingfold*, *Dulverton* and *Hurworth* being built at Vosper Thornycroft.

Name *Ledbury*; **Pennant number** M30; **Builders** Vosper Thornycroft; **Laid down** 1977; **Launched** December 5 1979; **Completed** 1980; **Commissioned** June 11 1981.

The second ship in the RN to bear the name, *Ledbury* was launched by Lady Berthon (wife of Admiral Sir Stephen Berthon). Still undergoing full work-up trials and having been displayed at the Royal Naval Equipment Exhibition at Whale Island, Portsmouth, in late 1981, the ship will be a valuable asset to the Fleet and the NATO MCM capability.

Name *Cattistock*; **Pennant number** M31; **Builders** Vosper Thornycroft; **Laid down** 1979; **Launched** January 22 1981; **Completed** December 1981; **Commissioned** 1982.

Class *Ton*
Name See below; **Pennant number** See below; **Standard displacement** 360 tons; **Full displacement** 425 tons; **Length** 46.3 m overall; **Beam** 8.8 m; **Draught** 2.5 m; **Propulsion** 2 × Mirrless 2,500 bhp or 2 × Deltic 3,000 bhp diesel; **Range** 2,300 nm at 12 knots; **Speed** 15 knots; **Complement** 4 officers and 25 ratings (minesweepers); 5 officers and 33 ratings

Bossington, *as half-leader of MCM 2 at Portsmouth* (RN).

(minehunters)*; **Armament** Either: None; 1 × 40 mm GP; 1 × 40 mm GP + 2 × 20 mm; 2 × 20 mm; 2 × 40 mm GP; **Sensors** Navigation radar and echo-sounder; MHs carry mine-locating sonar, such as Type 193M; **Small craft** Various combinations of Gemini craft; **Builders** Many small yards were contracting to build the *Ton* Class including: Camper & Nicholson; Cook, Welton & Gemmell; Doig; Dorset Yacht Co; Fleetlands; Harland & Wolff; Herd & McKenzie; Montrose;

* The complement figures also depend on the number of training billets in the flotilla/squadron; several years ago, a *Ton* was used for training Midshipmen and cadets from Dartmouth (BRNC).

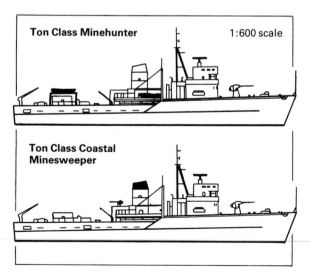

Philip; Pickersgill; Thornycroft; White and Wivenhoe, between July 1952 and September 1958.

The most numerically important class of warships in the RN since the end of World War 2, the *Ton* or *Coniston* Class have been the backbone of British mine warfare, offshore patrol and Fisheries' Protection for many years. They are now coming to the end of their useful lives and many are nearly 30 years in commission. Constructed of double hull mahogany and sheathed with copper or nylon, ships of the Class were constructed at numerous locations following the problems encountered with mines during the Korean War (1950–53). Many of the original Class have been sold off to friendly navies and still serve overseas.

In the early 1960s, the Class was sub-divided into minehunters (MH) and minesweepers (MCS) or (CMS) and several were converted to Patrol Ship standards for the Far East (*qv*). In addition, they were until a few years ago the standard vessel for training afloat of the Royal Naval Reserve (RNR) which forms the 10th Minesweeper Squadron (MCM10). The 'Fish Squadron' has used their very good seakeeping, if unpopular motion, to provide outer limit patrols in protection of British Fishery Limits (out to 200 nm) but the advent of the *Castle* Class OPV (*qv*) has lead to the *Tons* coming further inshore for their last years of service. The problem which the Admiralty now faces is that there are no suitable replacements for the MH and MCS role currently under construction in sufficient numbers to let the Class go. This is unfortunate because at Gibraltar, where many of the Class have been refitted over the years, the staff have noticed that the hulls are beginning to show signs of damage from the repeated battering of wave action/motion, especially on the supporting members of the hull. Nevertheless, there are a few years left in the Class yet.

Minehunters These vessels use special sonar, such as Type 193M, to detect mines and then use either submersible vehicles or clearance divers to knock them out. These ships carry full diving facilities and are usually not operated by the RNR.

The current minehunters with the RN are:

Name	Pennant number	Name	Pennant number
Bideston	M1110	*Gavinton**	M1140
Bronington	M1115	*Kedleston*	M1153
Hubberston	M1147	*Kellington*	M1154
Brereton	M1113	*Nurton*	M1166
*Bossington**	M1133	*Kirkliston*	M1157
Iveston	M1151	*Sheraton*	M1181
Brinton	M1114	*Maxton*	M1165

* Indicates that the vessel is earmarked for disposal in 1982–3.

In 1981–2, the following minehunters were used as training tenders by the RNR: M1113; M1153; M1154. All the above vessels were commissioned between April 1953 and August 1957.

Minesweepers The coastal minesweeper operations of the RN have to a large degree been overshadowed by the minehunting role, and it is an area which has been neglected by various Governments over the last 20 years. Until the new class of low-cost MCMVs is in service (about 1990), the remaining *Tons* will soldier on. MCSs carry large sweep gear on the aft end of the vessel together with davits for special decoys and for putting over the sweeper gear with otter boards, lines *et al*.

Upton *at the Silver Jubilee Review.*

Maxton *at sea* (FPU).

The current minesweepers are:

Name	Pennant number	Name	Pennant number
Alfriston	M1103	*Pollington*†	M1173
Cuxton	M1125	*Walkerton*†	M1188
Laleston	M1158	*Stubbington*†	M1204
Upton	M1187	*Crichton*†	M1124
Soberton†	M1200	*Hodgeston*	M1146
Crofton	M1216	*Shavington*†	M1180
Bickington†	M1109	*Wotton*†	M1195
*Glasserton**	M1141	*Lewiston*	M1208

* Indicates that the vessel is earmarked for disposal 1982–3.

† Indicates that the vessel serves with the Fisheries' Protection Squadron 1981–2.

RNR vessels in this sub-division are: M1103; M1125; M1146; M1158; M1208; M1216.

GRP Trials Ship

The specialist GRP trials ship *Wilton* (M1116) was built by Vosper Thornycroft in 1971–73 and commissioned in 1974 to prove that large vessels (*Wilton* has 450 tons displacement but the same dimensions as the *Ton* Class) could be constructed of the material. The ship paved the way for the *Hunt* Class (*qv*) and carried out very successful mine clearance operations in the Suez Canal following the 1973 Middle East war. Usually based at *Vernon*, *Wilton* now carries out regular squadron duties but is equipped as an MH or an MCS. She is powered by two Deltic 3,000 bhp diesels giving a recorded maximum speed of 16 knots and a range of 2,300 nm at 12 knots. Her usual complement is 5 officers and 32 ratings.

Class *Venturer*

Name *Venturer*; **Pennant number** M08; **Standard displacement** 134 tons; **Full displacement** 392 tons; **Length** 36.6 m overall; **Beam** 8.9 m; **Draught** 3.9 m; **Propulsion** 2 × Mirrless Blackstone diesels (2,000 hp); **Range** c2,500 nm at 12 knots; **Speed** 14 knots; **Complement** 4 officers and 23 ratings; **Armament** None (except GPMGs for mine destruction); **Sensors** Navigation radar; **Small craft** 1/2 Gemini; **Builders** Cubow; **Completed** 1973; **Purchased by MoD** 1978.

Name *St David*; **Pennant number** M07; **Builder** Cubow; **Completed** 1972; **Purchased by MoD** 1978.

These vessels are classed as Medium Minesweepers and are used exclusively by the RNR at Bristol and South Wales for training and to pioneer this form of sweeping. They were purchased by the Ministry of Defence in 1978 and remain unarmed.

St David is the former Stand-by Oil Rig Safety Vessel *Suffolk Monarch* and her sister ship *Venturer* is the former stern trawler *Suffolk Harvester*.

It is thought that these 392-ton vessels are the test ships for a class of similarly constructed stern sweep mines counter measures vessels for the RN and they could be used for deep sweeping. Certainly they have been operating from *Vernon*, the RN's School of Mine Warfare (*qv*) on occasions. Their future cannot be long-term but they have been very worthwhile additions to the Fleet and especially to the RNR.

Class *Ham*

Name See below; **Pennant number** See below; **Standard displacement** 120 tons; **Full displacement** 159 tons; **Length** 32.5 m (32.8 m for *Thornham*); **Beam** 6.5 m (6.7 m for *Thornham*); **Draught** 1.7 m (1.8 m for *Thornham*); **Propulsion** 2 × Paxman diesels (1,700 bhp; 1,100 bhp for *Thornham*); **Range** Circa 1,000 nm at 10 knots; **Speed** 13 knots (14 knots for *Thornham*); **Complement** 2 officers and 13 ratings; **Armament** Combination of 20 mm and 40 mm guns; **Builders** See below; **Completed** See below.

Over the years the *Ham* and *Ley* Classes have been whittled away to only a handful of craft, now used for training or as specialist tenders. There are still a few left with the RMAS (*qv*) and the RNXS (*qv*) but in RN service only *Dittisham*, *Flintham* and *Thornham* remain, being used to train University entrants at Southampton, Aberdeen and elsewhere. *Aveley* is now attached to the Naval Base at Plymouth. None of the vessels have long to go in RN service, being due for replacement in 1983.

At Liverpool, the former Inshore Survey Vessel, *Waterwitch* which had been converted from a *Ham* design, has replaced the former Seaward Defence Boat, *Dee* (P3104). *Droxford* of the latter type has a very limited future at Glasgow and will also be replaced in due course.

Replacement in the 25 m Class was expected to be announced in 1982.

Name *Dittisham*; **Pennant number** M2621; **Builders** Fairlie Yacht; **Completed** 1954

Name *Flintham*; **Pennant number** M2628; **Builders** Bolson; **Completed** 1955;

Name *Thronham;* **Pennant number** M2793; **Builders** Taylor; **Completed** 1955;

Name *Aveley;* **Pennant number** M2002; **Builders** White; **Completed** 1953;

Mines Countermeasures Support Ship

Class *Abdiel*
Name *Abdiel;* **Pennant number** N21; **Standard displacement** 1,375 tons; **Full displacement** 1,500 tons; **Length** 80.8 m overall; **Beam** 11.7 m; **Draught** 3.0 m; **Propulsion** 2 × Paxman diesels (2,690 bhp); **Range** 4,500 nm at 12 knots; **Speed** 16 knots; **Complement** 8 officers and 90 ratings; **Armament** None; **Sensors** 193M; 1006; HF/DF; **Aircraft** None (but there is a flight deck); **Small craft** 2 × survey workboats; **Ammunition** 44 exercise mines; **Builders** Thornycroft; **Laid down** May 23 1966; **Launched** January 27 1967; **Completed** 1967; **Commissioned** October 17 1967.

This is a multi-role ship, designed to act as a floating base for mine hunting and sweeping operations, such as in the Suez Canal exercise in 1974. Not only does *Abiel* carry exercise mines but she also is able to supply MCMVs in their work. She cost £1.5 m to build but has been refitted several times to keep her up to date. Originally flagship of MCM 1, she is now independent to support the other two RN MCM squadrons and she also operates with Standing Naval Force Channel.

Above left Wilton, *the 'plastic 'sweeper' at Vernon.* **Left** Lewiston *is now serving with London Division RNR* (RN).

Above Abdiel (HMS Excellent) **Right** *The RNR medium mine-sweeper* Venturer *on exercise in the Bristol Channel* (RNR).

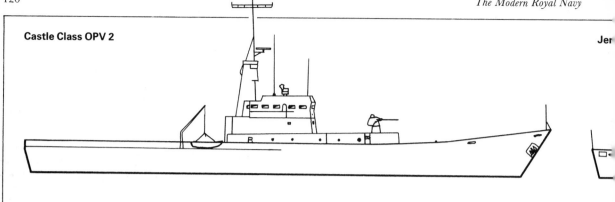

Castle Class OPV 2   Jer

Class *Castle*

Name *Leeds Castle*; **Pennant number** P258; **Flight deck code** LC; **Standard displacement** 1,450 tonnes; **Length** 81.0 m overall; **Beam** 11.0 m; **Draught** 3.0 m; **Propulsion** 2 × Ruston diesels (2,820 bhp) with controllable pitch propellor; **Range** Classified; **Speed** 20 knots (max); 15 knots (cruising); **Fuel** 180 tonnes; **Complement** 6 officers and 34 ratings; **Armament** 1 × 40 mm at present; 1 × 76 mm Oto Melara in due course; 4 × GPMG; **Sensors** Type 1006; MF/DF; Omega; CANE; **Small craft** 2 × Gemini (to be replaced by 2 × SR5M Seariders); **Builders** Hall Russell; **Completed** 1981; **Commissioned** 1982.

The *Castle* Class are a new class of £12 million specialist offshore patrol vessels (OPVs) which are due to take over the offshore element of the specialist role presently carried out by *Ton* Class warships. The order for the class was not confirmed until late 1979 and it is only thought two vessels—*Leeds Castle* and *Dumbarton Castle*—have been ordered to date, although a class of perhaps six is envisaged. Details are still somewhat unclear but without doubt the craft are superior to the earlier *Island* Class (*qv*), being capable of spending longer at sea and of operating a helicopter.

Although there is a flight deck there is no hangar accommodation, but helicopters of Sea King size have carried out trials aboard and the ship is equipped with stabilisers. It is no doubt envisaged that helicopters will use the ship as a platform from which to operate in the outer limits and where they can refuel or change aircrew. Sea Acceptance Trials in *Leeds Castle* are due to be completed in 1982 and it is thought, because there is a glide path indicator and horizon bar, night flying will be possible.

Name *Dumbarton Castle*; **Builders** Hall Russell; **Completed** 1982; **Commissioned** February 1982.

Class *Peacock*

Name Not yet allocated; **Pennant number** See below; **Standard displacement** Classified; **Length** 62.6 m overall; **Beam** 10.0 m; **Draught** 5.5 m; **Propulsion** 2 × APE Crossley Pielstick 18 diesels; **Range** 2,500 nm; **Speed** 25 knots; **Complement** 6 officers and 36 ratings; **Armament** 1 × 76 mm; 4 × GPMG; **Sensors** 1006; see text; **Small craft** 2 × SR5M Searider; **Builders** Hall Russell.

Of similar design and from the same shipyard as the *Castle*, Hall Russell at Aberdeen, is the *Peacock* Class for Hong Kong to replace the ageing *Tons*. Six units of this Class have been ordered and they will carry the 76 mm Oto Melara gun and Sea Archer fire control radar, but are also likely to be better equipped for more independent operations in Far Eastern waters; the Hong Kong Government is paying 75 per cent of the construction costs.

Besides the Type 1006 radar, the ships will be equipped with Kelvin Hughes MS45 Mk II Echo Sounder and a Racal-Decca radio/communication fit. The *Peacock* Class will be capable of RAS and

Leeds Castle, the first of the new OPV2s, seen off Rosyth (FOSNI).

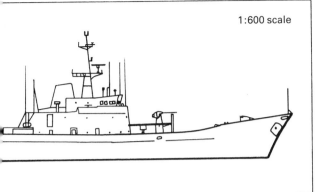

1:600 scale

Peacock *Class illustrated from artist's impression* (Hall Russell).

have two Avon Searider SR5Ms for boarding and independent patrol work. The lead ship has been given the pennant number P239 (following on from the naval hovercraft) according to the builder's artist's impression.

Class *Island*

Name *Jersey*; **Pennant number** P295; **Standard displacement** 925 tons; **Full displacement** 1,250 tons; **Length** 59.6 m overall; **Beam** 10.9 m; **Draught** 4.3 m; **Propulsion** 2 × diesels; **Range** 7,000 nm at 12 knots; **Speed** 17 knots; **Complement** 5 officers and 30 ratings; **Armament** 1 × 40 mm Bofors GP; 2 × GPMG; **Sensors** 1006; **Small craft** 2 × Gemini; **Builders** Hall Russell; **Launched** March 1976; **Completed** 1976; **Commissioned** October 15 1976.

The *Island* Class Offshore Patrol Vessels are designed to operate in the prtoection of the 270,000 square mile (699,300 sq km) economic zone in both the defence of natural gas/oil facilities and of the extensive fishing grounds. The shipyard of Hall Russell at Aberdeen was the main contractor using the earlier Scottish Department of Agriculture design as a basis. One of these *Island* Class ships, *Jura*, was operated by the RN from Rosyth in the mid-1970s with the old tug *Reward*.

The first of the class, *Jersey* was commissioned in 1976 and since then six others have been commissioned. Despite criticism that they are not large enough, fast enough or seaworthy enough for the role, the Class has been most successful in its task. Undoubtedly, the lack of a helicopter or flight deck facilities has been a great drawback to their effective operation. They are powered by conventional Rushton RK3 diesels which give good economy and produce 4,380 bhp through only one shaft. These ships all operate around the coast as part of the Fisheries' Protection Squadron and are nominally based at Rosyth.

Jersey, launched by HRH Princess Anne, is the seventh vessel to bear the name in the Fleet. On average one of these craft will board and inspect 150 vessels in any 12-month period. All ships carry a special computer-enhanced navigation system which allows the exact position of the ship and a potential law breaker to be recorded for possible use in Court later.

Name *Orkney*; **Pennant number** P299; **Complement** 4 officers and 31 ratings; **Launched** 1976; **Completed** 1977; **Commissioned** February 25 1977.

Orkney was the second *Island* Class OPV to be commissioned and in 1981 she underwent extensive refit at Rosyth to improve her communications and satellite navigation systems. Her stabilisers were also modified to make her a better platform for operating in the 12–200 nm EEZ. From 1977 to 1981, the ship steamed 85,000 miles and carried out 650 boardings and checks of fishing and other vessels. She was launched by Lady Troup, wife of the then FOSNI.

Name *Shetland*; **Pennant number** P298; **Complement** 5 officers and 29 ratings; **Laid down** 1975; **Launched** 1976; **Completed** 1977; **Commissioned** July 14 1977.

In 1981, *Shetland* was half leader of the Offshore Division, within the Fisheries' Protection Squadron, based at Rosyth. During her active service time, the ship has had the opportunity to go north to her namesake.

Name *Guernsey*; **Pennant number** P297; **Complement** As for *Jersey*; **Laid down** May 14 1976; **Launched** February 17 1977; **Completed** September 22 1977; **Commissioned** October 28 1977.

Launched at Aberdeen by Lady Martin, wife of the then Lieutenant Governor of the Island, *Guernsey* has been able to make several calls on the island during Fisheries' Protection work.

Name *Lindisfarne*; **Pennant number** P300; **Complement** As for *Jersey*; **Laid down** 1976; **Launched** June 1 1977; **Completed** 1978; **Commissioned** March 3 1978.

Launched by Mrs Patrick Duffy (wife of the then Secretary of State for the RN), *Lindisfarne* began operational patrols on April 10 1978. Later in the year she stood by a Soviet submarine in distress; she has also carried out over 175 boardings which have resulted in two prosecutions for illegal fishing.

Name *Anglesey*; **Pennant number** P277; **Complement** 4 officers and 29 ratings; **Laid down** 1977; **Launched** October 1978; **Completed** 1979; **Commissioned** June 1979.

On her first patrol in July 1979, *Anglesey* was operating in the South Western Approaches when the Fastnet Race was wrecked by bad weather and she was one of the first RN ships on the scene. Since then the ship has spent most of her time in the Atlantic/Channel approaches and Irish Sea.

Name *Alderney*; **Pennant number** P278; **Complement** As for *Jersey*; **Laid down** 1978; **Launched** 1978; **Completed** 1979; **Commissioned** 1979.

The last of the seven in the Class, *Alderney* was fitted with stabilisers in an attempt to cut down on motion in heavy sea conditions. Like her sistership, she is a member of the Offshore Division.

Class *Bird*
Name *Kingfisher*; **Pennant number** P260; **Full displacement** 190 tons; **Length** 36.6 m overall; **Beam** 7.0 m; **Draught** 2.0 m; **Propulsion** 2 × Paxman diesels; **Range** 2,000 nm at 14 knots; **Speed** 21 knots; **Complement** 4 officers and 19 ratings; **Armament** 1 × 40 mm Bofors GP Mk 9; 2 × GPMG; **Sensors** 1006; **Small craft** 2 × Gemini; **Builders** Richard Dunston; **Laid**

Above Alderney *at sea immediately after RN acceptance* (Hall Russell). **Left** Peterel *is reviewed by HM The Queen in 1977.* **Right** Beachampton *in the approaches to Hong Kong harbour.*

down 1974; **Launched** September 1974; **Completed** 1975; **Commissioned** October 8 1975.

Initially operating with the Inshore Division of the 'Fish Squadron', the *Kingfisher*, the 14th ship to bear the name in the RN, is now operational off Northern Ireland in a blockade and patrol role. The ship is a Lieutenant's command, costing over £1.1 million.

Name *Cygnet*; **Pennant number** P261; **Complement** 4 officers and 20 ratings; **Laid down** 1975; **Launched** October 1975; **Completed** July 1976; **Commissioned** July 8 1976.

The hull of *Cygnet* was constructed inverted at Thorne, South Yorkshire, and transported inverted to Hessle for final fitting out. The craft is the 16th to bear the name in the RN, and although originally with the Inshore Division of the Fisheries' Protection Squadron, she is now operational off Northern Ireland.

Name *Peterel*; **Pennant number** P262; **Complement** As for *Cygnet*; **Laid down** 1976; **Launched** 1976; **Completed** 1977; **Commissioned** February 7 1977.

This craft did not begin patrol duties but was transferred to the RNR as a training tender until a final decision on her future and that of the sister ship, *Sandpiper*, was reached. Both craft are now at Dartmouth as tenders to BRNC.

Name *Sandpiper*; **Pennant number** P263; **Complement** As for *Cygnet*; **Laid down** 1976; **Launched** 1976; **Completed** 1977; **Commissioned** September 16 1977.

Formerly an RNR Training Tender, *Sandpiper* is

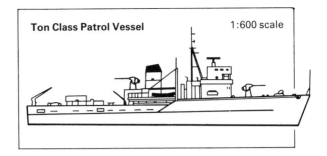

Ton Class Patrol Vessel — 1:600 scale

now one of the tenders to BRNC Dartmouth and is used for Cadet and Midshipman sea experience.

Class *Ton* (Patrol Vessel refits)
Name *Beachampton*; **Pennant number** P1007; **Standard displacement** 360 tons; **Full displacement** 440 tons; **Length** 46.3 m overall; **Beam** 8.5 m; **Draught** 2.5 m; **Propulsion** 2 × diesels; **Range** 2,300 nm at 13 knots; **Speed** 15 knots; **Complement** 5 officers and 25 ratings; **Armament** 2 × 40 mm Bofors GP; 2 × GPMG; **Sensors** 1006; **Small craft** 1 × Searider; 1 × Gemini; **Builders** Goole Shipbuilders; **Laid down** See *Ton* Class MCMVs; **Launched** Ditto; **Completed** Ditto; **Commissioned** 1953; **PV refit** 1969–70.

In 1969, five *Ton* Class minesweepers/patrol craft were transferred to Hong Kong to act in support of the Colony's Government and Marine Police. In 1971, the units were formed into the 6th Patrol Craft Squadron (they had been 6th MCM Squadron, Far East Fleet, until then). Of the original five, *Bossington*, *Hubberston* and *Maxton* were replaced by *Beachampton* and *Yarnton* and in 1972, *Wasperton*,

Wolverton and *Monkton* replaced *Kirkiston* and *Sheraton*. The new vessels had been refitted to suit them for patrol duties where they would be required to operate out into the South China Seas and carry LEP (Locally Enlisted Personnel).

Their main role over the last few years has been to assist in the capture of seaborne illegal immigrants (IIs), Vietnamese and Chinese boat people trying to land unnoticed, drug and currency smugglers and pirates. The latter have shown a resurgence in recent years and the new *Peacock* Class (*qv*) are needed to combat this menace especially. It would never be expected that the 6th Patrol Squadron would be in a position to operate with success for long against an invasion from the People's Republic of China, but luckily, today, relations between the Colony and its giant neighbour are as cordial as they have ever been. The ships have also been used for training Midshipmen and when operating against II or smugglers, even in the radar picket role (using Type 1006) they are under the control of the Royal Hong Kong Police (RHKP) Marine Wing.

Currently claimed to be the oldest ship in the RN, *Beachampton* has been at Hong Kong since 1981 and is due for replacement by a *Peacock* Class OPV in 1983. Like all HK-based *Tons*, she carries a mixed RN and LEP complement and has been most successful in apprehending IIs and smugglers.

Name *Yarnton*; **Pennant number** P1096; **Builders** Pickersgill; **Commissioned** 1956; **PV refit** 1969–70.

A former Persian Gulf-based minesweeper, *Yarnton* arrived in the Far East in 1971 with *Beachampton*. Like all the squadron, the ship has limited armour plating around the bridge area.

Name *Monkton*; **Pennant number** P1055; **Builders**

Herd and MacKenzie; **Commissioned** 1956; **PV refit** 1970–71.

Currently the half-leader of the Hong Kong Patrol Squadron, *Monkton* continues to provide support to the civil power of the Colony and will continue to do so until replaced by a *Peacock* Class OPV in 1982/3.

Name *Wasperton*; **Pennant number** P1089; **Builders** Samuel White; **Commissioned** 1956; **PV refit** 1970–71.

A former UK-based minehunter, *Wasperton* is now a stalwart member of the HK Patrol Squadron, and currently its leader.

Name *Wolverton*; **Pennant number** P1093; **Builders** Montrose; **Commissioned** 1957; **PV refit** 1971.

Another of the UK-based minehunters which joined the HK Squadron in 1972, *Wolverton* has been half-leader in her time at the Colony.

Survey craft

These ships fall into three categories: Ocean Survey Ships; Coastal Survey Ships; and Inshore Survey Craft. Without doubt, they carry out one of the most important peacetime naval tasks which also benefits the commercial shipping fleets of the world.

Class *Hecla*
Name *Hecla*; **Pennant number** A133; **Flight deck code** HL; **Standard displacement** 1,915 tons; **Full displacement** 2,733 tons; **Length** 79.3 m overall; **Beam** 15.0 m; **Draught** 4.7 m; **Propulsion** 3 + 1 diesel-electric; **Range** 12,000 nm at 11 knots; **Speed** 14 knots; **Complement** 12 officers and 105 ratings; **Armament** None; **Sensors** Navigation radars and

Monkton lying off one of the many islands of Hong Kong.

Hecla at the Silver Jubilee Review.

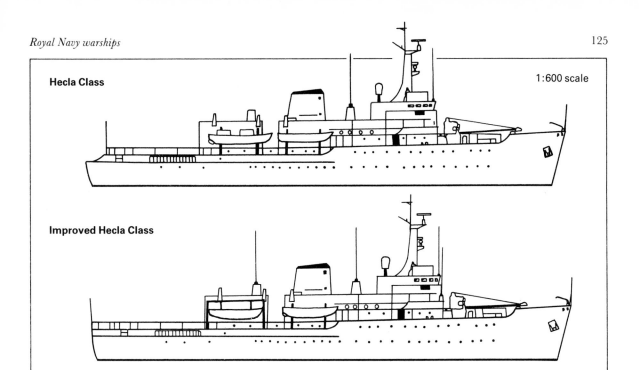

Hecla Class

1:600 scale

Improved Hecla Class

hydrographic equipment (see below); **Aircraft** 1 × Wasp HAS 1; **Small craft** 2 × 9.5 m Survey Craft; 1 × launch; **Vehicles** 1 × ⅓-ton Land Rover; **Builders** Yarrow; **Launched** 1964; **Completed** 1965; **Commissioned** September 9 1965.

This very successful Class of three plus one improved unit, have what are basically merchant hulls and therefore good stability, so important when charting and surveying the ocean bottom. As their name suggests, the Ocean Survey Ships operate in deep water locations and several deployments have been made in connection with the SSBNs and oceanographical work in the North Atlantic and elsewhere. The ability to operate a Westland Wasp HAS 1 helicopter is most important to the flexible use of these craft.

The average cost of each vessel in 1965–6 was £1.25 million, much of which was involved in fitting out the survey gear, ice protection, vehicle and helicopter provision, air conditioning and accommodation. The ships are powered by diesel-electric Paxman Ventura turbocharged diesels (3,840 bhp) and an electric motor (2,000 hp), which can be controlled directly from the bridge in order that accurate charting can be carried out. The single shaft is augmented by a bow thruster for manoeuvring. *Herald*, the improved *Hecla* Class, has additional gear for oceanographic work and was fitted with Hydroplot from building.

The usual specialist equipment fitted includes: Marconi Elliot Hydroplot, Hi-fix, Satellite Navigation, Decca Pulse 8, Decca Navigator Main-Chain, La-Coste Romberg Gravimeter and a Baringer Magnemeter. Coring equipment is also available.

The first of the Class, *Hecla* has seen service in a variety of locations, including the Gulf and the North Sea. Today, much of the survey work for the outer reaches of the UK EEZ has been carried out by the *Hecla* Class. In 1982, she acted as a hospital ship with the Falklands Task Force, ferrying wounded to Montevideo.

Name *Hecate*; **Pennant number** A137; **Flight deck code** HT; **Builders** Yarrow; **Launched** March 31 1965; **Completed** 1965; **Commissioned** December 20 1965.

The sixth ship to bear the name in the RN, *Hecate* was launched by Lady Yarrow. She has operated in the Celtic Sea (between the Irish Sea and Bristol Channel), and the Mediterranean, as well as the West Indies and off the North American coast. She also acted as a radar picket off Port Stanley.

Name *Hydra*; **Pennant number** A144; **Flight deck code** HD; **Full displacement** 2,844 tons; **Builders** Yarrow; **Launched** 1965; **Completed** 1966; **Commissioned** 5 May 5 1966.

The last of the Yarrow-built Ocean Survey Ships,

Herald *acting as sea ambulance for the Falklands Task Force.*

Hydra, like her sister ships, is a Commander's command, with almost all the deck officers being qualified surveyors. She also acted as a hospital ship in support of the Falklands operation.

Class *Improved Hecla*

Name *Herald;* **Pennant number** A138; **Flight deck code** HE; **Standard displacement** 2,000 tons; **Full displacement** 2,945 tons; **Draught** 5.0 m; **Complement** 12 officers and 106 ratings; **Builders** Robb Caledon; **Launched** October 4 1973; **Completed** October 31 1974; **Commissioned** November 22 1974.

The newest of the four RN Ocean Survey ships, *Herald* is the flagship of the Hydrographer to the Navy, and it was Mrs Hall, the wife of the then Hydrographer, who launched *Herald* at Leith in 1973. She is the fifth ship to bear the name and is equipped to a higher standard than her three half-sisters. The ship has been deployed to the Shetland-Orkney gap, the Mediterranean and locations further afield, including the South Atlantic as a hospital vessel.

Class *Bulldog*

Name *Bulldog;* **Pennant number** A317; **Standard displacement** 800 tons; **Full displacement** 1,088 tons; **Length** 60.1 m overall; **Beam** 11.4 m; **Draught** 3.6 m; **Propulsion** 4 × diesels; **Range** 4,000 nm at 12 knots; **Speed** 15 knots; **Complement** 4 officers and 34 ratings; **Armament** None (but fitted for 2 × 20 mm); **Sensors** Navigation radar and hydrographic equipment (see

below/above); **Small craft** 1 × Survey Craft (called *Wake*); 1 × launch; **Builders** Brooke Marine; **Commissioned** March 21 1968.

The coastal variants of the *Hecla* Class, yet not equipped for helicopters, the *Bulldog* Class has borne the brunt of surveying for the North Sea oil exploration and the safety channels for bulk oil carriers and rigs. In addition, the Class has operated in the Caribbean and Gulf waters.

Again using a merchant hull, the ships are powered by four Lister Blackstone 8-cylinder diesel engines each developing 660 bhp, driving two variable pitch propellors through reduction gearing. The service cruising speed is 15 knots and the propellor pitch and engine revolutions are controlled from the bridge (or the engine room). The ships are fitted with twin rudders and autopilot. The hull is designed for all-weather operation, being all-welded construction with a bulbous underwater bow and the high flared forecastle of a good seakeeper. A passive stabiliser system (anti-rolling tanks) is fitted to provide a stable platform for delicate hydrographical work.

The ships are equipped with echo sounders, fisherman's sonar (to search for and locate wrecks and underwater rock pinnacles—which could take the bottom out of an oil tanker), Hi-Fix (portable electronic surveying equipment to determine position), Decca radar with precision ranging attachment, and the two 9.5 m survey boats have echo sounding equipment.

The *Bulldog* Class have been designed to conduct hydrographic surveys throughout the world, they can make independent ocean passages and have limited capacity for scientific oceanographic work. They usually operate in pairs at home and abroad, although in the last few years much of their work has been concentrated on the UK EEZ.

The quarters of the crew are well designed and generally better than found in 'GreyFunnel Line' ships, and is especially conditioned for prolonged operations in the tropics, such as the Indian Ocean and the coast of Oman. Other ship facilities include a sick bay, self-service laundry and a drying room.

Bulldog normally works with *Beagle* and together they have operated off West Africa, in the Gulf and Indian Ocean. *Bulldog* is the eighth ship to bear the name and she was the first ship ever to be fitted with the highly sophisticated sector scanning sonar called Hydrosearch.

Name *Beagle*; **Pennant number** A319; **Complement** 6 officers and 40 ratings; **Small craft** 2 × Survey Craft (named *Darwin* and *Fitzroy*); **Builders** Brooke Marine; **Commissioned** May 9 1968.

The ninth ship to bear the name, *Beagle* is usually to be found in partnership with *Bulldog*. She has been deployed to various exotic locations such as the Maldives, the Seychelles, the Gulf and the west coast of Scotland.

Name *Fox*; **Pennant number** A320; **Complement** As for *Bulldog*; **Builders** Brooke Marine; **Commissioned** July 11 1968.

Usually in partnership with *Fawn*, *Fox* has been concentrating on 'western' hemisphere operations, including the Irish and North Seas.

Name *Fawn*; **Pennant Number** A325; **Complement** 5 officers and 37 ratings; **Small craft** 1 × Survey Craft; 1 × launch; **Launched** February

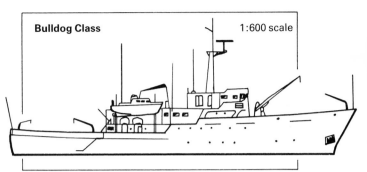

Bulldog Class   1:600 scale

1968; **Completed** September 10 1968; **Builders** Brooke Marine; **Commissioned** October 1968.

Fawn and *Fox* are usually to be found operating together in the western hemisphere, either around the UK coast or in the West Indies.

Class *E*

Name *Echo*; **Pennant number** A70; **Standard displacement** 120 tons; **Full displacement** 160 tons; **Length** 32.6 m; **Beam** 7.0 m; **Draught** 2.1 m; **Propulsion** 2 × diesels; **Range** 4,500 nm at 12 knots; **Speed** 14 knots; **Complement** 2 officers and 16 ratings; **Armament** None; **Sensors** 1006; echo sounders; Hi-Fix; **Small craft** Survey Craft; **Builders** White; **Commissioned** September 12 1958.

The Inshore Survey Squadron is made up of three *E* Class craft which are ideal for inshore work, especially in the Thames Estuary or the approaches to the East Anglian ports. The Dover Straits and the North Sea are also in their lists of deployments. They generally operate with two officers and 16 ratings, and there is a small survey launch available for close work or independent surveying.

Bulldog *at the Silver Jubilee Review.*

E-Class *inshore survey vessel provides a Royal escort* (RN).

The ships are powered by two Paxman diesels with contra-propellors and two shafts. They have a fuel capacity of 15 tons. The Class has been responsible for sweeping the Channel for wrecks of World War 2 ships which could prove a hazard to modern deep draught carriers and tankers.

Name *Enterprise;* **Pennant number** A71; **Builders** Blackmore; **Commissioned** 1959.

Name *Egeria*; **Pennant number** A72; **Builders** Weatherhead; **Commissioned** 1959.

Class *Ham*
Name *Woodlark*; **Pennant number** M2780; **Builders** White; **Commissioned** 1958 (as *Yaxham*); **Converted** Circa 1968; **Other details** See *Ham* Class MCMVs.

In addition to the *E* class, there are the two former *Ham* Class inshore minesweepers which have been converted for survey work: *Woodlark* (for the western coast) and *Waterwitch* (now a University tender). They are basically similar to the *E*s except in power and endurance, but the difference is not exceptional.

The need for more survey vessels as all types has at last been recognised by the Government and it is possible that new building will be announced in 1982. Some idea of the hectic pace of survey operations can be seen from the following table reproduced from an official list prepared for the "Chartered Surveyor" journal by the RN Surveying Service.

Ocean Survey Ships	Coastal Survey Vessels	Inshore Survey Craft
1976		
Shetlands	Dover Straits	Thames Estuary
Scotland North Coast	England East Coast	Dover Straits
Northern North Sea	English Channel	English Channel
Celtic Sea	Irish Sea	England East Coast
North Cornish Coast	Northern North Sea	Scotland East Coast
England South Coast	Wales West Coast	Firth of Forth
Scotland West Coast	England South Coast	Firth of Clyde
North West Approaches to North Channel	St George's Channel	Scotland West Coast
	Trinidad	Wales West Coast
Wales West Coast	Grenada	St George's Channel
Mediterranean	Anegada Passage-Anguilla	England South Coast
Persian Gulf	Sombrero Islands St Kitts	

Royal Yacht

Class *Britannia*
Name *Britannia*; **Pennant number** A00 (not worn); **Standard displacement** 3,990 tons; **Full displacement** 4,961 tons; **Length** 115.9 m overall; **Beam** 16.8 m; **Draught** 5.2 m; **Propulsion** Single reduction-geared steam turbines with 2 shafts and 2 boilers rated at 12,000 shp; **Range** 2,800 nm at 20 knots; **Speed** 21 knots; **Complement** 21 officers and 256 ratings; **Sensors** Navigation radar; HF/DF; MF/DF; **Small craft** 6 × launches (including special barge); **Builders** John Brown; **Laid down** June 16 1952; **Launched** April 16 1953; **Completed** January 1954; **Commissioned** January 14 1954.

HMY *Britannia* was laid down in July 1952 and launched on April 16 1953, but not completed until January 14 1954 when she was commissioned into the RN. She is based at *Excellent*, Portsmouth, and has a dual Royal Yacht-Hospital Ship role. Now one of the oldest ships in the RN, she is widely travelled and is crewed by specially selected volunteers who wear a special rig—soft shoes and navy blue (instead of black) socks. The 'Yachtsmen', as they are called, consider themselves to be an élite in an élite. *Britannia* is the only ship in the RN to be commanded by a Rear Admiral, the Flag Officer Royal Yachts.

The ship's turbines give a range, depending on speed and oil bunkage (normally 330 tons, but up to 510 tons can be carried in special tanks), of 2,800 nm at 20 knots; 3,200 nm at 18 knots; or 3,675 nm at 14 knots. The Royal Yacht is able to transit most seaways in the world, including the Suez Canal in 1981 with the honeymooning Prince and Princess of Wales. Her masts, which usually wear flags at all times, are specially hinged to allow passage under particularly low bridges. Unlike other naval vessels, *Britannia* wears a jack when under way, as do any escorting warships.

The ship is immaculate in appearance, being navy blue hulled with white upperworks and a buff funnel. The line beneath the gunwhale is gold leaf and the royal crest is borne on the stem. Despite the anti-Royalist 'knockers', the Royal Yacht is a special symbol of the nation and in war would fulfil an important role.

Fleet Tenders

The 1981 Defence White Paper confirms that three Fleet Tenders will enter service with the RN to take over from the former *Ham* Class Inshore Minesweepers already listed. They are *Manley* (commissioned March 2 1982), *Mentor* and *Millbrook*.

Submarine Tender Tug

Wakeful (see Chapter 8 for further details) was purchased from Swedish sources in 1974 for £6,000 to work in the Clyde submarine area as a tender, tug and target ship. Although British-built at Selby, North Yorkshire, *Wakeful* (then named *Herakles*, later *Dan*) was required to undergo a £1.6 million refit at Chatham two years after purchase. The 900-ton vessel was then used for Fisheries Protection duties until the commissioning of enough *Island* Class OPVs when she transferred to the Clyde. She is an ice breaker and retains a 50-ton bollard pull, but is often to be found shadowing Soviet warships. Without doubt she is an expensive warship to keep in service.

Diving Support Ships

Name *Seaforth Clansman*; **Standard displacement** 1,180 tons; **Full displacement** 1,977 tons; **Length** 78.6 m; **Beam** 14.1 m; **Draught** 5,0 m; **Propulsion**; 4 × diesels (1,830 bhp); 2 × contra-propellors and bow thruster; **Speed** 13 knots; **Armament** None; **Sensors** Commercial radar; **Other details** Unavailable.

With the disposal of *Reclaim*, the RN took a charter on a *Seaforth* Class diving support ship or Seabed Operations Ship. Manned by the RFA and a naval diving party, *Seaforth Clansman* (no pennant number) will remain in service until the commissioning of *Challenger* in late 1982/early 1983. Equipped with the latest technology in diving, firefighting and pollution control *Clansman* is of the type used in support of work in the North Sea and is owned by Seaforth Maritime of Aberdeen.

Her replacement, *Challenger* was ordered in October 1979 from Scotts of Greenock and launched in 1981. It is reported that she will be RFA-manned and wear the pennant number K07. She is designed to carry full saturation diving equipment, including a bell, decompression chamber and a special well for recovering objects on the seabed for salvage. Estimated specification is: **Displacement** 6,400 tons; **Length** 134.0 m; **Beam** 18.0 m; **Draught**

Above The new Fleet Tender Manley *was commissioned on March 2 1982; she will be joined by* Mentor *and* Millbrook *during 1982/3* (SPRO Plymouth).

Right Britannia, *the Royal Yacht and wartime Hospital Ship with HM The Queen and members of the Royal Family embarked* (RN).

5.0 m; **Speed** 15 knots; **Complement** 185 officers and men (including diving party).

It is reported that many RN divers would prefer to continue using the *Seaforth* Class which they say has many advantages and is cheaper; the cost savings being used to provide new equipment and carry out more research.

Warship disposals 1981–4

As a result of the 1981 Defence Review and subsequent statements by the Ministry of Defence (Navy), the RN is being forced to dispose of many of the older warships and some of its auxiliaries. This reduction has been caused by manning problems and a fundamental change of emphasis in Government planning by way of a reduction in the surface fleet, especially those units committed to NATO.

Blake (C99)	Helicopter cruiser (CCH)
Bulwark (R08)	Anti-submarine carrier (CVS/LPH)
Triumph (A108)	Heavy fleet maintenance ship
Lincoln (F99)	*Salisbury* Class frigate
Lynx (F27)	*Leopard* Class frigate
Ashanti (F117)	*Tribal* Class frigate
Gurhka (F122)	*Tribal* Class frigate
Mohawk (F125)	*Tribal* Class frigate
Nubian F131)*	*Tribal* Class frigate
Tartar (F133)	*Tribal* Class frigate
Zulu (F124)	*Tribal* Class frigate
Eskimo (F119)*	*Tribal* Class frigate
Glasserton (M1141)*	*Ton* Class MCMV
Isis (M2010)	Inshore MCMV/tender
Tenacity (P276)	Fast Patrol Boat (FPB)
Bacchus (A404)	Stores carrier

* Warships approved for scrapping.

Eddyfirth (A261)	Coastal tanker
Bacchante (F69)	*Leander* Class frigate (FF)
Naiad (F39)	*Leander* Class frigate (FF)
Dido (F104)	*Leander* Class frigate (FF)
Hermes (R12)	Anti-submarine carrier (CVS)
Norfolk (D21)	*County* Class destroyer (DLG)
Glamorgan (D19)	*County* Class destroyer (DLG)
Rhyl (F129)	*Rothesay* Class frigate (FF)
Berwick (F115)	*Rothesay* Class frigate (FF)
Londonderry (F108)	*Rothesay* Class trials ship
Torquay (F43)	*Whitby* Class trials ship
Tidepool (A76)	*Tide* Class fleet tanker
Tidespring (A75)	*Tide* Class fleet tanker
Stromness (A344)	*Ness* Class support ship

The exact dates of the withdrawals from the active list of the above-mentioned warships have yet to be announced but it is envisaged that *Hermes* will be decommissioned when *Ark Royal* is ready to join the Fleet. The two LPDs which have been used to deploy RM Commandoes and their supporting helicopters will be phased out; it is thought that *Intrepid* will go in 1985 and *Fearless* will follow within 18 months to two years.

Endurance, the RN's only vessel equipped for work in the Antarctic, was due for disposal after her 1981–2 patrol season although there is a vigorous campaign being run by former Hydrographer to the Navy, Rear Admiral Sir Edmund 'Egg' Irving and former explorer Sir Vivian Fuchs. The *Endurance* not only looks after British interests in the South Atlantic but also provides valuable surveying and SAR facilities to the whole world. As yet there is no announced replacement and she will remain in service until possibly 1983–4 at least.

By 1985, four more RFAs will be withdrawn from service and although this is only reasonable when the surface fleet is being cut down, the fact remains that many naval officers would argue that there are

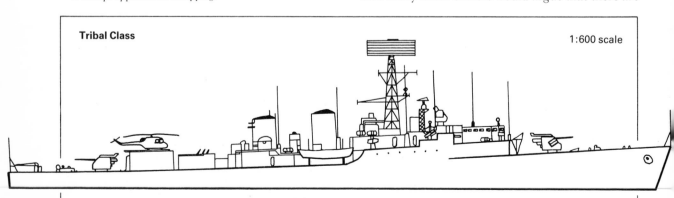

Tribal Class   1:600 scale

not enough in service now, especially with more and more emphasis being placed on Out of Area Deployments.

Further reductions will probably include the rest of the *Rothesay* Class FFs and several of the older *Leanders*. Various tugs and other RMAS vessels will also go but at least in this area of the RN there are more cost-effective craft on their way into service.

The Reserve

In recent years, the RN has been more short of manpower afloat than at almost any other time since the end of World War 2. The Reserve Ships Unit (RSU) provides a nucleus which could be made available to the Operational Fleet at short notice (weeks rather than days though). As these warships may be required at very short notice, the RSU has to provide for their maintenance to keep their first class condition. It is usual for warships entering the Reserve to be refitted and put through a short trials programme. The size of the warship denotes the method of preservation for the equipment:

Preservation by Operation PbyO is where the majority of the equipment and the ship's machinery is kept in full working order and operated regularly by the men of RSU. Occasionally, the warships are taken to sea for short periods.

Massive dehumidification Where the ship's larger openings are sealed to isolate the interior from the weather and the smaller ones treated in a similar way. Inside the atmosphere is kept dry to prevent deterioration by active corrosion. The machinery is preserved but unlike PbyO, it is not operated whilst the ship is in Reserve.

The worth of these operations was demonstrated in 1978 when *Bulwark* emerged from PbyO in very near perfect order.

The older ships of the Reserve are kept at Portsmouth and Plymouth, with former Chatham ships moving to the former in the near future. In recent years, several have been reactivated for accommodation duties.

RSU consists of a small Headquarters Group, a supply support group and each warship in reserve has a small maintenance crew. Large ships have tended to have been laid up at Portsmouth over the years and this role is thought to remain despite the down grading of the Dockyard in 1985.

The Standby Squadron

Ships of this squadron have been formed into a unit, known by their Aladin's lamp badge, which until 1984 will be based at Chatham and will then move to Portsmouth Harbour where many of the Reserve Fleet are at present. Some warships remain with the Standby Squadron from when they are decommissioned until they are approved for scrap, while others do on occasions return to the Fleet. All are maintained by maintenance personnel in PbyO and they are kept fully stored for immediate duty. Several were due to sail for duty off Iceland in 1976 and for this had wooden bows fitted; the Cod War was settled before they could be deployed.

In 1977, *Lynx* was brought forward for the Silver Jubilee Review at Spithead as a test for the system and *Hardy* (now an Accommodation Ship at Portsmouth) was brought forward from the Reserve twice in 1976–8 to replace warships in the fleet which had sudden need of deep maintenance. The Captain Fleet Maintenance is also Captain Standby Squadron.

In August 1981 the following ships were attached to the Squadron: *Falmouth*; *Lynx*; *Lincoln*; *Zulu*; *Nubian*; *Gurkha*; *Eskimo*; *Tartar*; *Berwick* and *Juno* (later rejoined the fleet as a Trials Ship).

Accommodation vessels

Over the years, a number of former warships have been employed in harbour training and accommodation roles and these are noted below as applicable today:

Rame Head (A134)	Accommodation Ship	Portsmouth
Berry Head (A191)	Accommodation Ship	Plymouth
Salisbury (F32)	Training Ship	Plymouth
Dundas (F48)	Accommodation Ship	Portsmouth
Hardy (F54)	Accommodation Ship	Portsmouth
Eastbourne (F73)	Training Ship	Rosyth
Duncan (F80)	Training Ship	Rosyth
Russell (F97)	Training Ship	Portsmouth
Ashanti (F117)	Training Ship	Portsmouth
Finwhale (S05)	Training Ship	Gosport
Kent (D12)	Training Ship	*Excellent*

All the above are non-seagoing vessels.

The former Harbour Training Ship *Diamond*, based at Priddy's Hard in Portsmouth Harbour to support *Sultan*, was sold for scrap in October 1981, arriving at the breaker's yard in Kent in November of that year.

The Fleet Air Arm

The history of British naval aviation can be traced to the origins of the Royal Naval Air Service (RNAS), which was formed on July 1 1914. When the Royal Air Force (RAF) was created from an amalgamation of the Royal Flying Corps (RFC) and the RNAS on April 1 1918, naval aviation went into the doldrums, despite the commissioning of the world's first flat-top aircraft carrier later the same year. In 1924, the Fleet Air Arm (FAA) was formed as a branch of the RAF but, by 1937, the Government of the day 'saw the light' and the FAA was passed over to RN control for training, organisation and equipment; tasking was already in naval hands. The Admiralty then dropped the term Fleet Air Arm throughout the wartime period and so between 1937 and 1953 (when the title was re-adopted), the service became known as the 'Air Branch' of the Royal Navy, later changed to 'Naval Aviation'.

Organisation

Today, the FAA consists of 17 operational front line squadrons and seven second-line support units, as well as a few specialist flights which are parented by other units but do retain some autonomy. The Fleet Air Arm is known as the Naval Air Command to the Admiralty, and as such has its own Flag Officer (FONAC) who has Commander-in-Chief status in a similar way to that of an Area Flag Officer.

FONAC has control over five Royal Naval Air Stations (RNASs) plus the Naval Aircraft Repair Organisation (NARO) with facilities at Royal Naval Aircraft Yard (RNAY) Fleetlands and the Royal Naval Aircraft Workshops (RNAW) Perth. There is also an input to the RAF's Maintenance Unit at Kemble for Hunters and Canberras and to RNAY Wroughton (a joint Service establishment) for helicopter storage. FONAC is tasked with keeping the RNASs functioning effectively and in this respect he reports to CINCNAVHOME. Additionally, he is responsible to CINCFLEET for providing aircraft and trained aircrews for the Fleet. Once an aircraft

leaves an RNAS to join a warship or an RFA, it becomes the responsibility of FOF3 (Fleet Aviation Authority for CINCFLEET) or of FOF1 and 2 in the case of small ship's flights; the latter still report to FOF3 for some tasking. There is also an interchange of ideas with DGA(N) and DNAW because FONAC is not charged with any direct responsibility for future policy.

FONAC flies his flag at a purpose-built complex, known as FONAC HQ, to the north of RNAS Yeovilton, being the Headquarters of Naval Air Command. To assist administration, the Captain of *Heron* (Yeovilton's naval name) is the Flag Captain to FONAC.

Air squadrons

Since 1933, the Fleet Air Arm has been divided for administrative and operational reasons into air squadrons which, whether afloat or ashore, operate in much the same way as a battalion of troops or a small company in industry. Every squadron is commanded by a Lieutenant Commander and has various other appointments including, as applicable, Senior Pilot, Senior Observer (SOBS), Air Warfare Officer, Air Engineering Officer (AEO) and Training Officer. Each squadron CO reports to the Commander (Air) of the parent station or ship and thus to Staff Air Operations officers and FONAC.

Each squadron is in commission in the same way as a ship is, and each is specifically charged by FONAC with tasks such as Air Commando, Training and Fleet Support. At sea, a squadron has a complicated reporting structure which includes FONAC, FOF3 and CINCFLEET, besides the Captain of the warship or RFA concerned. Today, even more than in the rapid progress which has been made since the end of World War 2, the RN is dependent on the Fleet Air Arm and its air squadrons for support, and as an extension of a warship's weapon systems, very often to over the

The FAA's Sea Harrier units—899 (mailed fist); 800 (gold tridents and crossed swords on red); 801 (blue winged trident). The aircraft are based at Yeovilton (tail code VL) but are deployed to carriers: 800 to Hermes *(H) and 801 to* Invincible *(N) (BAe).*

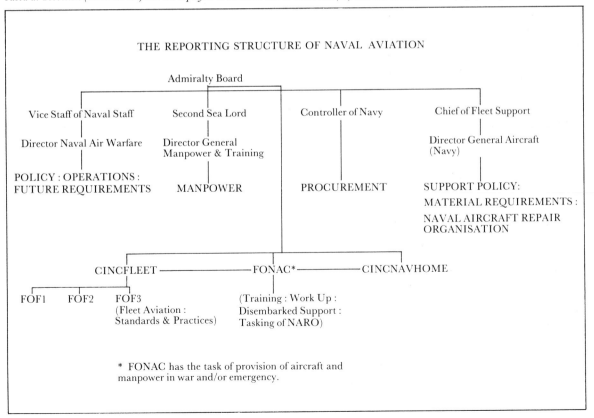

THE REPORTING STRUCTURE OF NAVAL AVIATION

Admiralty Board

Vice Staff of Naval Staff	Second Sea Lord	Controller of Navy	Chief of Fleet Support
Director Naval Air Warfare	Director General Manpower & Training		Director General Aircraft (Navy)
POLICY : OPERATIONS : FUTURE REQUIREMENTS	MANPOWER	PROCUREMENT	SUPPORT POLICY: MATERIAL REQUIREMENTS : NAVAL AIRCRAFT REPAIR ORGANISATION

CINCFLEET ————— FONAC* ————— CINCNAVHOME

FOF1   FOF2   FOF3
(Fleet Aviation :
Standards & Practices)

(Training : Work Up :
Disembarked Support :
Tasking of NARO)

* FONAC has the task of provision of aircraft and manpower in war and/or emergency.

horizon where the threat can be countered effectively.

In August 1982, the following units were in commission:

Sqdn	Aircraft	Primary role
800	Sea Harrier	Combat Air Defence
801	Sea Harrier	Combat Air Defence
809	Sea Harrier	Combat Air Defence
810	Sea King	ASW training
814	Sea King	Anti-Submarine Warfare
815	Lynx	ASW/ASVW (small ships)
819	Sea King	ASW (shore-based)
820	Sea King	Anti-Submarine Warfare
824	Sea King	Anti-Submarine Warfare
825	Sea King	Air Commando Logistics
826	Sea King	Anti-Submarine Warfare
829	Wasp	ASW and training
845	Wessex	Air Commando Assault
846	Sea King	Air Commando Assault
847	Wessex	Air Commando Logistics
848	Wessex	Air Commando Assault
899	Sea Harrier	Operational training
702	Lynx	Operational training
705	Gazelle	Basic training
706	Sea King	ASW training
737	Wessex	ASW training and DLGs
750	Jetstream	Observer training
771	Wessex	SAR training and operations
772	Wessex	Fleet Requirements and SAR

There are also a number of miscellaneous units without which the RN could not function and these are dealt with in the following paragraphs. It will be seen that the main emphasis is on ASW and this reflects the current thinking behind the Government's Defence Strategy of the United Kingdom. Today, however, fewer squadrons are afloat than possibly ever before, but the range of warships and RFAs is steadily increasing so that by 1985 most warships and auxiliaries will be air-capable.

Squadrons in the 800 series are deemed to be front-line operational units and those in the 700 series are second-line training units, whilst those in 1800 series (mentioned later) are RNR (Air Branch) units without individual aircraft of their own. Naturally, as with every system, this ruling is not hard and fast because, for example, 737 has deployed Wessex HAS 3s to *County* Class DLGs for operational duties for well over a decade, and 815 has a quite large HQ element at Portland for Advanced Operational training of Lynx crews.

800 Squadron This is the premier FAA squadron

which traces its history to the disbandment of 402 and 404 Flights in May 1933 to make the first FAA squadron. Since then the unit has had some notable 'firsts', including the pioneering of the first jets and the first high-altitude interceptors for the RN.

In April 1980, the squadron re-commissioned at Yeovilton with the latest in naval air warfare technology in the shape of the British Aerospace Sea Harrier FRS 1 which it then took to *Invincible* for Sea Acceptance Trials (SATS) in the autumn of that year. When not ashore at Yeovilton, 800's home is the newly refitted aircraft carrier *Hermes* and, during the latter part of 1981, both the ship and the squadron had a very successful shake-down in the Atlantic. The primary task of 800 NAS can best be described as Combat Air Defence of the Fleet— organic air power—as well as reconnaissance, limited ASW sonobuoy sowing, ground attack and surface strike against hostile warships. It is most probable that the squadron will be deployed to *Ark Royal* in 1984/5 when *Hermes* is phased out of service; this role would have originally gone to 802 whose re-formation has been cancelled in the 1981 Defence Review. Squadron battle honours are: Norway 1940–44; Mediterranean 1940–41; Spartivento 1940; Malta Convoys 1941–42; *Bismarck* 1941; Diego Suarez 1942; North Africa 1942; South France 1944; Aegean 1944; Burma 1945; Korea 1950 and Suez 1956.

801 Squadron The second operational Sea Harrier unit commissioned in February 1981 and is based at Yeovilton too. It also traces its history back to 1933 and was equally as active during World War 2, winning five battle honours: Norway 1940–44; Dunkirk 1940; Malta Convoys 1942; North Africa 1942–43 and Japan 1945. In addition, another honour was won for Korea 1952–53.

During 1981 the squadron was deployed in its floating home, *Invincible*, thus becoming the first fully worked-up Sea Harrier unit, as well as carrying out Blue Fox radar trials. The squadron also pioneered the use of the training ski-jump at Yeovilton and was the most successful air defence unit in the Falklands conflict.

Left *814 Sea King during the squadron's deployment to* Hermes *during the latter's time as a Commando/ASW carrier.*

Right *815—flying Lynx helicopters from Yeovilton and embarked flights—* Antelope *(321) and* Ambuscade *(323).*

Below right *819—the Scottish Sea King unit—celebrates the first Sea King with 4,000 hours' flying time: illustrates aircrew gear but champagne glasses are non-standard (819 NAS).*

809 Squadron The operational necessities of the Falklands Operation led to the formation of a fourth Sea Harrier FRS 1 unit in April 1982. Although previous information had led to the conclusion that 802 Squadron would be re-formed to fly the type from *Illustrious*, the 1981 Defence Review cast a shadow on this, as did the later cancelled move to sell *Invincible* to the Royal Australian Navy.

The aircraft transferred to the unit were originally painted in South Atlantic Air Defence Grey and transported south in the ill-fated container ship *Atlantic Conveyor* which was sunk on May 25 1982. The aircraft had, however, already been re-deployed to the carrier element of the Falklands Task Group—*Hermes* and *Invincible*.

Like the other Sea Harrier units, 809 is home-based at Yeovilton and is destined to join *Illustrious* when this ship reaches operational readiness.

810 Squadron This unit formed in December 1982 to augment the advanced operational flying training of ASW aircrew. Based alongside 706 Squadron at Culdrose, 810 has taken over the latter's Sea King HAS 5 helicopters to provide a concentrated training commitment on this advanced model, whilst 706 continues pilot and observer systems training sorties with the HAS 2.

Falklands commitments at the time of writing have precluded any detailed information on this unit being made available.

814 Squadron One of the illustrious 'Tiger Squadrons', 814 has had a long association with anti-submarine helicopters. It is now equipped with the Westland Sea King HAS 2 and has been trials unit for the new Jezebel passive sonar gear which is being introduced into the FAA's other Sea King squadrons in due course. During the last few years, the squadron has been afloat in *Hermes* (before modernisation) and the now defunct *Bulwark*, but today the unit provides additional aircraft and personnel for other embarked or shore-based units as required. It also takes its turn in the SAR roster at Culdrose where the unit is based. It usually has nine or ten aircraft on strength.

815 Squadron The newest helicopter unit in the FAA, 815 NAS is the operational parent unit for the Westland Lynx HAS 2 helicopter in small ships' flights and for operational training. It was formed at Yeovilton in January 1981 and moved to Portland during July 1982 so as to be nearer the Portland Sea Training Areas and the warships which it serves. The primary role is to form, train and support Lynx flights embarked in *Amazon*, *Leander*, *Broadsword* and *Sheffield* Class warships. The squadron deals with the engineering problems and training and maintains a pool of four Lynx for continuous training tasks; the squadron also parents 29JSTU (Joint Services Trials Unit) which is developing Lynx systems and operations. New small ships' flights continue to be formed monthly as the aircraft are delivered by Westland from nearby Yeovil; 51 flights are due to be formed in due course, but there are currently only half that number.

815 NAS, like most naval air squadrons, has a

very colourful past which includes the raid on Taranto in November 1940. The squadron insignia is the harp, based on the design of a famous Irish brewery's trade mark.

819 Squadron The squadron started life on January 14 1940 flying Swordfish aircraft from southern England and soon was at sea and in action, until 1945. In 1972, the unit re-formed again with Sea King helicopters at *Seahawk*, before moving north to *Gannet*, at Prestwick Airport on the Scottish west coast. It has remained here ever since and operates in a variety of roles, being the FAA's only permanent flying presence in Scotland. The primary role is ASW (the proximity of the Clyde submarine complex must have had something to do with the basing of the unit) but 819 is also required to be proficient in such secondary roles as external load lifting (including stranded light aircraft) and personnel winching; this latter application has some relevance to submarine operations, allowing personnel to be transferred without the warship having to enter port. In addition, the squadron plays a key role with RM Commandos, in the protection of Britain's offshore oil rigs and other installations, and 819 participates in regular exercises in Denmark and Norway to this effect. There is a 90-minute commitment to the Department of Trade for SAR missions and since 1975 a number of major rescues have been successfully performed by the unit, including the two Dutch naval Atlantique crashes in the North Atlantic. Snow relief work is also a forté of the squadron.

820 Squadron One of the four Sea King units based at Culdrose, 820 NAS is the first unit to fly the updated HAS 5 variant and its embarked home is the carrier *Invincible*. Its original embarkation was marred by a mid-air collision of two Sea Kings in bad weather. Since then, however, the unit has completed a successful cruise to the Western Atlantic and the United States. The unit's primary task is anti-submarine warfare and control of ASW air units in a task group scenario. It is here that the Decca radar (to be replaced by MEL Sea Searcher) is particularly useful.

824 Squadron This unit was seen by millions of television viewers when the series 'Sailor' was filmed aboard *Ark Royal* and 824 NAS was actually the first unit to equip with the Sea King HAS 1 in 1970. Again able to trace a history back to 1933, the squadron was present at Taranto and operated Swordfish almost throughout the whole of World War 2. 824 became a helicopter unit in 1958 and operated Whirlwinds until disbandment in 1963.

Today, the squadron has an ASW role which involves deployments of any of its three flights to RFAs or carriers to augment the usual ASW complement. During a deployment to the Arctic aboard an *Ol* Class RFA, the two Sea Kings were christened 'Hammer' and 'Sickle' because of the proximity of the Soviet Union. These names are not thought to have been officially adopted! When not at sea, the unit resides at Culdrose.

825 Squadron In order to strengthen the anti-submarine element of the Falklands Task Group, 825 Squadron was re-formed at Culdrose, its homebase, on May 7 1982 and the squadron of ten Sea King HAS 2 helicopters departed Devonport on May 13 1982 in the container ship *Atlantic Causeway*. Reports indicate that the helicopters were drawn from reserve storage, maintenance and 706 Squadron.

The squadron's role in the South Atlantic was to augment the logistic supply to the major elements such as troop transports, aircraft carriers and RFAs. It is not known whether this unit will continue to be operational in short-term, although the operational debut of *Illustrious* will call for an additional Sea King unit.

826 Squadron Originally flying Sea Kings from the helicopter cruiser *Tiger* and then from the Commando/ASW carrier *Bulwark*, 826 NAS now deploys Sea King HAS 2s and '5s to *Hermes*. Parented by Culdrose, the unit takes its place in the SAR standby routine when not at sea and will probably embark in *Illustrious* when that ship is OR (operationally ready). In 1981, the squadron carried out trials with airborne MAD (Magnetic Anomaly Detection) and the squadron strength rose from four

Below left *820—one of the Culdrose-based Sea King units, currently embarked in* Invincible.

Right *826—a Sea King HAS 5 of the* Hermes' *embarked squadron at Culdrose.*

Below *824—with rotors folded, an example of 'A' Flight of the squadron.*

aircraft to 12 (with 18 crews). By mid-1982, the re-equipment with the HAS 5 was complete giving the unit a passive and active sonar role.

829 Squadron When 703 Squadron disbanded in December 1980, there were 20 operational flights of Westland Wasp HAS 1 helicopters operating from Portland for Small Ships' Flights' duties. 829 NAS, the parent for the operational units, also took over the training duties of the now defunct 703. Although the more modern frigates and destroyers are now receiving the Lynx, there are still a number of *Rothesay* and *Leander* FFHs which will retain the Wasp until their demise. In addition, the four ocean-going survey craft have Wasp flights and 1982 saw the disbandment of the specialist *Endurance* Flight for Antarctic survey duties. The exact future of the squadron depends on the future of the ships which it serves and on the longevity of the Wasp, but there

should be another few years of life in squadron and aircraft yet.

845 Squadron This is the longest-serving Naval Air Commando Squadron and it has been flying the Westland Wessex since 1965 when the HU 5 variant was introduced to the FAA. Before it has been associated with both ASW and Air Commando rotary-wing types, but was originally formed in 1943.

845 NAS is tasked with short range troop movements, ferrying stores by internal and external means, paratrooping, helicopter gunship missions and search and rescue, as well as conventional Commando assault operations to beachheads or landing grounds further inland. Aircrew are also trained in depth charge and aerial torpedo dropping just to round off the skills required to be a 'Junglie' pilot.

829—now the only Wasp unit and with a very limited future: squadron aircraft undergoing routine maintenance at Portland (HMS Osprey).

Like most British Commando units, 845 is assigned to the Northern flank in wartime and much time is spent training for this role. In addition, the squadron is occasionally to be found operating in other roles, including troop transporting in Ulster. When not shore-based at Yeovilton the squadron is to be found aboard *Intrepid* or *Fearless*, although its most usual hunting ground was *Bulwark* before she decommissioned in 1981. It is not clear what the squadron's role will be in future with the demise of the Assault Ships and the continued use of *Hermes* and *Invincible* in the anti-submarine role. The helicopters can and have operated from other platforms.

The current strength of 845 is 21 Wessex and the unit has now taken over the spare cabs from 846 to become the only front-line Air Commando unit flying the HU 5. In early 1982, the strength of the Squadron was 275 personnel. It was very active, both at Ascension and in the Falklands.

846 Squadron Until November 1981, this unit was flying a mixed bag of Wessex HU 5s and Sea King Hc 4s, but now it has a full complement of ten Sea Kings. 846 Squadron started life in 1943 in an anti-submarine and anti-surface vessel role. It most recently re-formed, after several years of coming and going, in October 1978 with Wessex HU 5s in preparation for the phasing out of the Commando Carrier. Today, the squadron would, in time of war, tension or exercise, operate in the field alongside the Royal Marines which it supports in a trooping and heavy lift capacity. Despite its size, the Sea King HC 4 can be operated by a single pilot and its great asset is its ability to lift Land Rovers and field guns, as well as most other stores up to the 3.5-ton mark. Inside there is room for troops or stores, stretchers or other casualties. At least three aircraft were destroyed during the Falklands conflict, including one which inadvertently landed in Chile. The remaining helicopters moved 1,000,000 lb (453,600 kg) of stores.

847 Squadron To augment the Commando and logistic lift capability of the Falklands Task Group, 847 Squadron was re-formed in early May 1982 with Wessex HU 5 helicopters collected from various units (including storage locations). In all, 25+ aircraft went south, but sadly a number (which could have been as high as 17) were lost when the *Atlantic Conveyor* was sunk off the Fauklands. The long-term future of the unit is not clear, bearing in mind that its helicopters were formerly operating in training, communications and SAR roles with UK-based units. The home base is Yeovilton.

848 Squadron In April 1982, mainly as a result of the operational requirements dictated by the Falklands Operation in the South Atlantic, the advanced operational training unit, 707 Squadron, was disbanded and immediately re-formed as 848 Squadron. This squadron now has an operational air commando and support role, and the Wessex HU 5 equipment has been retained.

845—the largest helicopter unit in the FAA, operating in Norway, NI and from ships, including Hermes.

846—the Sea King heavy lift squadron seen here at Yeovilton Air Day.

It is believed that the unit operated from *Intrepid* during the re-occupation of East Falkland and later was involved in the advance towards Port Stanley. With 14 aircraft and a total of 315 staff (including Wren maintainers at Yeovilton), 848 Squadron is one of the larger FAA units. Its original expertise in operating with gun and rocket-armed helicopters was used in the South Atlantic, but it is mainly geared to operations in Northern Norway where front-line support to Commando units is vital. There is therefore a very close liaison with CTCRM Lympstone and other RM units.

899 Squadron Although the first Sea Harrier unit in the 800 series to be formed, 899 NAS is not destined to go to sea for any length of time. Its nickname is the 'Bunch with the Punch' which derives from its badge rather from any aggressive tendencies of the aircrew. The unit is the HQ part of the Sea Harrier force and has been based at Yeovilton since March 1980. Its complement consists of eight staff pilots, two fighter direction officers, four AEOs, 70 senior and 70 junior maintenance ratings. The aircraft used are Sea Harrier FRS 1s (seven on strength), Harrier T 4 (one) and a Hunter T 8M for Blue Fox radar training and trials. The primary task as given by FONAC is the operational training of Sea Harrier pilots for those who have already passed through RAF Wittering. The four-month course at Yeovilton encompasses air interception including combat techniques such as Viffing, air-to-ground firing, bombing, navigation and ski-jump techniques. These tasks are vital if the small Sea Harrier elements of only five aircraft which operate at sea are to be effective in the war or tension situation, as in the Falklands.

700 Squadron Although not currently in commission, a note on the role of this unit would not be out of place here. When a new naval aircraft is introduced into service it is the role of the Intensive Flying Trials Unit (IFTU) to examine all the possibilities for the aircraft and its operational role. These units are usually formed as part of 700 Squadron. For example, 700A (for 'Arrier) operated the Sea Harrier FRS 1 from June 1979 until March 1980; previously there has been 700L (for Lynx) which became 702 Squadron in 1978. 700L (1976–78) was a unique unit in that it was jointly run by the RN and the RNethN's MLD for Lynx operations by both nations.

702 Squadron Formed at Yeovilton in January 1978, 702 NAS has the task of carrying out pilot and observer conversion training for all Lynx flights parented by 815 Squadron. The squadron moved to Portland in late July 1982 to concentrate all the small ships' flights at one air station. Maintenance personnel are also trained at Portland with this unit. Aircrew complete a 23-week course which consists of conversion to flying the aircraft followed by operational training in one of seven Lynx HAS 2s kept specially for these tasks. DLPs are carried out aboard any frigate or destroyer which happens to be working up in the Portland Area during the course. On the job training for the maintenance personnel is somewhat longer and it is six months before either senior or junior rate is fit to take his place in a flight at sea, but that length of time is necessary if he is going to be able to fit into the specialist team afloat.

705 Squadron Helicopters have always been the business of 705 Squadron since it formed to evaluate the Sikorsky R4 in 1947. In 1959, the unit took up residence at RNAS Culdrose, and in 1975, the Anglo-French Gazelle HT 2 was introduced to replace the Westland Whirlwind and the Hiller HT 2.

705 NAS is today tasked by FONAC with training naval student pilots to fly helicopters and on average each year, some 76 students, like Midshipman HRH Prince Andrew in 1981, graduate with their coveted wings. Each flying training course syllabus lasts 19 weeks and about 80 hours of flying are accomplished in the Gazelle. From 750, the pilot will go on to do operational training with a *Junglies* Squadron or with 706 (for ASW work). In addition, it is possible for

Left *737—still flying Wessex HAS 3s in early 1982 but due to be decommissioned and replaced by 810 NAS in 1982/3 period. Antrim flight is one of the few remaining DLG Flights.* **Right** *750—carrying out navigation/observer training in a Jetstream T2 (BAe).*

graduated from the AFTC, takes seven weeks, part of which is spent aboard RFA *Engadine* at sea, practising ship-borne duties and DLPs (deck landing practice). DLPs are also carried out by Sea Kings from 706 on any passing ship with a deck large enough to accommodate the aircraft and with time available for the evolutions. Aircrew graduate to one of the four operations squadrons at Culdrose or to the unit at Prestwick.

Although flying the aircraft operationally is the *raison d'etre* for the FAA units having Sea Kings, they cannot operate for more than a few hours without the expert attention of the squadron maintainers. 706 NAS also trains Sea King maintainers at Culdrose and about 60 per cent of the unit's rating are, at any one time, undergoing 'on the job' training before going to one of the five operational squadrons.

706 NAS provides an important contribution to the United Kingdom Air Sea Rescue effort and, with the other Sea King units at Culdrose, the unit shares the task of providing long range (up to 200 nm unrefuelled) cover at 15 minutes' notice by day and 1½ hours by night or out of working hours. It has a 365-day, 24-hours-a-day, duty roster.

Although the foreign training of Sea King crews has been completed, the RN provides training facilities for the RAF's Sea King HAR 3 helicopter force in the guise of the Sea King Training Unit (RAFSKTU), and two HAR 3s are maintained at Culdrose for this purpose. In addition, 706 Squadron provides facilities for pilots and observers converting to the Sea King from other types of FAA aircraft and also provides basic type-training for the Naval Air Commando pilots who are destined to fly the Sea King HC 4 with 846 NAS at RNAS Yeovilton.

737 Squadron This unit is rather unusual in that it has an advanced and operational training role within the FAA flying training programme, as well as providing support for the embarked DLG Flights. The training programme includes conversion and refresher work for all Wessex HAS 3 aircrew and at any one time there are about 20 aircrew (pilots, observers and aircrewmen) undergoing training; additionally, there are perhaps 80 maintenance ratings being taught the skills needed to maintain the 'Camel' aboard ship.

The squadron has 12 staff pilots, eight observers and six aircrewmen, plus three AEOs, four senior

students to be assigned a small ships' flight role in which case they will proceed to 829 Squadron (for Wasps) or to 702 Squadron (for Lynx).

The squadron has a secondary role to train Maintenance Test Pilots ('Plumber' pilots) for helicopter test flying, Instrument Rating Instructors and the very few fixed-wing pilots who transfer to rotary wing operations.

In 1975, the squadron established the UK's only helicopter display team, called the *Sharks*, who are instructors from the unit. Details of the team will be found below.

The Gazelles of 705 NAS are maintained, not by ratings, but by civilian employees of the international firm Airwork Limited. The squadron's staff are all Qualified Helicopter Instructors (QHIs) who have completed the RAF course at Central Flying School, RAF Shawbury.

706 Squadron This is the only non-operational Sea King unit and its main task is to train Sea King personnel for the front-line squadrons. Based at RNAS Culdrose, 706 NAS is equipped with 13 Sea King HAS 2s and five Sea King HAS 5s. Its staff consists of 22 pilots, six observers, and seven aircrewmen. To maintain the 18 aircraft on strength, there are four AEOs, 20 senior and 120 junior maintenance ratings, plus ten Wrens.

With this hardware and personnel back-up, 706 takes a qualified pilot for a 13-week Advanced Flying Training Course, which is followed by a three-week tactical course. This is the operational training facet of 706's task. Observers and aircrewmen are also trained by the squadron; this facet, which is covered with the pilots who have

rates and 82 juniors for groundcrew. A senior Lieutenant Commander is in charge, and in the past several have been DLG Flight commanders before taking up this important post.

The 1980s have seen the gradual reduction of Wessex HAS 3 operational flying from *County* Class destroyers and by the end of 1981 there were only one or two Flights embarked, whilst on shore, about a dozen Wessex continued the training role (some temporarily embarked in RFA *Engadine*), provided support for FOST training tasks and for the Maritime Helicopter Warfare School.

It is envisaged that the unit will disband in December 1982 and re-form as 810 Squadron with the Sea King, when the Wessex HAS 3 will be phased out of service. As a matter of interest 737 NAS operated the Sea King between 1970 and 1974. Helicopters have been operated since August 1959, but before then the squadron was an Operational Flying School with a history running back to 1949.

750 Squadron Although formed as long ago as May 1939, 750 Naval Air Squadron has always been associated with the training of observers for the Fleet Air Arm. During the war, this important role was carried out in Trinidad, but the cessation of hostilities led to a disbandment of the squadron until February 1952. Since 1972, 750 NAS has been firmly established at RNAS Culdrose, near Helston in Cornwall. The combining of the squadron with RN Observer School in April 1981 has not changed the role of the unit, which is to provide the front-line and other units with first-class observers—what the RN now calls airborne tacticians. The aircraft used for this role is the Scottish Aviation Jetstream T 2,

which replaced the Hunting Sea Prince in 1979–80.

Each Observer Course lasts 23 weeks and it is designed to teach students the fundamentals of flying, low- and high-level navigation, general principles of radar and radio communications. At least 100 hours of flying takes place, and ports of call include Gibraltar and Berlin. The Basic Observers' Course is run five times a year with about ten students (direct entrants, Special Duties and General List officers) per course. Besides the CO and the Training Officer, there are four specialist instructor officers (usually Lieutenant Commanders) plus an officer for each course.

The Air Squadron has a complement of 11 staff pilots, two Qualified Flying Instructors (QFIs—although twin-engined conversion flying tends to be carried out by *Seahawk* Flight at the moment), besides the CO. It is possible that all 12 Jetstreams could be operational together, but it is more usual, especially for trips abroad, for four or six aircraft to deploy together.

The Advanced Flying Training Course for observers is carried out with 737 Squadron at Portland (shortly to be at Culdrose with 810 NAS which assist 706 NAS).

771 Squadron The Wessex HU 5s of 771 NAS are a familiar sight to the holidaymakers on the Cornish and Devonshire coasts, especially as they are marked in dayglo with an 'Ace of Clubs' motif behind the cockpit. Although primarily a training unit, the squadron is very active in the SAR scene, operating from its home base at RNAS Culdrose, near Helston, Cornwall.

Originally based at Portland, the unit has been

long associated with mercy operations and its aircrew have received several gallantry awards for daring rescues—the average scramble time is less than two minutes. Normally, however, the squadron's ten Wessex are engaged in the Aircrewman School's training programme and in the training and drilling of SAR specialist, including the unique SAR diver. Normal crews for SAR missions are a pilot, a winchman and one diver. The squadron's complement, on the other hand, is ten pilots, an observer and 11 staff aircrewmen. In the hangars, the AEO has a deputy, 39 senior and 42 junior maintenance ratings (and administrators), plus 16 Wrens.

772 Squadron Based at Portland and flying the Wessex HU 5 in a mixed SAR and support role for FOST, 772 NAS also provides aircraft for RFAs to carry out vertrep tasks. For example, either or both *Regent* Class ammunition and stores ships carry a Wessex flight aboard, and in 1981 one helicopter (named 'Bumble') was deployed to *Invincible* as a COD (Carrier Onboard Delivery) aircraft during the ship's work-up and initial operations.

The Air Stations

During the years following the 1957 and 1966 Defence White Papers, the FAA shrank as the RNASs were turned over to the RAF and in some cases to the Army, one by one. By 1980, there were only five remaining: RNAS Culdrose (HMS *Seahawk*), RNAS Lee-on-Solent (HMS *Daedalus*), RNAS Portland (HMS *Osprey*), RNAS Prestwick (HMS *Gannet*) and RNAS Yeovilton (HMS *Heron*).

Each Air Station is commanded by a Captain RN*, with usually four senior Commanders: the

---

* Because of its size, *Gannet* has a senior Commander RN in command.

Executive Officer (responsible for the day-to-day management); the Commander (Air) (responsible for all flying, squadron and airfield activities); the Base Supply Officer—or BSO—(responsible for the supply and secretariat back-up). In addition, there are other Commanders for training (as at Culdrose), medical and dental services and specialist units such as the Flight Safety Centre (Yeovilton) or the Weather Centre (Culdrose).

The Air Department Under the Commander (Air)—known as 'Wings'—the Lieutenant Commander (Flying)—or 'Little F' at *Daedalus*, is responsible for the administration and operational efficiency of the airfield. Other sections which come under the Department's control are: air traffic control, airfield fire and rescue, flight planning and meteorological forecasting. In addition, the efficient all-weather, day and night operation of the airfield with the various requirements of visiting aircraft, aircrew and personnel come under the aegis of the department.

Above *Home of many of the Air Department functions is the control tower complex. During all flying operations, the tower is usually manned with a full complement of controllers and loggers, as here at Yeovilton (HMS Heron).*

Left *771—the Culdrose-based SAR unit with Wessex HU 5s marked with the 'Ace of Clubs'.*

Right *The Met Office with Wren Meteorological personnel at work (RN).*

The Air Engineering Department Provides continuous technical and logistical support for an Air Station which in turn has to meet a series of operational tasks as dictated by FONAC. As a generalisation, an Air Station's AED would consist of: Inspection Department (quality assurance); mechanical workshops (aircraft components and airframes); ground radio section (airfield radars and radios); instrument and electrical workshops (testing, repair and calibration); air weapons section (aircraft ordnance); air radio workshops (including sonars); refuel section (bowsers and fuel installations); air equipment control (spares service); ground equipment control (includes chocks and ground supply units); air stores control office (admin); survival centre (safety equipment and flying clothing).

Air Traffic Control On an Air Station ATCs undertake all normal control duties, that is for the safety of aircraft operating to, from and around the Air Station, including aircraft in transit through the airfield's zone. Ground movements are controlled by air traffic as are all aircraft in 'local control' in the five-mile circuit. Radar control of aircraft can overlap, especially at Yeovilton where Portland traffic is relatively close. There is a direct landline link to civilian and national air traffic control centres. During exercises, each squadron will provide, or be provided with, its own controller and at Yeovilton—where there is the Fighter Direction School as well—exercises are handled by one controller (RN or WRNS), but he does keep in touch with what is happening in the area. The daily flying programme is co-ordinated with the Operations Department so that each squadron, whether fixed-wing or rotary, can be allocated the right amount of time for the particular task which it has to perform.

In addition, the Senior Air Traffic Controller (SATCO), who is usually a Lieutenant Commander, is responsible for firefighting and rescue; at Yeovilton and Culdrose his duties also include bird control by the Falconry Unit. The firefighting chain of command is:

SATCO

|

ATC

|

Fire Station

The fire officer is usually a Special Duties (SD) branch officer with firefighting experience as a rating. This is considered most important.

Three sections within the tower complex provide the necessary information and control for the smooth running of the flying programme. Detailed planning is undertaken before every flight and the ATC staff can brief aircrew on routes and hazards.

Royal Naval Air Stations

Perth

Pitreavie

HMS Gannet

Wroughton

HQNAC Heron

HMS Daedalus

Fleetlands

BRNC FLT

HMS Osprey

HMS Seahawk

Mountbatten

● Royal Naval Air Stations/Airfields
▲ Royal Naval Aircraft Yards
■ Maritime Headquarters
★ R.N. Aircraft Workshop

Yeovilton is home for six squadrons, including 899 NAS with Sea Harrier aircraft.

The Operations Room keep a log of air movements and has the ability to task aircraft for SAR (or just search in the case of fixed-wing) at any time.

The Visual Control Position (VCP) on top of the tower is manned by an officer (Duty Air Traffic Controller—DATCO), a senior and three junior ratings (RN or WRNS) during all flying operations, and it is from here that the team controls all aircraft within the circuit. Radar control is maintained and every Air Station provides a ground-controlled approach (GCA) which gives a talk-down during bad weather or in the event of an emergency. Yeovilton tower handles an average of 6,000 movements a month with a complement of 17 officers and two FCPO/CPOs as qualified controllers, plus assistants and loggers. The team is split into two watches of eight, although manning does vary, especially at night, during exercises, air days and at weekends.

Bird Control Unit Under the control of the ATC Department, the Falconry units at Yeovilton (formed 1972) and Culdrose (formed 1975) perform a very useful task in reducing the number of unwanted birds around the airfield, thus reducing the risk of bird strike. In addition, the beautiful falcons are assisted by conventional tactics, such as taped distress calls, pyrotechnic crackers, propane gas cannons and rotary bird scarers. Without doubt, this sub-unit makes a substantial and cost-effective contribution to flight safety.

Naval Aircraft Support Unit Comes under the control of the Commander (AE) but its role at Culdrose and Yeovilton is to provide local deep maintenance facilities for the individual squadrons. The work is varied and widespread with, for example, NASU at *Seahawk* being responsible for the Sea Kings at *Gannet*. The actual work can be maintenance, modification or conversion. In the latter respect, NASU (*Seahawk*) has collaborated

with RNAY Fleetlands in the conversion of Sea King HAS 2 airframes to HAS 5 standard in recent months. When all work in the hangars has been completed, the aircraft are test flown by Maintenance Test Pilots.

Supply and Secretarial Department No Air Station could function for more than a few minutes without the direct, but inconspicuous support of the Pusser's Department. Basically, the Commander (S) has to provide domestic stores and administrative support to the Air Station. The Stores Accountants sub-unit provides stores and accounting facilities—everything from a rotorblade to a new hat. The food served in the FAA is the responsibility of the Catering sub-unit whilst the Writers deal with pay, service documents and general administration duties. A large proportion of WRNS personnel are employed in the Dept.

Sick Bay Every Air Station has a specially equipped sick bay to give a comprehensive medical service for the airfield and lodger units. At the major Air Stations the Medical Department is commanded by a Surgeon Commander and many SAR operations use their facilities and personnel. There is also a medical input to Health and Safety at Work. Ambulance drivers are provided by the Motor Transport Section. Most air stations also have a Dental Department under a Surgeon Commander (D) and mobile clinics are also used.

Meteorological Department The met office is situated in the tower and provides weather information for flying. It is manned during and usually before all flying operations. An Instructor Lieutenant Commander ('Schollie') is usually in command with a team of rating observers, including many WRNS.

Air Station defence Unlike RAF stations, there are no missile batteries or AA guns defending Britain's Naval Air Stations, but in time of war or tension it is assumed that elements of the Royal Marines, particularly the Bands Service, would be employed in this role.

HMS Heron Yeovilton is known to the RN as HMS *Heron* and as the HQ of both Naval Air Command and its Flag Officer. There has been an airfield on this site in Somerset since 1940* when FAA fighter training was commenced there. The Air Station has steadily grown through the jet era when it was home to the squadrons of Sea Vixens and later Phantoms (before the latter moved to RAF Leuchars). Today, it is the base for the RN's Naval Air Commando helicopters and for the Sea Harrier force.

By the end of 1982, the following are envisaged to be in residence at Heron; 800 Squadron—British Aerospace Sea Harrier FRS 1; 801 Squadron—British Aerospace Sea Harrier FRS 1; 845 Squadron—Westland Wessex HU 5; 846 Squadron—Westland Sea King HC 4; 847 Squadron—Westland Wessex HU 5; 848 Squadron—Westland Wessex HU 5; 899 Squadron—British Aerospace Sea Harrier FRS 1 and T 4 plus Hawker Siddeley Hunter T 8M.

However, the future of the Naval Air Commando training unit, 707 Squadron, which was disbanded to provide aircrew and helicopters for the South Atlantic operations, is in doubt. It may be that this unit will re-form if and when 847 and 848 Squadrons disband. The future of the Wessex HU 5 is thought to be limited in any case and it was envisaged that the pre-Falklands situation of one front-line Wessex HU 5 squadron (845) would not continue beyond the middle of 1984.

In addition to the usual Air Station functions, *Heron* is host to the following specialist and lodger units: Aircraft Direction School; Air Training Section; *Heron* Station Flight; Sea Harrier Training Ski-Jump; Fleet Requirements and Direction Unit (see separate section); FONAC's Royal Marines Band; Fleet Air Arm Museum; Royal Naval Flight Safety Centre; and Tactical Air Control Party (Mobile Air Operations Team).

Aircraft Direction School Known to the FAA as the D School, this unit, which shares the tower complex with ATC, has been a part of Yeovilton's make-up for many years. The Fighter Controller is borne in most large ships of destroyer size and above where he is responsible for controlling the combat air patrols (CAPs) of friendly fighters, or in the case of *Invincible*, *Illustrious*, and *Hermes*, for controlling the organic air element. The responsibility for training

these men who are as much a part of the defence as, say, the Sea Harrier pilot, rests with the ADS at Heron. Incidentally, women members of the RN—the WRNS—are trained as ATCO but as they do not go to sea they have little requirement for direction duties.

The training staff consists of four officers (of whom one is always an exchange member from the RAF) and one CPO. Using Hunters from FRADU (*qv*) and front-line RAF types, as well as the Sea Harrier, the student Fighter Direction Officer (FDO) will achieve 80 hours of controlling before joining his ship. Refamiliarisation courses are also run at the D School.

The Air Training Section Monitors the training standards of the various squadrons and schools based at *Heron*. Young officers are also trained in tactics and weapons used by NATO aircraft, but special emphasis is placed on RN types. The level of training can vary from the detailed and specialised aviation warfare and weaponry courses to short acquaint visits. At the present time the Sea Harrier programme is in full swing at Yeovilton.

Heron Station Flight Like all station flights, *Heron* takes care of all visiting aircraft but it also has another role—that of hosting the RN's Historic Flight (*qv*). With the disbandment of 781 Communications Squadron, several aircraft have been passed to *Heron* Flight including a Sea Heron and a Sea Devon; FONAC's 'barge' is a Sea Heron and this is also hosted by the flight. Handling VIP flights is a very important part of everyday routine at Yeovilton.

Flight Safety Centre During the early postwar era, there were a large number of flying accidents in the RN, especially aboard warships. The Admiralty Accident Advisory Board which had been set up previously developed an offshoot called the Flight Safety Centre to carry out the prevention work before an accident occurred. Today, the centre still does important work in flight safety, although the number of flying accidents have greatly reduced in number.

Tactical Air Control Party. Known as the 'Motleys' to the Naval Air Commando squadrons, TACP(MAOT) operates wherever and whenever a Commando group goes into action, be it tropics or arctic. The team is a mixture of RN and RM specialists, all of whom have passed the Commando course at CTCRM Lympstone and are eligible to wear the green beret. The unit is the link between the squadrons ashore, the parent ship and the ground forces HQ; their main task being to control air space during and after a Commando airlift. The RN element are the controllers whilst the RM provide the technical and tactical back-up. TACP is split

---

* Historical details of Yeovilton and the other RNASs can be found in the *Action Stations* series of books, also published by Patrick Stephens, which cover all military airfields in the UK.

Lee-on-Solent is next to the sea and there is even a slipway which has prompted the FAA to use the station for hovercraft trials work (HMS Daedalus).

into five-man groups based around an HF, VHF and UHF equipped ¾-ton Land Rover of the air-portable type. During exercises, the 'Motleys' provide air safety control and training is generally carried out with Air Commando squadrons.

Fleet Air Arm Museum The museum at Yeovilton was established in 1964 with only three aircraft but today it probably contains the greatest exhibition of naval aviation in the world. It is open every day except Christmas Eve and Christmas Day. Of particular importance is the Vampire used for the first jet-aircraft deck landing and the collection of naval aero engines.

The Sea Harrier Support Unit Handles all support and maintenance of the three Sea Harrier squadrons at Yeovilton, especially the newly delivered aircraft or those which have undergone major overhaul. It was formed in March 1980 and operates along the lines of a mini-NASU but is administered by 899 Squadron.

Merryfield Yeovilton's training satellite airfield situated about 12 miles to the west adjacent to a low flying area. Helicopter training by both Yeovilton- and Portland-based aircraft is carried out. The airfield is completely self-contained with its own ATC and fire/crash set-up. The opening hours are 09:00 until the cessation of night flying at Yeovilton, which could be 04:00 the next morning. The Mobile

Air Operations team can provide lighting for night flying because the airfield has no permanent lighting of its own. The normal complement of the airfield is a Duty Officer, a CPO, a PO, four ATC junior rates, six firemen, a driver and the most important cook.

HMS Daedalus The last vessel to bear the name *Daedalus* was a depot ship for the Royal Naval Air Service later named *Thunderbolt*, so it is fitting that the former HQ of Naval Air Command should retain a link with the beginnings of the Fleet Air Arm.

When the former RAF station at Lee-on-Solent was handed back to the RN in 1938, the depot ship's name was revived and apart from a period between 1959–65 (when Wykeham Hall was so-named) the name has remained at Lee.

The main task of *Daedalus* today is the technical training of FAA ratings, as well as supplying base facilities for a number of lodger units. Very little flying is carried out since the disbandment of 781 Squadron—the Naval Clippers—in early 1981. Only the important Solent Search and Rescue Flight and the Royal Naval Gliding and Sailplane Association (RNGSA) remain as permanent flying units.

As at April 1 1981, the following units were based at Daedalus: Accident Investigation Unit; Air Engineering School; Air Medical School; Central Air Medical Board; Mobile Aircraft Repair, Transport and Salvage Unit; Naval Aircraft and Marine Examination Board; Naval Aircrew Advisory Board; Naval Air Technical Evaluation Centre; Naval Air Trials Installation Unit; Naval Hovercraft Trials Units (see separate section); Royal Naval Mass Miniature Radiographics Service; Royal Naval Microfilm Unit; Royal Naval Schools Presentation Team; Royal Naval Survival Equipment School; and Search and Rescue Flight.

The Air Engineering School This moved to Lee from Arbroath (formerly *Condor*, now RM Condor) in 1970 and was merged with the Air Electrical School to form a single larger unit. It is tasked with training all maintenance ratings for the FAA and many courses are run at the school, ranging from four-year apprenticeships to one-day acquaintance courses. The staff consists of about 110 engineer and instructor officers, plus civilians; in addition there are about 200 ratings. The AES is divided into three units: the Basic Training Group which trains ratings who have completed basic training at *Raleigh*; the Mechanical, Electrical and Air Weapons Groups which are responsible for providing career courses for mechanics, mechanicians, and artificer apprentices for airframe, engines, air electrical and air weapons; and the Training Design Group which designs all the courses.

With the recent air engineering branch restructuring, the courses are changing to keep pace with technology, especially with the introduction of the Sea Harrier FRS 1, the Lynx HAS 2 and the Sea King HAS 5 aircraft. A larger degree of uniformity within the naval engineering organisation has now been achieved. AEOs are trained at RNEC Manadon (*qv*).

MARTSU This rather long-winded but accurately named unit is responsible for the repair, transportation and salvage of aircraft (not just naval ones) from locations as different as mountain tops and jungle clearings worldwide. It was this unit which rescued an Army Gazelle helicopter from the depths of the Gambian jungle some years ago.

The unit has about 50 civilian and 100 Service members and in one year alone reckons to survey over 200 aircraft and repair 165, travelling 500,000 miles to do so. Many of their vehicles are manned by personnel from PSTO(N).

Royal Naval Survival Equipment School For the FAA, survival equipment is most important because a complete safety system (ejection seat, parachute, dinghy/life raft and flying clothing) is vital should aircrew be forced to abandon an aircraft. The unit is actually housed at Seafield Park, only a stone's throw from *Daedalus* proper at Hill Head. RNSES trains personnel who in turn will be responsible for the training and maintenance of survival equipment at an Air Station or with an embarked squadron or flight. They will be a part of the Survival Equipment Branch. Additionally,

General Service ('fishhead') personnel and ratings of friendly foreign navies are trained on naval inflatable lifesaving equipment at Seafield Park. Civilian organisations can, of course, also benefit from the experience of RNSES.

Royal Naval Air Medical School Also situated at Seafield Park, the RNAMS is responsible for basic and refresher training of aircrew in first aid and aviation medicine. The Army Air Corps is also trained at Seafield. SAR personnel are trained and refreshed on first aid which is an important aspect of their day-to-day work. The school is conveniently close to RNH Haslar and to the Institute of Naval Medicine at Alverstoke.

Mention must also be made of the Fleet Air Arm Field Gun Crew who are based at *Daedalus* during their season.

HMS Seahawk Commissioned in 1947 at Culdrose, near Helston on the Lizard peninsula, initially as the Naval Air Fighter School, but in 1953, the Air Station became the centre for operational anti-submarine and observer training. Helicopter flying has also long been associated with Culdrose and today it is the largest such base in Britain.

In addition, Culdrose is the largest Air Station and its modern role is to act as parent for the four afloat operational Sea King squadrons, to provide observer/aircrewman training facilities, search and rescue cover and the home for several minor, but important, units, such as: Royal Naval Helicopter School; Royal Naval Observer School; Royal Naval

In 1979, Culdrose mounted a massive SAR assistance operation for the Fastnet Race and this picture illustrates the many people and items of equipment involved. Actually, only one quarter of those actually involved are shown here! (HMS Seahawk).

Aircrewman School; Royal Naval School of Meteorology and Oceanography; Royal Naval School of Aircraft Handling; Royal Naval Telephonist School; Naval Air Command Motor Transport Driving School; Naval Air Command Firefighting School; Station Engineer Training School; Naval Aircraft Support Unit; HMS *Seahawk*/Culdrose Station Flight; and Royal Naval Aircraft Direction Centre.

The current NASs in residence are: 705 Squadron—Westland Gazelle HT 2; 706 Squadron—Westland Sea King HAS 2 and HAS 5; 750 Squadron—British Aerospace Jetstream T 2; 771 Squadron—Westland Wessex HU 5; 814 Squadron—Westland Sea King HAS 2; 820 Squadron—Westland Sea King HAS 5; 824 Squadron—Westland Sea King HAS 2; and 826 Squadron—Westland Sea King HAS 5. (737 Squadron will disband in December 1982 and its function will be taken over by the newly re-formed 810 Squadron at Culdrose flying Sea King HAS 2 helicopters.)

Royal Naval Flying Training School This unit provides centralised co-ordination of all basic flying training for pilots, observers and aircrewmen carried out at Culdrose. 705 Squadron provides instructors for basic training of student pilots in helicopter flying using Gazelles. 771 Squadron's Wessex are tasked to complete the flying training of the Aircrewman School. Observers learn their art in the back of Jetstreams of 750 Squadron whilst advanced flying training is carried out by 706 Squadron in Sea Kings*. The FTS also handles the Sea King simulator and sonar training and analysis centre. 706 Squadron embraces the RAF Sea King Training Unit (RAFSKTU—or 'Crab TU') which for some years has been co-ordinating RAF SAR training using three yellow-painted Sea King HAR 3s. Maintenance Test Pilots are trained by 705 NAS and this squadron is somewhat unique in that it uses civilian maintainers.

Seahawk Station Flight The reception, servicing and despatch unit for all visiting aircraft to Culdrose. In addition, several aircraft are kept on strength for local duties, such as the station's Chipmunk T 10 glider tug, two Sea Devon C 20s for RNR (Air) and twin-engined training and the sole Sea Heron C 1 for Ministry of Agriculture Fisheries and Food-tasked Fisheries' Protection duties in south-western and Irish Sea waters.

Part of the RN Historic Flight is kept at Culdrose

in the shape of the last Sea Hawk FGA 6 flying in the western hemisphere (the type still serves in a limited capacity with the Indian Navy). There are also several Sea Hawks to be found at the SAH (*qv*).

NAC Weather Centre Culdrose is one of a worldwide network of meteorological observing stations which exchange information on actual weather. The centre makes extensive use of satellite information and radar pictures for forecasting. During weekends and leave periods, the weather for other air stations is provided from Culdrose.

RN School of Meteorology and Oceanography For over 50 years, the RN has been at the forefront of specialist predictions for ships and aircraft. Today, in the era of the nuclear submarine, the science of oceanography is particularly important. The primary task of the RNSOMO is to train the officers and ratings who run the RN Meteorological Service, both ashore and afloat. Specialist officers undergo a six-months course at the school before going to frigate squadrons, Air Stations and the larger ships of the Fleet. Both WRNS and RN assistants are trained for five months at Culdrose whilst Hydrographic Officers (who train initially at *Drake*), and some aircrew, undergo more specialist courses.

School of Aircraft Handling Established at Culdrose in 1959, the SAH has a special dummy deck near the airfield which is currently marked to depict the flight deck of an *Invincible* Class CVL—former models have been *Hermes*, *Bulwark*, *Ark Royal* and *Eagle*.

The school is divided into four sub-sections which cover New Entry Airmanship Training (where ratings, straight from *Raleigh*, learn the tricks of aircraft handling); Firefighting (where fire prevention, firefighting and rescue techniques are taught); Aircraft Handling (where the art of manoeuvring and securing a naval aircraft is taught on the dummy deck—the emphasis is currently on Sea Harriers and helicopters operating in conjunction; Motor Transport (where aircraft and vehicle handling in restricted areas above and below deck is taught). Fork lift drivers are taught to use their vehicles in ammunitioning and provisioning operations. Aboard ship the vehicles come under the AE Department whose organisation is:

Sub-section officer (AE)
|
Ground Equipment Section (CPO i/c)
|
Flight Deck Motor Vehicle Section

The Naval Airman (Aircraft Handler) course lasts three weeks and recruits learn to drive the JCB

---

* It will be remembered that during October 1981, HRH Acting Sub-Lieutenant Prince Andrew, undertaking operational training with 706 Squadron aboard RFA *Engadine*, flew a rescue sortie for a submariner who had been washed overboard from an SSK off Scotland.

520, All Wheel Drive (AWD), Hyster fork lift, and the Coles crane.

Predannack This is Culdrose's satellite airfield and is situated on the southern Lizard peninsula. The original airfield was constructed in 1941 for RAF Coastal Command operations in the South-Western Approaches. In 1959, the airfield was taken over by Culdrose for flying training during busy periods. So active did Predannack become that in 1972 a new control tower was constructed and runway improvements were carried out in the late 1970s.

HMS Osprey The Royal Naval Air Station at Portland and the name of the base establishment for the Portland area; it is the only RNAS without a main runway facility, although doubtless Sea Harriers could operate from here if necessary.

Helicopters have been flown from Portland area since the very first trials in 1945/6, but it was not until 1957 that an ASW helicopter unit first commenced operations, based at nearby Chickerell. When Eglinton closed in 1958, the Naval Air ASW School moved to Portland and 737 Squadron took up residence. Two new hangars were erected in front of the Old Fleet Canteen and the RNAS Portland was commissioned on April 24 1959.

It was evident from the beginning that flying training was compatible with sea training once small warships began to operate helicopters at sea. In addition, the helicopter is a first rate transport and communications aircraft and thus it provided a good means of moving FOST and his staff about. A Search and Rescue School was formed at Portland in the 1960s, although this has now moved to *Seahawk*.

Between 1969–74, there was a major airfield re-development which cost £2.3 million and which transformed the facilities into a modern, well-equipped Air Station capable of operating at least three helicopter units, including an important training task for FONAC; the Observer Operational Training. The Westland Lynx HAS 2 began its service career with the RN at Yeovilton with 700L Squadron for initial trials before the unit was formed into 702 Squadron in 1978. In 1981, the operational and trials element was moved to a new front-line unit, 815 Squadron; both 702 and 815 moved to Portland in July 1982; thus putting all the Small Ships' Flights in the same air station. 829 NAS, the Wasp parent and training unit, has been in residence for many years.

This move notwithstanding, *Osprey* will still be the base of 772 NAS which is a Fleet Requirements Unit operating on behalf of FOST and for parenting the three detached flights to RFAs. The squadron's many roles include SAR in the Portland Sea Areas and helicopter controller training. The SAR

Osprey—both Wessex HAS 3s and Wasps operate from the heli-strip at Portland.

operations are controlled from Mountbatten Rescue Co-ordination Centre, Plymouth.

In addition, *Osprey* is the base establishment for all naval personnel serving at the naval base and in the immediate area. RNAS Portland, then, is an integral part of *Osprey* and the Captain is responsible for various elements of Flying Training to FONAC. He is also Flag Captain to FOST and supplies assistance, when necessary, to HM ships visiting Portland for Sea Training.

Osprey is the home of the Fleet Target Group (*qv*) and the naval base, having no dockyard facilities, has a Fleet Maintenance Group for warship engineering and technical problem-solving and routine maintenance; the latter reporting to Captain of *Osprey* in his FOST role.

Air Training Department This unit has the task of co-ordinating the training of Observers and Aircrewmen 702 and of pilots in 829 NAS. In addition, it undertakes the ground school instruction of these personnel. The department has overall charge of three separate units which help to train aircrew and flight deck personnel.

The 1075 Sonar Simulator is used to train Wessex HAS 3 and Sea King HAS 2/5 observers and aircrewmen for their 'back-seat' jobs; the unit will relocate at Culdrose in 1982/3.

The Helicopter Control Unit trains seagoing personnel of the radar branch to control helicopters in tactical situations by radar; it has its own simulator. The Flight Deck Training Unit trains FDOs and flight deck crews of small ships in all aspects of helicopter deck operations in the RN and RFA.

Left Gannet—*the Station's flight line which is adjacent to Prestwick International Airport* (HMS Gannet).

Below right *A Sea King (819 NAS) carrying out flight deck trials in* Leeds Castle *on what must be one of the narrowest decks on which the helicopter has ever had to operate* (FOSNI).

HMS Gannet There have been *Gannets* in the RN since 1800, but it was not until May 1943 that the name was first associated with the Fleet Air Arm. It was then that *Gannet* was the commissioned name of RNAS Eglinton in Northern Ireland and this connection continued until 1958 when the airfield was handed back to civil use. In 1971, the former USAF(E) base at Prestwick International Airport was taken over by the RN and renamed *Gannet* and it is here that the name remains.

Today, the Naval Air Station is the home of 819 NAS, equipped with Sea King HAS 2 helicopters on operational shore-based duties for FOSNI and for SAR operations in the North Atlantic and the west coast of Scotland. The unit and the base have close connections with the Royal Marines at RM Condor, Arbroath, on the east coast, and from here are used in offshore protection operations. *Gannet* commenced its SAR role in April 1975 and has through 819 NAS one aircraft at a maximum of 90 minutes alert for either civil or military operations.

By comparison with the other RNASs, *Gannet* is a small establishment and is commanded by a Commander RN, rather than a Captain as with *Seahawk, Heron, Daedalus* and *Osprey*.

Fleet Air Arm afloat

Despite the pressure put upon the FAA by successive Governments and the recent Defence Review, the Fleet still requires aircraft at the scene of any action, and that is at sea. Basically, the FAA afloat consists of Small Ships' Flights, embarked ASW units, ASW units aboard RFAs and a miscellany of other deployments and temporary embarkations.

Small Ships' Flights Hardly able to be classified in this role and now reaching the end of a hectic and useful life is the Westland Wessex HAS 3 which has been used with great effect afloat in *County* Class DLGs. The use of an ASW helicopter was a late addition to the design of the first of the Class,

Devonshire, and hangarage is only achieved by careful manhandling along the port side of the ship's aft superstructure. In this class of DLG, the ASW helicopter is the only anti-submarine asset available to the Captain, although all units do have hull-mounted sonar. The Wessex can be used as an independent unit in the ASW screen around a Task Group or as an airborne command and guidance centre using both its own input and that from the sensors carried aboard ship.

Today, the era of the Wessex HAS 3 is rapidly coming to its close, although the aircraft, well fitted out with Type 195 sonar and Ferranti radar (in the characteristic hump), has a limited endurance of about 83 minutes in a 50:50 hover:cruise mode and allowing sufficient fuel reserves for more than one recovery attempt. There is provision to fit a drop tank to give another 90 nm range, but this means a sacrifice in the weapons load.

In terms of organisation, the Flight Commander (usually a Lieutenant Commander), either the observer or the first pilot, is directly responsible to the Captain for the Ship's Flight. This consists of the aircrew: pilot, second pilot, observer and aircrewman (usually of PO rank); and the groundcrew who are divided into three sub-units under the SMR (Senior Maintenance Rating). The trades are: airframes and engine fitters; electrical mechanics (who also deal with the ordnance) and the radio and sensor fitters. The bulk of the maintenance at sea is carried out in one of the most cramped hangars ever conceived but this does not prevent a good record of serviceability provided that the spares are available; in this connection, there was a problem for *Antrim* Flight during the Group Deployment to the Far East in 1980.

At sea, then, a DLG Flight acts rather in the same way as a mini-Sea King squadron in an RFA, but it also has a surface search role which would be accomplished by a Sea Harrier in a carrier or Task Group. This role is especially important against missile-armed gunboats which must be detected and if possible attacked well out of their missile range. Whilst in the air, the Wessex is controlled from the ship's Operations Room by the Helicopter Controller (usually a Leading hand) whilst the landing and launch operations are monitored on the flight deck by specially trained personnel, such as the Captain's Secretary or Master-at-Arms, doubling as Flight Deck Officer (FDO). Sorties are tasked by the Principal Warfare Officer (underwater)—or PWO(U)—or in the secondary search role by PWO(A).

Another helicopter which, although long in the tooth, is still actively embarked in *Rothesay* and certain *Leander* Class frigates, is the Westland Wasp HAS 1. In fact, there is a specially equipped unit of three Wasps aboard the Ice Patrol Ship *Endurance* and in addition there are non-combatant support and utility Wasps in the Ocean Survey Ships of the RN. Today, though, a large question mark hangs over the Wasps' future, especially with the move of Lynx flights to Portland.

The Wasp Small Ship's Flight gives a comparatively junior officer, in his late twenties, the opportunity to command and exercise independence not otherwise possible in the mainstream squadron. This allows important

chances at man management so necessary in the modern Royal Navy. Usually, the Flight will consist of the Flight Commander, the Wasp's pilot, an aircrewman/missile aimer (who also navigates), with a maintenance team of seven or eight. In *Endurance* Flight there is also an Observer. In the Squadron Leader, there can be two pilots because of the duties required of the 'Squavo'.

The roles which this helicopter can perform are limited and well defined; it is basically a weapons platform, either in the ASW or the ASVW roles. It can of course be used for communications and some light stores transfers—ship-to-ship or ship-to-shore—and like all helicopters at sea it has a limited SAR role to play. Wasps attached to Survey Flights are used primarily to transport survey teams to remote locations and to ferry supplies from the parent ship to the remote party to sustain shore-based surveying work.

Although the number of Wasp flights is steadily diminishing, especially with their replacement by Lynx in the *Amazon* and *Sheffield* Classes, there are still several homes from which they can be replaced until that particular warship leaves service. A Wasp is a difficult helicopter to replace because of its simple technology, but having said that it is interesting to reflect that during its service life (it

first went to sea in *Tribals* in 1964) it has seen just about everything. It is a well-proven aircraft and can withstand rough treatment though it has been known to 'bite the hand of an unwary pilot on occasions!' The usual restriction to Wasp flying from ship's flight decks was (and is) usually the high sea state, rather than wind or rain blowing across the deck. It is a matter of getting the wind across the deck within the limits laid down by Flight Safety manuals. What may seem like a heavily rolling and pitching deck can be a little misleading, inasmuch as providing the movement is not too rapid or unpredictable, one times one's take-off or landing to coincide with the ship moving through the vertical. This is, of course, where the Lynx's Harpoon deck attachment device is so useful because with a Wasp, there is a dangerous period in heavy seas whilst the deck party put the nylon lashings on the aircraft. Not only the aircraft and its crew, but the handlers are also at risk. In general though, a Small Ship's Flight would not fly if conditions were such that the aircraft was put at risk.

The Lynx at sea has provided the RN with a most valuable weapon and the newly equipped flights with MAD have an aircraft which is second to none in the ASW and ASVW roles. In 1978, the helicopter went to sea for the first time operationally aboard the *Sheffield* Class DLG *Birmingham* and now the helicopter is well established. It is a most important asset and with a twin-engine capability, the helicopter has been operated in pitching and rolling seas with winds gushing up to 50 knots. The

Embarked Sea King ASW squadrons are often asked to perform other duties, like lifting ½-tonne Land Rovers for the RM.

Harpoon system already mentioned is especially important as is the Ferranti Sea Spray radar (similar to the Sea Harrier's Blue Fox). This latter set is designed for the tactical overwater role when the pilot can be conned back to the ship by the observer who always sits beside him; a significant departure from the older Wasp.

In modern warships, the Lynx flight consists of a pilot and an observer (either of whom can be the Flight Commander) with a maintenance party of seven, led by the SMR. Because the aircraft's complex nature there are a large number of POs and above in the modern ship's flight. The normal breakdown is two electrical fitters/maintainers; two for radio/sensors and two for engines and airframe. The Type 22s are destined for two Lynx when sufficient aircraft are available from the manufacturer, but in the meantime they have an extra aircraft embarked for exercises; then 11 maintainers are carried. Usually one aircraft would be operated turn and about by the two aircrews until it needed servicing when the second would be brought out. This means that the deck could be kept clear at all times, which could be important as the Lynx is not equipped for in-flight refuelling from the deck of a ship like the larger helicopters. The Type 42s have a pool of three FDOs to take charge of the deck at flying stations but the pilot still retains the ultimate veto. The PWO will control the helicopter's flying from the Ops Room via a radio link with the pilot and Helicopter Controller. Occasionally, one of the maintenance personnel will fly with the aircraft to perform routine maintenance if the helicopter is going to be away from 'mother' for any length of time and one or two are always kept trained up to act as 'winch weights' or winchmen for SAR missions, when a lightweight hoist can be fitted to the Lynx, controlled by the observer. All Flight Commanders will also try and make each member of the ship's flight familiar with the aircraft as part of general training and so air experience flights will be arranged.

Embarked squadrons The number of platforms from which helicopters can work at sea in squadron strength will be three by 1984/5, where there is a major role to be played by the Sea King HAS 2/5 and to some extent by the HC 4. The latter is a Commando Assault/Logistics aircraft which is primarily designed to operate in the field alongside the troops which it supports, but it has taken part in operations aboard *Hermes* and even *Invincible*. The Wessex HU 5 formerly found a home in the LPHs or Commando Carriers which have now disappeared from the Fleet, and their future is in any case in doubt. During the Falklands operations, Wessex were embarked in several types of ships, including

Sea Kings have found a useful new ASW platform in the shape of RFAs—a Sea King from Fort Grange.

requisitioned container vessels, like *Atlantic Conveyor*, as well as in assault ships. Today, then, it is the large Sea King ASW units aboard *Hermes* (826), *Invincible* (820) and *Illustrious*, which are important. At sea, they act in just the same way as they do ashore and take with them a full maintenance party led by the AEO (Air Engineering Officer). Perhaps over 200 personnel will be necessary in this role. With only limited airframes, it is especially important to keep as many 'cabs' in the air as possible. The Sea King does, of course, take more people aloft with it—a pilot and a second pilot, observer and aircrewman. Besides the carriers, Sea Kings will be hosted by the OPV2s of the *Castle* Class, although the flight deck is small (even by Canadian Navy standards where Sea King operations have been run from ships of about the same size for 15 years). The problem is that once over the deck the pilot has to rely solely on perception of perspective for picking up fore and aft drift unless there is a crew member conning the aircraft from the back cargo door. Experience is limited in respect of the OPV2s at present, but it is clear that protracted operations from the Class might pose problems of corrosion because there is no hangarage or protection for the aircraft nor for the maintenance ratings working on it. The *Castles* must therefore be used as refuelling and landing platforms for the Sea King in connection with other missions concerned with the guarding of Britain's offshore economic installations.

Aboard many of the RFAs there are now facilities for air operations by both Sea Kings and Wessex HU 5s, the latter only in the vertrep role with, for example, *Regent* Class carriers. The new *Fort* Class have facilities for operating several Sea Kings and accommodation (the best that any FAA personnel are likely to encounter in the 'Andrew') is available for both aircrew and groundcrew; the number of the latter depend on the length of the deployment and the number of aircraft embarked. Certainly, the

Wessex aircrew of two (pilot and aircrewman) plus about ten maintainers are all that a non-ASW RFA carries. Most RFA Captains feel that a helicopter is well worth the trouble of having one officer always manning the radar (as HCO) and one on the flight deck as FDO. In this decade we shall see the continued use of RFAs as platforms for putting ASW helicopters to sea, especially after the experience in the South Atlantic.

Squadron deployments The RN has been devoid of true fixed-wing air cover—organic air—since the decommissioning of *Ark Royal* in December 1978. In 1980, the first operational Sea Harrier squadron (800 NAS) was re-formed to bring some semblance of a Fleet fighter back to sea.

The 1981 Defence Review has implied that only two jet squadrons will be deployed at sea, which means that just ten aircraft (plus reserves) will be available. There will be another ten aircraft units ashore for operational training and the two afloat units will also be ashore, at Yeovilton, when their parent carriers are in port. Current Sea Harrier deployments are: 800 NAS—*Hermes* (perhaps to *Ark Royal* (V) on commissioning), 801 NAS—*Invincible*, and 809 NAS—South Atlantic/*Illustrious*.

ASW helicopters The mainstay of the current Fleet Air Arm squadrons afloat is the large Westland Sea King which operates in the ASW role from carriers and certain RFAs. The original HAS 1 airframes have now been completely replaced or converted to HAS 2 standard and ultimately new tactical gear will be incorporated to up-rate these aircraft to HAS 5 standard; there will also be new aircraft acquired. Today, the deployment afloat of the operational Sea King squadrons is as follows: 814 NAS—*Illustrious*; 820 NAS—*Invincible*; 824 NAS—RFAs and carriers as required; and 826 NAS—*Hermes* (later *Ark Royal*).

Helicopters have become a very important asset in the ASW fight and they have a great many advantages over surface or even sub-surface warships. The main advantage to the cost-conscious FAA today is that they are comparatively cheap to operate and require less manpower to run. They do, however, require platforms from which to operate and these are expensive pieces of kit. Like ASW warships, they search for, locate and kill submarines. Here again, they have the advantage in that the dipping Type 195 sonar of the Sea King and the Wessex HAS 3 can penetrate different levels and layers in the ocean, as well as remain almost static in rough weather, when hull-mounted sets may even have difficulty remaining in the water!

The helicopter is still, at the present time, undetectable to the submerged submarine between dips or 'jumps' and they are unpredictable as to

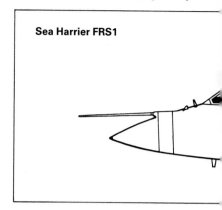

Sea Harrier FRS1

Sea Harrier FRS 1—the only organic air cover for the Fleet; this example from 899 NAS at Yeovilton.

where they will probe next. Despite recent advances in submarine-launched weaponry, the ASW helicopter is still virtually invulnerable to attack from the submarine it is stalking. There is, however, evidence to show that even at 122 knots (a Sea King's maximum rated airspeed), they could have difficulty in remaining in a suitable position to successfully attack the latest high speed Soviet submarines which it is thought will enter service in the mid-1980s.

The front-line ASW helicopters are deployed to provide an effective hunter-killer screen around a Task Group and the Sea King's long endurance makes it ideal for this task. The usual squadron complement varies, but is generally taken to be 12 aircraft with perhaps 18 crews. Each squadron has a party of maintainers, dependent on mark of airframe, deployment and purpose of embarkation, and these engineers are led by the squadron Air Engineering Officer (AEO) with the support of the Senior Maintenance Rating (SMR). The embarked squadron is a self-contained unit capable of remaining serviceable as long as spares are available and the airframes are within servicing life. RFAs which accompany carriers usually carry additional spares, including aero engines for embarked aircraft. Today, the Sea King is the only RN/ASW helicopter embarked in squadron strength, although 824 NAS usually operates with detached flights of two or four aircraft (two flights) in RFAs or to 'top up' other squadrons.

Normal operations against possible threats are by means of a regular screen around the Task Group as discussed in Chapter 2 (ASW). The pilot (not necessarily the Captain of the aircraft) will fly the helicopter to a predetermined search position, usually about 20 nm ahead of the TG, where an attacking submarine is considered most likely to be

lurking near the surface. Although a Sea King or Wessex HAS 3 from a DLG can work alone, it is more usual for it to co-operate with an LRMP aircraft, such as an RAF Nimrod or Canadian Aurora, but the preferred tactical unit appears to be for two ASW helicopters to co-operate together in a search, one trying to maintain contact with a target at all times.

On station, the sonar is operated by the underwater controller (the aircrewman), and the search is directed on set bearings and ranges by the observer, usually in the adjacent seat, in the darkened interior of the helicopter's after cabin. Target information can be fed directly to the observer's plot and this can be transmitted to other units. The observer can direct other helicopters, LRMP aircraft or ships to an attacking position whilst co-ordinating the whole effort, including the continued tracking of target and friendly units. The recent development of passive ASW gear and the LAPADS anaylsis equipment has meant that more information is now available to the tactical co-ordinator, but it also means that the aircrewman has more than his usual work cut out monitoring the systems; if there was the manpower and fuel available, one supposes that there might be five-man aircrews for Sea Kings rather than the present four.

In addition, embarked ASW helicopters have a secondary task in that they can be used against hostile surface ships, but this is really the province of the smaller helicopters like the Lynx HAS 2 and the venerable Wasp HAS 1, which make up Small Ships' Flights.

Aircraft

Since the demise of the aircraft carrier was first mooted in the mid-1960s, the number of fixed-wing aircraft in the Fleet Air Arm has dropped to the low level of today. Without doubt, the modern Royal

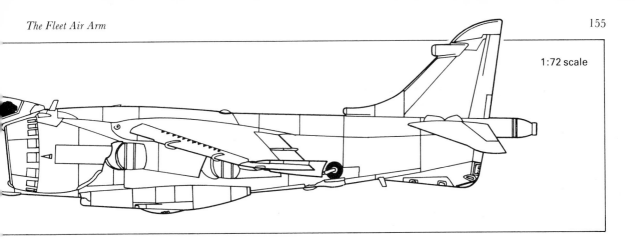

1:72 scale

Navy has a Naval Air Command in which the helicopter predominates. Nevertheless, there are still fixed-wing aircraft in service, particularly the operational Sea Harriers. Each aircraft is described below.

Front-line fixed-wing type: Sea Harrier FRS 1.

Second-line jet fixed-wing types: Hunter T 8C; Hunter T 8M; Hunter GA 11; Canberra T 4; Canberra TT 18; Canberra T 22; Harrier T 4.

Second-line utility and training types: Jetstream T 2; Chipmunk T 10; Sea Devon C 20; Sea Heron C 1/C.4.

Front-line helicopters: Lynx HAS 2; Sea King HAS 2; Sea King HAS 5; Sea King HC 4; Wessex HAS 3; Wessex HU 5; Wasp HAS 1.

Sea Harrier FRS 1

Manufacturer British Aerospace; **Purpose** Shipborne V/STOL strike fighter; **Crew** 1 pilot; **Squadrons** 800; 801; 809; 899; **Range** 750 km (depending on sortie profile); **Endurance** Classified; **Max speed** 625 knots (1,158 kmh); **Cruise speed** 485 knots (900 knots kmh); **Service ceiling** 6,000 m (normal ops); **Rate of climb** Classified; **Length** 14.5 m; 12.9 m (folded); **Height** 3.7 m; **Span** 7.7 m; **Weapons** 2 × 30 mm Aden cannon; flares; AIM-9L Sidewinder; Cluster bombs; 68 mm Matra rockets; (underwing load of 2,268 kg); P3T Sea Eagle; Martel; Harpoon ASM; **Engine** 1 x RR Pegasus 104; **Fuel capacity** 2,277 kg; **All-up weight** 10,433 kg; **Embarked** *Invincible, Illustrious, Hermes*; (*Atlantic Conveyor* during Falklands' operations).

It has taken the Sea Harrier a long time to come into operational service with the RN, because as long ago as 1968 an Admiralty working party had conceived the idea of Sea Harriers based on small aircraft carriers like the present *Invincible* Class. The Sea Harrier has an antecedence going back to the Hawker P.1127 and flight deck trials in *Ark Royal* during 1963, although the actual model in service today is directly descended from the RAF's Harrier GR 3. The main visible changes have been centred on the cockpit area which was completely redesigned to accommodate the Blue Fox radar and other new avionics. The electrical equipment has been altered for the new role and to keep pace with modern developments. V/STOL flying characteristics have been improved by providing increased roll reaction (useful for dog-fighting) and allowing 2° more nose-down pitch control via greater tailplane positive travel. Most importantly from the nautical point of view, only four magnesium components remain in the Sea Harrier; the RR Pegasus accessory gearbox, the nosewheel, and the two outrigger legs. All this navalisation has only resulted in 50 kg of extra weight, which must be a remarkable achievement in modern aviation.

In May 1975, 24 single-seat Sea Harrier FRS 1s and one Harrier T 4 were ordered from British Aerospace. The attrition replacement order for ten more was temporarily shelved in the Defence Review of 1981, although the order was placed in May 1978. As a result of the losses in the South Atlantic, the order is proceeding. The first flight was August 20 1978 and the first deck landings took place in *Hermes* on November 13 1978. The first production aircraft was handed over to the RN for service with 700A Squadron (Intensive Flying Trials Unit) on June 18 1979. The first Sea Harrier went aboard *Invincible* on May 20 1980. Trials were run at sea during 1980 and 1981 as well as operations from the ski-jump trainer at Yeovilton, from which the first Sea Harrier was launched on October 30 1980.

The first front-line Sea Harrier FRS 1 unit was 800 Squadron which formed at the RN's Harrier base at Yeovilton on March 31 1980, followed by 899 Squadron (the training and HQ unit) a matter of

Sea Harrier mission profiles

Role	Probable target	Radius of action
Air Interception and Fleet Fighter	Long range maritime patrol aircraft, including mid-guidance aircraft	400 nm at 6,000 m
Reconnaissance and probe	Search for surface/air threat and the gathering of intelligence against the enemy	20,000 nm² of sea can be covered in one hour's flying at low level
Strike and ground attack	Fast patrol boats, or warships, or shore targets (perhaps for RM landing operations)	250 nm+ depending on sortie profile and armaments.

hours later. In January 1981, the second unit, destined for *Invincible*, 801 Squadron, was formed. 800 had previously been earmarked for *Hermes* and later *Illustrious*. 809 Squadron was formed in April 1982 for service in the South Atlantic, sailing in the container ship, *Atlantic Conveyor*; this was the first such embarkation for V/STOL aircraft and the squadron provided air defence and reconnaissance for that part of the Task Group.

The RN have specified that quick reaction alerts (QRAs) will be necessary and in this role the duty Sea Harrier would always use STO via the ski ramp of the parent ship and be recovered by vertical landing (in the same way as a helicopter does on any flight deck at sea).

Like most subsonic fighters, the Sea Harrier can cruise at 6,000 m at Mach 0.8+ for well over an hour on internal fuel of 2,277 kg, although there is provision for the aircraft to take combat external loads of 730 kg extra. In terms of armaments, the Sea

Harrier carries two 30 mm Aden guns and can take up to 2,270 kg of external war load. Trials have been carried out with the new British Aerospace Dynamics Group Sea Eagle ASV missile which it is thought the Sea Harrier will carry in 1983. Another possibly under consideration is the use of the aircraft for ASW sorties where its QRA ability via ramp take-off means that if it were fitted for deploying sonobuoys, it could be at the action area far quicker than any helicopter yet in service. With the rumoured high submerged speeds of the new generation of Soviet submarine, this will undoubtedly be a special bonus to the Task Group commander. Total time from alarm to a 30 nm distant drop point is under six minutes, assuming that the Sea Harrier was already fitted for the task.

During the Falkland operations, Sea Harriers flew 2,376 sorties totalling 2,675 hours, and made 2,088 deck landings.

Hunter T 8C

Manufacturer Hawker; **Purpose** Fleet Requirements and Air Direction; **Crew** 1/2 pilots; **Squadrons** FRADU; **Range** 1,800 nm (3,333 km); **Endurance** Circa 3 hours; **Max speed** 590 knots (1,100 km/h); **Cruise speed** 500 knots (926 km/h); **Service ceiling** 14,326 m; **Rate of climb** 1,100 m/min; **Length** 14.9 m; **Height** 4.0 m; **Span** 10.3 m; **Weapons** Unarmed but equipped with arrestor hook; **Engine** 1 × RR Avon 122 rated at 3,425 kg static thrust; **Fuel capacity** Classified; **All-up weight** 7,802 kg; **Embarked** Shore-based.

The Hunter T 8 is the navalised variant of the RAF's very successful T 7 and in this mark is a dual-seat side-by-side trainer. When first delivered in 1958, the T 8 was used as an advanced operational trainer for the swept-wing carrier aircraft programme; several were converted to Admiral's barges at one time. In all 41 were delivered to the RN, being conversions of F 4 and T 7 aircraft, and today they are based at Yeovilton with FRADU.

Sea Harrier Operations

Air Defence Role

1½hr. cap

Transit

100NM   Invincible

ASV Strike Role

Transit

Enemy vessel   250NM   Invincible

Reconnaisance Role

Search air   Transit

Invincible

Two sub-marks were originally delivered—the T 8B (with TACAN) and the T 8C (with partial TACAN), both being unarmed when the Aden cannon were removed on conversion. Today, the aircraft are all officially known as T 8Cs and about a dozen are carried on strength at FRADU, with others in store at RNAY Wroughton.

Hunter T8M

Purpose Radar training; **Squadrons** 899; **Length** Circa 15 m.

This is a modified Hunter T 8 airframe which now incorporates the cockpit arrangement and Blue Fox radar of the Sea Harrier FRS 1. Initially, 899 Squadron at Yeovilton is due to have only one on strength for pilot training but it is probable that at least two others are available for Blue Fox trials. It is reported that the Hunter T 8M is a very cost-effective way of putting fixed-wing pilots through much of their Sea Harrier tactical and operational training.

Hunter GA 11

Purpose Fleet Requirements and Air Direction, pilot training; **Crew** 1 pilot; **Squadrons** FRADU; **Service ceiling** 15,240 m; **Rate of climb** 1,392 m/min; **Length** 14.0 m; **Weapons** Practice bombs only, equipped with arrestor hook; **Engine** 1 × RR Avon 113 rated at 3,402 kg static thrust; **Fuel capacity** Classified; **All-up weight** 7,757 kg; **Embarked** Shore-based.

The prototype Hawker Hunter (then called the P.1067) first flew as long ago as July 20 1951 and since then it has become a world beater. Those flying in Royal Navy colours are crewed by civilians under contract to Airwork as part of the FRADU organisation. The GA 11s are the RN weapons trainer variant of the Hunter F 4, from which they

were converted, and the former originally served in the same role with 738 Squadron. Today, the GA 11 is used to provide target and tracking facilities and requirements to the Fleet, especially for warships during refit and post-refit trials. Of the 40 aircraft originally converted, about 18 remain active with several more in store at RNAY Wroughton. During the conversion, the guns and gunsights were removed, but a large Harley Light fitted into the nose for visual tracking. Some of the aircraft first flew as long ago as 1954 and they are now painted dark sea grey and white with red/white/blue roundels and white serials and codes. First deliveries to the RN were made in 1962 and, between 1975–1980, the RN operated the world's only civilian crewed jet aerobatic team called very appropriately the 'Blue Herons', coming as they did from HMS *Heron* (RNAS Yeovilton).

Canberra T 4

Manufacturer English Electric; **Purpose** Fleet Requirements and Air Direction training; **Crew** 1/2 pilots; 1 observer; **Squadrons** FRADU; **Range** Circa 3,300 nm (6,112 km); **Endurance** Circa 6 hours; **Max speed** 500 knots (926 km/h); **Cruise speed** 450 knots (833 km/h); **Service ceiling** Classified; **Rate of climb** Classified; **Length** 19.8 m; **Height** 4.9 m; **Span** 19.5 m; **Weapons** Unarmed; **Engine** 2 × RR Avon; **Fuel capacity** Classified; **All-up weight** Circa 24,750 kg; **Embarked** Shore-based.

Over the years, a number of former RAF Canberra T 4 trainers were delivered to the Royal

Below *Canberra T4—used for training.* **Overleaf: Top** *Hunter T 8C—a FRADU-operated type.* **Centre** *Hunter T 8M used for Sea Harrier radar training with 899 NAS but operated by FRADU.* **Bottom** *Hunter GA 11, civilian-crewed, seen here at Gibraltar.*

Hunter T8C

Hunter T8M

Hunter GA11

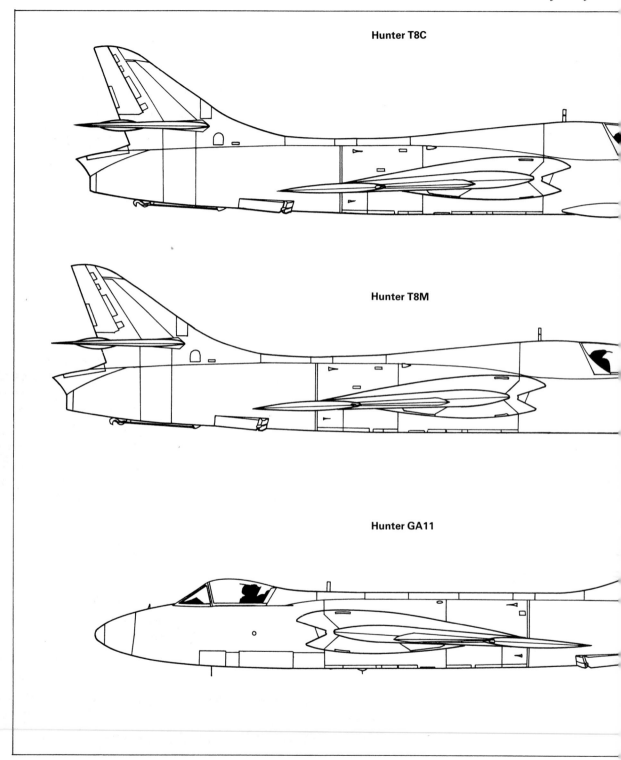

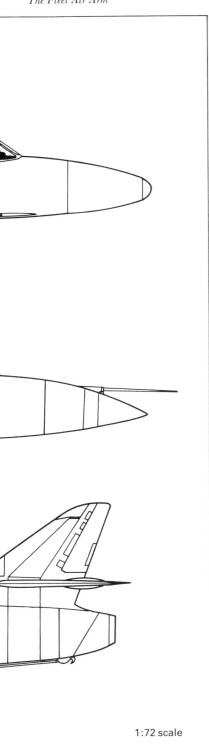

1:72 scale

Canberra T4/TT18

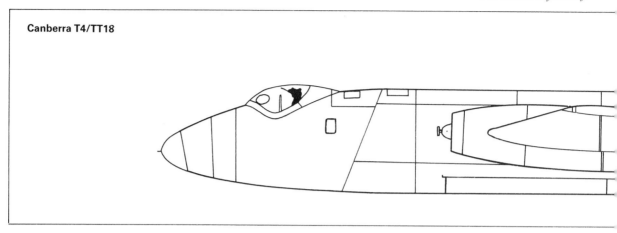

Navy. The T 4 is based on the B 2 (hence is similar in flying characteristics to the TT 18 and T 20) which was first delivered to the RAF in the early 1950s. Today, the Canberra T 4s fly with FRADU at Yeovilton where they are used to train the civilian aircrew and to provide additional targets for radar calibration as required. The T 4 has dual controls.

Canberra TT 18

Purpose Target-towing; **Crew** 1 pilot; 1 observer; **All-up weight** 24,800 kg.

The Canberra TT 18 is a special conversion of the English Electric Canberra B 2 bomber designed for service with the RAF, and 16 were converted for use by FRADU at Yeovilton. Usually equipped with the Flight Refuelling Rushton drone, the Canberra TT 18 fulfils a very useful role by providing warships in work-up with targets for gunnery practice. The aircraft are painted a light aircraft grey colour with

very prominent black/yellow stripes over all the undersurfaces.

Canberra T 22

Purpose Fleet Requirements, Air Direction and pilot familiarisation; **Crew** 1 pilot; 1 observer.

When the RAF updated its fleet of photo-reconnaissance Canberras, a number of airframes were made available to the RN and converted for a special training role at the British Aircraft Corporation base at Samlesbury. Several of the airframes first flew in the early 1950s, whilst the first conversion took to the air in June 1973. At that time only six were converted, but more were worked on later. The aircraft are flown by the civilian aircrew of FRADU and can be distinguished by the pointed nose and light aircraft grey finish with dayglo bands. (Note: Six Canberra U 10 drones were converted from B 2 airframes in the 1960s and were all

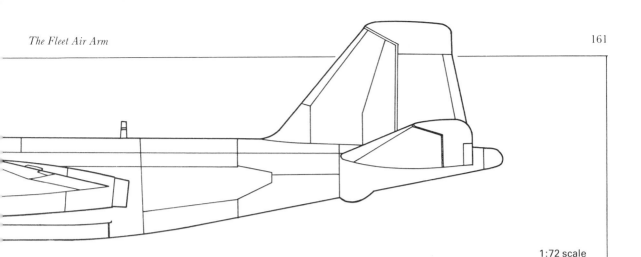

1:72 scale

expended during the Seacat missile trials in the Mediterranean.)

Harrier T 4

Manufacturer British Aerospace; **Purpose** Operational training; **Crew** 1/2 pilots; **Squadrons** 899 (SHSU/FRADU); **Range** 2,000 nm (3,704 km); **Endurance** Circa 4 hours; **Max speed** 625 knots (1,158 km/h); **Cruise speed** 480 knots (889 km/h); **Service ceiling** 5,000 m; **Rate of climb** Classified; **Length** 17.0 m; **Height** 3.71 m; **Span** 7.7 m; **Weapons** As for Sea Harrier FRS 1; **Engine** 1 × RR Pegasus 104; **Fuel capacity** 2,955 litres; **All up weight** 6,168 kg; **Embarked** Shore-based.

Although most of the Sea Harrier training and conversion work is carried out with the RAF at Wittering, Northants, there is one Harrier T 4 aircraft which is operated by the Fleet Air Arm's 899 Squadron at both Yeovilton and one at Wittering.

They are, however, marked in RAF camouflage at the moment. The Harrier T 4 is the dual seat (tandem) version of the Harrier GR 3. Because this type has not been specially adapted for embarkation, it remains shore-based even when 899 deploys for work-up aboard a carrier. It is, however, very useful for co-ordinated air weapons and warfare training.

Jetstream

Manufacturer BAe (Scottish Division); **Purpose** Observer training/communications; **Crew** 1/2

Left *Canberra T 22—the Blue Parrot-equipped variant.* **Below** *Canberra TT 18—the target-towing variant, seen here at Gibraltar.* **Overleaf: Centre** *Harrier T 4 operated in RAF colours to assist centralised servicing at RAF Wittering.* **Bottom** *Jetstream T 2 at home at Culdrose, prior to a navigation exercise.*

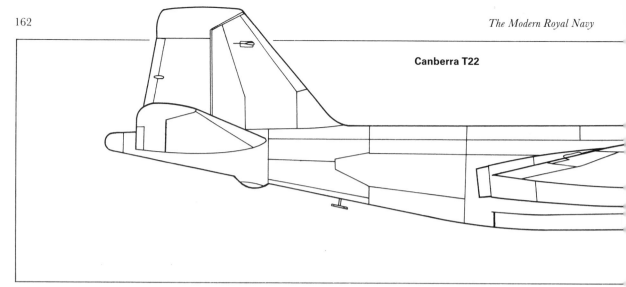

Canberra T22

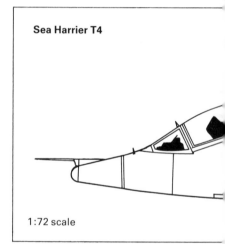

Sea Harrier T4

1:72 scale

1:72 scale

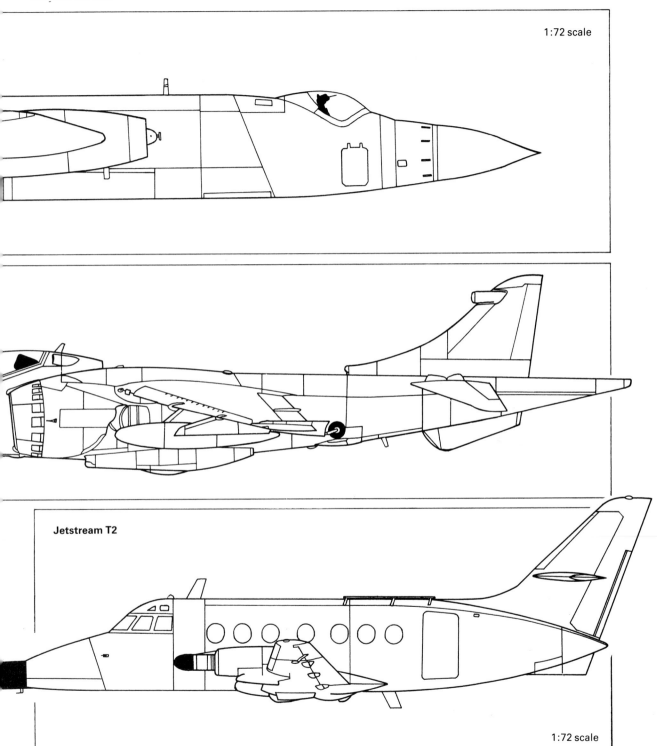

Jetstream T2

1:72 scale

pilots; 1/2 instructors; 2/3 observer pupils; **Squadrons** 750; **Range** 1,380 nm (2,555 km); **Endurance** Circa 5 hours; **Max speed** 250 knots (463 km/h); **Cruise speed** 240 knots (444 km/h); **Service ceiling** 7,925 m; **Rate of climb** 762 m/min; **Length** 14.36 m; **Height** 5.32 m; **Span** 15.85 m; **Weapons** Unarmed; **Engine** 2 × Turbomeca/RR Astazou XVI rated at 940 shp; **Fuel capacity** Classified; **All-up weight** 5,693 kg; **Embarked** Shore-based.

The Scottish Aviation Jetstream began life as a product of the Handley Page company and was ordered originally by the RAF as a multi-engine trainer. It did not enter FAA service until 1979, when several RAF airframes which had been in storage were refitted for service with 750 Squadron, then flying the Hunting Sea Prince. Today, the Jetstream is used as a flying classroom for the RN Observer School at Culdrose for low and high level navigation, general airmanship and radio/radar operations. The medium range of the aircraft enables training flights to be made to various European landfalls including Berlin, Munich, Valkenburg (Netherlands), Wildenrath (West Germany), Oporto (Portugal) and Gibraltar.

There is currently speculation that a small number of Jetstreams will be purchased for the FAA to act as communications aircraft in place of the Sea Devons and Sea Herons which are now feeling the ravages of age. Time will tell if another squadron will be formed or whether the aircraft will be taken on strength by Station Flights.

Chipmunk T 10

Manufacturer de Havilland Canada; **Purpose** Training and air experience; **Crew** 1/2 pilots; **Squadrons** RNR Flight; BRNC; Station Flights; **Range** 260 nm (482 km); **Endurance** 2 hours; **Max**

Sea Devon and Sea Heron—originally based at Daedalus, *but now operated by station flights or in store, this pair are seen over the Solent.*

speed 120 knots (222 km/h); **Cruise speed** 100 knots (185 km/h); **Service ceiling** Circa 3,000 m; **Rate of climb** Circa 240 m/min; **Length** 7.82 m; **Height** 2.16 m; **Span** 10.47 m; **Weapons** Unarmed; **Engine** DH Gipsy Major B rated at 145 hp; **Fuel capacity** 82 litres; **All-up weight** 908 kg; **Embarked** Shore-based.

The Chipmunk elementary trainer was designed and built in Canada and then in the United Kingdom for the RAF, RN and Army. The RN received 12 for the Britannia Royal Naval College Flight now based at Roborough, near Plymouth. In addition, several are in use around the various Air Stations for glider towing and air experience. The RNR (Air Branch) has also been using them and for a time one was based at Lee-on-Solent with 781 Squadron for this purpose. The aircraft is very manoeuvrable and provides the FAA with an

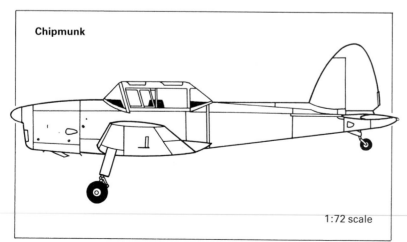

Chipmunk

1:72 scale

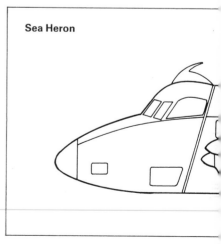

Sea Heron

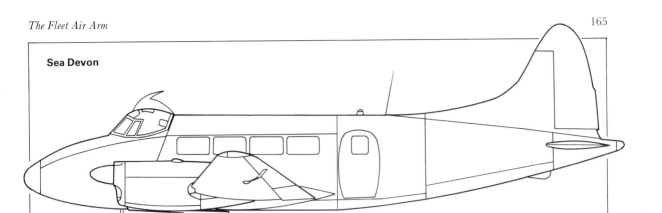

Sea Devon

1:72 scale

opportunity to teach basic airmanship to young officers at Dartmouth and at Manadon. It is expected to continue in service for several more years until, presumably, the Scottish Aviation Bulldog on which naval pilots learn to fly with the RAF becomes available.

Sea Devon C 20

Manufacturer de Havilland; **Purpose** Communications and fisheries' protection; **Crew** 1/2 pilots; 1 attendant and up to 8 passengers; **Squadrons** Station Flights; **Range** 765 nm (1,417 km); **Endurance** Circa 3 hours; **Max speed** 200 knots (370 km/h); **Cruise speed** 170 knots (315 km/h); **Service ceiling** 6,000 m; **Rate of climb** Circa 260 m/min; **Length** 11.96 m; **Height** 4.06 m; **Span** 17.37 m; **Weapons** Unarmed; **Engine** 2 × DH Gipsy Queen 70 rated at 340 shp each; **Fuel capacity** Classified; **All-up weight** 4,060 kg; **Embarked** Shore-based.

The Sea Devon is the navalised version of the highly successful de Havilland Dove light transport and was first acquired by the Fleet Air Arm in 1955 for light communications duties. Since then it has carried out a number of tasks, including VIP transport, air ambulance, Fisheries' Protection and HM Coast Guard surveillance of the Dover Straits. At one time there were about a dozen in service with Station Flights and with the now defunct 781 Squadron—the 'Naval Clippers'. The aircraft has also been used for twin-engine conversion flying and, although this is now carried on by Culdrose/*Seahawk* Station Flight, it is a declining role.

Sea Heron C 1/C 4

Purpose Communications; **Crew** 1/2 pilots; 1 attendant and up to 14 passengers; **Squadrons** FONAC; Station Flights; **Range** 400 nm (741 km); **Endurance** Circa 2 hours; **Max speed** 175 knots (324 km/h); **Cruise speed** 159 knots (295 km/h);

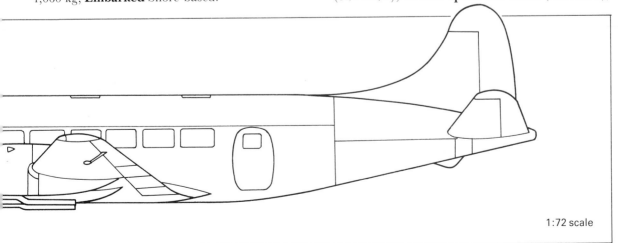

1:72 scale

Left *Chipmunk T 10—this example is operated by the BRNC flight but others operate with station flights.*

Below right *Lynx HAS 2 operating aboard RFA Engadine whilst on a training sortie with 702 NAS; it is reported that a search Lynx (the HAS 5) will be operational in 1983/4 (HMS Heron).*

Service ceiling 5,639 m; **Rate of climb** 323 m/min; **Length** 14.8 m; **Height** 4.32 m; **Span** 21.8 m; **Weapons** Unarmed; **Engine** 4 × DH Gipsy Queen 30 rated at 250 hp each; **Fuel capacity** Classified; **All-up weight** 6,124 kg; **Embarked** Shore-based.

In 1961, the Fleet Air Arm introduced this aircraft to communications and VIP work with 781 Squadron, as a supplement to the Sea Devon which had already been in service for six years. With the phasing out of FONAC's jet VIP Hunter T 8, one Sea Heron was transferred to *Heron* Flight for his use. Today, with the disbandment of 781 Squadron, the aircraft is still in service with Culdrose/*Seahawk* and Yeovilton/*Heron* Flights for communications, Fisheries' Protection and surveillance duties. It is not anticipated that the Sea Heron will remain in service beyond 1985 and the supposed replacement is the Scottish Aviation Jetstream already operated by the FAA in an observer training role.

Lynx HAS 2

Manufacturer Westland; **Purpose** Ship-borne surface and ASW strike; **Crew** 1 pilot; 1 observer; 1 aircrewman; up to 10 passengers; **Squadrons** 702; 815; **Range** 320 nm (593 km); **Endurance** 2.83 hours; **Max speed** 135 knots (250 km/h); **Cruise speed** 125 knots (232 km/h); 122 knots (226 km/h) on one engine; **Service ceiling** 2,920 m; **Rate of climb** 660 m/min; **Length** 11.92 m; 15.16 m (rotors); **Height** 3.58 m; **Width** 12.8 m; 2.95 m (rotors folded); **Rotor diameter** 12.8 m; **Weapons** Mk 44, Mk 46, Stingray torpedoes; Sea Skua ASM; Nord AS 11 ASM; nuclear depth bombs; GPMG; 20 mm cannon; Miniguns; **Engine** 2 × RR Gem rated at 1,120 shp; **Fuel capacity** 726 kg; **All-up weight** 4,309 kg; **Embarked** *Leander*, *Amazon* and *Broadsword* Class frigates; *Sheffield* Class destroyers; can operate from all decks; also shore-based.

The Westland Lynx was the third of the Anglo-French helicopters of the 1960s/1970s (the other two being the Gazelle and the Puma) and is a new technology design specifically designed to meet worldwide requirements as a light shipborne helicopter. It is, then, a second generation, but greatly improved Wasp and as such is embarked in Small Ships' Flights. Unlike the Wasp, it is a twin-engine, all-weather, high-performance helicopter. It can be successfully deck-landed when the parent ship is rolling at 20° or more and can land on the deck independently without restricting the tactical

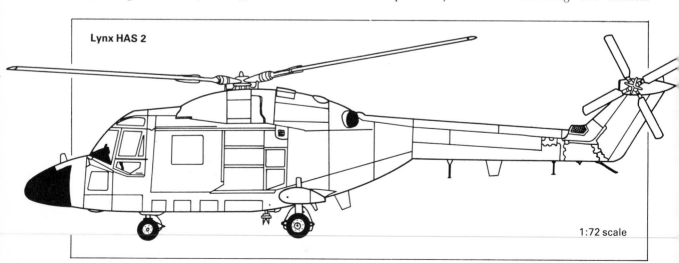

Lynx HAS 2

1:72 scale

movement of the warship. The tricycle undercarriage arrangement with two-stage oleos provides high energy absorption and stability, especially when linked to the Harpoon deck handling device. Immediately after landing the pilot can apply 1,360 kg downward thrust to keep the helicopter on the deck. It is quite amazing to watch the helicopter rotate on its own axis for positioning prior to take-off or to align with the hangar. The main rotors fold simply and the tail pylon folds back to give an overall stowage space of 10.61 m; this is most useful in the refitted *Leanders* and other small ships of the RN from which the Lynx has been operating since 1979. It first went to sea in *Birmingham* although much of the initial operational experience was gained in *Sirius*.

Primarily, the Lynx is used in the RN for surface search and attack sorties and for this it is equipped with Seaspray radar (derived from the Blue Fox in the Sea Harrier). This gives the parent ship an over-the-horizon search capability. In the ASW role, the Lynx is designed to localise, classify (with assistance from 'mother' or another sonar-equipped helicopter, such as the Sea King) and then attack underwater targets. For ASW strike, the Lynx can be equipped with Mk 44, Mk 46 or Stingray torpedoes. In addition, it is possible to take marine markers, Mk 10 depth charges and other light stores up. In this mode, the radius of action is 40 nm, but without heavy armament the Lynx can stay on station for 2½ hours. The ever-increasing threat from small warships which are missile-equipped has led to the development of the high technology Sea Skua lightweight missile, of which the Lynx can carry four. Using its own radar resource, the Lynx would search out these over-the-horizon targets before they became a serious threat to the parent warship.

Its rapid reaction time means that the Lynx can be used for SAR and rescue support roles. For this a lightweight hoist is usually fitted which has a 272 kg lifting capacity, ie, aircrewman and survivor. There is seating for up to eight passengers, although if the

depth bombs; GPMG; **Engine** 2 × RR Gnome
rated at 1,660 shp; **Fuel capacity** 680 kg; **All-up
weight** 9,300 kg; **Embarked** *Invincible, Illustrious,
Hermes, Fort* Class and other similar decks.

The sea King helicopter is the primary airborne
ASW system in the modern RN and is embarked in
both the major warship platforms, as well as certain
RFAs. On shore, the helicopter fulfils a similar role,
but its secondary task of SAR comes more to the
forefront. It has a reputation as a dependable
helicopter with low maintenance requirements.

*Sea King HAS 2—the forerunner of the now-standard HAS 5, but
still in service with several units; in time they will be converted to
Mk 5 standard.*

helicopter is ECM-equipped one will have to mind
his feet because the 'black box' is positioned
immediately behind the observer, but in front of the
first port-side pax seat! A typical SAR sortie would
have radius of action of 100 nm.

At sea, the Lynx also has a limited vertical
replenishment (vertrep) role and can carry up to
1,586 kg internally if the cabin seats are removed, or
externally as an underslung load from the cargo
hook. It is possible for a Lynx to transfer 4,536 kg of
stores between two ships 50 nm apart in 2½ hours
without the need to refuel or land.

Modern technology has made the Lynx relatively
easy to maintain and thus the number of
maintainers in a ship's flight has been reduced (see
above). New equipment recently adopted for service
by 815 Squadron, the operational parent NAS at
Portland, includes an airborne, towed magnetic
anomoly detector (MAD) which is positioned on the
starboard rear undercarriage sponson. Details of
this are still secret. An uprated Lynx variant, known
as the HAS 3, is due to enter service in 1983 and all
further Lynx production for the RN will be to this
standard.

Sea King HAS 2

Purpose ASW, SAR and training; **Crew** 1/2 pilots;
1 observer; 1 aircrewman; up to 25 passengers;
Squadrons 706; 814; 819; 824; 825; **Range**
600 nm+ (1,111 km); **Endurance** 4 hours; **Max
speed** 112 knots (207 km/h); **Cruise speed** 100
knots (185 km/h); **Service ceiling** 3,200 m; **Rate of
climb** 911 m/min; **Length** 17.01 m; 22.15 m
(rotors); **Height** 5.13 m; **Width** 5.0 m (rotors
folded); **Rotor diameter** 18.9 m; **Main cargo door**
1.72 m × 1.52 m; **Weapons** Mk 44, Mk 46,
Stingray torpedoes; Mk 11 depth charges; nuclear

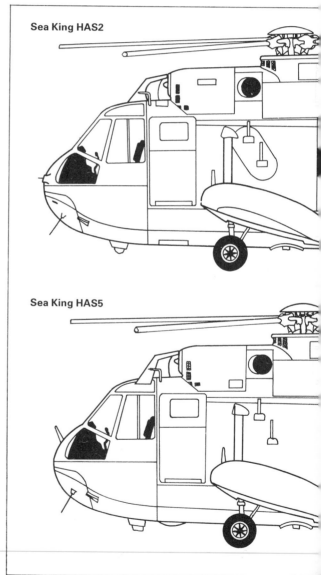

Sea King HAS2

Sea King HAS5

The Sea King HAS 2 was a development of the HAS 1 which entered service in 1969; some aircraft were retro-fitted to Mk 2 standards whilst others were specially built. Today, the HAS 2 is being replaced in service by the HAS 5 (*qv*) in a similar fashion. The Sea King integrates sonar, radar, doppler, automatic flight control and ASW weapons into a complete hunter-killer aerial platform. It has an all-weather ability and can detect, classify and attack even the fastest of the present day nuclear submarines. In this role, the Sea King carries two pilots, an observer/ASW controller and an aircrewman to operate the dunking sonar or drop the mini-sonobuoys. The role of the Sea King in the tactical scenario has been discussed above, but without doubt the system does give the RN an edge on the opposition.

In terms of armament, the Sea King can be fitted for Mk 44 or Mk 46 (the more usual load) lightweight torpedoes and it will deploy the new Stingray in due course. Depth charges can also be carried but these are very much last-ditch weapons.

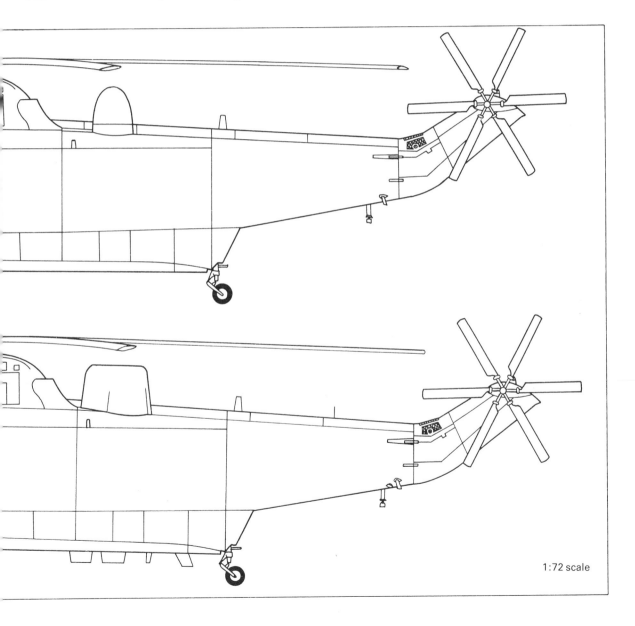

1:72 scale

The RN has experimented with command-control missions for missiles, but one suspects that the afloat ASVW role is limited at present, with the Lynx being the primary system here.

An important secondary role for the Sea King is that of SAR and both the shore-based and the afloat squadrons have practised this to a fine art, as has been demonstrated on numerous occasions. The automatic flight control system allows the aircraft to hover above a survivor for winching day or night, just as easily as it hovers for the dunking sonobuoy to do its work. Famous rescues include the Fastnet Race in 1979; the two Dutch Navy Atlantique sorties (1979 and 1981) and the first Royal rescue when Midshipman Prince Andrew successfully piloted a Sea King HAS 2 of 706 Squadron during a rescue of a submariner swept overboard in September 1981.

The Sea King represented a number of firsts for the RN and the FAA: a retractable undercarriage; a boat-shaped hull which can be used in emergency for take-off and landing on the sea (but with two engines turning preferably!); a fully automatic blade folding system and realistic long-time endurance on the ASW screen.

Sea King HAS 5

Crew Up to 22 passengers; **Squadrons** 706; 820; 825; 826; **Range** 664 nm (1,230 km); **Endurance** 5 hours; **All-up weight** 9,526 kg; **Underslung load** 2,948 kg.

The Sea King HAS 5 is updated variant of the basic Sea King airframe and, although several have been derived from Mk 2 airframes, the initial order

Above *Sea King HAS 5, the latest Sea King variant, this example is from 826 Squadron.* **Below left** *Wessex HAS 3—the old warhorse of the DLG flights: Antrim's example illustrated.*

was for 17, the first being handed over to the RN at Culdrose on October 2 1980. The enhanced design has a new radome for the provision of the MEL Sea Searcher radar in due course, but at present the Ferranti radar and Racal Decca 71 Doppler are employed. Internally, the cabin has been lengthened to provide space for passive mini-Jezebel sonobuoy dispensers and its associated Marconi LAPADS data processing equipment. The new equipment is designed to allow the aircrew to pinpoint an enemy submarine at far greater range than at present. In addition to monitoring the signals from its own sonobuoys, the Sea King HAS 5 will be able to handle information from buoys dropped by RAF Nimrod aircraft in a joint search operation. During the search the Sea King can stay on station for long

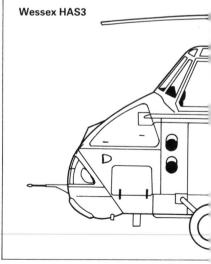

Wessex HAS3

periods (say 2½–3 hours depending on crew stamina) and operate about 100 nm from the Task Group. A crew of four will still operate the aircraft with the aircrewman operating the LAPADS equipment at an additional crew station. Future developments of the aircraft include the carriage of more powerful torpedoes and MAD gear, currently on trials.

Wessex HAS 3

Purpose ASW/surface search; training; **Crew** 1/2 pilots; 1 observer; 1 aircrewman; **Squadrons** 737; DLG Flights; **Range** 300 nm (555 km); **Endurance** 1.75 hours; **Max speed** 128 knots (237 km/h); **Cruise speed** 100 knots (185 km/h); **Service ceiling** Circa 4,000 m; **Rate of climb** 500 m/min; **Length** 11.73 m (tail folded); 20.08 m (rotors); **Height** 4.39 m; **Width** 3.66 m (wheel track); **Rotor diameter** 17.07 m; **Weapons** Mk 44, Mk 46 torpedoes; Mk 11 depth charge; nuclear depth bomb; GPMG; **Engine** 1 × Napier Gazelle gas turbine rated at 1,600 shp; **Fuel capacity** Classified; **All-up weight** 6,123 kg; **Embarked** *County* Class DLGs; *Engadine* (for training).

Based on the successful Wessex HAS 1 airframe, which was itself a licence-built Sikorsky S-51, the Wessex HAS 3 has provided initially carriers and later *County* Class DLGs with an effective if somewhat limited ASW vehicle. The Wessex HAS 3, like so many of the RN's helicopters, was built by Westland Helicopters at Yeovil, Somerset, and first entered service in 1967. The characteristic hump behind the main rotors gives the helicopter its

Service nickname of the 'Camel', but this seemingly ugly appendage contains a lightweight but sophisticated Ferranti radar. The dunking sonar carried aboard the helicopter is the Type 195, as used in the Sea King which has replaced the HAS 3 in four operational squadrons. Today, its future is very limited and the DLG Flights' parent squadron—737—will disband in December 1982.

At sea, the Wessex HAS 3 is an integrated part of the DLG's weapons system, in fact their only ASW system, and for offensive load carries a variety of air launched AS weapons including the unloved Mk 10 depth charge and the Mk 46 homing torpedo. The helicopter's role is to locate, track and kill hostile submarines, but facilities exist for it to be used in the surface search, rescue, vertrep and air controller roles as well. Without doubt, the Westland Wessex HAS 3 has been a reliable and adaptable workhorse in FAA service.

Wasp HAS 1

Purpose ASW/surface attack; communications; **Crew** 1 pilot; 1 aircrewman; 1 observer (*Endurance* only); up to 3 passengers; **Squadrons** 829; **Range** 415 nm (770 km); **Endurance** 2.4 hours; **Max speed** 120 knots (222 km/h); **Cruise speed** 100 knots (185 km/h); **Service ceiling** 3,810 m; **Rate of climb** 183 m/min; **Length** 7.85 m (folded); 12.29 m (rotors); **Height** 3.61 m; **Width** 2.64 m (folded); **Rotor diameter** 9.83 m; **Weapons** Mk 44 torpedoes; Mk 11 depth charge; nuclear depth bomb; Nord AS 12 ASM; GPMG; **Engine** 1 × RR Nimbus; **Fuel capacity** 562 kg; **All-up weight**

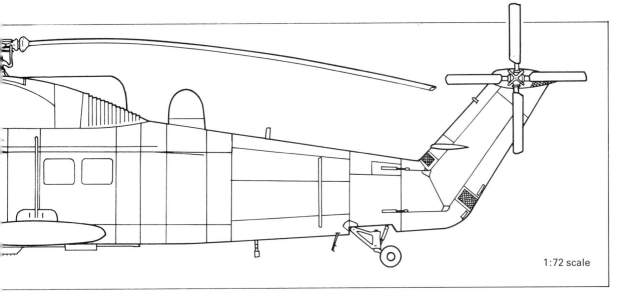

1:72 scale

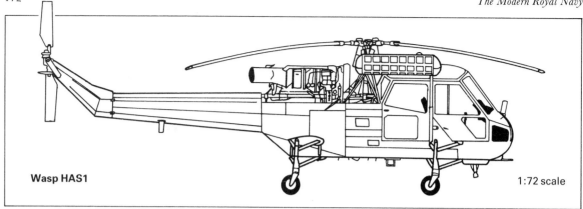

Wasp HAS1

1:72 scale

2,457 kg; **Embarked** *Leander* and *Rothesay* Class frigates; *Endurance* and RFAs; Survey ships.

The Westland Wasp HAS 1 is now approaching the end of its life with the FAA. The first naval version flew in October 1962 and it is now reduced to operating from the older FFHs of the RN, Ocean Survey vessels and the Ice Patrol ship *Endurance* (which is due to be put into reserve in 1982/3). In addition, several RFAs can operate the Wasp in the vertrep, communications or utility role but their lack of ASW sonar, etc, would make them a platform for the Wasp at best. The early use of embarked helicopters of this type has given the RN a leading role in modern ASW operations and many young FAA officers were given their first chance of command in Wasp flights. The helicopter is, however, very much first generation, being purely a weapons carrier without any sensors of its own. The weather conditions in which it has operated in the past have varied from tropical calm to North Sea gale, but in every environment the Wasp has acquitted itself well. At Dartmouth the helicopter still provides cadets with their first taste of naval helicopters whilst RNR Air Branch officers continue to use the aircraft for continuation training. The air-to-surface missile firing role with the AS 12 ASM will now be phased out rapidly as the Lynx replacement with its Sea Skua system is brought into service in ever-increasing numbers.

Sea King HC 4

Purpose Air Commando; **Crew** 1/2 pilots; 1 aircrewman; 28 fully armed troops; **Squadrons** 846; **Range** 664 nm (1,230 km); **Ferry range** 814 nm

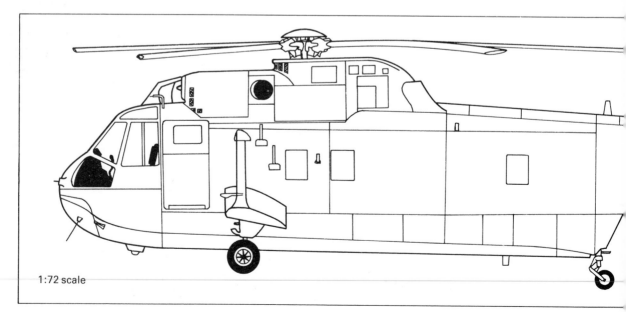

1:72 scale

Wasp HAS 1—the first RN helicopter embarked for small ships' flights: note flotation bags and missile sight.

(can operate from any amphibious ship or RFA; during Falklands Deployment operated from *Canberra* and *Queen Elizabeth 2*).

For the first time, the Royal Marines have a means of transporting their heavier equipment without needing the assistance of ASW Sea Kings. The Sea King HC 4 (known commercially as the Westland Commando) is the first heavy lift air commando aircraft and has become an outstanding troop transport even in the north of Norway during the winter months. Typically, the Sea King HC 4 can carry 28 fully armed men into action and de-plane them through the large cargo door, or it can carry their equipment internally or their vehicles as underslung loads (up to 3,600 kg). It has an all-weather day or night capability and automatic flight control systems for easy operation in the hover.

In the casevac role, the aircraft can carry a total of 16 injured with their medical attendant over a distance of 610 km or 329 nm at sea level.

In the RN, the Sea King HC 4 operates in the field

(1,507 km); **Endurance** 5.9 hours; **Max speed** Circa 125 knots (232 km/h); **Cruise speed** 112 knots (208 km/h); **Service ceiling** 1,525 m; **Rate of climb** 616 m/min; **Length** 17.02 m; 22.15 m (rotors); **Height** 5.13 m; **Cabin height** 1.9 m; **Width** 18.9 m (rotors turning); **Rotor diameter** 18.9 m (main); 3.15 m (tail); **Main door size** 1.72 m × 1.52 m; **Personnel door** 0.92 m × 1.67 m; **Weapons** GPMG (door-mounted); **Engine** 2 × RR Gnome turboshafts rated at 1,660 shp; **Fuel capacity** 3,636 litres; **All-up weight** 9,525 kg; **Basic aircraft** 5,070 kg; **Embarked** Shore-based

Sea King HC 4 provides the RM with heavy lift, especially in Norway (Westland).

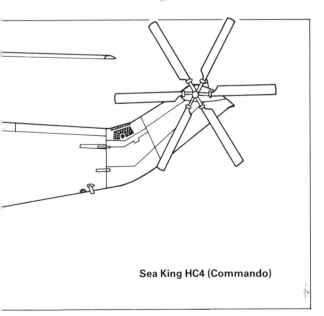

Sea King HC4 (Commando)

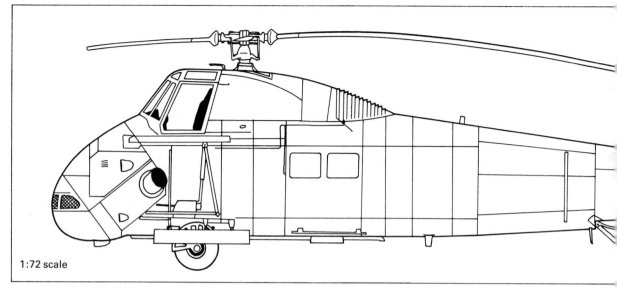

1:72 scale

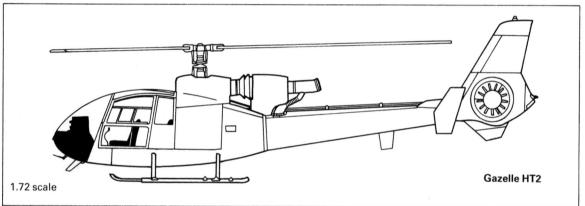

1.72 scale   **Gazelle HT2**

alongside the Royal Marines but it can be embarked for short periods in *Hermes*, *Invincible* or *Illustrious* or one of the Assault Landing Ships (LPDs). It first flew on September 26, 1979 and 15 have been ordered for the RN to serve with 846 NAS; three were lost in the Falklands operations, including one which forced-landed in Chile and was destroyed by its crew.

Wessex HU 5

Purpose Air Commando; logistic support; helo delivery; **Crew** 1/2 pilots; 1 aircrewman; 16 troops; **Squadrons** 771; 772; 845; 847; 848; **Range** 270 nm (500 km); **Endurance** 2.25 hours; **Max speed** 132 knots (245 km/h); **Cruise speed** 121 knots (225 km/h); **Service ceiling** 1,676 m; **Rate of climb** 500 m/min; **Length** 14.74 m; **Height** 4.93 m; **Width** 3.7 m; **Rotor diameter** 17.07 m; **Weapons**

GPMG; Nord AS 11 ASM; 2.75-in/70 mm rocket launchers; flares; **Engine** 2 × RR Gnome turboshafts; **Fuel capacity** Classified; **All-up weight** 6,120 kg; **Embarked** Assault ships; CVLs; RFAs; LSLs; SAR Flights.

Although the Wessex airframe has been around for a long time, it was only in 1963 that the first RN squadrons were equipped with the twin engined (1,350 shp) Wessex HU 5 for the Commando assault and logistical support role, mainly from the newly developed Commando Carriers. Today, the role of the helicopter has changed and more emphasis has been placed on operating in the field alongside RM units and in SAR duties from Lee-on-Solent, Culdrose and Portland, as well as providing ships' flights for *Invincible*, *Illustrious* and *Hermes*. The main limiting feature is that the Wessex has, in modern terms, limited lift capability, being capable

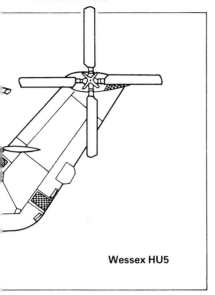

Wessex HU5

only of 1,588 kg as opposed to the Sea King HC 4's 3,600 kg. Nevertheless, the Wessex has an operational life until the early 1990s in the vertrep and support roles, although it is possible with defence cuts this may be shortened by several years. What is particularly important about these aircraft, is the way in which it is easy for the aircrew to become familiar with them and the way in which they have been flown with flair and daring along Norwegian fjords during arctic exercises and into trouble spots in Aden, Cyprus, Northern Ireland and the Falklands. Truly an outstanding aircraft.

Gazelle HT 2

Purpose Training/utility; **Crew** 1/2 pilots; 1 aircrewman and up to 4 passengers; **Squadrons** 705 ('Sharks' team); **Range** 350 nm (648 km); **Endurance** 2.5 hours; **Max speed** 168 knots (311 km/h); 25 knots (46 km/h) (backwards); **Cruise speed** 130 knots (240 km/h); **Service ceiling** 3,650 m; **Rate of climb** 540 m/min; **Length** 9.52 m; 12.09 (rotors); **Height** 3.02 m; **Rotor diameter** 10.5 m; **Weapons** Unarmed (but could mount GPMG); **Engine** 1 × Turbomeca/RR Astazou IIIN rated at 600 shp; **Fuel capacity** 445

Above *Wessex HU 5 marked with low visibility colours—an example from 845 NAS.* **Below** *Gazelle HT 2—the type used by Prince Andrew for flying training.*

litres; **All-up weight** 1,800 kg; empty 1,040 kg; **Embarded** Shore-based.

This is the naval helicopter training variant of the Anglo-French Westland Gazelle AH 1* and all RN examples are based at RNAS Culdrose where they form 705 Squadron. The helicopters are painted red and white with black serials and codes, in addition to which they all have a black shark emblem on their tails. The latter feature is* to assist pooled maintenance in the summer flying season when the Gazelles are the mounts of the 'Sharks' (*qv*) helicopter aerobatic team. In 1981, Prince Andrew (with the rank of Midshipman) completed a very successful flying course with 705 Squadron and their Gazelles. Maintenance at Culdrose is carried out by civilians under contract to the RN. The Gazelle HT 2 first entered service in 1975 and 36 were delivered to the RN.

Future ASW helicopter developments

Although it is conceivable that both the Sea King HAS 5 and the Lynx HAS 2 will continue in RN service until the turn of the century, the Fleet Air Arm, more specifically DNAW and DGA(N), have been considering the long-term replacement programme. Without doubt the HAS 5, with active and passive sonar as well as MAD, is the best ASW helicopter in the world in this role, but it is now a dated design. The airframe can probably take more development but not in the propulsion side. The Lynx HAS 2, on the other hand, could be uprated in terms of engine power, and this would be needed if the helicopter were to be equipped with the light dunking sonar, as are French and West German equivalents; this version in RN use would be designated HAS 5.

In 1978, plans were announced for a design called the Westland WG 34 which would be the ASW helicopter for the 1990–2010 period with special features including active/passive sonar, three engines and an enclosed weapons bay. The requirement was that the helicopter should be capable of operating at greater ranges than the present Sea Kings—600 nm/1,111 km—and in an independent environment. The use of sonobuoys would be exploited and automatic data information handling would be used to lessen the workload on the observer-aircrewman team so that they could fight the ASW battle. The use of MAD and other

Agusta/Westland EH-101 (formerly WG 34) Sea King replacement helicopter for the RN and other navies (Westland).

sensors would be incorporated, thus making the helicopter heavier but not larger because of the deck limitations posed by existing warship design.

At the 1980 Farnborough Air Show it was announced that Westland Helicopters and Agusta of Italy would co-operate to design and build the new aircraft under the banner of European Helicopter Industries with the project called the EH-101. Basic data so far published includes: **Speed** 172 knots; **Range** 1,100 nm; **Endurance** 9 hours; **Max take-off weight** 28,660 lb; **Engine** 2 × General Electric T700 or 2 × RR RTM 321 turboshafts; **Weapons** Stingray and other ASW systems.

It is envisaged that the first aircraft will fly in mid-1985 and that production delivery could begin in 1987/8 as long as the Governments of both countries do not cause any delays because of funding. The RN intends to use the following equipment: AQS-901 acoustic processor (LAPADS); Blue Kestrel radar; Electronic Support Measures (ESM); data link and secure speech; Electronic Counter Measures (ECM); ASQ 81 towed MAD; and automatic data handling for sensors. It has been announced that the EH-101 will be part of the armament of the new Type 23 frigate which should enter service in 1988.

At present there would seem to be a requirement for a crew of three—pilot, observer and sonar operator—but recent trials and operational flying with the Sea King HAS 5 has shown that even four aircrew (the extra being the second pilot) are not enough in bad weather on prolonged patrols on a distant ASW screen.

---

* It should be noted that several second-line units operate helicopters which can really be considered front-line types as it is important to conduct operational training in aircraft which will actually be flown in service with a front—800-series—squadron. In this account, the three helicopter types operated by the Royal Marines are dealt with separately in Chapter 6.

Naval search and rescue

Ever since the first naval use of the helicopter in the late 1940s, the FAA has played a part in both civilian and military SAR. During the days of the fixed-wing carrier it was particularly important and it was during this time that the specialist aircrew-diver trade was developed; and it is still believed that the FAA is the only user of this highly trained life-saver.

Although specifically designed for military operations, the SAR helicopter flights at Culdrose and Lee-on-Solent have now been seconded in daylight hours for Department of Trade (DoT) civilian lifesaving and rescue operations at 15 minutes' notice when on the ground or at immediate notice when flying. SAR missions can be over land as well as over water in search of a missing child on a cliff or one who has floated out to sea on a rubber lilo. The aircraft in this role are converted Wessex HU 5s from 771 Squadron at Culdrose and from the Solent SAR Flight (formerly parented by 781 NAS) at Lee. In addition, the remaining seven of 771's Wessex are available together with eight Wessex at Portland with 772 Squadron; this includes the three

Helicopter Delivery Flights normally attached to RFAs. All the resident Sea King HAS 2/5 aircraft at Culdrose and Prestwick are available for SAR operations, especially those at long range, like the now world famous Fastnet Race of 1979. The Operations Rooms of all Air Stations are aware of the SAR-status of all aircraft flying in their areas so that should an emergency arise, an aircraft can be detailed off immediately. Even fixed-wing aircraft can be used in the search role and, at sea, all ships would make their helicopters available should this be important or necessary.

An additional DoT obligation is for long-range day or night cover in the South Western Approaches and off the west coast of Scotland where Sea Kings are at 1½ hours' notice (or 1 hour's notice if the airfields are open) from Culdrose and Prestwick respectively.

The Wessex aircraft employed carry a pilot (two at night); an aircrewman and an aircrewman-diver for SAR missions, and the helicopter has all the necessary equipment aboard, such as Sproule net, stretcher, medical equipment and oxygen. In certain circumstances it is possible for aircraft to carry a

SAR—the men who keep the SAR service from Culdrose operating every day. Left to right: Groundcrewmen, aircrewman/winch operator, pilot, HMCG liaison officer, SAR diver, groundcrewmen (RN).

naval doctor to assist, for example, with a casevac (casualty evacuation) of a pregnant woman to hospital during snow conditions.

A close liaison is maintained with HM Coastguard Service and the co-operation with RNLI (Royal National Lifeboat Institution) is always good. At Culdrose there are two Coastguard officers attached to the SAR control and calls for assistance are passed to Culdrose Ops by direct land line from Coastguard stations and the Rescue Co-ordination Centre at Mountbatten in Plymouth Sound. At Prestwick information is passed from MHQ Pitreavie which is also a RCC. For the longer-range missions, the Sea King is an excellent tool being able to fly 200 nm and to accommodate 11 survivors. At Yeovilton, trials have been carried out with the Commando version of the Sea King and this aircraft could be used if the Culdrose or Lee facilities were unable to cope (for example, another Fastnet Race which caused over 200 flying hours in 1979). The Sea King HC 4 has room for 18–20 survivors and can cover another 100 nm.

Naval Air Commando Squadrons

Since the landing and assault operations at Suez in November 1956, and the supply and troop movements carried out by Whirlwind helicopters from Naval Air Squadrons in Malaya, the RN has built up a considerable expertise in the use of helicopters for Commando and troop operations. Today, an assault landing in the teeth of enemy action is not anticipated because by that time the 'war' will have been lost. So the role of the helicopter, both the Wessex HU 5s and Sea King HC 4s of 846 Squadron, is to move troops in from transport at sea or move them up to the front line during a period of tension. The main operating area is Norway and the Atlantic/Baltic Islands in support of 3 Commando Brigade and other NATO-dedicated units.

Originally, the squadrons used the LPHs for a base but with the demise of these vessels and the eventual demise of the LPDs, it is obvious that they will have to be able to operate from ground areas adjacent to the troops which they are supporting. It may well be that by the end of 1983, the Wessex will have been retired from service in this role and replaced by a smaller number of Sea King HC 4s giving the same lifting power to the Marines. It is important that this lift capacity is continued but because of the HC 4s' improvements over the Wessex, especially in the weight of the underslung loads which can be carried, this will be possible with a smaller number of more sophisticated aircraft.

Naval Air Commando aircrew have mostly carried out the RM Commando course at RM Lympstone and many are able to wear the special and coveted 'Royal Naval Commando' shoulder flashes. It is important, of course, that the aircrew are able to operate in the battlefront area with the same range of skills and expertise as the men whom they fly around. To this end a number of RM personnel are to be found at Yeovilton providing training for the aircrew in Commando scenarios.

Naval aircrew engaged in this kind of flying are dubbed 'Junglies' by the rest of the FAA and their role is both taxing and exciting; flying is very often by the seat of the pants in mountainous and often otherwise inaccessible terrain. The NATO operating area in northern Norway is one of the most demanding helicopter areas in the world, especially when flying at 15 m (50 ft) or less to avoid radar at an air speed of 100 knots.

A great deal of experience was gained in the Falklands where both Wessex and Sea King helicopters performed well in all their design roles. The use of the requisitioned ships, such as car ferries and container vessels, was pioneered successfully despite the sad loss of about half the squadron complement of 847 Squadron in *Atlantic Conveyor*. The Sea Kings were especially useful in moving troops and supplies around East Falkland and are credited with moving 1,000,000 lb (453,600 kg) of stores per day during the campaign.

RNR Air Branch

One of the most constructive amendments to the RN in recent years was the re-formation of the Royal Naval Reserve Air Branch in 1980. In 1957, the former Royal Naval Volunteer Reserve Air Squadrons were disbanded and in the meantime there was no pool of experienced pilots and observers on whom the FAA could draw in times of emergency.

The Defence Council Instruction (DCI) which led to the re-formation of the RNR Air Branch defined the new role as providing a reserve aircrew officers trained to an acceptable state of readiness to augment embarked and disembarked squadrons in time of tension or war. The aim then would be to let the RNR man the communications and home-based SAR and ASW units, leaving the regular and thus more experienced aircrews for front-line operations where their recent knowledge could be put to more beneficial use.

Aircrew attend two-week training periods at several Naval Air Stations, including Lee and Yeovilton, and are divided into 1831 and 1832 Naval Air Squadrons for this purpose. Originally, they were re-trained on de Havilland Chipmunks and Westland Wasps attached to 781 NAS's RNR Flight

FRADU in action—two Canberra T 22s rendezvous with Coventry *prior to a fleet requirements exercise in the Bristol Channel* (Malcolm English).

at Lee, but with the disbandment of the parent unit, they now operate with training squadrons or station flights.

The RNR officers are certainly keen—700 applied for 40 vacancies when the scheme was first announced. They have all departed the FAA only a maximum of five years before and most are still flying—commercial helicopters in the North Sea, air taxi firms, smaller airlines, etc. There are currently 50 aircrew on the register.

The RNR Air Branch is today tasked with providing a pool of semi-trained aircrew to supplement regular aircrew in times of national emergency.

The Fleet Requirement and Air Direction Unit

This unit, known as the FRADU, is situated at RNAS Yeovilton, and is operated by Airwork Ltd under Contract to the Ministry of Defence. The FRADU flies Hunter GA 11s, T 8s and a T 7*, also Canberra TT 18s and T 22s and a T 4, comprising some 33 aircraft. All the aircrew and engineering personnel are civilian (although usually former Service), making this a unique organisation.

It is the function of the FRADU to assist ships of the Royal Navy and many foreign navies to work up to full operational status by carrying out radio/radar trials, visual and radar tracking followed by live weapon firings at a variety of towed targets. Participation in major maritime and air defence exercises also takes place on a regular basis at several overseas locations, as well as in UK waters.

Practice interceptions at high and low levels are provided to train RN officers as Fighter Controllers

* This aircraft has now been identified as a composite T 7/8 and the data in respect of T 8 is applicable.

and the aircraft are also provided for use by RN officers of the Naval Flying Standards Flight also based at Yeovilton. In addition, the unit maintains a Hunter T 8M and Harrier T 4 for radar and continuation training respectively, in support of the Sea Harrier squadrons.

Britannia Flight

Without doubt, the oldest aircraft on the FAA's current inventory is the DHC-1 Chipmunk, which continues to be operated by a number of flights. The majority are, however, to be found at Plymouth Roborough where the Britannia Royal Naval College (BRNC) Flight has been based since the 1950s.

Originally, the Flight flew DH Tiger Moths which, like the present red and grey Chipmunks, were passed on to the RN from the RAF. Today, the Flight has ten of these most suitable aircraft and is commanded by a senior Lieutenant Commander— the Naval Flying Grading Examiner (NFGE). The rest of the staff consists of a Chief Flying Instructor (CFI) and nine Qualified Flying Instructors (QFIs) who are all A2-rated flying instructors, either ex-RN or ex-RAF. The whole operation is run to a MoD contract by Airwork Limited, who have retained the contract for nearly 18 years. The basis of the contract is that the RN provides the aircraft and spares, whilst the company recruits instructors and a staff of ten maintainers. The hangar is leased from Plymouth Airport Limited and accommodation supplied by Airwork.

The main task of the Flight is to grade naval personnel to establish their potential as naval service pilots before they proceed to primary training with the RAF. This system ensures that only the best candidates are filtered through from BRNC at Dartmouth, or from RNEC at Manadon in the case of naval maintenance test pilots. These courses last three weeks to give each candidate about 12 hours in the air before a final handling test. In order to complete the task, especially during the winter months, it is often necessary to work and fly at weekends, but the system is flexible enough to allow flying 364 days a year—the exception being Christmas!

In addition to the naval flying grading, the Flight also provides a small amount of conversion training when, for example, a rotary-wing pilot has been selected to return to fixed-wing duties. There are also air experience flights for all candidates at BRNC and the air engineering students at RNEC, and in the past this has sometimes resulted in a cadet volunteering for aircrew duties on completion of his seamanship training; each Wednesday, the BRNC General List cadets fly in the Chipmunks. This way,

The Sharks—flying Gazelles from 705 NAS.

the Flight flies, on average, 3,500 hours per annum and has to date graded an incredible 2,400 potential pilot candidates.

Roborough is a convenient base because of its proximity to both colleges and RNEC students have the opportunity of putting their theoretical work into practice. There is every indication that the Flight will remain with its Chipmunks, at Roborough, for the forseeable future.

Display teams

Although, in the 1950s and 1960s, there were regular fixed-wing aerial display teams working up for such events as the Farnborough Air Show, the decline in that type of operation flying led to a complete reduction in teams. In the 1970s and early 1980s, the Fleet Air Arm did sponsor the only jet-equipped civilian-manned display team in the world, known as the 'Blue Herons' after their base at Yeovilton which is the 'stone-frigate' *Heron*. The aircraft were Hawker Hunter GA 11s of the FRADU.

Today, there are only the following units providing the various functions which can be described as display activities: The 'Sharks' from RNAS Culdrose; The Royal Naval Presentation Team's Wessex HU 5; The Fleet Air Arm Historic Flight; and The Fleet Air Arm Mobile Display.

The Sharks With the introduction of the high performance French-designed but British-built Westland/Aerospatiale Gazelle HT 2 into squadron service with 705 NAS at Culdrose, the possibility of forming a display team became a reality. Originally only formed to give displays at Naval Air Days and

base Navy Days, the team has branched out into the commercial display season with many daring and spectacular evolutions. Today, they are the only helicopter team in the United Kingdom, being made up of a team manager and four pilots, all QHIs from the squadron, plus a navigator/timekeeper who is an Observer School instructor. The team carries out formation display flying in addition to the normal duties of the staff; the lengthy and continuous training and practice flights taking place in the early morning prior to the Squadron's normally early start to the working day. The Sharks believe that the high performance of the Gazelle gives them the ability to perform many high speed jet formations, but also gives them the added ability to operate sideways and backwards. They also carry out solo and pairs routines. Maintenance is carried out, as with the normal squadron operations, by Airwork Ltd, and for ease of maintenance all 705's Gazelles are marked with the distinctive shark emblem on the tail.

Fleet Air Arm Historic Flight This unit, originally set up with a Fairey Swordfish II, now has the following additions: Hawker Sea Fury FB 11; Hawker Sea Fury T 22 (for pilot training); Fairey Firefly AS 5; and de Havilland Tiger Moth—all these aircraft residing at Yeovilton and being administered via *Heron* Flight. At Culdrose is the latest addition to the Flight, which appropriately enough is handled by *Seahawk* Flight—a Hawker Sea Hawk FGA 6.

The Swordfish was built in 1943 and did not actually see active service but was retained by the manufacturers for ferrying people and for historic interest. It is now flown by the Royal Navy and operates most weekends during the display season. The Sea Fury FB 11, on the other hand, did see service and action over Korea with *Theseus'* air group before being returned to Hawker. The RN bought it back in July 1971 and by 1972 the aircraft was airworthy again, thanks to the spare-time efforts of many FAA maintainers and the donations of spares from the manufacturers.

The Firefly has had a far more illustrious history because, after service with the Royal Australian Navy, the aircraft was due to be scrapped in the late 1960s. It was rescued by members of *Victorious'* air group and RAN aviators who sent it to England and the Fleet Air Arm Museum. The first flight was eventually made in 1972. Up until only a matter of years ago the BRNC Flight at Roborough were operating the de Havilland Tiger Moth for naval aircrew grading, so it could be argued that this aircraft is the most recent in the Flight! Many thousands of pilots have been trained on the type and it is fitting that it should remain in an airworthy condition with the Flight.

After completing a front-line tour with 806 NAS—the Ace of Diamond Squadron—the Culdrose-based Sea Hawk was acquired for apprentice training by the RAF until returned to the RN in 1976. By 1978, the maintainers and civilian employees at Culdrose had completed a very fine restoration job and now the aircraft regularly delights crowds at air shows. It should be noted that at the time of writing the type is still in service with the Indian Navy and that until the early 1970s, the type was operated by the Fleet Requirements Unit at Hurn, the forerunner of FRADU.

RN Presentation Team The RN Presentation Team is a very important part of the Navy's effort to communicate what it is doing and why it is doing it to the general public. In order to facilitate rapid transit from one presentation to another, the team uses a Wessex HU 5, appropriately coded RN for this work. It can also be used for schools displays and other similar operations. On average the RNPT reaches an audience of 31,000 people and a further 27 million via the media of television and radio. It is not within the FAA organisation.

Mobile displays Part of the recruiting drive by the RN and the FAA in particular is the display of large models representing the current aircraft carrier. Carried on the back of a low-loader with a Bedford prime mover, the current ship displayed is *Invincible* complete with aircraft models. In the past, the same hull (but with different fittings) has represented *Ark Royal*, *Eagle* and *Hermes*.

Naval hovercraft

The debate about whether a hovercraft ranks as an aeroplane or as a warship in terms of its use by the RN raged for several years, and many thought the former to be the case because the RN had identified its hovercraft with aircraft-type serials and, for practical reasons, had based the Naval Hovercraft Trials Unit (NHTU) at *Daedalus*, Lee-on-Solent. In 1979/80, this changed when all five of the RN's hovercraft reverted to warship pennant numbers with flag superior 'P' indicating that they were considered patrol vessels.

The classing of hovercraft as ships made no difference to the command structure position of NHTU, which was headed by a Commander RN, as the involvement of FONAC had been administrative at all times. This was mainly because the unit has made use of the facilities at *Daedalus*, a former seaplane station with a large ramp leading from the airfield complex directly into the Solent, and because the aviation-type engines and systems used by a hovercraft make the use of FAA technical ratings beneficial. The unit was disbanded in June 1982 leaving only the BH-7 in service.

NHTU was funded by Director General Ships and programmed by the Naval Hovercraft Committee on which FONAC had no representative. In terms of operational control, once a hovercraft has left the slipway at Lee, it is under the operational direction of CINCFLEET. (As an historical note, the unit was originally formed as long ago as 1962 under the title of Tri-Service Hovercraft Trials Unit or Interservice Hovercraft Unit (IHU). In 1975, due to defence cuts and other budgetary problems, the RAF and the British Army withdrew their support and so the NHTU was formed that January.)

RN Presentation Team—Wessex HU 5 marked 'RN' used to carry personnel from one venue to another.

MCM role Despite long and useful trials, especially during the autumn exercise season in such places as the Hebrides and Shetland, the hovercraft has yet to convince anyone in the Admiralty as its amphibious assault potential, although a number of Middle Eastern nations have large fleets in operation and the Soviet Union is proud of its 'monster' craft. The role to which official favour is now turning is that of mines countermeasures (MCM) and it is expected that this will be the role of the future for the hovercraft with the RN.

The main contender for the MCM role would seem to be the British Hovercraft Corporation BH-7 which is still in service at Lee, although the Corporation's SRN Military-4 would also seem to have potential. The reason why the BH-7 is currently being evaluated in the MCM role is due to the need to find a cost-effective alternative to the expensive warship type MCMVs, such as the *Hunt* Class which will be few in number and will need support. The current thinking is that to obtain full utilisation from the *Hunts* it will be useful to have hovercraft available. The advantage of 'hoovers' is that they have a rapid transit time from contact to contact and are relatively invulnerable to mine detonation. They are also easily re-supplied at sea and move back into the 'thick of it' with ease, thus significantly extending their time on task.

Hovercraft MCM is a concept supported by the specialists at MoD and by BHC as the many trials so far completed have demonstrated their capability. The current absence of the appropriate weapon systems for hovercraft minehunting (MCMH) at speed is an obvious hindrance to the progress of this concept at present.

BHC have adopted a system of pallet-mounted MCM gear and have developed a minelaying potential for their craft. The Military-4 will use an integrated computer-based navigation and action information system with inputs from the heading gyro compass.

Effective MCM by hovercraft necessitates that the craft maintain a good track across the water and trials have shown that this is possible in winds of 20 knots to within a standard deviation of 8.0 m.

BHC BH7 Wellington

Pennant number P235; **Overall length** 23.9 m; **Overall Beam** 13.9 m; **Overall height** 11.8m (hovering); 10.4m (on pad); **Propulsion** 1 × RR Marine Proteus; **All up weight** 60 tons (61.1 tonnes); **Endurance** 8–10 hours with 10 tons of fuel; 10–12 hours with max fuel of 11.8 tons; **Max speed** 65 knots (calm water); **Capacity** 14 tons combat load; 16 tons logistics load; 50 troops; 4 Land Rovers; **Propulsion rated** 4,250 shp; **Crew** 3 (inc load master).

This is a fast amphibious military craft designed to meet a wide range of defence needs, including logistic support to isolated posts. In trials, loads of up to 20 tons have been accommodated at speeds of around 60 knots. It has a central vehicle bay which can take three ¾-ton trucks and their trailers and there is an assault-type door for beach disembarkation. In addition, in the side cabins there is room for 50 fully armed troops; in fact, with four ¾-ton trucks it is possible to take 69 troops. The Mk 4 is the logistic support type as delivered to the RN. Abroad, there have been sales of the Mk 5 which is missile-equipped and used for combat as a fast patrol vessel. Currently, there are trials underway to check the craft's suitability for MCM work using the stern door and there is provision for a 5 m Searider craft to be accommodated on davits. It is normal for operating personnel to wear flying gear.

BH-7 Wellington—operating at speed in the Solent (HMS Daedalus).

Fleet Target Group

The Fleet Target Group (FTG), originally the Pilotless Target Aircraft Squadron, moved to its present base at Portland in 1974. Its role is to provide radio-controlled surface and airborne targets to the fleet wherever its services are required. The air task is to provide Chukar (MQM 74C) and Shelduck (KD2R-5) target drones to meet the missile and gun training requirements of the Fleet. Its surface task is to administer the allocation and repair of surface towed targets ('splash targets') and to operate remotely the controlled target vessels.

The Group consists of a Headquarters unit, two flights and a surface unit. All are mobile and capable of operating throughout the world. The Flights generally operate from Royal Fleet Auxiliaries on

Chukar drone—recovery aboard a British warship (RN).

long deployments but can also operate from warships or from ashore.

In addition to the aerial target drones described below, the RN also uses a number of Seaflash naval target systems as manufactured by Flight Refuelling Limited of Bournemouth-Hurn. These small craft (overall length 8.99 m) are remotely-controlled via a radio data-link with six or more functions and optional on-board manual control. It is designed to simulate the attack profile of many classes of fast patrol boats and the electro-magnet signatures of conventional surface warships from corvette to frigate. For the latter task it employs special gear carried within the GRP hull. Other data: **Beam** 2.21 m; **Height** (from waterline to top of control mast) 5.79 m; **Propulsion** inboard/overdrive petrol engine—minimum 93 octane; **Speed** 30 knots plus, decreasing to 20 knots in sea state 5. The drone has a remote control range of 10 nm and typical payloads include visual tracking flag, passive radar enhancement and smoke flares. Limited EW and ECM gear can be carried but details are secret. Seaflash is certainly a cost-effective way of practising wartime scenarios in peacetime.

Ashore the system is portable on a trailer similar to the average large dinghy and is towed behind a number of vehicles including the ubiquitous Land Rover.

Shelduck D1

Manufacturer Northrop-Ventura; **Purpose** Target drone; **Crew** Pilotless; **Squadrons** FTG; **Range** 333 km; **Endurance** 60 mins; **Max speed** 436 km/h; **Cruise speed** 324 km/h; **Service ceiling** 7,000 m; **Rate of climb** 1,065 m/min; **Length** 3.84 m; **Span** 4.27 m; **Weapons** Unarmed; **Engine** McCullough air-cooled; **Fuel capacity** Classified; **All-up weight** 163 kg; **Embarked** Operates from warships or RFAs.

The predominant drone in the RN inventory is the Northrop-Ventura Shelduck, which is known to the USN as the MOM-36A. Initially 85 were ordered for the RN in the 1960s, which were followed by repeat orders of similar drones until about 550 had been delivered. The propellor-driven Shelduck is considerably cheaper than the jet-powered Chukar and is also more versatile. Guidance is by means of VHF radio linked to either visual or radar control. The drone can be equipped with smoke generators, infra-red tow-target, night light or radar augmentation pods. Recovery is by parachute which can be triggered by command, engine failure or near-miss. Take-off is very often rocket-assisted from the special cradle aboard ship.

Chukar D1

Manufacturer Northrop-Ventura; **Purpose** Target drone; **Crew** Pilotless; **Squadrons** FTG; **Range** 450 km max; **Endurance** 96 mins; **Max speed** 760 km/h at sea level; **Cruising speed** 390 km/h at sea level; **Service ceiling** Classified; **Rate of climb** 2,000 m/min; **Length** 3.81 m; **Wingspan** 1.73 m; **Weapons** Unarmed; **Engine** Williams turbojet plus JATO; **All-up weight** 213.6 kg; **Embarked** Operates from warships and RFAs.

The Chukar drone as flown by the Fleet Target Group is manufactured in the United States by the Ventura Division of Northrop. The drone, a direct equivalent of the USN's MQM-74A, was ordered for the RN in two batches, the last deliveries being in the mid-1970s. Serials run in the XW and the XZ series.

Described as a lightweight target drone, the Chukar is designed for anti-aircraft gunnery practice as well as for missile training. It is radio-controlled and the turbojet motor with jet assisted take-off (JATO) facilities make it a useful aid to ships in work-up. The drone is recoverable after its mission, or if it is near-missed by missile or gunfire, when it descends to the sea where it is collected by either helicopter or launch.

The Royal Marines

'If ever the hour of real danger should come to England, they will be found the country's sheet anchor.'

Admiral Lord St Vincent, 1802.

The history of the Corps goes back to 1664 and the Duke of York's Regiment, later called the Lord High Admiral's Regiment, when soldiers first fought at sea in an organised manner after being specially raised. The present Corps' true roots began in 1755, though, when former soldiers from Maritime Regiments were brought under Admiralty control. Since then the Royal Marines have given sterling service to the Crown and the nation and must be rated today as the best sea soldiers in the world. The Commando role is, incidentally, a comparatively recent one stemming from the needs of World War 2.

The Corps has the following roles, several of which have been demonstrated admirably in recent months—to provide: Commandos for amphibious operations but with the ability to work worldwide in an infantry role; special detachments for HM Ships

The Captain General Royal Marines, HRH Prince Philip, visits a Royal Marines unit in the field in Norway during the winter exercise season (RM).

and for a number of important shore establishments; specialist amphibious units for raiding and small craft work; a special quick reaction force to protect the United Kingdom's offshore installations and in the nautical anti-terrorist role; and a Bands Service for the RN and RM.

RM establishments

The Headquarters of the Commandant General Royal Marines (CGRM) is at the Ministry of Defence, London, but the major concentration of facilities is in the West Country where there are establishments at Plymouth (Seaton, Coypool, Bickleigh and Stonehouse) and at Lympstone, near Exeter, where the RM has its Commando Training Centre (CTCRM). Moving further east there is RM Poole, another training establishment. In Kent, RM Deal still functions as the HQ for the RM Band Service whilst Training and Reserves are administered from RM Eastney near Portsmouth; this is also the location of the Corps Museum. In Scotland, RM establishments are limited to Arbroath, known as RM Condor after the former Naval Air Station.

Operationally, 40 Commando is based at Seaton Barracks; 42 Commando at nearby Bickleigh Barracks with 45 Commando and the M&AW cadre at Plymouth. The HQ 3 Commando Brigade RM, is at Stonehouse Barracks, Plymouth. Amphibious and certain trade training is carried out at RM Poole whilst the 3rd Commando Brigade Air Squadron (CBAS) was based at Bickleigh but planned to move to a more permanent base during 1982; the original base was Coypool which was congested at the best of times, and has recently been encroached by civilian development.

Commando Forces comprise: HQ 3 Commando Brigade; 40 Commando, RM; 42 Commando, RM; 45 Commando Group; Commando Brigade Air Squadron; Air Defence Troop, RM (3 Commando Brigade HQ); Signals Squadron, RM; 1 Raiding Squadron, RM; and Commando Logistics

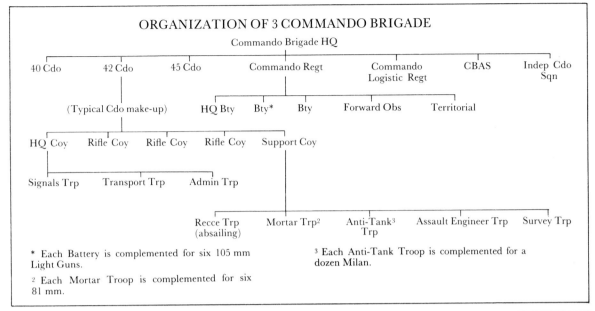

ORGANIZATION OF 3 COMMANDO BRIGADE

Commando Brigade HQ

40 Cdo — 42 Cdo — 45 Cdo — Commando Regt — Commando Logistic Regt — CBAS — Indep Cdo Sqn

(Typical Cdo make-up)

HQ Bty — Bty* — Bty — Forward Obs — Territorial

HQ Coy — Rifle Coy — Rifle Coy — Rifle Coy — Support Coy

Signals Trp — Transport Trp — Admin Trp

Recce Trp (absailing) — Mortar Trp[2] — Anti-Tank[3] Trp — Assault Engineer Trp — Survey Trp

* Each Battery is complemented for six 105 mm Light Guns.

[2] Each Mortar Troop is complemented for six 81 mm.

[3] Each Anti-Tank Troop is complemented for a dozen Milan.

Regiment, RM. In addition there are the Army units; 29 Commando Regiment, RA; 59 Independent Commando Squadron, RE; and 131 Independent Commando Squadron, RE(TA); which are covered in Terry Gander's companion volume to this work.

The Commando Logistic Regiment is manned by a joint force of RN, Army and RM personnel and thus is unique in the United Kingdom order of battle. It provides workshop, ordnance, transport and medical back-up. The RN also provides air lift support in the form of 845, 847 and 848 Squadrons (Wessex HU 5) and 846 Squadron (Sea King HC 4), and these units are covered in the FAA section of this book.

Commando units The three remaining Commando units (41 Commando was disbanded in 1981) are basically tasked with Mountain and Arctic Warfare (M&AW) and with Temperate Climate Operations which would involve operations in Norway during the summer, the Baltic Approaches and, as recent events have shown, the Atlantic Islands. All Commando units are trained and ready to operate in other areas even those outside the present NATO boundaries.

M&AW is the popularly acclaimed role of the Marines and today there are two Commandos trained in this role, together with Commando Brigade HQ, 3 CBAS and supporting elements. In addition, the RM is ably supported in Norway by elements of the Royal Netherlands Marines Corps (RNLMC), known as 1 Amphibious Combat Group (1ACG) and Whiskey Company which is an

Royal Marines Facilities

Condor Arbroath

Commando Brigade
● Air Squadron
▲ Commando Establishments

Yeovilton
Lympstone
Plymouth
Poole
Deal
Coypool
Stonehouse

The role of the Royal Marines today is very much concentrated on the Northern Flank (RM).

the Soviet Union—in time of war. This would then prevent the 'Bear' from projecting its influence into the Norwegian Sea and the North Atlantic proper; the Kola Peninsula is not the best place in the world to do so if the NATO powers still control the Northern Flank. The daunting threat of outflanking NATO by land and of stopping reinforcements to the Central Front by sea is recognised, but the Corps neither overestimates nor underestimates the threat.

Each Commando is variously rostered to the UK Army 'Spearhead' battalion and thus sees service as and when requested; in 1981 a Commando was flown by the RAF to Vanuatu (New Hebrides) to assist in keeping the peace. During the 'Spearhead' period, operational control passes to the HQ of UK Land Forces (UKLF) at Wilton. United Nations peacekeeping tours in Cyprus and elsewhere have also been undertaken by Commandos in the normal course of Service life.

The British operations in the South Atlantic to recover the illegally taken Falkland and South Georgia Islands provided the RM with active service in conditions which, although harsh, they were trained to fight in. Almost every facet of the Commando system was used in the campaign and the General Officer Commanding the British Forces was well pleased with the performance of the RM Commando Brigade. It was typical of the 'Out of Area' operations for which these troops are especially suited.

independent unit slightly larger than a regular rifle company. Each year during January-March, the force trains in Northern Norway, centred on Bardufoss, and the exercises which are held usually test the reinforcement, deployment and contingency planning of the NATO and/or Anglo-Norwegian arrangements. The modern Marine is capable of working at temperatures of −46°C using current oversnow vehicles and techniques.

In peacetime, operational control of the majority of units in Commando Forces is delegated to the Commander of 3 Commando Brigade, but full command is maintained by MGRM CF in any event. In war or even time of tension, 3 Brigade could comprise all the available Commandos plus 1 ACG with the associated logistic and combat support. Such are the number of options which are available to SACLANT and SACEUR that the Marines have to be ready for almost any contingency. It is important that the Royal Marines are not seen as a specialist M&AW or other similar role element of the UK order of battle. The Corps moves with the developing situation worldwide and it must continue to do so. The most likely wartime scenario is that the Brigade will have the M&AW trained units whilst the other 'temperate' Commandos will operate separately and probably independently in other theatres; there could even be a role on NATO's Southern Flank.

Without doubt, though, operations in the South Atlantic notwithstanding, the Northern Flank is the most important area in which the Corps is likely to operate in the foreseeable future. Both SACLANT and SACEUR feel that this area is very important because it has facilities such as ports and airfields which must be denied to the potential aggressor—

Organisation

The Corps is organised along Army lines but with a curious blend of naval traditions and functions. It is commanded by a Lieutenant General who is known as Commandant General Royal Marines (CGRM); he does not have a place on the normal Admiralty Board, but is tasked with advising the Board on all Amphibious and RM matters. The organisation is split into two: Commando Forces; and Reserves/Training. The Headquarters of Commando Forces, RM, is at Plymouth and this element is commanded by a Major General whose HQ is at Mount Wise. Responsibility for planning and mounting all amphibious operations and exercises comes under this control with the assistance of FOF3. He also provides advice to the Staff on amphibious operations.

Based at Eastney, near Portsmouth, Training and Reserves Forces are also commanded by a Major General who acts as a link for CINCNAVHOME but with additional Home Defence tasks. The five major Royal Marine establishments come under MGTRF, who is also responsible for training of individuals, specialists, tradesmen, musicians and for command.

Commando Forces

The landing force element of the United Kingdom Amphibious Force, which is declared to NATO and would be assigned to SACLANT in time of global war, is the primary Commando Forces' task. It is envisaged that the assignment would be to Northern European Command (NEC) which encompasses Norway, Denmark and North Germany. This will aid the trans-Atlantic resupply routes in time of war or tension. Commando Forces have an important role to play in NATO thinking at this time.

It is not possible for CF to acquire all the necessary expertise that is required from within the Corps so there are elements of the RN and of the British Army involved. Nevertheless, all those from other services are expected to undergo the rigorous Commando training course at RM Lympstone and most personnel are therefore entitled to wear the coveted green beret.

Comacchio Company As part of the UK forces' effort to prevent tampering with the numerous offshore and inshore economic installations, the RM formed a special sub-unit in May 1980. Named Comacchio Company in typical Corps tradition

An RM recruit undergoing the assault course for the award of a Green Beret at CTC Lympstone (RM).

after a battle in the past, the unit is made up of specially trained units of Commando Forces, the Special Boat Squadron (SBS) and LC Company. Based at RM Condor, Arbroath, this unit is not only involved with offshore installations, but numbers the protection of other facilities of vital importance to the UK's wellbeing amongst its charges.

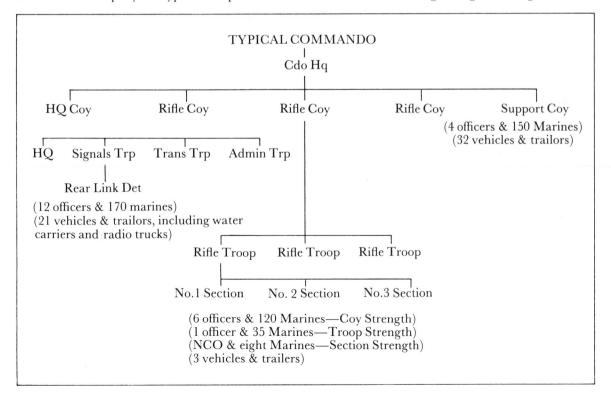

TYPICAL COMMANDO
Cdo Hq

HQ Coy — Rifle Coy — Rifle Coy — Rifle Coy — Support Coy

(4 officers & 150 Marines)
(32 vehicles & trailors)

HQ — Signals Trp — Trans Trp — Admin Trp

Rear Link Det

(12 officers & 170 marines)
(21 vehicles & trailors, including water carriers and radio trucks)

Rifle Troop — Rifle Troop — Rifle Troop

No.1 Section — No. 2 Section — No.3 Section

(6 officers & 120 Marines—Coy Strength)
(1 officer & 35 Marines—Troop Strength)
(NCO & eight Marines—Section Strength)
(3 vehicles & trailers)

Special Boat Squadron This 'cloak and dagger' unit is based at RM Poole and is classified as an amphibious special forces unit which is capable of undertaking any operation at sea or up to a limited distance inland. The Special Air Services Regiment (SAS) of the British Army is the land-based equivalent. It has such an important operational role that elements are always available to NATO or national commanders for special operations. The main role is to provide the RM with amphibious reconnaissance and intelligence about the enemy, as in the Falklands, and the men assigned to the SBS are specialists in many trades, including photography and explosives. They also have a 'direct action' role against specific targets but today are probably better known for their counter-terrorist role; a particular forté is assumed to be the relief of hijacked ships and port installations. All ranks are classed as swimmer-canoeists, trained in parachuting and the use of small craft such as the Gemini or Rigid Raider. They would travel to the

A swimmer-canoeist of SBS with Klepper canoe and Armalite rifle (RM).

target area in any vessel and/or aircraft which would seem appropriate to the task and have been known to be dropped from helicopters over the horizon or to canoe out of a partly submerged landing craft. There is a Reserve SBS unit.

Raiding Squadrons The Corps currently operates three raiding squadrons equipped with Rigid Raider and Gemini craft: 1 RSRM (UK); 2 RSRM(R) (UK); 3 RSRM (Hong Kong). The role of the squadrons is to operate small craft including those impressed into service for raiding and other allied duties. All the personnel are thoroughly trained in the use of small boats at LC Company, RM Poole. The squadrons would operate in all climatic conditions including the Arctic and the tropics. One of their secondary roles is that of internal security by providing boat patrols when required, such as during the Jubilee Fleet Review of 1977.

Embarked detachments Whilst all ships of the RN and RFA have the capability to embark amphibious troops, even the *Invincible* Class CVLs, there are certain warships which carry an RM detachment of one Sergeant, a Corporal and eight Marines; the original system of an officer and 20 men was terminated in 1978. Currently the following classes are specially prepared for RM detachments but with a maximum of 19 detachments at sea at any one time it is obvious that not every warship will be 'occupied' at the same time: *County* Class DLGs; *Bristol* Class DLG; *Broadsword* Class FF (except Squadron Leaders); *Leander* Class FF (Exocet and Broad-beamed, except Squadron Leaders); *Rothesay* Class. In addition, there was a Marine detachment aboard *Endurance* which regularly exercised with and reinforced NP8901 on the Falklands prior to the Argentine invasion.

Comacchio Company deploys by abseiling from a Sea King HAS 2 of 819 NAS. This is just one mode of transport used by this specialist force (Commando Forces).

Selection for the embarked detachments is via the regular sea roster although volunteers are welcomed. Training is carried out at RM Poole where the course is split between two weeks at Poole to do the administrative side, including medicals, four weeks at *Raleigh*, where the standard eight weeks' Junior Seaman course is completed in four weeks for RMs, followed by a further two weeks at Poole learning weapons drill, signals and using the ranges. There is then a ceremonial pass-out before the warship's Captain or Commander. This completes Pre-Embarkation Training (PET) and several courses a year will continue their training (PJT) before joining the warship at *Cambridge*, where they are taught aspects of naval gunnery. In the days of the RM gun turret detachments this was an important part of the sea service routine, but today the detachment is expected to do different duties including providing the shore security party and manning the small craft of a particular ship; they will still provide members for the turret crew if required. Their duties are very much in the hands of the warship's CO, and a naval officer is appointed OCRM for each detachment. The length of time that each detachment remains with a warship depends on the ship's programme but the average recently has been 18 to 20 months, although it can be as long as two years or as short as 12 months.

Perhaps one of the likeliest operations to be carried out by the RM detachment is disaster relief in, say, the West Indies, although it is possible that the detachment would be landed at the request of a friendly power to preserve law and order until reinforcements arrived, such as the 'Spearhead' Battalion from the UK. The job is not as popular today as it was when the Navy was still regularly east of Suez, but there are still volunteers. The equipment is the standard RM section type—personal SLRs, a GPMG and an 84 mm Carl Gustav anti-tank weapon. In addition there are Clansman radios available (the signaller or radio operator being the only specialist aboard); these radios have replaced the old A40/A41 sets for ship-to-shore and ship-to-small craft communications. It should be noted that there can be an RM officer aboard a warship as a watchkeeper and then he would take over the responsibility of OCRM.

Naval shore establishment detachments There are a number of key establishments whose installations require safeguarding by RM detachments and one presumes that these must include the nuclear submarine bases and HQ complexes. No further details are available.

3 Commando Brigade Air Squadron Equipped with Westland Gazelle AH 1 light observation helicopters and recently re-equipped with the Westland Lynx AH 1 anti-tank and utility type, the 3rd CBAS is one of the best-equipped mini air forces in the NATO alliance. This unit is closely associated with the Army Air Corps at Middle Wallop but is independently based at RNAS Yeovilton. The squadron is organised into four flights, three in Devon and the fourth with 45 Commando and Comacchio Company at Arbroath; the latter being equipped exclusively with Gazelles. Each flight is named after an important battle in which the Royal Marines took part.

The wartime role would be to operate with 3 Commando Brigade in the Northern Flank areas and thus much of the flying training reflects M&AW in either Norway or the Pyrenees. Aircrew also fly Army helicopters in Ulster as and when required. Various procedures have been adopted for amphibious and embarked operations and the aircrews are trained to fly from all amphibious ships including the LSLs. Special modifications have been incorporated into the aircraft to assist their flying environments, including inflation bags (these take only 2.5 seconds to operate) and radio altimeters to assist landing and hovering above snow covered areas.

In wartime conditions, the aircraft would be camouflaged white over their existing green/black paint scheme if operating in the Norwegian snow. In peacetime the use of this emulsion type covering causes problems for the maintainers.

Part of Endurance's *Embarked Detachment in Falkland waters prior to the Argentine invasion.* (RM).

Air Defence Troop Based on the equivalent units within the Royal Artillery, the ADT in the Royal Marines is also Blowpipe SAM-equipped and is attached to HQ 3 Commando Brigade for point defence of Brigade HQ, a strongpoint, bridge or other tactically important location. It is commanded by a senior Lieutenant and consists of about 36 men. Training is carried out by the Army at Larkhill.

The Marines and Naval helicopters

The concept of using naval helicopters for transporting elements of an RM force ashore, or within an operational area, goes back to the days of the Suez landings and to the later operations on the Malayan Peninsula and Borneo. Today, the Naval Air Commando Squadrons (*qv*) and the Corps work as a tightly knit community.

The RN provides two squadrons, one each of Sea King HC 4 and Wessex HU 5 (with the wartime emergency addition of a second Wessex unit normally in training at Yeovilton). The Wessex is now rather long in the tooth but could continue until the end of the decade whereas the Sea King provides the Corps with good lift and range facilities in a larger and better airframe. It is important that ski-troops are able to embark and disembark readily from a helicopter; the HC 4's large rear cargo door certainly makes this possible. Now that the RM can combine its lift helicopter with the introduction of the missile-armed Lynx in a utility role, the scope for airborne operations has widened.

It is likely that the Defence Review of 1981 will see, in the longer term, the withdrawal of the Wessex

The majority of aircrew are recruited from SNCOs and young officers who fly as part of their normal tours; there are no career aviators. NCOs are also trained as missile firers for the TOW system being introduce in the Westland Lynx.

The current dispostion of 3 CBAS is as follows:

HQ Flight	2 × Scout AH 1
Brunei Flight	4 × Scout AH 1 with AS 11*
Dieppe Flight	3 × Gazelle AH 1
Montfortebeek Flt	3 × Gazelle AH 1†
Kangaw Flight	3 × Gazelle AH 1
Salerno Flight	3 × Gazelle AH 1

The move of 3 CBAS to RNAS Yeovilton was made possible by the fact that RN Lynx squadrons moved to Portland in August 1982, thus making the accommodation available. Yeovilton is also well situated for military exercise areas in the West Country.

In addition to aircraft, 3 CBAS is an integral part of 3 Commando Brigade and is equipped with the usual personnel weapons as well as 7.62 mm GPMG mountings for use by helicopters; variant L7 (see Chapter Ten). In addition to RM personnel, there are also Royal Artillery, Royal Army Ordnance Corps, Royal Electrical and Mechanical Engineers and WRNS personnel attached to the squadron, making a total of over 100.

---

* In late-1982, the composition of 3 CBAS was due to change with the arrival of the TOW-equipped Lynx AH 1 and it is envisaged that HQ and Brunei Flights will convert to the new helicopter 1982–3; training to take place at AAC Centre, Middle Wallop.

† Montfortebeek Flight is attached to 45 Commando at RM Condor, Arbroath.

The Royal Marines

Left *A GPMG fitted in the doorway of a Sea King HC 4 during the Goose Green operations* (RN).

Below left *Royal Marines coming ashore at San Carlos on May 21 1982* (Popperfoto).

Right *Commando Forces are air-minded and use such types as the Sea King HC 4 for mobility, even in Norway* (Westland).

from Commando lift operations, but as long as this is eventually remedied with additional Sea King airframes to give the same lift the situation will not be drastically altered. The advantage with an all-Sea King fleet is that the aircraft has superior manpower economics and longer flying intervals between the service and maintenance periods. Whereas the Wessex payload is only a little over 35,00 lb (1,588 kg), ten fully equipped troops or a ½-tonne underslung load, the Sea King can cope with some 7,500 lb (3,402 kg) for short transit or 6,000 lb (2,722 kg) for longer runs, 25 fully equipped troops in better conditions or an underslung load such as a 1-tonne Land Rover or field gun and support. The range differs from 40 nm (74 km) to 65 nm (120 km) fully loaded respectively. Both aircraft can be fitted with close support weapons such as GPMG and/or AS 11, although neither is in the gunship class of the American AH-1 Cobra or the Russian Mi-24 'Hind'.

Landing Craft Company

The specialist amphibious ships of the RN carry landing craft which are manned exclusively by the Royal Marines of the Landing Craft Company. The whole branch is controlled from RM Poole via the sponsorship of the Commanding Officer. The company is commanded by a Major, RM. LC Company is responsible for the training of crews for the LCVPs (Landing Craft Vehicle and Personnel) and LCUs (Landing Craft Utility—formerly LCM9s).

The LC Assault Squadrons are attached to *Hermes* (9 Assault Squadron), *Fearless* (4 Assault Squadron) and *Intrepid* (6 Assault Squadron). These warships carry LCVPs at davits and have four craft each. Each 12-tonne craft is crewed by a Corporal and two Marines. In addition, the LPDs are equipped to

carry four LCUs in the dock-type compartment beneath their flight decks and they operate in and out of this when the ship is 'flooded down'.

Recent events have led to a reappraisal of the Landing Craft element of RM and it is thought that a special LC Assault Squadron (on the lines of the Commando Brigade Air Squadron) could be formed to support Commando Forces. This will involve a concept known as the Forward Landing Craft Operating Base which will enable 3 Commando Brigade to deploy to, for example, Norway, with limited assistance from LPDs and LPHs.

In order to facilitate this concept, one presumes that, in addition to the new aluminium LCVPs undergoing trials at RM Instow, the need for a larger LCU will be realised. During the period 1980–2, the RM operated a converted LCU—known as the 'Black Pig'—in Norway during winter exercises to prove that the Forward Base was sound. In 1981, the 'Pig' was even deployed to Norway via Scotland under her own power. This trip took about 36 hours but proved that it could be done. A new LCU, displacing about 350 tonnes, could act as flotilla leader and carry 4-tonne trucks, Land Rovers and a full Commando Company with a crew of 12 at 12–15 knots. If funding is available, then this would seem to be an answer to the lack of LPDs.

Marines who specialise in LCs are at the lowest level qualified to cox Rigid Raiders and Gemini whilst the highest level is the Officer i/c Landing Craft aboard an LPD. Corporals usually provide the cox'ns for LCVPs and LCUs. This use of smaller craft enables the LC Company to provide a nautical element to Comacchio Company (qv), RM units in Northern Ireland, the SBS (qv) plus a three-man detachment (before the recent fighting) to NP8901 in the Falkland Islands, consisting of a Corporal and two Marines with their Gemini craft. In addition to

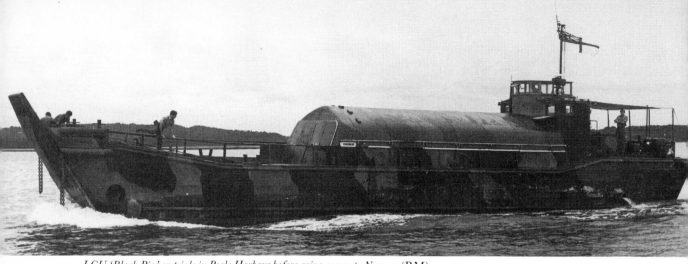

LCU 'Black Pig' on trials in Poole Harbour before going across to Norway (RM).

military tasks, LC Company is always ready to provide assistance to the civil powers for disaster relief and casevac. In line with Britain's assistance to foreign powers, the Company provides men on secondment to the small boats' section of the Royal Brunei Malay Regiment.

Royal Marines on patrol in Northern Ireland with SUIT equipped SLRs (45 Commando).

The Marines and Northern Ireland

Since the recent resurgence of trouble in 1969, the Royal Marines have been deployed in the Province in rotation with Army units spending four-month emergency tours. They have also carried out duties as Resident Battalion in Londonderry. In the turn of events, the RM is also liable for duty in Ulster as the 'Spearhead' Battalion. Their duties are those of any Army unit and in addition they do provide a nautical element to lough and sea patrols. Sea-going intelligence officers with the regular naval patrols are often RMs whose primary duty is to assist in the prevention of arms smuggling and terrorists in coastal and inshore waters. Those wishing to research this subject further are advised to study the section on Ulster deployments in the companion volume, *Encyclopaedia of the Modern British Army* by Terry Gander.

The Marines and logistics

Every Commando unit deployed, even in peacetime, requires the support of specialist logistic personnel and the RM have the Commando Logistic Regiment to do this task. This support is based on a fixed time back-up which is available to each Commando, Commando Air Squadron and 1 ACG. In addition logistic support is supplied to RFAs with amphibious roles, and the LPH. During and following an assault it is important to maintain administrative and distribution functions at peak efficiency. Supplies can either be ferried ashore from RFAs or impressed merchant vessels, or host nation assistance can be given. The latter will mainly be concentrated on combat support and medical back-up. Logistics are just as important a role as combat.

Amphibious operations

Until 1985, the amphibious lift capability for the RM will be provided by the specialist amphibious ships—the two LPDs with additional assistance from the LSLs. These vessels, except the LSLs which are RFA-manned, form part of the Third Flotilla and hence FOF3 is responsible for the naval planning and operating of them. The Commodore Amphibious Warfare (COMAW) functions as the naval amphibious group commander (CATF) for brigade-scale amphibious operations. SACLANT will actually assign the use of amphibious warships in a war situation.

The 'naval' role on the Northern Flank is still there even though the idea of an assault against enemy forces is no longer NATO doctrine. The new *modus operandi* is for the amphibious troops to land on a friendly, coast without the use of ports and/or airfields. In time of tension the UKNL Force (*qv*), mainly operating with an LPD, Commando lift helicopters and LCs, would sail before a political decision to mount an amphibious operation had been taken. They would then be posed over the horizon, being uncommitted yet there. All these operations would be with the assistance of Britain's allies, especially Norway, Denmark, Canada and the United States. The new role for landing craft is discussed in the LC Company section.

The use of *Hermes* in her secondary role of LPH would be used, presumably for 'quick dash' operational reinforcement or initial deployment to Norway. In normal events the ship is declared to NATO for anti-submarine and Task Group operations. The LPDs are designed to operate as the Joint Headquarters of an Amphibious Group together with providing troop lift, amphibious docking and a platform for support helicopters. The RFA man six LSLs of the *Sir Lancelot* Class which

A Royal Marine light anti-aircraft gunner overlooking a landing point in San Carlos Bay (Popperfoto).

could be available to support amphibious operations with their clamshell doors and the use of multi-purpose Mexeflote pontoons. Their availability would be a decision for the Chiefs of Staff because they are important for reinforcing the Central Front forces cross-Channel. Although it is unlikely that she would be deployed, the CVLs like *Invincible* could be used in their war emergency overload situation with up to 1,000 men embarked for a short period. Such large hulls are, however, too important to be used in this role, one would think. In the late 1970s when the government of the day decided to begin the cut-down of the Amphibious Forces and their lift capability, a number of civilian ships were identified for use in the troop deployment role. Such vessels, of course, have no real amphibious capability and neither are their crews trained for same; however, every little helps to support the amphibious ships. The type of vessel under consideration is obviously the Ro-Ro ferry type which could be used to run stores and battle loss replacements to Norway or Denmark provided that port facilities were available.

The RN/RM operations in the Falklands during May and June 1982, have shown how quickly merchant vessels can be phased into operations leading to amphibious landings. Perhaps one should define the difference between these operations, and those which would be envisaged in Europe: the Falklands situation was a limited police action designed to remove an aggressor from a small group of islands at some distance from the UK home base. Any operations in Europe would see merchant ships in a far more vulnerable position, where repeated air and sub-surface attacks would occur.

Several vessels were requisitioned or chartered by the UK government, including the liners *Canberra* and *Queen Elizabeth 2* which were used as assault

An LCU is manoeuvred out of an LPD's flooded well deck. The ship, Fearless, *is also operating Wessex HU 5 and Scout AH 1 helicopters* (Commando Forces).

troop and garrison troop transports respectively. Although vulnerable, the ships with their mixed merchant/military crews were also used as hospital ships. One vessel which lent its services to the Task Group was the schools' cruise ship *Uganda*, which had its dormitories converted to wards for the duration. Ro-Ro and Container vessels were pressed into service to carry heavy equipment, such as British Army light combat reconnaissance vehicles and helicopters to the Falklands. The early loss of *Atlantic Conveyor* was a serious blow to the Task Group and confirms the vulnerability of such large (15,000-tonne) vessels. Without doubt, however, the ability to use merchant ships for transportation of men and supplies to a war zone does exist.

Amphibious Trials and Training Unit Based at RM Instow, this unit, known as ATTURM, is responsible for research and development, as well as trials into the technical work connected with amphibious operations; much of this work is necessarily classified. One aspect which is important is the waterproofing of vehicles and associated equipment and the recovery of same in the beach landing environment; this work is pioneered at Instow. One of the recent projects has been trials of the new aluminium LCVP which is little different from the present one except that it is designed to travel at more than 15 knots instead of a sedate 9 knots which the current LC crews are used to (see Chapter Ten).

Amphibious tactics It is suggested that, following the political decision to land RM forces on foreign soil, the amphibious ships deployed in the quick dash would either return to ASW duties or pick up a second wave. This latter function will more likely be carried out by the LPDs—the so-called dedicated amphibious ships. Most of the support helicopters—Wessex HU 5s, Lynx AH 1s, Gazelle AH 1s and Sea King HC 4s—will be disembarked to work in the field with their respective units. In addition the embarked and the pre-deployed LCs will operate in some instances as independent commands, especially in the NEC and Island areas.

If naval gunfire support is required it is more than likely that the spotting will be carried out by elements of 148 (Meiktila) Commando Forward Observation Battery, RA, which is an independent sub-unit of 29 Commando Regiment but is based at RM Poole. Its personnel are, of course, Commando-trained and wear the green beret.

Amphibious Beach Unit Both *Fearless* and *Intrepid* carry an ABU with a Captain RM in command to be transferred ashore to co-ordinate the landing operations. Their role is being considered but it is clear that if beach landings are to continue so will these units.

Royal Marines Reserve

The RMR is a commando-trained volunteer force which in time of war or tension—or 'mobilisation'—is ready and able to join the regular Corps, either as specialist sub-units or as individual reinforcements. Under the terms of the Royal Marines Act 1947, two units of reserve RMs were formed at Glasgow and London under the aegis of the Royal Marines Forces Volunteer Reserve (RMFVR). In 1963, the RMR was formed from the sure foundations of the RMFVR, which title had lost some of its message with the disbandment of National Service.

Today there are five units and ten detachments with some 70 officers and 1,100 other ranks. The units and detachments are:

RMR City of London Portsmouth Detachment; Chatham Detachment.

RMR Scotland Dundee Detachment; Greenock Detachment; Arbroath Detachment.

RMR Bristol Cardiff Detachment; Poole

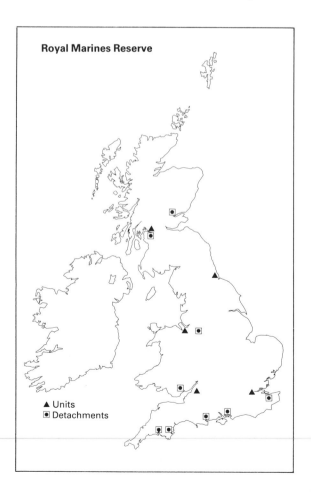

On exercise on Salisbury Plain with a Wessex of 845 NAS, a section of Commando Company, London RMR, deploys to an assault position.

Detachment; Lympstone Detachment; Plymouth Detachment.

RMR Merseyside Manchester Detachment.

RMR Tyne No Detachments.

The RMR has a good, close relationship with neighbouring RNR units, and in several cases they share common establishments. In addition, the RNR has always provided medical assistance and back-up for the RMR and several Reserve Medical Assistants have won the coveted green beret and the right to wear the exclusive 'Royal Naval Commando (R)' shoulder flash.

Recruiting is from all walks of life from Chartered Surveyor to butcher, but the applicant must be physically fit and mentally alert. He must also be dedicated to his part-time vocation because he must attend a 15-day continuous training period each year, a weekly training night and about one weekend in three. Most employers realise the benefit to the nation, themselves and society in general—but not all have any real idea of how dedicated and professional the RMR really is in a modern warfare context.

Every recruit must undergo about two years' training in order to complete the tough Commando course (at CTCRM Lympstone) and it is after this period that final selection for officer training (a further two years) takes place. Once trained, the Marine Reservist joins Commando Company and is able to train as a specialist in one of many fields including Mountain and Arctic Warfare (M&AW). The initial service is four years with re-engagement until 50 years of age.

2 Raiding Squadron RM(R) 2 RSRM(R) is a recently formed but fully fledged Raiding Squadron which, unlike its regular sister units, is equipped with inflatable raiding craft—the Gemini—powered by 40 hp Johnson engines. This difference of equipment enables the squadron to operate by different means and in different roles to that of the regular Corps and thus is a useful addition. Detachments are based at all RMR units, and the Headquarters element is at RMR City of London. Transportation is provided by Bedford RL 4-tonne trucks in which the Gemini can be easily stowed. The unit was formed in 1978.

4 Special Boat Section (Reserve) The RMR's connection with the SBS is a long and useful one. 4 SBS(R) acts in support of the regular squadron and trains highly skilled frogmen and parachutists who can approach their objectives by parachute, submarine, canoe or by swimming under water in order to carry out their mission.

608 Tactical Air Control Party (Reserve) RMR Bristol provides 608 TACP(R), a four-man team led by a subaltern, which provides air liaison to land forces and an aircraft control facility in forward areas. In 1979 this team deployed to Belize with a Regular Army battalion on a Regular Arms Plot Tour. This was the first time that a Reserve or TA unit had done this, and 608 TACP carried out a further tour in 1981.

The RMR offers the opportunity for civilians to undertake arduous training in parachuting, skiing and cliff climbing which would otherwise not be possible in their normal occupations. In addition, they can specialise as Assault Engineers, Signallers, PT Instructors, Cooks or in supporting weapons (mortars) or platoon weapons.

The RMR frequently detaches officers and men to the regular Corps and occasionally to units of the RNLMC and USMC for exercises. Training has recently been carried out in Belize, Canada, Cyprus, Hong Kong, Holland and Norway. There are opportunities for Staff College training and, indeed, senior officers must pass a Staff College Course before taking up their appointments. The RMR units are commanded by Lieutenant Colonels and come under the auspices of Major General Royal Marines Training and Reserve Forces (MGRM TRF) at Royal Marines, Eastney, Southsea.

In 1976, following the Defence Review, RMR units were affiliated to Commando Forces RM as follows:

City of London 41 Commando Group (disbanded May 1981*); 42 Commando, RM; Commando Logistic Regiment, RM.

*See also next page.

Scotland 45 Commando Group; Commando Logistic Regiment, RM.
    Bristol 3 Commando Brigade HQ and Signals Squadron, RM; 41 Commando Group(*); Commando Logistic Regiment, RM.
    Merseyside 40 Commando, RM; 41 Commando Group(*).
    Tyne 45 Commando Group; Commando Logistic Regiment, RM.

*Disbanded May 1981.

Typical of the co-operation between NATO allies is the UK/NL Amphibious Force exemplified by this photograph taken during Exercise 'Teamwork' (Commando Forces/PO Holdgate).

The Royal Marines and the Royal NL Marines

Some years ago a Memorandum of Understanding was agreed between the British and Dutch Governments for the operational and training deployment of elements of the Royal Netherlands Marine Corps (RNLMC) under the command of Commando Forces RM for NATO purposes. Two elements are usually earmarked for such duties—1 ACG and Whiskey Company, both based at Doorn in the Netherlands. The combining of all these elements has resulted in the UK/NL Amphibious Force whose joint training is often held up as a good example of NATO co-opertion. In addition, the RM has seconded and training officers with the forces of Brunei, Nigeria and Oman, plus participation in exchange programmes with the United States Marine Corps, RNLMC and the Australian Special Forces.

Royal Marines Band Service

The primary purpose of the Band Service is to provide Naval units and establishments with military bands and orchestras for formal occasions. The Corps currently maintains ten bands: Chatham (FO Medway), Deal (RM Band School), Portsmouth (CINCNAVHOME), Yeovilton (FONAC), Lympstone (CTCRM), Dartmouth (BRNC), Plymouth (CFRM), Rosyth (FOSNI), FOF3 and the RM at Deal. In wartime, the instruments would be put away and the Band Service would take on a role of internal security at Naval establishments; each bandsman is weapons-trained but not Commando-trained. They could also provide additional medical orderlies. RM Buglers, unlike bandsmen, have the opportunity of joining Commando units. Band Service officers are commissioned from the ranks to the Special Duties List, RM. One of the most prestigious venues is HMY *Britannia*. Two bands went to the Falklands.

Marine specialists

Although all Royal Marines except the Band Service are Commando-trained, it is possible for a Marine to undertake training for a Specialist Qualification (SQ) or to undergo trade training with Technical Training Company (TT Coy) at RM Poole. The Marines have three levels of specialist—Grade 3 (ordinary Marine); Grade 2 (usually a Corporal);

The Royal Marines band of Commander-in-Chief Naval Home Command (RM).

Grade 1 (usually a Sergeant or Colour Sergeant). In addition, there are artificers who are usually Warrant Officers, but their training is progressive because, unlike the RN, the Corps does not recruit direct into the artificers grade.

NCO and Marine specialisations are:

General Duties Branch Air Crewman; Assault Engineer; Drill Instructor/Leader; Helicopter Pilot (SNCOs); Heavy Weapons Instructor; Landing Craft; Provost/Marine Police; Physical Training Instructor; Platoon Weapons Instructor*; Mountain Leader (M&AW); Swimmer Canoeist/Para-

* Weapons up to and including 84 mm.
† Equipment.
‡ Pay and Records.

chutist; Driver; Signaller; Radio Operator; and Groom.

Technical Branch Bugler; Clerk (CQ†); Clerk (CPR)‡; and Musician (Band Service).

Tradesmen Illustrator; Carpenter; Metalsmith; Printer; Armourer; Vehicle Mechanic; Artificer (Vehicle); and Telecomm Technician.

The Mountain Leader SQ is to provide a cadre of M&AW personnel (at Plymouth) for long-range patrol, leadership and training tasks. Most of the technical training is carried out at RM Poole, or administered from there but actually carried out with the Army at Borden, where Armourers are trained, or Netheravon for support weapons, whilst RM cooks are trained with the RN at *Pembroke* (soon to move, perhaps to Aldershot).

Auxiliary Services

The Royal Fleet Auxiliary, Royal Maritime Auxiliary Service
and Royal Naval Auxiliary Service

Royal Fleet Auxiliary Service

The Royal Fleet Auxiliary Service (RFA) is operated and controlled by the Directorate of Supplies and Transport (Fuel, Movements and Victualling); DST is one of five Directorates which make up the Royal Naval Supply and Transport Service (RNSTS) which is headed by the Director General of Supplies and Transport (Naval). DGST reports to the Chief of Fleet Support who has a seat on the Admiralty Board.

The RFA is a fleet of merchant ships—tankers, stores support ships and landing ships—used to supply the needs of the RN at sea. The Fleet is owned by the Ministry of Defence but is manned by merchant officers and seamen (called ratings in most cases). Stores support ships also carry RNSTS civil servant officers to control stores.

Origins

The RFA can trace its history back to the days of Elizabethan exploration when ships known as 'pinks' accompanied fleets. This service was developed during the Napoleonic Wars and following the development of oil-burning warships, especially during the First World War. In the Second World War, RFAs were in the thick of the action, especially on the convoys to Russia and across the North Atlantic. During the Pacific Campaign, under US Navy guidance, the RN/RFA began 'Fleet Train' operations to keep the active Fleet in operation several thousand miles from a dockyard.

The tanker and logistic fleets have expanded into new roles since the war and today the task includes giving support to the Commonwealth and NATO navies as well as the RN. By 1957, the year after Suez, the RFA had reached a peak in terms of numbers of hulls and the list included a number of tugs and allied craft now under the control of the Royal Maritime Auxiliary Service (RMAS).

As the RN surface fleet, especially the aircraft carrier task groups, decreased, the use of RFA fell and the specialisation increased. This is now recognised to have been a move in the wrong direction and the future may lie in 'one stop' vessels, combined tanker/supply ships which enable a warship to pick up all its supplies in one replenishment at sea (RAS); the methods used would be jackstay and helicopter Vertrep.

Service

The RFA's motto is 'Ready for Anything' and this is their proud boast 365 days a year. They now follow the RN on deployment all over the world in whatever conditions—Arctic or Tropics.

The most important service provided by the RFA is underway replenishment at sea—the RAS—which can either be for solids (RAS(S)) or liquids (RAS(L)). This involves precise seamanship as fuel, water, food, ammunition and stores are transferred at sea whilst both vessels are underway. During RAS(L), the two vessels (or more if a group RAS is taking place) are linked by a flexible hose for the transfer of FFO (furnace fuel oil—larger warships), AVGAS (aviation gasoline) or fuel oil for the gas turbine engined frigates and destroyers. The ships maintain a steady course but can manoeuvre if required—in this technique the RN/RFA leads the world.

RAS(S) is carried out by means of jackstay rigs and today the weather is not the problem that it used to be and the methods and the rigs are constantly being uprated. The increasing use of helicopters, either borne by the RFA or by another ship, has meant that a technique called VERTREP (vertical replenishment) has been refined for the transfer of bulky items and of items to and from several sources when it is not possible to come alongside. On RFAs the helicopter landing pads are served by special lifts and loads are assembled on the flight deck using rope slings and nets. Weight limits are important, especially for the older Westland Wessex HU 5 helicopters of 772 NAS which are available for RFA work. It is interesting to reflect that the flight decks of most RFAs are about 60 ft (18 m) above sea level, or higher than the average aircraft carrier at 50 ft (15 m) above sea level. For helicopter operations RN personnel are carried but this does not alter the ships' unique position of being classified as merchant ships and thus able to visit foreign ports without the need for diplomatic clearance.

The supplying ship usually maintains a steady course—the role of 'guide' and the recipient takes 'station' on her, whether for abeam or astern replenishment, the latter only being available for liquids when the transfer line is 'floated' aft. Lines are put across by using the standard SLR 7.62 mm with a special attachment and various wires to show position are also sent across as well as the fuel lines.

Personnel

The opportunity to work with the RFA is open to all UK merchant seamen who can transfer from their own merchant companies or to cadets who can enlist from school or college. The work is unusual and interesting; deck officers especially are expected to undertake demanding jobs such as becoming a Helicopter Controller (HC) or a Flight Deck Officer (FDO). There are about 3,500 merchant navy personnel employed, including some 1,250 officers, and these men serve under the National Maritime Board conditions of service—Merchant Navy Articles of Agreement. It is possible that women will make the RFA their first inroad into the male world at sea in the next decade; this is already happening with the naval manned auxiliaries of Canada and the Netherlands.

Deck Officers These men carry out the navigational, tactical and watchkeeping duties in RFAs. Their life differs considerably from life in a regular merchant company; how many officers are allowed to deliberately beach a ship? LSL* officers have to as part of their job! Deck officers are responsible for the cargo in all ships (but in stores support vessels, only during RAS).

Engineer Officers These men control the propulsion and auxiliary systems aboard RFAs, whether they are motor ships with modern diesels like the *Rover* Class or steamships like the *01* Class. Most ships have automatic machinery control and in the main the engines are more powerful than those found in other merchant ships of the same tonnage.

Radio Officers RFAs, because of the naval connection, have quite complex radio gear for communications with the Fleet. Training is sometimes carried out at *Collingwood*. Some ships even carry electronic test and maintenance gear. maintenance gear.

Electrical Officers This is a sub-specialisation of the Engineering Department aboard RFAs where the 'greenie' is responsible for the maintenance of modern sophisticated electrical machinery.

Pursers These men manage the catering and the pay/accounting functions in the ships. The Ship's Office is the Purser's base and there is a large personnel management function involved.

* LSL officers are those with extra training to man the *Sir Lancelot* Class Landing Ships Logistics—most of whom have experienced South Atlantic waters in 1982.

The RFA of the future would seem to be a mixture of replenishment at sea and the more naval role of helicopter carrier. This is Fort Grange *with an 824 Sea King HAS 2 (Fleet Photo Unit).*

Ranking structure
Officers

Deck Branch	Engineer Branch	Electrical Branch	Purser	Radio	Surgeon
Commodore	Commodore	No equivalent	-	-	-
Master	Chief Engineer	-	-	-	-
Chief Officer	Second Engineer	-	-	-	Ship's Surgeon
First Officer	-	Senior Elect. Off	Senior Purser	Senior RO	-
Second Officer	Third Engineer	First Elect. Off	Purser	Radio O(A)	-
Uncertificated SO	Uncert. Third Eng	-	-	-	-
Third Officer	Fourth Engineer	Second Elect. Off	Asst. Purser	RO (B) Junior RO	-
Uncert. Third Off	Uncert. Fourth Eng	Junior Elect. Off	-	-	-
Fourth Officer	Junior Engineer				

Ratings

(NB: RFA Carpenters rank above all other craftsmen including CPO Deck and this position does not 'go through the ranks'.)

Deck Dept	Engineer Dept	Catering	Catering
CPO Deck	CPO	-	Chief Cook
PO Deck	PO Motorman	PO Steward	Ship's Cook
Quartermaster	-	-	-
Seaman IA	Motorman IA	Catering Storekeeper	Second Cook and Baker
Seaman IB	Motorman I	-	-
Seaman II	Motorman II	Steward	Assistant Cook
Junior Seaman	-		Junior Catering Rating (JCR)

Officers at work: a bridge briefing by the Captain of an RFA during exercises in the Portland area (RFA).

Ship's Surgeons All RFAs carry medical personnel and most of the large ones have a surgeon who looks after the ship's company and can on occasions be required to perform emergency surgery when an RFA goes to the assistance of a ship in trouble. RFA surgeons work closely with their RN counterparts ashore and afloat.

The Seaman grades are specialist as well, dealing with the Deck, Engine Room and Catering Departments. There is a rating uniform but it is not used in practise and enforcement is difficult because of the unionisation of the RFA. Many ratings do find the standard RN working rig a useful 'uniform' when working the ship.

Ships

RFAs are to be found all over the world in company with RN warships, and for many years they have been accompanying Group Deployments to the South Atlantic, Indian Ocean and Far East. At the present time there are two RFAs on duty in the Arabian Sea with the Gulf Patrol, and they use Mombasa, Kenya, as a base port. During the large-

Fort Grange *in company with RN frigates* (PRO Portsmouth).

scale NATO exercises carried out in the autumn of 1981, both *Fort Austin* and *Fort Grange* were deployed for the first time with a full complement of four Sea King anti-submarine helicopters and it was reported that they performed very well and led the then FOF3, Rear Admiral J. C. Cox, to comment that they were almost like having two extra aircraft carriers available. Without doubt then, the role of the RFA (in terms of ships) is changing and the combined RFA/carrier concept may well continue to be developed into a ski-ramp-equipped, missile-armed 'one stop' ship capable of its own defence and that of a convoy of merchant ships. British Aerospace is already taking a containerised defence system around 'the bazaars' and this scheme could well be adapted for RFA use.

In the last several years, the RFA has lost a number of ships due to defence cuts and the general rundown of the surface fleet which means that less and less RFA hulls are required. In 1981, *Bacchus*, the dry cargo freighter/wartime amphibious support ship, was paid off and in 1982 *Stromness* followed *Lyness* and *Tarbatness* out of service as Stores Support Ships and into the US naval transport and supply service. The older fleet tankers are being withdrawn steadily, including *Tidepool* and *Tidespring*; the former in 1981 and the latter in 1983. On the other hand, there are new ships coming along

including the charter of another *Leaf* Class ship built be Cammell Laird.

Stores Support Ships
Class *Fort*
Name *Fort Grange*; **Pennant number** A385; **Flight deck code** FG; **Standard displacement** 8,300 tons; **Full displacement** 22,749 tons; **Length** 184.0 m overall; **Beam** 24.0 m; **Draught** 9 m; **Propulsion** 1 × diesel (23,200 hp); **Range** 10,000 nm at 20 knots; **Speed** 20 knots; **Complement** 140 RFA, 45 RNSTS (civilians); **Armament** None; **Sensors** Navigation radar only; **Aircraft** 1–4 Sea King HAS 2/5 or 1–4 Wessex HU 5; **Small craft** 8 × ship's boats; **Vehicles** Logistic and stacking; **Builders** Scott-Lithgow; **Laid down** November 9 1973; **Launched** December 9 1976; **Completed** November 1978; **Commissioned** April 6 1978.

The two vessels of the *Fort* Class are the nearest yet to the one stop/ASW ships which it is thought will be the mainstay of the RFA in the 1990s. The *Fort Grange* and *Fort Austin* are designed to replenish RN warships with naval armaments and victualling (including refrigerated) stores underway. Stores are palletised for greater efficiency in handling. Accommodation standards are high, with individual cabins for officers and senior POs.

Shelduck drone—launch from an RFA (RN).

Olmeda at sea with Wessex HU 5 embarked on the flight deck aft (RN).

Bomb Alley—an Argentine attack on RFAs, the requisitioned ferry Norland *and the assault ship* Fearless *(RN/HMS* Fearless*).*

Both saw service in the South Atlantic and *Fort Grange* was the centre of unwanted attention from an Argentine C-130 Hercules whilst still an estimated 1,000 nm (1,852 km) from San Carlos water. Luckily the aircraft did not attack the unarmed ship; the latter was carrying a flight of 824 Squadron Sea Kings during this time. *Fort Austin* actually served as an ammunition ship during the San Carlos landings and was also attacked.

Name Fort Austin; **Pennant number** A386; **Flight deck code** FA; **Standard displacement** 8,300 tons; **Full displacement** 22,890 tons; **Length** 184.0 m overall; **Beam** 24.0 m; **Draught** 14.9 m; **Propulsion** 1 × diesel (23,200 hp); **Range** 10,000 nm at 20 knots; **Speed** 22 knots; **Complement** 140 RFA, 45 RNSTS (civilians); **Armanent** None; **Sensors** Navigation radar only; **Aircraft** 1–4 Sea King HAS 2/5 or 1–4 Wessex HU 5; **Small craft** 8 × ship's boats; **Vehicles** Logistic and stacking; **Builders** Scott-Lithgow; **Laid down** December 9 1975; **Launched** March 8 1978; **Completed** January 1979; **Commissioned** May 11 1979.

Large Fleet Tankers

Class *Ol*

Name Olwen (ex-*Olympus*); **Pennant number** A122; **Flight deck code** OW; **Standard displacement** 10,890 tons; **Full displacement** 36,000 tons; **Length** 197.5 m overall; **Beam** 25.6 m; **Draught** 11.1 m; **Propulsion** 2 × steam turbines (26,500 shp); **Range** 10,000 nm at 16 knots; **Speed** 19 knots; **Complement** 25 officers and 62 ratings (FAA aircrew extra); **Armament** None; **Sensors** Navigational radar only; **Aircraft** 1–4 Sea King HAS 2/5 or 1–4 Wessex HU 5 or 1–4 Wasp HAS 1; **Small craft** 8 × ship's boats; **Vehicles** May be stored in starboard hangar; **Builders** Hawthorn Leslie; **Commissioned** June 21 1965.

The *Ol* Class were the largest and fastest ships in the RFA when first commissioned; *Olwen* and *Olmeda* were originally named *Olympus* and *Oleander* respectively when built in 1965 but due to confusion with *Olympus* (SSK) and *Leander* (FFH), they were

Green Rover, the first of a class of modern, fast tankers (RFA).

Tidespring *entering Portsmouth at dusk* (RN).

renamed in 1967. Aircraft hangarage is split into two: three helicopters on the port side and a fourth or vehicles on the starboard. These ships provide training billets for naval helicopters as well as homes for detached Wessex used for Vertrep. Each vessel can carry 24,260 tons of oil.

Name *Olna*; **Pennant number** A123; **Flight deck code** ON; **Complement** 27 officers and 62 ratings; **Aircraft** 1–4 Sea King HAS 2/5 but more usually Wessex HU or Wasp HAS 1; **Vehicles** May be stored in hangars; **Builders** Hawthorn Leslie; **Commissioned** April 1 1966; **Other details** As for *Olwen*.

Name *Olmeda* (ex-*Oleander*); **Pennant number** A124; **Flight deck code** OD; **Builders** Swan Hunter; **Commissioned** October 18 1965; **Other details** As for *Olna*.
    Acted in support of the Falklands Task Force.

Class *Tide*

Name *Tidespring*; **Pennant number** A75; **Flight deck code** TS; **Standard displacement** 8,531 tons; **Full displacement** 27,400 tons; **Length** 177.6 m overall; **Beam** 21.6 m; **Draught** 9.8 m; **Propulsion** 2 × steam turbines (15,000 shp); **Range** 8,000 nm at 15 knots; **Speed** 18 knots; **Complement** 30 officers and 80 ratings; **Armament** None; **Sensors** Navigational radar only; **Aircraft** 1–4 helicopters, usually Wessex HU 5 or Wasp HAS 1; **Small craft** 8 × ship's boats; **Vehicles** May be stored in hangar; **Builders** Hawthorn Leslie; **Commissioned** January 18 1963.
    Sadly, the *Tide* Class will soon be gone from the lists of the RFA, for they are surely one of the most graceful designs possible in a tanker. *Tidepool* was paid off in early 1982 and *Tidespring* is due to follow in 1983. *Tidereach* was laid up in Portsmouth Harbour in the late 1970s following earlier defence cuts. Like the *Ol* Class, they have Babcock & Wilcox boilers and double reduction geared turbines. *Tidespring* is capable of carrying 18,860 tons of oil stores. She formed part of the support force for the Falklands Task Force.

Name *Tidepool*; **Pennant number** A76; **Flight deck code** TP; **Commissioned** June 28 1963; **Other details** As for *Tidespring*.

Small Fleet Tankers

Class *Rover*

Name *Green Rover*; **Pennant number** A268; **Flight deck code** GN; **Standard displacement** 4,700 tons; **Full displacement** 11,522 tons; **Length** 140.6 m overall; **Beam** 19.2 m; **Draught** 7.3 m; **Propulsion** 2 × diesels; **Range** 15,000 nm at 15 knots; **Speed** 18 knots; **Complement** 16 officers and 31 ratings; **Armament** None; **Sensors** Navigational radar; 16 in (406 mm) true motion; 12 in (305 mm); D/F; Decca navigator; Loran; **Aircraft** Helicopter-capable up to Sea King size; **Small craft** 2 × ship's boats; **Vehicles** None; **Builders** Swan Hunter; **Commissioned** August 15 1969.

    The *Rover* Class are the small fleet tankers which are used to replenish frigates on deployment and cost between £3 million and £7 million to build, the German engines having had to be replaced on several. They have controllable pitch propellors (one shaft each) and a bow thruster for berthing. The two Pielstick diesel engines develop 15,300 bhp. They can be recognised by the large funnel which occasionally bears a badge, such as the 'Children Warning' road sign of *Black Rover* during her time at Portland on sea training duties.

The ships were specially designed to meet the needs of the RFA and are capable of supplying 6,600 tons each of the usual liquids: furnace fuel oil, diesel, aviation spirit, lubricating oil, fresh water and some limited dry cargo which can be handled via Vertrep from the flight deck; there is no hangar.

Name *Grey Rover*; **Pennant number** A269; **Flight deck code** GY; **Commissioned** April 10 1970; **Other details** As for *Green Rover*.

Name *Blue Rover*; **Pennant number** A270; **Flight deck code** BE; **Complement** 17 officers and 30 ratings; **Commissioned** July 15 1970; **Refits** 1979; **Other details** as for *Green Rover*.

Name *Gold Rover*; **Pennant number** A271; **Flight deck code** GV; **Complement** 16 officers and 38 ratings; **Commissioned** March 24 1974; **Other details** As for *Green Rover*.

Name *Black Rover*; **Pennant number** A273; **Flight deck code** BV; **Commissioned** August 23 1974; **Other details** As for *Green Rover*.

Support Tankers
Class *Leaf*
Name *Appleleaf* (ex-*Hudson Deep*); **Pennant number** A79; **Standard displacement** Unknown; **Full displacement** 40,200 tons; **Length** 170.7 m overall; **Beam** 25.9 m; **Draught** 11.9 m; **Propulsion** 2 × diesels; **Range** 15,000 nm at 12 knots; **Speed** 15.5 knots; **Complement** 60 officers and ratings;

Top left Gold Rover *at the 1977 Spithead Review.* **Centre left** Regent *at a buoy in Portland harbour.* **Left** Resource, *also at Portland.* **Below** Plumleaf *is one of the older tankers and is due to be replaced* (MoD).

Appleleaf *running light on sea trials* (HMS Osprey).

Armament None; **Sensors** Navigational radar only; **Small craft** 4 × ship's boats; **Builders** Cammell Laird; **Launched** July 24 1975; **Completed** September 1979; **Commissioned** December 1979.

These vessels are usually chartered to the Ministry of Defence for the transportation of FFO, Dieso and AV fuel in bulk between oil terminals and MOD(N) storage facilities, such as Gosport. They are also used for consolidating Fleet tankers and for replenishment at sea in a limited capacity. On chartering, the vessels have been refitted with RAS gear for the transfer of liquids, mail, personnel and light loads. They have no helicopter facilities. The two older vessels, *Pearleaf* and *Plumleaf*, are generally tasked with bulk freighting, whilst the two newer vessels are more flexible in their operations.

A new vessel, *Bayleaf*, which has been constructed at Cammell Laird, entered service in 1982, its operational debut having been advanced following the Falkland operations.

Appleleaf, *Brambleleaf* and *Pearleaf* took part in the Falklands operation, in support of the Task Force.

Name *Brambleleaf* (ex-*Hudson Cavalier*); **Pennant number** A81; **Launched** January 22 1976; **Completed** September 1979; **Commissioned** May 6 1980; **Other details** as for *Appleleaf*.

Name *Pearleaf*; **Pennant number** A77; **Nett displacement** 7,215 tons; **Full displacement** 25,790 tons; **Length** 173.2 m overall; **Beam** 21.9 m; **Draught** 9.2 m; **Propulsion** 1 × diesel (8,800 bhp); **Range** 15,000 nm at 14 knots; **Speed** 16 knots; **Complement** 55 officers and ratings; **Builders** Blythswood, Scotstoun; **Launched** October 15 1959; **Completed** 1960; **Commissioned** January 1960; **Other details** As for *Appleleaf*. (*Pearleaf* is owned by Jacobs and Partners.)

Name *Plumleaf*; **Pennant number** A78; **Gross displacement** 12,459 tons; **Full displacement** 26,480 tons; **Length** 170.8 m; **Beam** 22.0 m; **Draught** 9.2 m; **Propulsion** 1 × diesel (9,500 bhp); **Range** 15,000 nm at 12 knots; **Speed** 16 knots; **Complement** 55 officers and ratings; **Builders** Blyth Drydock; **Launched** March 29 1969; **Completed** 1960; **Commissioned** July 1960; **Other details** as for *Appleleaf*.

Fleet Replenishment Ships

Class *Regent*
Name *Regent*; **Pennant number** A486; **Flight deck code** RG; **Gross displacement** 18,029 tons; **Full displacement** 22,890 tons; **Length** 195.1 m overall; **Beam** 23.5 m; **Draught** 8.0 m; **Propulsion** 2 × steam turbines (20,000 shp); **Range** 12,000 nm at 18 knots; **Speed** 21 knots; **Complement** 119 RFA, 52 RNSTS, 11 RN; **Armament** Fitted for 2 × 40 mm GP; **Sensors** Navigational radar; SCOT; **Aircraft** 1 × Wessex HU 5; **Small craft** 8 × ship's boats; 1 × supply craft; **Vehicles** Logistic and stacking; **Builders** Harland & Wolff; **Commissioned** June 6 1967.

The two Fleet Replenishment Ships of the *Regent* Class were ordered on January 24 1963 to operate in support of the Fleet, particularly the larger units such as aircraft and Commando carriers. They carry ammunition, explosives, food and naval stores, including aircraft spares. Replenishment is carried out at sea using large jackstay rigs or the ships' helicopters. These are usually Wessex HU 5s drawn from the specialist support flight of 772 NAS at Portland. These vessels only occasionally go alongside at special facilities because of the nature of their cargoes. *Resource* acted in support of the Falklands Task Force.

Name *Resource*; **Pennant number** A480; **Flight deck code** RS; **Builders** Scotts, Greenock; **Commissioned** May 16 1967; **Refits** Several, including 1980–81.

RFA Engadine—a merchant aircraft carrier (well, almost!) (RFA).

Helicopter Support Ship

Class *Engadine*

Name *Engadine*; **Pennant number** K08; **Flight deck code** EN; **Nett tonnage** 2,848; **Full displacement** 9,000 tons; **Length** 129.3 m overall; **Beam** 17.8 m; **Draught** 6.7 m; **Propulsion** 1 × diesel (5,500 bhp); **Range** 8,000 nm at 14 knots; **Speed** 16 knots; **Complement** 15 officers and 48 ratings; 2 officers and 12 ratings (RN staff); 29 officers and 84 ratings (RN training); **Armament** None; **Sensors** Navigational radar only; **Aircraft** None allocated; accommodation for 4 × Wessex HAS 3 or 3 × Lynx HAS 2 or 2 × Sea King HAS 2/5 or 2 × Wasp HAS 1; **Small craft** 6 × ship's boats including crash boat; **Vehicles** ML aircraft handlers; **Builders** Henry Robb; **Laid down** August 9 1965; **Launched** September 15 1966; **Completed** 1967; **Commissioned** December 15 1967.

Engadine, the first Helicopter Support Ship in the RFA, was designed to meet a naval requirement for training helicopter aircrew and groundcrew, without involving costly operations from larger carriers. The ship was ordered in August 1964 and launched by the wife of the then FOST, Mrs. P. G. Sharp. Since being commissioned in 1967, more than 22,000 helicopter landings have been carried out on her decks. She is usually to be found operating 737 NAS (Wessex HAS 3) or 706 NAS (Sea King HAS 2/5). In late 1981 her helicopters were twice called out to render assistance, and in one incident Acting Sub-Lieutenant the Prince Andrew flew a rescue mission with 706 Squadron.

Engadine is powered by a two-stroke, turbocharged 5RD68 Sulzer diesel engine built by Wallsend Slipway and Engineering Co Ltd with five cylinders; it develops 4,400 shp and drives a single shaft. Stabilisers are also fitted to enable helicopter operations to be carried out in most weather conditions. The vessel also carries naval stores for the Sea King, Wessex and Lynx aircraft which may be operating from her at any time. She is also equipped with bunkers for aviation fuels. *Engadine* has RAS-fittings on the foremast and light jackstay transfers are possible.

Landing Ships Logistics

Class *Sir Lancelot*

Name *Sir Lancelot*; **Pennant number** L3029; **Flight deck code** LN; **Light displacement** 3,270 tons; **Full displacement** 5,550 tons; **Length** 125.6 m overall; **Beam** 19.6 m; **Draught** 4.3 m (beaching ability); **Propulsion** 2 × diesels (9,520 bhp); **Range** 8,000 nm at 15 knots; **Speed** 17 knots; **Complement** 18 officers and 50 ratings; war load of 340 troops; **Armament** Fitted for 2 × 40 mm GP; **Sensors** Navigational radar only; **Aircraft** Accommodation for 3 × Wessex HU 5 or 2 × Sea King HC 4 or 3 × Gazelle AH 1; **Small craft** 4 × ship's boats; **Vehicles** All types of military vehicle may be carried; **Builders** Fairfield; **Laid down** March 1962; **Launched** June 23 1963; **Completed** 1963; **Commissioned** January 16 1964.

These ships, known as Landing Ship Logistics (LSLs), were originally ordered by the Ministry of Transport for use by the Army but in 1970–1 management and manning was taken over by the RFA. The *Sir Lancelot* Class (all vessels are named for knights of the Round Table) are designed as multi-purpose troop and heavy vehicle carriers and are employed in peacetime on regular voyages from their home base at Marchwood, near Southampton, to Antwerpen and Northern Ireland. They are fitted for roll-on-roll-end traffic with bow and stern doors and can undertake vehicle maintenance; helicopters of the Wessex type can be operated by day or night from the decks and there is a helicopter deck on the stern. Mexeflotes can be used as pontoons for ferrying troops and vehicles ashore or the craft can beach in the traditional landing craft mode.

LSLs have a unique and vital role anywhere in the world, including east of Suez, where *Sir Lancelot* played an essential part in the East Pakistan flood relief operations in 1970. In wartime, it is not sure what the exact role of the Class would be, whether supporting the Army for the Central Front or the Royal Marines and amphibious forces in Norway or the Atlantic islands; the Chiefs of Staff will have to decide the priority.

All six LSLs were heavily involved in the Falkland Islands during 1982, where *Sir Tristram* was badly damaged and *Sir Galahad* sunk in June.

Name *Sir Bedivere*; **Pennant number** L3004; **Flight deck code** BV; **Full displacement** 5,674 tons; **Propulsion** 2 × diesels (9,400 bhp); **Small craft** 4 × ship's boats; 2 × Gemini; **Builders** Hawthorn Leslie; **Laid down** October 1965; **Launched** July 20 1966; **Completed** 1967; **Commissioned** May 18 1967; **Other details** As for *Sir Lancelot*.

Name *Sir Galahad*; **Pennant number** L3005; **Flight deck code** GD; **Small craft** 4 × ship's boats; 1 × Gemini; **Builders** Alex Stephen; **Laid down** February 1965; **Launched** April 19 1966; **Completed** 1966; **Commissioned** December 17 1966; **Lost** South Atlantic June 1982; **Other details** As for *Sir Bedivere*.

Name *Sir Geraint*; **Pennant number** L3027; **Flight deck code** GR; **Small craft** 4 × ship's boats; **Laid down** June 1965; **Launched** January 26 1967; **Completed** 1967; **Commissioned** July 12 1967; **Other details** As for *Sir Galahad*.

Name *Sir Percivale*; **Pennant number** L3036; **Flight deck code** PV; **Builders** Hawthorn Leslie; **Laid down** April 1966; **Launched** October 4 1967; **Completed** 1968; **Commissioned** March 23 1968; **Other details** As for *Sir Galahad*.

Name *Sir Tristram*; **Pennant number** L3505; **Flight deck code** TM; **Small craft** 4 × ship's boats; **Laid down** February 1966; **Launched** December 12 1966; **Completed** 1967; **Commissioned** September 14 1967; **Other details** As for *Sir Bedivere*.

Sir Bedivere with one of Fearless' LCUs at the stern doors (Commando Forces).

RFA ship designations

The RFA, in common with other NATO associated organisations, uses abbreviations to describe ships and their role: **AEFS** Fleet Replenishment Ships; **AOF(L)** Large Fleet Tankers; **AOF(S)** Small Fleet Tanker; **AOS** Support Tanker; **AO(H)** Coastal Tanker (there are no longer any in RFA service); **AVS/AFS** Stores Support Ship (the last was paid off in early 1982); **AK** Stores Carrier (the last was paid off in 1981); **LSL** Logistic Landing Ship.

Sir Lancelot moves up to a disembarkation point during an exercise (HMS Osprey).

Royal Maritime Auxiliary Service

In October 1976, the Port Auxiliary Service combined with the Royal Maritime Auxiliary Service (RMAS) under the latter's banner to form a support service for the RN of about 170 craft by 1981. One could be forgiven for thinking that the RMAS only operates tugs, but, in fact, there are a small fleet (bigger than many navies) of other craft from general support fleet tenders to the specialist and highly developed craft, such as underwater weapons trials ships.

The Service is civilian-manned but operates within MOD(N) and is tasked with providing local maritime support at the following: HM Naval Bases Chatham, Portsmouth, Plymouth, Gibraltar, Rosyth, Portland and Hong Kong; plus Greenock, Pembroke Docks, Poole, Birkenhead, Belfast and other ports as necessity dictates.

It should be noted that RN officers and ratings are often carried as part of special duties' crews or for special work, including sea salvage and submarine rescue.

RMAS craft are quite distinctive in their colour scheme of black hull and buff upperworks, and they are often seen around the coasts of the United Kingdom and occasionally 'going foreign' as needs dictate. In the latter category are the powerful and majestic ocean tugs, such as *Typhoon* and the *Roysterer* Class. Alas, the paddlewheel harbour tugs of the *Director* Class are no longer in naval service and their demise could well be linked to that of the aircraft carrier which they were designed to handle in the narrow confines of naval ports. They were the only paddlewheel tugs operated by any navy and the last, *Faithful*, was decommissioned in September 1981.

The RMAS is surprisingly modern although there are a few types remaining which began life in the wartime era; as warships have developed since World War 2, so have their support vessels. Today, the roles played by these craft have widened and have grown more complex. Several ships are now RN-manned for specialist jobs, such as diving tenders, but the majority are manned by professional seamen who have, in the RMAS, an excellent career structure and a responsible job. They are civil servants and have been known to take industrial action nonetheless. The RMAS is vital to the smooth and efficient running of the modern RN. The most intriguing roles are played by the trials ships and in many cases their exact tasks are closely guarded secrets.

The following list gives an indication of the potential and wide spectrum of maritime work carried out by the RMAS: ocean tugs; harbour tugs; water tractors; Fleet tenders; diving tenders; degaussing vessels; tank cleaning vessels; water carriers; boom defence ships; coastal tankers; trials ships; torpedo recovery vessels; armament carriers; target ships; cable ships. They are described Class by Class below.

Ocean tugs

Class *Roysterer*

Name *Roysterer*; **Pennant number** A361; **Displacement** 1,630 tons; **Length** 55.0 m; **Beam** 11.7 m; **Draught** 5.5 m; **Propulsion** 2 × Mirrless diesels (4,500 bhp); **Range** 13,000 nm at 12 knots; **Speed** 15 knots; **Complement** 10 officers and 21 ratings; **Armament** None; **Builders** Holmes; **Completed** April 26 1972.

Particularly well-suited for ocean salvage, towing and rescue duties, these powerful craft cost about £2 million each. Their bollard pull is 50 tons and they can work in harbours as easily as other large tugs. In fact, they are the largest and certainly the most powerful such vessels to operate with the RMAS or the RN. In addition to their normal merchant crew, they can accommodate ten RN salvage crew and a large number of survivors for short periods.

Name *Robust*; **Pennant number** A366; **Builders** Holmes; **Completed** February 1973.

Name *Rollicker*; **Pennant number** A502; **Builders** Holmes; **Completed** April 6 1974.

Class *Typhoon*

Name *Typhoon*; **Pennant number** A95; **Standard displacement** 800 tons; **Full displacement** 1,380 tons; **Length** 61.0 m; **Beam** 13.0 m; **Draught** 4.0 m; **Propulsion** 2 × Vee diesels (2,750 bhp); **Range** Unknown; **Speed** 16+ knots; **Complement**

Right Typhoon *leaves her home base at Portland.* **Centre right** *The ocean tug* Roysterer (RMAS). **Bottom right** *The former harbour tug* Agile, *now rated ocean tug.*

35 officers and ratings plus salvage crew; **Armament** None; **Builders** Robb & Co; **Launched** October 14 1958; **Completed** 1960.

The Scottish shipbuilding form of Henry Robb & Co of Leith built this tug for ocean towing, salvage and firefighting/rescue to augment the earlier designs. Her two turbocharged Vickers-designed diesels drive a single shaft but give the tug a handsome speed in excess of 16 knots. This system was the first of its kind in a naval tug. The bollard pull is 32 tons and *Typhoon* has a heavy derrick for working the towing deck. She is usually based at Plymouth.

Class *Confiance*
Name *Confiance*; **Pennant number** A289; **Displacement** 760 tons; **Length** 47.2 m; **Beam** 10.7 m; **Draught** 3.4 m; **Propulsion** 4 × Paxman diesels (1,800 bhp); **Range** Unknown; **Speed** 13 knots; **Complement** 29 officers and ratings plus salvage crew; **Armament** Fitted for 1 × 40 mm GP; **Builders** Inglis; **Completed** March 27 1956.

Originally a Class of two—*Confiance* and *Confident*—the similar harbour tugs were added to the Class in 1971 and can be distinguished from the original pair by their mainmasts. They are all classed as ocean-going tugs and, indeed, could be used as such, but today they seem to spend their time docking the RN's larger warships, such as DLGs and carriers. Their appearance is that of the 'traditional' tug.

Name *Confident*; **Pennant number** A290; **Builders** Inglis; **Completed** January 1956.

Name *Agile*; **Pennant number** A88; **Builders** Goole; **Completed** July 1959.

210

Name *Advice*; **Pennant number** A89; **Builders** Inglis; **Completed** October 1959.

Name *Accord*; **Pennant number** A90; **Builders** Inglis; **Completed** September 1958.

Class *Bustler*
Name *Cyclone*; **Pennant number** A111; **Standard displacement** 1,118 tons; **Full displacement** 1,630 tons; **Length** 62.5 m; **Beam** 12.3 m; **Draught** 5.1 m; **Propulsion** 2 × Atlas Polar diesels (4,000 bhp); **Range** 17,000 nm; **Speed** 16 knots; **Complement** 42 officers and ratings; **Armament** None; **Builders** Robb; **Launched** September 10 1942; **Completed** September 1943.

Cyclone was originally named *Growler* and chartered commercially in the name of *Caroline Moller*, later changed to *Castle Peak* before being returned to the RMAS in 1957. Between then and 1964, she was renamed *Welshman* whilst again on charter. Others in the eight-strong Class were chartered at times during their careers, but their main purpose was ocean towing and rescue. Of wartime construction also, *Cyclone*'s sister ship *Mediator* will be remembered as the last tug to sail under the White Ensign and classmate *Reward* as the converted tug-cum-patrol vessel which sank in the Firth of Forth in 1976, only to be salvaged later. These craft were of single-shaft design.

Harbour tugs

Class *Girl*
Name *Alice*; **Pennant number** A113; **Standard displacement** 40 tons; **Length** 18.6 m; **Beam** 5.0 m; **Draught** 2.2 m; **Propulsion** 1 × diesel (495 bhp); **Range** Unknown; **Speed** 10 knots;

Complement Circa 6; **Armament** None; **Builders** P. K. Harris; **Completed** 1961.

This is a Class of eight smaller harbour tugs, built at the same time, as the larger *Dog* Class (*qv*) to replace the obsolete World War 2 tugs for harbour duties. They have no funnels.

Name *Agatha*; **Pennant number** A116; **Builders** P. K. Harris; **Completed** 1961.

Name *Audrey*; **Pennant number** A117; **Builders** P. K. Harris; **Completed** 1961.

Name *Agnes*; **Pennant number** A121; **Builders** P. K. Harris; **Completed** 1961.

Name *Bridget*; **Pennant number** A322; **Builders** Dunston; **Completed** May 10 1963.

Name *Betty*; **Pennant number** A323; **Builders** Dunston; **Completed** April 25 1963.

Above *The harbour tug* Doris *at Devonport* (RMAS).

Left Alice, *the first of eight harbour tugs* (RMAS).

Above right Adept *newly arrived at Portsmouth* (RN).

Name *Barbara*; **Pennant number** A324; **Builders** Dunston; **Completed** May 10 1963.

Name *Brenda*; **Pennant number** A325; **Builders** Dunston; **Completed** June 27 1963.

Class Modified *Girl*

Name *Daisy*; **Pennant number** A145; **Standard displacement** 38 tons; **Length** 18.6 m; **Beam** 5.0 m; **Draught** 2.2 m; **Propulsion** 1 × diesel (495 bhp); **Range** Unknown; **Speed** 10 knots; **Complement** Circa 6; **Armament** None (except *Clare*, see text); **Builders** Dunston; **Completed** November 12 1968.

Although lighter than the earlier *Girl* Class, the modified eight are more similar to the *Dog* Class in appearance, having twin uptakes on the after end of the small deckhouse. HM Tug *Clare* is RN-manned at *Tamar* (Hong Kong) and was used mainly for anti-smuggling and anti-illegal immigrant operations, mostly in the Pearl River estuary 1929–81. In 1980 the tug strayed across into Chinese waters due to a navigation error but, after discussions with the People's Militia, she was allowed to return to Hong Kong waters. In this patrol vessel role, *Clare* was equipped with a Gemini dinghy and could mount light machine-guns; she was commanded by a Lieutenant Commander and mainly crewed by Submarine Service ratings on rotation and LEPs (locally enlisted personnel, ie, Chinese seamen).

Name *Edith*; **Pennant number** A177; **Builders** Dunston; **Completed** June 5 1969.

Name *Charlotte*; **Pennant number** A210; **Builders** Pimblott; **Completed** 1966.

Name *Christine*; **Pennant number** A217; **Builders** Pimblott; **Completed** 1966.

Name *Clare*; **Pennant number** A218; **Armament** See text; **Small craft** See text; **Builders** Pimblott; **Completed** 1966.

Name *Doris*; **Pennant number** A252; **Builders** Dunston; **Completed** March 19 1969.

Name *Daphne*; **Pennant number** A156; **Builders** Dunston; **Completed** December 19 1968.

Name *Dorothy*; **Pennant number** A173; **Builders** Dunston; **Completed** April 24 1969.

Class *Adept*

Name *Adept*; **Pennant number** A224; **Displacement** Unknown; **Length** 38.82 m overall;

Beam 9.1 m; **Draught** 4.2 m; **Propulsion** 1 × diesel (984 kw brake); **Range** Unknown; **Speed** 12.5 knots; **Complement** 9 officers and ratings; **Armament** None; **Builders** Dunston; **Laid down** July 23 1979; **Launched** August 27 1980; **Completed** October 20 1980.

The latest tugs (or twin tractor units) to enter service, the *Adept* Class are dual coastal or harbour towing craft with a bollard pull of 28 tons. Their appearance is characterised by a large bridge and swat uptakes of twin design. They utilise a Voith-Schneider propellor at the end of a single shaft.

Name *Bustler*; **Pennant number** A225; **Builders** Dunston; **Launched** February 20 1981; **Completed** April 14 1981.

Name *Capable*; **Pennant number** A226; **Builders** Dunston; **Launched** July 2 1981; **Completed** September 11 1981.

Name *Careful*; **Pennant number** A227; **Builders** Dunston; **Launched** January 12 1982; **Completed** March 5 1982.

Class *Dog*

Name See below; **Pennant number** See below; **Full displacement** 170 tons; **Length** 28.7 m; **Beam** 7.5 m; **Draught** 3.7 m; **Propulsion** 2 × Lister Blackstone diesels (1,320 bhp); **Range** Unknown; **Speed** 12 knots; **Complement** 8 officers and ratings; **Armament** None; **Builders** See below; **Completed** See below.

Name *Airedale*; **Pennant number** A102; **Builders** Scarr; **Completed** 1962.

Name *Alsatian*; **Pennant number** A106; **Builders** Scarr; **Completed** 1962.

Name *Cairn*; **Pennant number** A126; **Builders** Doig; **Completed** 1965.

Name *Dalmatian*; **Pennant number** A129; **Builders** Doig; **Completed** 1965.

Name *Deerhound*; **Pennant number** A155; **Builders** Appledore; **Completed** 1965.

Name *Elkhound*; **Pennant number** A162; **Builders** Appledore; **Completed** 1966.

Name *Labrador*; **Pennant number** A168; **Builders** Appledore; **Completed** 1966.

Name *Husky*; **Pennant number** A178; **Builders** Appledore; **Completed** 1966.

Name *Mastiff*; **Pennant number** A180; **Builders** Appledore; **Completed** 1967.

Name *Saluki*; **Pennant number** A182; **Builders** Appledore; **Completed** 1969.

Name *Pointer*; **Pennant number** A188; **Builders** Appledore; **Completed** 1967.

Name *Setter*; **Pennant number** A189; **Builders** Appledore; **Completed** 1969.

Name *Sealyham*; **Pennant number** A197; **Builders** Appledore; **Completed** 1967.

Name *Spaniel*; **Pennant number** A201; **Builders** Appledore; **Completed** 1967.

Name *Sheepdog*; **Pennant number** A250; **Builders** Appledore; **Completed** 1970.

Name *Basset* (ex-*Beagle*); **Pennant number** A327; **Builders** Dunston; **Completed** 1963.

Name *Collie*; **Pennant number** A328; **Builders** Rowhedge; **Completed** 1964.

Name *Corgi*; **Pennant number** A330; **Builders** Rowhedge; **Completed** 1964.

Name *Foxhound* (ex-*Boxer*); **Pennant number** A394; **Builders** Dunston; **Completed** 1964.

Foxhound *was named* Boxer *when she first entered service in 1964* (RMAS).

These craft are classed as medium berthing tugs and are found in the dockyards and ports around the UK where naval vessels operate. In addition, two (*Airedale* and *Sealyham*) are at Gibraltar. The craft have a bollard pull of 16 tons, which means that two are usually used for FFHs and above. It should be noted that *Foxhound* was renamed in October 1977 so that *Boxer* could be released for the Type 22 FFH.

Water tractors

Class *Triton*
Name See below; **Pennant number** None; **Standard displacement** 107.5 tons; **Length** 17.6 m; **Beam** 5.5 m; **Draught** 2.4 m; **Propulsion** 1 × diesel (330 bhp); **Range** Unknown; **Speed** 8 knots; **Complement** Circa 5; **Armament** None; **Builders** Dunston; **Completed** 1972–73.

These are small water tractors* although, like the *Felicity* Class, they are fitted with twin screws. They can be identified by a small funnel adjoining the bridge structure. The last one was delivered to the RMAS in August 1974.

* A water tractor is defined as a vessel having the point of application of the tow positioned aft of the propellor units, while a conventional screw tug has this point forward of the propellor(s).

Name	Completed
Irene	June 15 1972
Isabel	August 17 1972
Joan	September 15 1972
Joyce	October 11 1972
Kathleen	November 16 1972
Kitty	December 15 1972
Lesley	March 29 1973
Lilah	May 10 1973
Mary	May 25 1973
Myrtle	May 25 1973
Nancy	August 31 1973
Norah	December 19 1973

Class *Felicity*
Name *Felicity*; **Pennant number** None; **Standard displacement** 80 tons; **Length** 22.0 m; **Beam** 6.4 m; **Draught** 3.8 m; **Propulsion** 1 × diesel (600 bhp); **Range** Unknown; **Speed** 10 knots; **Complement** Circa 6; **Armament** None; **Builders** Dunston; **Completed** 1968.

These are medium water tractors for use at the three main naval bases to move warships and other craft in harbour. They are characterised by their large funnel set clear of the bridge and aft of it. By means of the Voith-Schneider propellor these (and

The water tractor Irene *at work* (RMAS).

the *Triton* Class) are able to use full power in any direction.

Name *Fiona*; **Builders** Hancock; **Completed** 1973.

Name *Georgina*; **Builders** Hancock; **Completed** 1973.

Name *Gwendoline*; **Builders** Hancock; **Completed** 1974.

Name *Helen*; **Builders** Hancock; **Completed** 1974.

Fleet tenders
Class *Aberdovey*
Name See below; **Pennant number** See below; **Displacement** 117.5 tons; **Length** 24.0 m; **Beam** 5.4 m; **Draught** 1.7 m; **Propulsion** 1 × Lister Blackstone diesel (225 bhp); **Range** Unknown; **Speed** 10.5 knots; **Complement** 6 officers and ratings; **Armament** None; **Builders** See below; **Completed** See below.

Name *Aberdovey*; **Pennant number** Y10; **Builders** Pimblott; **Completed** 1963.

Name *Abinger*; **Pennant number** Y11; **Builders** Pimblott; **Completed** 1964.

Name *Alness*; **Pennant number** Y12; **Builders** Pimblott; **Completed** 1965.

Name *Alnmouth*; **Pennant number** Y13; **Builders** Pimblott; **Completed** 1966.

Name *Appleby*; **Pennant number** A383; **Builders** Pimblott; **Completed** 1967.

Name *Ashcott*; **Pennant number** Y16; **Builders** Pimblott; **Completed** 1968.

Name *Beaulieu*; **Pennant number** A99; **Builders** Doig; **Completed** 1966.

Name *Beddgelert*; **Pennant number** A100; **Builders** Doig; **Completed** 1967.

Name *Bembridge*; **Pennant number** A101; **Builders** Doig; **Completed** 1968.

Name *Bibury*; **Pennant number** A103; **Builders** Doig; **Completed** 1969.

Name *Blakeney*; **Pennant number** A104; **Builders** Doig; **Completed** 1970.

Name *Brodick*; **Pennant number** A105; **Builders** Doig; **Completed** 1971.

Name *Cartmel*; **Pennant number** A350; **Builders** Pimblott; **Completed** 1971.

Name *Cawsand*; **Pennant number** A351; **Builders** Pimblott; **Completed** 1971.

Occasionally called the *Cartmel* Class, these were the first postwar design of Fleet tenders and have accommodation for 200 standing passengers, 25 tons of cargo and/or two standard heavyweight torpedoes. *Aberdovey* is at present carrying out a training role with RM Poole while *Alnmouth* has a similar function for the Sea Cadet Corps at Devonport, and *Bembridge* at Portsmouth. Like all Fleet tenders, these vessels are capable of short coastal voyages and have a single screw.

At Gibraltar, *Alness* and *Ashcott* are attached to *Rooke* for general duties including providing FPB targets for passing warships to exercise with— operations known as Passexs.

Class *Clovelly*
Name See below; **Pennant number** See below; **Displacement** 143 tons; **Length** 24.1 m; **Beam** 6.4 m; **Draught** 2.0 m; **Propulsion** 1 × Lister Blackstone diesel (320 bhp); **Range** Unknown; **Speed** 10.5 knots; **Complement** 6 officers and ratings (12 if training tender); **Armament** None; **Builders** See below; **Completed** See below.

Name *Ettrick*; **Pennant number** A274; **Builders** Cook; **Completed** 1972.

Right Holmwood *seen alongside at Portland in 1981 (*Engadine *is in the background)*.

Name *Elsing*; **Pennant number** A277; **Builders** Cook; **Completed** 1971.

Name *Epworth*; **Pennant number** A355; **Builders** Cook; **Completed** 1972.

Name *Elkstone*; **Pennant number** A353; **Builders** Cook; **Completed** 1971.

Name *Froxfield*; **Pennant number** A354; **Builders** Dunston; **Completed** 1972.

Name *Felsted*; **Pennant number** A348; **Builders** Dunston; **Completed** 1972.

Name *Dunster*; **Pennant number** A393; **Builders** Dunston; **Completed** 1972.

Name *Holmwood*; **Pennant number** A1772; **Builders** Dunston; **Completed** 1973.

Name *Horning*; **Pennant number** A1773; **Builders** Dunston; **Completed** 1973.

Name *Clovelly*; **Pennant number** A389; **Builders** Pimblott; **Completed** 1972.

Name *Criccieth*; **Pennant number** A350; **Builders** Pimblott; **Completed** 1972.

Name *Cricklade*; **Pennant number** A381; **Builders** Holmes; **Completed** 1971.

Name *Cromarty*; **Pennant number** A488; **Builders** Lewis; **Completed** 1972.

Name *Denmead*; **Pennant number** A363; **Builders** Holmes; **Completed** 1972.

Name *Dornoch*; **Pennant number** A490; **Builders** Lewis; **Completed** 1972.

Name *Fintry*; **Pennant number** A394; **Builders** Lewis; **Completed** 1972.

Name *Fotherby*; **Pennant number** A341; **Builders** Dunston; **Completed** 1972.

Name *Fulbeck*; **Pennant number** A365; **Builders** Holmes; **Completed** 1972.

Name *Glencoe*; **Pennant number** A392; **Builders** Pimblott; **Completed** 1972.

Name *Grasmere*; **Pennant number** A402; **Builders** Lewis; **Completed** 1972.

Name *Hambledon*; **Pennant number** A1769; **Builders** Dunston; **Completed** 1973.

Name *Harlech*; **Pennant number** A1768; **Builders** Dunston; **Completed** 1973.

Name *Headcorn*; **Pennant number** A1766; **Builders** Dunston; **Completed** 1973.

Name *Hever*; **Pennant number** A1767; **Builders** Dunston; **Completed** 1973.

Name *Lamlash*; **Pennant number** A208; **Builders** Dunston; **Completed** 1974.

Bee *at sea on a coastal route* (RMAS).

The specialist fleet tender Dolwen (RMAS).

Name *Lechlade*; **Pennant number** A211; **Builders** Dunston; **Completed** 1974.

Name *Llandovery*; **Pennant number** A207; **Builders** Dunston; **Completed** 1974.

These were a general improvement over the *Aberdovey* Class and have been designed to fulfil a range of tasks including passenger tenders, passenger/cargo tenders and/or training tenders. At Gibraltar, *Elsing* and *Ettrick* are deployed in a two-tone grey scheme rather than the usual buff and black; they are directly under *Rooke*.

Class *Insect*
Name See below; **Pennant number** See below; **Displacement** 450 tons; **Length** 34.1 m; **Beam** 8.5 m; **Draught** 3.4 m; **Propulsion** 1 × Lister Blackstone diesel (660 bhp); **Range** Unknown; **Speed** 10 knots; **Complement** 10 officers and ratings; **Armament** None; **Builders** See below; **Completed** See below.

Name *Bee*; **Pennant number** A216; **Builders** Holmes; **Completed** 1970.

Name *Cicala*; **Pennant number** A263; **Builders** Holmes; **Completed** 1971.

Name *Cockchafer*; **Pennant number** A230; **Builders** Holmes; **Completed** 1971.

Name *Cricket*; **Pennant number** A229; **Builders** Holmes; **Completed** 1972.

Name *Gnat*; **Pennant number** A239; **Builders** Holmes; **Completed** 1972.

Name *Ladybird*; **Pennant number** A253; **Builders** Holmes; **Completed** 1973.

Name *Scarab*; **Pennant number** A272; **Builders** Holmes; **Completed** 1973.

These craft are capable of coastal or even short sea voyages and for this role *Bee*, *Cicala* and *Cockchafer* have been fitted with two cargo handling cranes, whilst *Cricket*, *Gnat* and *Ladybird* are deployed as ammunition carriers at Faslane and Devonport. Based at Pembroke Dock, but soon to move under the 1981 Defence Review, *Scarab* is used for mooring duties and for this role she was fitted with a 3-ton crane which is capable of dealing with 10-ton loads over the bows.

Class *Dolwen*
Name *Dolwen*; **Pennant number** None; **Standard displacement** 115.9 tons (net); **Full displacement** 602 tons; **Length** 41.1 m; **Beam** 9.0 m; **Draught** 4.4 m; **Propulsion** 1 × National diesel; **Range** Unknown; **Speed** 14 knots; **Complement** Circa 10; **Armament** None; **Builders** P. K. Harris; **Completed** 1962.

This vessel was built as the stern trawler *Hector Gulf* and purchased by the RN for use as a buoy tender using its special stern davits. Today, it is employed as a range safety vessel at the Aberporth missile firing range of the mid-Wales coast.

Diving tenders
Class *Clovelly*
Name See below; **Pennant number** See below; **Displacement** 143 tons; **Length** 24.1 m; **Beam** 6.4 m; **Draught** 3.0 m; **Propulsion** 1 × Lister Blackstone diesel; **Range** Unknown; **Speed** 10 knots; **Complement** 6 officers and ratings; **Armament** None; **Builders** Gregson; **Completed** 1974.

All except the externally similar *Datchet* are of the same *Clovelly* Class as the 27 Fleet tenders of the same group (*qv*). All are RN-manned but the hulls remain on the RMAS list. In this role, some operating from *Vernon* carry one or more Gemini craft on racks forward of the bridge.

Name *Ilchester*; **Pennant number** A308.

Name *Instow*; **Pennant number** A309.

Name *Ironbridge*; **Pennant number** A310.

Name *Invergordon* **Pennant number** A311.

Name *Ixworth*; **Pennant number** A318.

Name *Datchet*; **Pennant number** A357.

Degaussing vessels

Class *Ham*

Name *Warmingham;* **Pennant number** M2737; **Standard displacement** 120 tons; **Full displacement** 159 tons; **Length** 32.4 m; **Beam** 6.5 m; **Draught** 1.7 m; **Propulsion** 2 × Paxman diesels (1,100 bhp); **Range** Unknown; **Speed** 14 knots; **Complement** 2 officers and 13 ratings; **Armament** None; **Builders** Appledore (?); **Laid down** Circa 1954; **Completed** Circa 1955.

This craft represents one of the many conversions which were carried out on the basic *Ham* Class MCMV (Inshore) hulls after the craft had reached the end of their useful lives for the operational side of the RN. In wartime, such vessels would be

Magnet is the first of a new class of degaussing vessels (RN).

responsible for degaussing warships and other vessels using naval ports in order that they would not trigger magnetic mines. *Warmingham* has a specially built-up superstructure.

Class *Magnet*

Name *Magnet*; **Pennant number** A114; **Displacement** 700 tons; **Length** 54.8 m; **Beam** 11.4 m; **Draught** 3.0 m; **Propulsion** 1 × diesel; **Range** Unknown; **Speed** 15 knots (estimated); **Complement** 10 (estimated); **Armament** None; **Builders** Cleland; **Launched** July 12 1979; **Completed** 1980.

When it was established that the *Ham* Class conversions were coming to the end of their useful lives, the RN commissioned a study into replacements which resulted in these two vessels

With characteristic derrick, Instow *is a diving tender; note Gemini dinghy in tow* (RN).

from Cleland S.B. Co Ltd of Wallsend. *Magnet* operates in the Clyde area and *Lodestone* was recently delivered to Portsmouth. Their use is as the *Ham* Class above.

Name *Lodestone*; **Pennant number** A115; **Builders** Cleland; **Launched** November 20 1979; **Completed** 1981.

Tank-cleaning vessels
Class *Isles*
Name *Caldy*; **Pennant number** A332; **Displacement** 770 tons; **Length** 49.0 m; **Beam** 8.4 m; **Draught** 4.2 m; **Propulsion** Triple expansion (850 ihp); **Range** Unknown; **Speed** 12 knots; **Complement** Circa 6; **Armament** None; **Builders** Lewes; **Completed** 1943.

These are the last two of over a hundred wartime construction vessels which were originally used in the minesweeping and coastal convoy escort roles. Today, they have a limited future as tank cleaning vessels and are due to be replaced by tank cleaning lighters in the near future.

Name *Lundy*; **Pennant number** A336; **Builders** Welton; **Completed** 1943.

Water carriers
Class *Water*
Name See below; **Pennant number** See below; **Gross displacement** 285 tons; **Length** 40.1 m; **Beam** 7.5 m; **Draught** 2.4 m; **Propulsion** 1 × diesel (600 bhp); **Range** Unknown; **Speed** 11 knots; **Complement** 11 officers and ratings; **Armament** None; **Builders** See below; **Launched** See below; **Completed** See below.

Watercourse, *a water carrier* (RMAS).

Name *Watercourse*; **Pennant number** Y15; **Builders** Drypool; **Launched** 1973; **Completed** 1974.

Name *Waterfowl*; **Pennant number** Y16; **Builders** Drypool; **Launched** 1972; **Completed** 1974.

Name *Waterfall*; **Pennant number** Y17; **Builders** Drypool; **Launched** 1966; **Completed** 1967.

Name *Watershed*; **Pennant number** Y18; **Builders** Drypool; **Launched** 1965; **Completed** 1967.

Name *Waterspout*; **Pennant number** Y19; **Builders** Drypool; **Launched** 1966; **Completed** 1967.

Name *Waterside*; **Pennant number** Y20; **Builders** Drypool; **Launched** 1966; **Completed** 1967.

Name *Waterman*; **Pennant number** A146; **Builders** Dunston; **Launched** 1977; **Completed** 1979.

These craft are designed for transporting supplies of fresh water to warships and other vessels in naval bases and anchorages. *Waterfall* and *Watershed* have their after deckhouses extended forward, whilst *Waterfowl* and *Waterman* have another deckhouse towards amidships. The latter, built by Dunston at Hessle, has a dry stores carrying ability. They were ordered to replace wartime construction of the *Spa* and *Fresh* Classes.

Class *Fresh*
Name *Freshburn*; **Pennant number** None; **Standard displacement** 594 tons; **Length** 38.5 m; **Beam** 7.8 m; **Draught** 3.3 m; **Propulsion** Triple expansion (450 ihp); **Range** Unknown; **Speed** 9 knots; **Complement** Circa 10; **Armament** None; **Builders** Unknown; **Completed** 1939–45.

Vessels of this Class were of wartime construction and steam-powered. *Freshburn* cannot have much longer to serve with the RMAS and is due to be struck from the list in the immediate future.

Boom defence ships
Class *Wild Duck*
Name *Mandarin*; **Pennant number** P192; **Standard displacement** 283 tons; **Full displacement** 950 tons; **Length** 55.4 m; **Beam** 12.2 m; **Draught** 4.2 m; **Propulsion** 1 × Paxman diesel (550 bhp); **Range** 3,000 nm at 10 knots; **Speed** 10 knots; **Complement** 6 officers and 18 ratings; **Armament** None; **Builders** Cammell Laird; **Launched** September 17 1963; **Completed** March 5 1964.

These vessels and their near sister-ships (see below) are employed in a variety of roles at the major naval bases; in particular, mooring buoys, salvage, boom defence and submarine rescue come under their 'horns'. All vessels are designed with the same lifting capacity (over 200 tons at the bow) but their internal arrangements differ.

Name *Pintail*; **Pennant number** P193; **Builders** Cammell Laird; **Launched** December 3 1963; **Completed** March 5 1964.

Class Improved *Wild Duck*
Name *Gargancy*; **Pennant number** P194; **Standard displacement** 283 tons; **Full displacement** 950 tons; **Length** 57.9 m; **Beam** 12.2 m; **Draught** 4.2 m; **Propulsion** 1 × Paxman diesel (550 bhp); **Range** 3,000 nm at 10 knots; **Speed** 10 knots; **Complement** 6 officers and 18 ratings; **Armament** None; **Builders** Brooke Marine; **Completed** September 20 1966.

The second group of modern boom defence vessels to be built for the RN, this time by Brooke Marine of Lowestoft. As can be seen from their dimensions, they are slightly different to *Mandarin* and *Pintail*.

Name *Goldeneye*; **Pennant number** P195; **Builder** Brooke Marine; **Completed** December 21 1966.

Class Later *Wild Duck*
Name *Goosander*; **Pennant number** P196; **Standard displacement** 300 tons; **Full displacement** 1,125 tons; **Length** 60.2 m; **Beam** 12.2 m; **Draught** 4.2 m; **Propulsion** 1 × Paxman diesel (550 bhp); **Range** 3,000 nm at 10 knots; **Speed** 10 knots; **Complement** 6 officers and 12 ratings; **Armament** None; **Builders** Robb; **Completed** September 10 1973.

The Later *Wild Ducks* are larger than the four

Based in Scotland, Goosander *is a boom defence and salvage vessel* (RMAS).

earlier craft and have a different appearance even to the casual observer; they are both based in Scottish waters.

Name *Pochard*; **Pennant number** P197; **Builders** Robb; **Completed** December 11 1973.

Class *Kin*
Name *Kingarth*; **Pennant number** A232; **Standard displacement** 950 tons; **Full displacement** 1,050 tons; **Length** 54.8 m; **Beam** 10.7 m; **Draught** 3.7 m; **Propulsion** 1 × Polar Atlas diesel (630 bhp); **Range** Unknown; **Speed** 9 knots; **Complement** 34 officers and ratings; **Armament** None; **Builders** Hall; **Completed** 1944.

Originally classified as coastal salvage vessels, these four ships are all that remain of a wartime building programme of eight.

Name *Kinbrace*; **Pennant number** A281; **Builders** Hall; **Completed** 1945.

Name *Kinloss;* **Pennant number** A482; **Builders** Hall; **Completed** 1945.

Name *Uplifter*; **Pennant number** A507; **Builders** Smiths; **Completed** 1944.

Coastal tankers
Class *Oil*
Name See below; **Pennant number** See below; **Standard displacement** 280 tons; **Full displacement** 530 tons; **Length** 41.5 m; **Beam** 9.0 m; **Draught** 2.5 m; **Propulsion** 1 × Lister Blackstone diesel (405 bhp); **Range** Unknown; **Speed** 9 knots; **Complement** 2 officers and 7

ratings; **Armament** None; **Builders** Appledore; **Launched** See below; **Completed** 1969.

Ordered in 1967 to provide rapid and cost-effective transmission of oil products between coastal installations, these vessels are now operated as bunkering craft in the major naval bases.

Name *Oilpress*; **Pennant number** Y21; **Launched** June 1968.

Name *Oilstone*; **Pennant number** Y22; **Launched** June 1968.

Name *Oilwell*; **Pennant number** Y23; **Launched** January 1969.

Name *Oilfield*; **Pennant number** Y24; **Launched** September 1968.

Name *Oilbird*; **Pennant number** Y25; **Launched** November 1968.

Name *Oilman*; **Pennant number** Y26; **Launched** February 1969.

Trials ships (sonar)

Class *Newton*

Name *Newton*; **Pennant number** A367; **Full displacement** 3,940 tons; **Length** 98.6 m; **Beam** 16.0 m; **Draught** 5.7 m; **Propulsion** 3 × Blackstone diesels (4,350 bhp); **Range** 5,000 nm at 14 knots; **Speed** 15 knots; **Complement** 64 including MoD scientists; **Armament** None; **Builders** Scott Lithgow; **Launched** June 25 1975; **Completed** June 17 1976.

All trials craft carry out secret defence and associated government work, so it is often difficult to glean information on their exact roles. Therefore, the basic data on each ship is all that can be recorded below. *Newton* was out of action 1979–81 with engine problems and *St Margarets* (*qv*) replaced her in a trials role.

Class *Auricula*
Name *Auricula*; **Pennant number** A285; **Full displacement** 1,100 tons; **Length** 52.0 m; **Beam** 11.0 m; **Draught** Classified; **Propulsion** 2 × Blackstone diesels (1,300 hp); **Range** Unknown; **Speed** 12 knots; **Complement** 7 officers and 15 ratings plus 10 trials party; **Armament** None; **Builders** Ferguson; **Launched** November 22 1979; **Completed** 1980.

Trials ship (torpedoes)
Class *Whitehead*
Name *Whitehead*; **Pennant number** A364; **Full displacement** 3,040 tons; **Length** 97.3 m; **Beam**

14.6 m; **Draught** 5.2 m; **Propulsion** 2 × Paxman diesels (3,400 bhp); **Range** 4,000 nm at 12 knots; **Speed** 15.5 knots; **Complement** 10 officers and 32 ratings plus 15 scientists; **Armament** 1 × 53 cm torpedo tube; 3 × Mk 32 STWS; **Builders** Scott; **Launched** May 5 1970; **Completed** 1971.

Trials ship (acoustic)
Class *Crystal*
Name *Crystal*; **Pennant number** RDV01; **Full displacement** 3,040 tons; **Length** 126.1 m; **Beam** 17.1 m; **Draught** 1.7 m; **Propulsion** None; **Range** Towed only; **Speed** Towing ship's; **Complement** 60 including scientists; **Armament** None; **Builders** Devonport; **Laid down** March 1970; **Completed** November 30 1971.

Torpedo recovery vessels
Class *Tornado*
Name *Tornado*; **Pennant number** A140; **Displacement** 698 tons; **Length** 40.0 m; **Beam**

Above left *Used for harbour and coastal bulk fuel work is the* Oil *class coastal tanker (RMAS).* **Above** Newton *is a sonar trials ship (RMAS).*

Far left *A modern sonar trials vessel—* Auricula *(RMAS).* **Left** *Sea-going torpedo recovery vessel* Tornado *(RMAS).* **Right** Whitehead *is a torpedo trials ship.*

9.2 m; **Draught** 3.3 m; **Propulsion** 2 × Blackstone diesels (2,200 hp); **Range** Unknown; **Speed** 14 knots; **Complement** 17 officers and ratings; **Armament** None (10 torpedoes stored on deck); **Builders** Hall Russell; **Launched** May 24 1979; **Completed** November 1979.

These craft are operated by the RMAS and RN for the recovery of exercise and trials torpedoes fired from *Whitehead* (*qv*) and HM submarines acting in this role.

Name *Torch*; **Pennant number** A141; **Builders** Hall Russell; **Launched** August 7 1979; **Completed** February 1980.

Name *Tormentor*; **Pennant number** A142; **Builders** Hall Russell; **Launched** November 6 1979; **Completed** May 1980.

Name *Toreador*; **Pennant number** A143; **Builders** Hall Russell; **Launched** February 1980; **Completed** July 1980.

Class *Torrent*
Name *Torrent*; **Pennant number** A127; **Gross displacement** 550 tons; **Length** 46.1 m; **Beam** 9.6 m; **Draught** 3.4 m; **Propulsion** 2 × Paxman diesels (700 bhp); **Range** Unknown; **Speed** 12 knots; **Complement** 19 officers and ratings; **Armament** None (can store 32 torpedoes); **Builders** Cleland; **Completed** September 10 1971.

Name *Torrid*; **Pennant number** A128; **Builders** Cleland; **Completed** January 1972.

Class *Ham*
Name *Everingham*; **Pennant number** M2626; **Standard displacement** 120 tons; **Full displacement** 159 tons; **Length** 32.4 m; **Beam** 6.5 m; **Draught** 1.7 m; **Propulsion** 2 × Paxman diesels (1,100 bhp); **Range** Circa 1,000 nm at 10 knots; **Speed** 14 knots; **Complement** 2 officers and 13 ratings; **Armament** None (torpedoes stored); **Builders** Various, *qv* earlier entries; **Completed** 1952–55.

Everingham and her sister ships *Haversham* (M2635) and *Lasham* (M2636) will be retired by the end of 1982.

Class *Endeavour*
Name *Endeavour*; **Pennant number** None; **Full**

displacement 88 tons; **Length** 23.2 m; **Beam** 4.4 m; **Draught** 3.0 m; **Propulsion** 1 × Lister Blackstone diesel (337 hp); **Range** Unknown; **Speed** 10.5 knots; **Complement** 4; **Armament** None; **Builders** Dunston; **Launched** 1966; **Completed** 1966.

Endeavour has operated from Portland since August 1974.

Armament carriers
Class *Throsk*
Name *Throsk*; **Pennant number** A379; **Standard displacement** 1,150 tons (deadweight); **Full displacement** 1,968 tons; **Length** 64.3 m; **Beam** 11.9 m; **Draught** 4.6 m; **Propulsion** 2 × Blackstone diesels (3,000 bhp); **Range** 5,000 nm at 10 knots; **Speed** 14 knots; **Complement** 22 officers and ratings; **Armament** None; **Builders** Cleland; **Completed** September 20 1977.

These craft are used to provide a supply of naval armaments around the United Kingdom for naval establishments. They are relatively modern and designed specifically for the task.

Name *Kinterbury*; **Pennant number** A378; **Builders** Cleland; **Completed** November 1980.

Target ship
Class *Cochrane*
Name *Wakeful* (ex-*Dan*, ex-*Heracles*); **Pennant number** A236; **Standard displacement** 493 tons (gross); **Full displacement** 900 tons; **Length** 38.9 m; **Beam** 10.7 m; **Draught** 4.7 m; **Propulsion** 2 × Rushton diesels (4,750 bhp); **Range** Unknown; **Speed** 14 knots; **Complement** 5 officers and 22 ratings; **Armament** None; **Builders** Cochrane; **Purchased** 1974; **Refitted** 1976.

Wakeful has been a very costly investment for the RN, considering that she was acquired third-hand. Although RMAS, she is operated by the RN and occasionally publicly denoted 'HMS' *Wakeful*. The main purpose for her acquisition was in support of the Clyde Submarine Base as a target ship and occasional icebreaker. She did serve in the 'Fish Squadron' for a while.

Cable ship
Class *Bull*
Name *St Margarets*; **Pennant number** A259; **Net displacement** 590 tons; **Full displacement** Circa 2,500 tons; **Length** 77.0 m; **Beam** 11.1 m; **Draught**

Top left *Torrent entering harbour* (RMAS), **Centre left** *Throsk is one of two armament carriers* (RMAS). **Left** St Margarets, *although a cable ship, looks more like a steam yacht* (RMAS).

5.0 m; **Propulsion** Triple expansion; 2 × Babcock & Wilcox boilers (1,260 bhp); **Range** Unknown; **Speed** 10 knots; **Complement** 12 officers and 52 ratings; **Armament** Fitted for 4 × 20 mm Oerlikon; **Builders** Swan Hunter; **Launched** October 13 1943; **Completed** February 1944.

St Margarets is one of the finest RMAS craft afloat and must certainly have the most pleasing lines. She is nicknamed 'Maggie' and is based at Plymouth. During 1979–81 she replaced *Newton (qv)* in a trials role.

Harbour launches

There are a large number of dumb and miscellaneous vessels and smaller craft to be found at naval bases. They often work in the inner parts of the naval dockyards, transferring personnel and stores. For example, at Portsmouth there is a regular service to and from the submarine base at *Dolphin*, which is on the Gosport side of the harbour, away from the Dockyard proper. Some launches are used to tow lighters and for communications and administrative reasons they are marked with reference numbers. It is outside the scope of this book to list them all, but a general precis follows.

Chatham Two basic designs are in use here and four craft are in service.

Clyde Three small craft are operated here.

Plymouth Devonport uses two standard types, including one from New Zealand; 14 craft in service.

Portland Although there are the same actual number of craft, there are four types, including two from New Zealand.

Portsmouth By far the greatest user and its craft even include specially designed ambulance craft equipped for stretchers; 20 craft in service.

Rosyth A half dozen craft used.

Gibraltar Two craft, one used by the Fire Brigade.

RMAS craft deployment

The list below, given by location, is representative only because the situation is continuously changing as support craft are moving from location to location as the need of the RN arises.

Chatham *Collie; Mastiff; Barbara; Betty; Brenda; Joyce; Kathleen; Lesley; Caldy; Kinloss; Cicala.*

Clyde *Accord; Deerhound; Elkhound; Husky; Labrador; Spaniel; Daisy; Daphne; Mandarin; Pochard; Kingarth; Brodick; Cartmel; Cawsand; Felsted; Fintry; Fotherby; Glencoe; Gnat; Everingham; Haversham; Lasham; Magnet.*

Plymouth *Robust; Advice; Confiance; Capable; Typhoon; Charlotte; Christine; Doris; Georgina; Lilah;*

Mary; Myrtle; Nancy; Switha; Pintail; St Margarets; Abinger; Alnmouth; Beddgelert; Bibury; Cromarty; Fulbeck; Headcorn; Hever; Clovelly; Cricket; Ladybird.

Portland *Basset; Sheepdog; Agatha; Agnes; Kinbrace; Cricklade; Dunster; Harlech; Holmwood; Lechlade; Cockchafer.*

Portsmouth *Roystere; Agile; Confident; Sea Giant; Dalmatian; Foxhound; Setter; Alice; Audrey; Bridget; Dorothy; Felicity; Fiona; Helen; Irene; Isabel; Joan; Kitty; Norah; Lundy; Goldeneye; Appleby; Beaulieu; Bembridge; Denmead; Elkstone; Epworth; Froxfiled; Hambledon; Horning; Lamlash; Bee; Lodestone.*

Rosyth *Rollicker; Cairn; Corgi; Pointer; Gwendoline; Goosander; Laymoor; Kingarth; Blakeney; Dornoch; Llandovery.*

Gibraltar *Airedale; Sealyham; Edith; Alness; Ashcott; Elsing; Ettrick.*

Hong Kong *Clare.*

The Royal Naval Auxiliary Service

The Royal Naval Auxiliary Service (RNXS) is a civilian volunteer organisation trained and administered by the Royal Navy. Its role in wartime is to protect merchant ships, harbours and anchorages and to play an important part in the control of civilian shipping. This role will therefore relieve Service personnel of this task and thus enable more regular sailors to be used at sea.

Membership of the RNXS is open to both men and women, between the ages of 18 and 55 and training occupies one evening per week and usually every third weekend. As the Service is voluntary, there is no pay in peacetime but allowances are made and certain expenses, including travel and uniform, are paid for by the RN.

Shore service This involves the RNXS in plotting and communications duties, as well as the general administration of a port or naval base.

Sea service Using *Ham* Class auxiliary vessels (former inshore minesweepers), the RNXS trains volunteers as engineers, seamen, or communicators for port duties. Women are equally welcome and in 1981 one rose to command a *Ham* Class craft.

In wartime, besides manning the Port Headquarters facilities, the RNXS would provide the crews for Naval Boarding Officers and Reporting Officers. Night time surveillance of port area shipping would also be in the tasks allotted to the Service.

The organistion is divided into areas and administratively comes under the Ministry of Defence and CINCNAVHOME. The Service is commanded by a Captain RN who is known as Head of RNXS.

RNXS craft Portisham *coming alongside at* Excellent (CU Pontoons).

Area	Port
Portsmouth	Solent
	Portland
Plymouth	Mersey
	Anglesey
	South Wales
	Severn
	Cornwall
	Torbay
	Channel Islands
Scotland & Northern Ireland	Tees
	Tyne
	Forth
	North-East Scotland
	Orkney Islands
	Clyde
	Belfast
Medway	Sussex
	Dover
	Thames
	East Anglia
	Humber

It will be seen that the RNXS areas correspond to the RN's Sea Areas controlled by the four Flag Officers.

Currently the RNXS operates a number of vessels, mainly for training and exercise purposes and these are prefixed with term XSV (Auxiliary Service Vessel).

Class *Ham*

Name See below; **Pennant number** See below; **Standard displacement** 120 tons; **Full displacement** 159 tons; **Length** 32.1 m overall; **Beam** 6.6 m; **Draught** 1.8 m; **Propulsion** 2 × Paxman diesels (1,100 bhp); **Range** Circa 1,000 nm at 10 knots; **Speed** 14 knots; **Complement** 2 officers and 13 ratings; **Armament** None; **Builders** Various, *qv* earlier entries; **Completed** 1952–55.

The *Ham* Class vessels are due for replacement during the next few years by *Loyal* Class tenders, but at the time of writing were as follows: *Shipham* (M2726), based at Chatham; and *Portisham* (M2781), based at Portsmouth.

Class *Loyal*

Name See below; **Pennant number** See below; **Full displacement** 143 tons; **Length** 24.1 m overall; **Beam** 6.4 m; **Draught** 3.0 m; **Propulsion** 1 × Lister Blackstone diesel (320 bhp); **Range** Unknown; **Speed** 10.5 knots; **Complement** 1 officer and 5 ratings; **Armament** None; **Builders** Various small ship builders.

In appearance very similar to *Clovelly* Class tenders and diving tenders (*qv*), these vessels are ideal for boarding and patrol duties, and three, whose names have been changed for obvious political reasons, operate in Northern Irish waters. These are *Supporter* (ex-*Loyal Supporter*), *Alert* (ex-*Loyal Governor*) and *Vigilant* (ex-*Loyal Factor*).

Name *Supporter*; **Pennant number** A158; **Based at** N/A; **Builders** N/A; **Completed** N/A.

Name *Alert*; **Pennant number** P254; **Based at** N/A; **Builders** Pimblott; **Completed** 1970.

Name *Vigilant*; **Pennant number** P252; **Based at** N/A; **Builders** Holmes; **Completed** 1970.

Name *Loyal Helper*; **Pennant number** A157; **Based at** Medway, **Builders** N/A; **Completed** N/A.

Name *Loyal Watcher*; **Pennant number** A159; **Based at** Birkenhead; **Builders** N/A; **Completed** N/A.

Name *Loyal Volunteer*; **Pennant number** A160; **Based at** Scotland; **Builders** N/A; **Completed** N/A.

Name *Loyal Mediator*; **Pennanant number** A161; **Based at** Portsmouth; **Builders** N/A; **Completed** N/A.

Name *Loyal Moderator*; **Pennant number** A220; **Based at** Plymouth; **Builders** Dunston; **Completed** 1973.

Name *Loyal Chancellor*; **Pennant number** A1770; **Based at** East Coast; **Builders** N/A; **Completed** N/A.

Name *Loyal Proctor*; **Pennant number** A1771.

Name *Scotland*; **Builders** Dunston; **Completed** 1973.

Other Services

The Women's Royal Naval Service, Queen Alexandra's Royal Naval Nursing Service, the Royal Naval and Women's Royal Naval Reserves and the Sea Cadet Corps

The Women's Royal Naval Service (WRNS)

The Women's Royal Naval Service (WRNS) can trace its ancestry back to 1917 when ladies were recruited to do clerical and support jobs. It was not until the Second World War that 'Wrens' were employed in more unusual jobs, including aircraft maintenance and cypher work. The 65 years* of the WRNS' existence has therefore seen many changes—in role, emphasis, position and status for the Service 'within a Service'.

The WRNS have a complete rank structure from Director (Commodore RN equivalent) to Wren†, Ordinary Rate (although on enrolment Wrens are termed Probationary until the completion of specialist training). Now part of the RN proper, WRNS are subject to the Naval Discipline Act, although exempt from the Sex Discrimination Act, and do not serve on the complement of warships at sea; however, certain WRNS *do* go to sea as Weapons Analysts in all types of vessels including submarines (for day running only). It is thought that the first vessels in which WRNS will serve at sea will be RFAs. There are no 'Wren' pilots, although they are trained as Stewardesses for VIP and 'Clipper' flights. The FAA, in fact, does have a large

---

* As a peacetime economy measure the WRNS were disbanded 1919–39 and established as an integral part of the RN in 1949 by Order in Council.

† In 1980, the Admiralty issued a Defence Council Instruction (DCI) to indicate the correct terms for refering to members of the WRNS:

'The correct abbreviation for the Women's Royal Naval Service is WRNS. The letters WRNS may be used both as a collective noun and as an adjective (for example, WRNS Officer, WRNS quarters and the WRNS). The term 'Wrens' should only be used as a noun when referring to a rating member of the WRNS, eg, Petty Officer Wren. The official designation of a member of the WRNS is either WRNS officer or WRNS rating.'

It therefore follows that there is no such rate as CPO Wren or FCPO Wren, as the correct title must be Chief Wren or Fleet Chief Wren respectively.

The Chief Commandant of the Women's Royal Naval Service is HRH The Princess Anne (RN official).

Flying in the left-hand seat of a Sea King on SAR standby, this Wren photographer would record any rescue on film (RN/Culdrose).

A WRNS Air Engineering Mechanic (Mechanical) at work on the engine of a Sea King helicopter at Culdrose (RN).

proportion of WRNS in Air Mechanic, meteorological and photographic roles.

Today, WRNS drafting is carried out at *Centurion*, along with their male counterparts, and WRNS officers are trained at Dartmouth (the Britannia Royal Naval College) alongside their male colleagues, the first course moving from Greenwich in 1976. This was a year before the Service came under the Naval Discipline Act.

The WRNS are proud to have HM Queen Elizabeth The Queen Mother as their Commandant-in-Chief and as Chief Commandant, HRH The Princess Anne. The command structure consists of a Director‡ (DWRNS) and a Deputy Director (DDWRNS), with Commandant, Superintendent, Chief Officer, First, Second and Third Officers (3/0)—or Sub-Lieutenant RN equivalent—at the bottom of the officer scale. Rank equivalents and the corresponding ranks of the WRNS and RN are described in Chapter Eleven.

The rating structure follows more easily the RN male rating, with Fleet Chief Wren, Chief Wren, Petty Officer Wren, Leading Wren and Wren (ordinary Rate).

‡ DWRNS holds Commandant rank.

Despite the limitations put on the Service by the 1981 Defence Review, the recruiting of WRNS will continue and it is expected that by the end of the decade 12–15 per cent of the RN will be made up of female members. It may be at this time that some will go to sea: for example, the aircraft maintenance functions aboard RFAs, currently employing male ratings, could be carried out by similarly trained Wrens, many of whom are already trained in this work.

WRNS specialisations

The careers open to Wrens who have passed out of initial training at *Raleigh* have been steadily increasing since the Second World War:

The Wren Air Engineering Mechanic serves at Naval Air Stations, with Naval Air Squadrons (NAS) and at such units as the Naval Aircraft Support Unit (NASU). There are three trades available, in parallel with the male members of the Fleet Air Arm—Mechanical (M), Radio and Radar (R) and Weapons Electrical (WL). Basically, the job entails the servicing and repair of naval aircraft, both fixed and rotary wing. Training is carried out at *Daedalus* followed by a posting to a Naval Air Station.

The Wren Photographer provides a photographic service at Naval Air Stations and to various units of the RN and RM. Both still and movie photography is taught at the Photographic School at *Excellent*. Besides the usual PR (public relations) work for which Wrens are particularly suited, the Branch, part of the Fleet Air Arm, covers fault* and aerial photography, giving a wide range of opportunity.

Also attached to the FAA is the Wren Meteorological Observer who serves at Naval Air Stations and at certain headquarters facilities, including NATO. At present there are no Wren 'METs' at sea. Training is carried out at *Seahawk*, where the finer points of collecting rainfall, sunshine and temperature data are taught, as well as how to interpret the weather and the preparation of weather charts for aircrew and command briefing. Met Offices, usually run with both RN and WRNS ratings, are under the command of a specialist Instructor Officer.

In the dental line, there are two skills for Wrens— Dental Surgery Assistant (DSA) and Dental Hygienist (DH), both of whom serve alongside Dental Officers (both male and female) at all UK and overseas dental facilities. Both specialisations are trained at *Nelson*. Dental Hygienists are automatically promoted Acting Leading Wren on the successful completion of the one year training course as they work unaided to promote the education and care of teeth, in both service personnel and dependents†.

At operational headquarters, Naval Air Stations

A Wren Radar Operator at work in Culdrose's tower (RN).

and specialist establishments, the Wren Radar monitors the displays of surface radar for air traffic, safety, warning, trials and other purposes. The role additionally requires the keeping of logs and is open to Cadet entry (entry as a Wren for training with a guaranteed place for selection at Admiralty Interview Board for promotion to officer after 12–15 months). Training takes place at *Dryad*. Serving at a similar location will be the Wren Radio Operator whose work is mainly carried out in the Main Signals Office. Again a Cadet entry position or ordinary entry trade, the Wren who selects this post will be trained at *Mercury*.

The Wren Telephonist serves in Service telephone exchanges at virtually every Naval and RM establishment, and is often called upon to work overseas, especially with NATO. The trade is, however, of limited entry although it is important in

At work on a patient at Gibraltar is a Wren Dental Surgery Assistant.

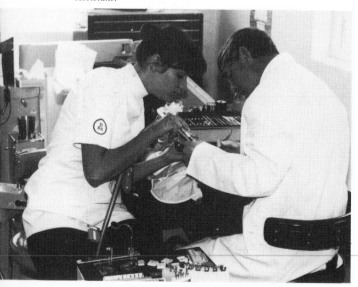

---

* The use of pictures to illustrate faults in ships, aircraft, etc, both for training and for evidence in an enquiry.

† DHs are usually DSAs with three 'O' levels, selected by a special board and then put forward for DH, or they can also be qualified before entry.

the naval communications net. Training is carried out at *Seahawk*.

The use of audio and visual aids is increasingly important in the teaching and training function of the RN, and most probably any slides or displays seen will be the responsibility of the Wren Training Support Assistant (TSA) who is trained at *Nelson*. The trade is open to Cadet entry.

The Supply and Secretariat Branch of the RN makes use of the talents of several sub-specialisations within the WRNS, including Wren Writer (Pay) who serves at Naval, Naval Air and RM establishments dealing with the pay and records of officers and ratings. This trade is open to Cadet entry and training takes place at *Pembroke* at the present time. The Wren Writer (Shorthand)* and the Wren Writer (General) are both trained at *Pembroke*, although only the latter trade is open to Cadet entry. Again, both these Wrens would be employed at headquarters facilities and other establishments throughout the UK and overseas. The Wren Writer (Shorthand) or ST, transfers to the (General) branch to be promoted to Petty Officer Wren. In the administrative branch there are also Wren Stores Accountants who train at *Pembroke* and have similar duties in terms of requisitioning, storing and issuing as the Naval Stores Accountant, also trained at Chatham. Two other specialisations are trained at *Pembroke* for WRNS, the Wren Cook (who only serves ashore) and the Wren Steward.

The Wren Quarters Assistant serves at most Naval and RM establishments and deals with the everyday needs of the personnel, especially in terms of the standards of Service quarters. Training used to take place at *Dauntless* which closed in 1981, but it is now carried out at *Raleigh*. Many training establishments have Leading Wren Education Assistants on their books and she is responsible to the Education Officer of other establishments for the administration of the education centre. She is promoted to Acting Leading Wren immediately on completion of training at *Pembroke* (the Writer's course) and at *Nelson* (the Education course). Other Leading Wren specialisations are Regulators who are advanced to Acting Leading Wren on completion of their training at *Excellent*, and the Physical Trainer, part of a very small branch in the RN, now that PT is no longer compulsory. Wren PT instructors are very able to deal with the recreational and expeditionary roles now required and on completion of training at *Temeraire*, the PT Wren will be promoted to Acting Leading Rate. Both these two Leading Wren specialisations require transfer from the Able Rates in other trades, skills or branches.

Family Services Wrens wear the letters FS in the centre of circular branch badges and they are very much involved in the welfare of the RN, RM and WRNS and their dependants. Training is carried out at *Drake*, with further training at Plymouth or Portsmouth Polytechnic.

The Wren Weapon Analyst, a Cadet entry position, serves at Naval Air Stations, ranges and in the Gunnery Data Reduction and Torpedo Trials Units of the Fleet. Her job may require brief periods at sea to assess the programmes to which she is assigned. Basically, the job requires a practical application of mathematics and training is carried at the Fraser Gunnery Range, Portsmouth Harbour.

Although many Flag Officers have, for security reasons, Royal Marines drivers, there are still a large number of general purpose and staff car drivers who are Wrens. Promotion is, however, limited, and there are no drivers beyond PO Wren rate. Driving training is carried out at *Seahawk*, although there is a possibility that all RN driving courses will be concentrated at RM Poole, the home of the RM Training Branch, in the mid-1980s.

The RN has a tremendous reputation for good food—a Wren Cook puts the finishing touches to a strawberry dessert (RN).

---

* Good typing and shorthand qualifications are required.

Queen Alexandra's Royal Naval Nursing Service (QARNNS)

QARNNS are greatly respected and well loved, being an important part of the Royal Naval Medical Service, primarily responsible for the health and fitness of RN, RM, WRNS and dockyard personnel. Establishments at home and overseas have QARNNS' staff, including the major hospital complexes at Gibraltar, Plymouth and Gosport. Their work is very similar to that within a National Health Service hospital but conforms to Naval conditions and practises. Male nurses are now being encouraged to join QARNNS and this aspect will see a major, but quiet, revolution in the next few years. The whole structure of QARNNS is due to change in the 1980s, so it is only possible to describe here the Service as it exists in early 1982; the QARNNS opened their ranks to male entrants on April 1 1982.

Until now, entry has been restricted to female applicants who may be selected for entry as student nurse, pupil nurse or as a qualified State Enrolled Nurse (General)—SEN(G) or SEN(M)—(Mental). Applicants enter a Service with a long and highly commendable record since Naval nurses went to the Crimea in 1854. QARNNS were not formed however, until 1902 when the then Queen Alexandra became President of the Naval Nursing Service. The Queen Consort took up the cause of Naval nursing with great enthusiasm and designed the uniform and badges of the Service. Despite the antique look of the present uniform, there are many who would not change it for anything. This continuity can only be good for the Service.

During World War 2, 1,200 QARNNS served all over the world and later, HRH Princess Alexandra took over the role of active Patron with the same enthusiasm as her great-grandmother. In 1974, a non-nursing category known as the Clerical and Quarters (C&Q) branch was introduced to manage nursing quarters and to deal with the ever increasing administrative workload of the Naval nurse. At present the Medical Branch of the RN still provides all the male nursing and paramedical staff in the roles of radiography, physiotherapy, hygiene, laboratory technicians, and pharmacy dispenser. SRN (State Registered Nursing) and mental nursing are carried out jointly. QARNNS come under the Naval Discipline Act; they do march and salute, albeit occasionally!

QARNNS' Nursing Officers are selected from SRN applicants and trained at Haslar, then appointed as Nursing Sisters or Senior Nursing Sisters dependant on post-qualification experience.

The initial engagement is for a short service commission but Career appointments are possible and hence the opportunity to advance to Superintending Sister, Matron and Principal Matron. Like the WRNS, QARNNS do not serve at sea, but there are possibilities for tours at Gibraltar (RNH), Family Clinics at Hong Kong and Naples and Sick Bays in RN establishments. QARNNS officers are usually given responsibilities for wards, departments and the appropriate staffs. Initial appointment is for single women but it is possible for QARNNS officers to marry during a commission in certain circumstances.

Naval nurses, with their characteristic cap designed by Queen Alexandra, also train at Haslar for SRN, or Haslar or Plymouth for SEN. Those without previous experience are given a two- (Pupil Nurse) or three-year training (Student Nurse) also with the rate of Probationary Naval Nurse. Direct entry SENs are accepted as Acting Naval Nurses. Again, entry is usually for single women (unmarried, divorced or widowed) but it is possible to marry and to remain in the Service.

The Quarters Officers of the QARNNS supervise the running of nurses' 'homes', called quarters or messes by the RN. They are hotel and catering trained and the rank of Quarters Officer equates to that of Nursing Sister. Advancement is limited to Senior Quarters Officer. These officers are supported by C&Q assistants whose work is mainly clerical and administrative.

A superintendent Sister on duty at the Royal Naval Hospital, Gibraltar; in 1982 the QARNNS opened their ranks to men, but with a revised uniform.

The corresponding ranks of WRNS, QARNNS and the RN are shown in tabular form in Chapter Eleven, but it is useful to show the WRNS/QARNNS/C&Q equivalents below:

QARNNS	WRNS	C&Q
Matron-in Chief	Commandant	-
Principal Matron	Superintendent	-
Matron	Chief Officer	-
Superintending Sister	First Officer	-
Senior Nursing Sister	Second Officer	Senior Clerical and Quarters' Officer
Nursing Sister	Third Officer	Clerical and Quarters' Officer
	Fleet Chief Wren	
Head Naval Nurse	Chief Wren	Head C&Q Asistant
Asst Head Naval Nurse	Petty Officer Wren	Asst Head C&Q Assistant
Senior Naval Nurse	Leading Wren	Senior C&Q Assistant
Naval Nurse	Wren	C&Q Assistant

The Royal Naval Reserve and the Women's Royal Naval Reserve (RNR and WRNR)

The Royal Navy and the Women's Royal Naval Service is supplemented in times of war, national need or emergency by personnel of the Royal Naval Reserve (RNR) and the Women's Royal Naval Reserve (WRNR). The Reserves are split into lists according to training and branch commitments:

List 1 These are professional Merchant Navy officers of the seaman and engineering branches with a seagoing connection. Their training commitment is between two weeks every year (junior officers) to two weeks every four years (senior officers).

List 2 This was the old Patrol Service and disbanded in 1971.

List 3 These are the 'civilians' who volunteer for RNR service in Divisions, Headquarters or

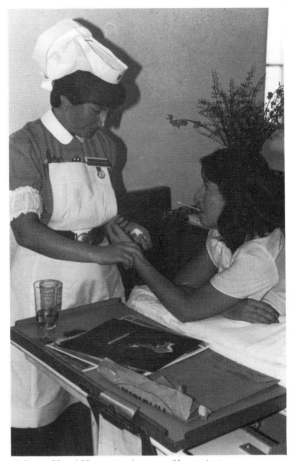

A Senior Naval Nurse attends to one of her patients.

Communications units. Their commitment is 100×1 hour drills per annum, with 14 days' continuous training. This list forms the bulk of the RNR and WRNR.

List 4 These are the professional volunteers from the medical, dental and ecclesiastical fields. In addition, there are intelligence and PR officers included in this list, if they can not make the normal training commitments of List 3. Students may also be in this situation, but the commitment in List 4 is 50 drills per annum, plus 14 days' continuous training.

List 5 This category is for those fully trained in their war task who are only required to undertake 14 days' continuous refresher training every two years, plus attendance three times a year. Officers are usually in the NCS and 'Special' duties or are RNR Postal Branch.

List 5A These are officers in 'shortage' categories who are above the retirement age, who do no training and do not receive the 'bounty' but who augment the other Lists as required.

List 6 These are officers who are temporarily unable to complete training due to absence abroad on business.

The WRNR became integrated with the RNR on January 1 1976 following the disbandment of the Royal Naval Volunteer Reserve (RNVR) and the change of command to CINCNAVHOME from Admiral Commanding Reserves.

The RNR's role today is **Seagoing**: to man the 10th MCM Squadron, a large part of Britain's MCM defence; to assist the RN in a variety of offshore tasks; to provide ships' crews from commerce in time of war; and to train in Naval terms, the officers of the Merchant Navy; **Ashore** Naval Control of Shipping (NCS) form port headquarters; to provide mobile surgical teams for the RM and amphibious ships; to organise the Fleet Mail Organisation in time of war; to provide key staff for headquarters and establishments.

The history of the RNR and WRNR goes back many years, if not centuries to the times when there was no standing Navy, only a few officers retained on half-pay during peacetime. It was not until the First World War that the Reserve forces really came into their own, with service throughout the conflict. In 1936, the RN Supplementary Reserve was formed from those wishing to place themselves at their country's disposal in emergency. The RNR and RNVR also played an important part in the Second World War, especially in the communications, Naval Air Command and Coastal Forces organisations. On November 1 1958, the RNR and RNVR were combined under the title RNR.

Today, seapower is still one of the most effective ways of preventing war and the RNR and WRNR are an added insurance to back up the deterrent of the Fleet in being, especially the SSBMs. The RNR and WRNR are trained to assist and supplement the active service in communications, postal and Mines Counter Measures duties, but they could be equally required to operate anywhere at any time. The operational side of the RNR is today made up of the Tenth Mines Counter Measures Squadron (MCM10) under the control of the Captain Mines Counter Measures at Rosyth; the days of a separate Reserve force under the Admiral Commanding Reserves has gone. The Divisional Headquarters of the RNR are under the control of Area Flag Officers. The Reserve is commanded by CINCNAVHOME and administered by the Reserves Division.

The opportunities open to civilian volunteers include the Engineering, Weapons, Communications, Operations (Seaman), Medical, Supply and Secretariat Branches, as well as the Air Branch RNR for former Naval aircrew officers (see Chapter Five).

The RNR and WRNR are organised under two Commodores RNR, one presently at Chatham (*Wildfire*) and the other at Barry (*Cambria*) but each training Division is commanded by a senior Commander RNR or a Captain RNR depending on the size of the unit. There is a unit at Gibraltar (*Calpe*), which is described in Chapter Three.

RNR Divisions

Each Division of the RNR is a sea training unit which generally has a *Ton* or *Venturer* Class minesweeper attached to it, although the number of hulls available does vary from time to time. This being so, the former special names given to individual MCMVs used in this connection have been discontinued and the warships continue to use their own commissioned names. The RNR is the only user of the *Venturer* Class. Other craft such as the former Seaward Defence Boats and other tenders attached to universities are borne on the books of the

RNR minesweepers on patrol during a NATO exercise—Glasserton (now paid off), Kellington, Upton, Crofton, and Brereton (RNR).

The diver is an important part of the team fighting modern mines—
the minehunter illustrated behind is Brereton (RN).

relevant RNR establishment for administrative
reasons. Although old and a little prone to
seasickness, the *Ton* Class are excellent ships in
which to learn navigation, seamanship and the
RNR's war role of Mines Counter Measures.

Division	HQ Name	Location	Former name of ship
London	*President*	London	*Thames*
Clyde	*Graham*	Glasgow	*Clyde*
Forth	*Claverhouse*	Edinburgh	*Killiecrankie*
Mersey	*Eaglet*	Liverpool	*Mersey*
Severn	*Flying Fox*	Bristol	*Venturer**
Solent	*Wessex*	Southampton	*Solent*
South Wales	*Cambria*	Sully, Nr Barry	*St David*†
Sussex	*Sussex*	Hove	*Curzon*
Tay	*Camperdown*	Dundee	*Montrose*
Tyne	*Calliope*	Gateshead	*Northumbria*
Ulster	*Caroline*	Belfast	*Kilmorey*

* *Venturer* is retained as the commissioned name of the MCMV
presently attached to Severn Division.

† *St David* is the commissioned name of the other MCMV of the
Venturer Class, attached to South Wales Division.

The location of several of the Divisional
Headquarters makes it impossible for the attached
MCMV to be based there and so the following
Divisions have other bases:

Division	Base
London	Southampton, may temporarily change to Chatham until 1984
Clyde	Greenock
Forth	Leith
South Wales	Cardiff
Tyne	Newcastle-upon-Tyne

NB: *President* is a former warship used as a
Headquarters ship.

In addition to the RNR Divisional Training
Centres, there are a number of training centres on

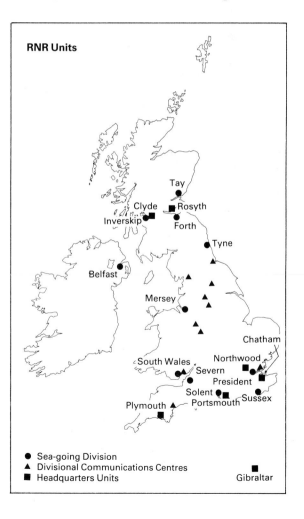

RNR Units

Tay
Clyde Rosyth
Inverskip Forth
Belfast
Tyne
Mersey
Chatham
South Wales Northwood
Severn President
Solent Sussex
Plymouth Portsmouth
Gibraltar

● Sea-going Division
▲ Divisional Communications Centres
■ Headquarters Units

shore at which the Communications personnel of the RNR and the WRNR are trained and regularly parade.

Training centre	Location
Westcliff-On-Sea	Southend, Essex
Swansea	South Wales
Exeter	Devonshire
Nottingham	Nottinghamshire
Birmingham	West Midlands
Coventry	West Midlands
Sheffield	South Yorkshire
Yeadon	Leeds, West Yorkshire
Preston	Lancashire
Manchester	Greater Manchester
Stockton	Cleveland

Men and women are recruited for service in the Onshore Training Centres mainly for communications duties: Tactical Communications (visual or voice communications); Radio Communications (morse telegraphy); General Communications

Part of a realistic exercise to test the skills of a Surgeon Lieutenant Commander RNR. The Ton's *sweep gear is seen in part behind and the quick-release Gemini fuel containers can also be seen* (RN).

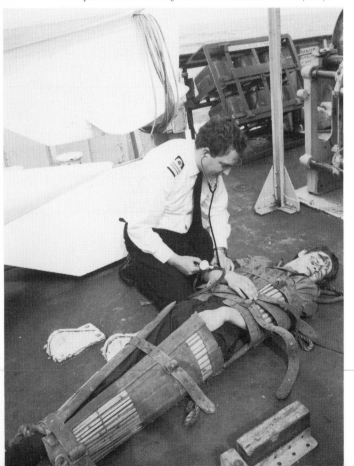

(teleprinters); Radio Electrical Mechanics (radio maintenance). Both Tactical and Radio Communicators are carried at sea, and therefore in line with the RN, these billets are only open to males. Training is carried out at any of the above-mentioned centres and trainees are appointed as ratings in the RNR Communications Branch. Ex-Service Communication ratings are appointed to a special list. Training requirements are 40 two-hour periods per annum and four periods of continuous training to 56 days during the five-year enrolment period.

Headquarters units In order to provide a comprehensive back-up for the RN in Naval Control of Shipping (NCS) and other onshore, headquarters functions, the RNR mans seven Headquarters Units in the UK and Gibraltar. In times of war and tension, Commanders-in-Chief would control all maritime operations from these Headquarters where the normal complement would be brought up to war-footing level with RNR and WRNR personnel. Civilian volunteers serve as Plotters, Communicators and Writers (General) for five years (male) and three years (female). Promotion is only to Chief Petty Officer rate.

Headquarters	Name	Location
Northwood	*Northwood*	Middlesex (adjacent to *Warrior*)
Southwick	*Southwick*	Portsmouth
Mount Wise	*Vivid*	Plymouth
Chatham	*Wildfire*	Gillingham, near Chatham
Rosyth/Pitreavie	*Scotia*	Dunfirmline, Fife
Inverkip	*Dalriada*	Greenock, Scotland
Gibraltar	*Calpe*	Gibraltar

All are under the command of a Commander RNR. In addition, there are RNR Naval Liaison Officers based at Southampton Docks, London, Liverpool and Cardiff.

Women's Royal Naval Reserve

Female ratings are accepted into the WRNR, which reinforces the WRNS in time of war, in following categories: Writer (General); Stores Accountant; and Radio Operator. In addition, WRNR personnel carry out work in connection with degaussing (protection against magnetic mines) of all types of vessels. There are opportunities for advancement from Wren to Chief Wren, and to officer status. In the event of mobilisation, members of the WRNR would serve anywhere in the world required by the

Co-operation with the RN is vital: here Upton *makes a rendezvous with a Sea King HAS 2 from 706 Squadron at Culdrose* (RNR).

Admiralty. The WRNR became fully integrated in January 1976 although only onshore appointments are possible.

RNR Postal Branch

This unusual and unique organisation caters for a small group who are already employed by the Post Office and would be prepared to form the nucleus of a Fleet mail organisation in time of war. Ratings enter as Postal Assistants (equivalent to Able Rate) and men with administrative experience may enter as officers, on selection.

Obligations

Members of the RNR and WRNR have all agreed to the following obligations: to make themselves efficient in each year of enrolment; to carry out the prescribed periods of continuous training with the Fleet or ashore; to keep kit in good order; not to leave the UK without obtaining written leave of absence; to notify change of address; to report in the event of Calling-up or on the Queen's Order in an emergency.

RNR on exercise

The Royal Naval Reserve, in the shape of the MCM10 and the Headquarters' Units, has recently been involved in several major NATO exercises in the autumn season, and the *Ton* Class vessels then have the opportunity of operating at sea together. The regular exercising of the RNR gives all those in the Seaman (Operations), Communications (Operations), Marine Engineering, Weapons Engineering, Medical, Instructor and Supply & Secretariat Branches the opportunity to work together.

Corresponding ranks
List 1

Seaman Branch	Engineering	S & S Branch	Special Duties
Commodore	-	-	-
Captain	Captain	Captain	-
Commander	Commander	Commander	-
Lieutenant Commander	Lieutenant Commander	Lieutenant Commander	Supply Lieutenant Commander
Lieutenant	Lieutenant	Lieutenant	Supply Lieutenant
Sub-Lieutenant	Sub-Lieutenant	Sub-Lieutenant	Supply Sub-Lieutenant
Midshipman	Midshipman	Midshipman	-

Lists 3–6

Seaman Branch	Engineering	Electrical	S & S Branch	Instructor	Medical*	Special Duties
Commodore						
Captain	Captain	Captain	Captain	-	Surgeon Captain	Captain (Sp)
Commander Commander	Commander	Commander	Commander	Instructor Commander	Surgeon Commander	Commander (SP)
Lieutenant Commander	Lieutenant Commander	Lieutenant Commander	Lieutenant Commander	Instructor Lieutenant Commander	Surgeon Lieutenant Commander	Lieutenant Commander (SP)
Lieutenant	Lieutenant	Lieutenant	Lieutenant	Instructor Lieutenant	Surgeon Lieutenant	Lieutenant (Sp)
Sub-Lieutenant	Sub-Lieutenant	Sub-Lieutenant	Sub-Lieutenant	-	Surgeon Lieutenant	Sub-Lieutenant (Sp)
Midshipman	Midshipman	Midshipman	Midshipman	-	-	Midshipman (Sp)

* Dental officers in the RNR are known as Surgeon (D)s.

Members of the WRNR are commissioned into WRNS ranks up to Superintendant WRNR.

Sea Cadet Corps (SCC)

The Royal Navy has been encouraging young boys (and to a certain extent girls—the Girls' Naval Training Corps) to take a look at a nautical career since the Navy League first introduced the Sea Cadet Corps in 1919. Whitsbale, in Kent, was the first town to have a Corps in 1926. The original idea was to provide the nation with a number of experienced young men capable of being readily trained to enter the RN in the event of war. By 1939, there were 100 units and 10,000 cadets.

In 1942, the original Navy League name prefix was dropped and the Girls' Naval Training Corps was formed; the latter has changed its name and formation several times, until 1980 when the MoD agreed to girls being admitted to the Sea Cadets Corps to form Girls' Nautical Training Contingents.

In 1955, the Royal Marines agreed to the formation of Marine Cadet sections within Sea Cadet Corps units. Today there are 392 units with 22,500 instructors, officers and cadets in the United Kingdom of which 2,000 are girls and 1,000 are Marine Cadets.

Today, the organisation is a charity called the Sea Cadet Association with significant assistance from the MoD, including training and ship visits. The Association is a worthwhile facet of Britain's nautical heritage.

Right *Cadets from the Sea Cadet Corps act as programme sellers at the Yeovilton Naval Air Station open day.*

Naval equipment, weapons and sensors

The RN uses a variety of specialist and utility pieces of equipment from Land Rovers to specially mounted GPMGs, from Clearance Diving Geminis to aircraft trolleys.

Personal Weapons

The RN has a long reputation for being able and willing to land a Naval Patrol to support the civil power in the case of unrest or disaster ashore. The warships which do not carry RM detachments are equipped with 7.62 mm SLRs, pistols and SMGs. Naval boarding parties have even been known to carry cutlasses during the Beira Patrol in the Indian Ocean. Today, the Fisheries Patrol and Hong Kong anti-smuggling patrols do not, as a rule, carry firearms unless they have definite evidence that there will be 'trouble' aboard the boarded vessel. Weapons and IS training is carried out at *Cambridge*, where RN ratings and officers are even taught the use of anti-riot gear and equipment.

The basic provision of personal weapons to the RN is: 9 mm Automatic Pistol (L9A1); 9 mm Sub-Machine Gun (L2A3); and 7.62 mm SL Rifle (L1A1). These weapons can be used for exploding tethered mines which come to the surface after a sweep, or for firing lines across to other warships and RFAs for jackstay transfers and line transfers. Details of the above weapons will be found in the RM Equipment section (pages 277–286).

Pintle-mounted GPMG

The pintle-mounted GPMG is designed primarily as an effective policing weapon for patrol boats of the *Ton*, *Island*, *Bird* and *Castle* Classes. It is readily adapted for aircraft or hovercraft uses. The gun itself is the L7A2 infantry version of the 7.62 mm general purpose machine gun which can be mounted on a buffered tripod (L4A1) or on the bulwark pintle. The mounting is specially designed and manufactured for the RN, being robust and able to stand sea poundings. It has all-round traverse, height adjustment and a detachable spent cartridge container. Details of the L7A2 GPMG can be found in the RM equipment section, but the mount has the following characteristics: **Elevation** −10° to +45°; **Height of gun axis** 1,270 mm to 1,676 mm; **Ammunition** 200 rounds.

Naval small craft

The RN, not surprisingly, has a large number and several different types of small craft, from Gemini to Huntress Class launches. Landing craft and assault craft are described in the RM Water Craft section, but the following will be considered here: Gemini (Mine Clearance) and Avon Searider.

A pintle-mounted GPMG in a sandbagged position on Fearless' *superstructure to provide additional anti-aircraft cover in Bomb Alley—San Carlos Water (RN).*

Gemini

The mine-clearance Gemini is produced from the original RAE Farnborough design by Dunlop Rubber. There is a six-man craft known as the Type 9728 and a ten-man type 9729, their specifications being as follows:

	Type 9728	Type 9729
Length	3.8 m	4.6 m
Beam	1.6 m	1.9 m
Inside length	2.38 m	3.0 m
Cockpit area	2.0 m²	3.0 m²
Total weight	96.05 kg	137.4 kg

These craft are kept inflated with special boards on the main decks of MHs and are fitted with 40 hp Johnson outboards; spare fuel cans are carried in special racks, so that they may be jettisioned in the event of fire. The General Purpose Gemini is a ten-man craft, known as the Type 9730, manufactured by Avon and Dunlop. These are kept aboard frigates and destroyers for use by naval parties, RM detachments and working parties, being transferred over the side by lightweight davit. Such craft are carried by Type 22 frigates and *Leanders*. Their specification is as the RM Type 9727 described in the RM Water Craft section.

Avon Searider SR5M

This is almost identical in every detail to the RM craft, which are RN property as described previously and operated in Hong Kong waters. The Searider was selected by the Tri-Service Small Boat Committee for use as a boarding craft, especially for the Hong Kong Squadron and the Fisheries' Protection Squadron operating in British EEZ waters. The craft is robust and is capable of travelling at 12 knots through seas up to Force 8. They are kept on the decks of patrol craft with a lightweight davit to handle them. The standard power pack is the 90 hp Johnson outboard. They are used as crash boats by some frigates during flying operations, being capable of beating the maxima laid down for crash-launches, currently standing at six minutes from ditching to attendance. The specification is described in the RM Water Craft section. The normal coxswain for these craft, many of whom are trained at RM Poole or at *Vernon*, are the Buffers (senior Leading Rates) of the warship.

Motor boats and motor cutters

There are a number of these craft in service both aboard larger craft, such as warships, and for transporting stores and personnel around naval bases and from warship to warship.

Huntress 7 m FMB The Huntress Fast Motor Boat has been in service a number of years, being carried on several Classes of FF and DLG; it is also used for harbour training and is well loved for its speed and manoeuvrability.

Pacific boats The Pacific type are used for training and aboard older warships: they are designated Pacific 22 (6.5 m) and Pacific 27 (8 m), and there is now the possibility of a larger boat for harbour service.

Cheverton 7.5 m MB/MC This craft comes with a 4 or 6-cylinder engine, depending on the task required of it. It is used for harbour training and is carried aboard large warships.

10 m Fast Motor Launch A craft used for harbour training, as a senior officer's barge and for the sad duty of funerals at sea.

Bottom far left *Avon Searider used in Hong Kong waters for boarding.* **Bottom left** *Mine clearance Gemini with 40 hp Johnson outboard.*

Right *Seen aboard* Danae, *the 24 ft Cheverton Motor Boat, now known to the RN as the 7.5 m Motor Boat for liberty and general duties in frigates and destroyers.* **Below right** *The standard Whaler Mk II ready for lowering into the water.*

11 m workboat A utility craft as used by the Army and the Royal Air Force Marine Unit for transporting stores and personnel in a similar way to the LCVP, which it resembles; most of modern construction and are driven from the stern.

8 m Motor Whaler Formerly known as the Whaler Mk II, this is the standard crash boat and utility craft for the older warships of the RN, including *County* Class DLGs and the newer Type 21s. It is launched from davits on the main deck and has the following specification: **Length** 8.23 m; **Weight** 2.5 tonnes; **Crew** 3; **Max capacity** 26; **Power** Inboard diesel. The craft is manned by a coxswain, bowman and radio operator and has many uses including panic boat for man overboard, crash boat for flying stations and picket boat for patrols in potentially unfriendly harbours.

Survey craft There are currently two major types: the 9.5 m Survey Craft for independent work away from the parent Ocean Survey Craft and the 6 m craft for use by Coastal Survey Vessels.

Dory 17 A utility, training and patrol craft seen almost everywhere.

Specialist projectiles

Head Rocket Flare No 3 Mk N6

This is the parachute flare used as an illuminator for the Corvus launcher system. It incorporates a timing device for range settings and has a burning time of 70 seconds. It is used to illuminate surface targets and incidents.

Thunderflash

For safe and effective training the RN use a lighter, smaller Thunderflash than the RM (see RM equipment). It can even be used inside a hangar.

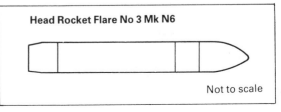

Head Rocket Flare No 3 Mk N6

Not to scale

Aircraft handlers

There are numerous types of aircraft handling device, but the two most commonly used by both the RN and the RM are manufactured by ML Aviation: Utility Handler and the Aircraft Handler Type EN.

Utility Handler

This is mainly used for the Lynx AH 1, Scout AH 1 and Gazelle AH 1 aircraft, being tractive and quickly engaged with a skid-mounted helicopter. It comprises a battery-powered drive unit and steering arm, with an electro-hydraulic jacking system. Dolly wheels are attached to the aft ends of the skids and the aircraft is manoeuvred with the handler at the forward end. **Tractor unit length** 1.302 m; **Width** 0.9 m; **Height** 0.425 m; **Weight** 508 kg; **Motor** Electric 48v 6kW (8 hp); **Max speed** 4.8 km/h/ 3.5 km/h (loaded aircraft).

Aircraft Handler Type EN

This is an airfield or flight deck aircraft handling device which is capable of handling a number of different types of aircraft including the Sea King and the Sea Harrier. It is highly manoeuvrable, especially in the confined space of a ship's hangar, whether on a Type 42 destroyer or the helicopter support ship *Engadine*. It is electrically driven and can travel 20 km between battery charging. **Length** 2.54 m; **Width** 1.6 m; **Height** 0.77 m; **Weight** 1,918 kg; **Tractive effort** 2,268 kg; **Power** 10 hp electric; **Max lift load** 5,560 kg; **Speed** 6.4 km/h.

Ford Tractor

On airfields, the commonest aircraft tug is the Ford 222 tractor which is used for the full range of naval aircraft, from Sea Heron to Lynx HAS 2. Every Naval Air Station has at least three on strength.

Although most Naval aircraft can taxi under their power for the pre-flight phase of normal flying operations, it is necessary for there to be a number of specially adapted vehicles available for the tugging of aircraft which are not under their own power. At Yeovilton, for instance, there are about 30 tractors available to act as aircraft tugs. These are predominantly Ford types, with the older 2600 and more powerful 4100 series being replaced by the

Top left *Specialist ground equipment for 899 NAS's Sea Harriers.* **Centre left** *Other ground support equipment includes 'dollies', stairs and wheel-extinguishers.* **Left** *One of many Ford-produced aircraft-towing tractors.* **Top right** *An All-Wheel Drive (AWD) tractor towing a Sea Harrier during flying operations in* Invincible *(RN).* **Right** *The standard RNAS airfield Rescue Land Rover which also acts as a 'Police' vehicle.*

medium-powered Ford 3600 type. These vehicles are basically Service adaptions of commercially available types, and they are compared below:

Type	Ford 2600	Ford 3600	Ford 4100
Length	3.221 m	3.228 m	3.444 m
Width	2.25 m	2.25 m	2.355 m
Height	2.489 m	2.489 m	2.642 m
Weight	2,418 kg	2,422 kg	2,638 kg

Airfield vehicles

There are several major types of vehicle to be found on the Royal Naval Air Stations around the UK. Besides the large number of non-powered accessories, like the mobile compressors, starters, water and fuel tankers, there are a number of specialist vehicles which deserve special mention.

The RN Fire Service, famous for its sterling work with the 'Green Goddess' appliances during the two Firemen's Strikes, is equipped with two major types:

Thornycroft Nubian (Crash-type)

This is an all-wheel drive fire tender which can quickly respond to incidents on or off the airfield. It is equipped with foam-spreader and has a crew of four including the driver. It is usually commanded by a Leading Rate. **Length** 8.73 m; **Width** 2.6 m; **Height** 3.54 m; **Weight** 20,774 kg.

Land Rover (Rescue-type)

These reflective red-painted vehicles with a good four-wheel drive facility are used for emergency work and can be considered to be the first vehciles to reach a crash. Their aim is then to make a safety path to the crew and effect a rescue. The vehicle has a three-man crew, including driver and a firesuited

member who rides in a special seat at the rear of the vehicle. They are also used in a security role being able to move about the airfield at speed. **Length** 4.42 m; **Width** 1.92 m; **Height** 2.59 m; **Weight** 2,520 kg.

A typical air station like Yeovilton will have three Thornycrofts and four Land Rovers on strength at any one time. They are deployed to strategic points on the airfield during flying, being alternated with those in the Fire Station.

Flight deck vehicles

There are four types of flight deck vehicle used in *Hermes*, *Invincible* and *Illustrious*: All Wheel Drive Tractor; JCB 520 Lifter; Coles Crane; and Hyster Fork Lift.

Air-launched weapons

The technology involved in air-launched weapons, as has so vividly been demonstrated in the South Atlantic, has increased to such an extent that there is really no comparison with the basic developments of World War 2. It was during this time that the first realistic air-to-surface systems began to be developed, primarily for ASW work and later for strikes against land targets. There had, of course, been bombs carried by Naval aircraft ever since they were first established in the Royal Naval Air Service,

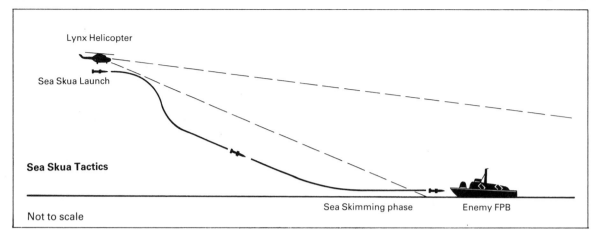

Lynx Helicopter

Sea Skua Launch

Sea Skua Tactics

Sea Skimming phase   Enemy FPB

Not to scale

but the rocket projectile of the second half of the war was the forerunner of the sophisticated vehicles costing sums of six figures each which are carried by today's Sea Harrier and Lynx. Air-launched weapons can be divided into two categories: missiles and free-fall devices, such as bombs.

Missiles

The primary missile systems carried by Naval aircraft in the modern RN are the anti-surface ship devices which combat the threat posed by warships of a hostile force at a position far enough away from the friendly force that the threat is not able to launch its own missiles. The RN also uses a licence-built AAM, the Sidewinder, on Sea Harrier aircraft.

Sea Skua (CL 834)

Role ASM (helicopter-launched); **Status** In production; **Weight** 210 kg at launch; **Length** 2.83 m; **Body diameter** 0.20 m; **Warhead charge** HE 20 kg; **Velocity** Classified; **Rate of fire** Classified; **Range** Medium; **Manufacturer** BAe Dynamics; **Aircraft equipped** Lynx HAS 2.

The Sea Skua is a semi-active, air-launched, all-weather sea-skimming, anti-ship homing missile which entered front-line service with the Lynx HAS 2s of 815 Squadron during 1981, each of which can carry four missiles. It is a very cost-effective medium-range weapon which provides the Fleet with an over-the-horizon potential against small missile-armed warships. The missile can also inflict severe if not disabling damage on large vessels.

The missile is designed to be operated in conjunction with the Lynx's Ferranti Seaspray radar which illuminates the target for the semi-active homing guidance. Sea skimming is achieved by the use of a small radar altimeter at one of four pre-selected heights which can be chosen in the

aircraft by the pilot. The missile has powered control surfaces on the body with fixed fins at the tail.

The propulsion system comprises a solid-fuel boost and sustainer motors which ignite simultaneously after launch, the missile having first dropped clear of the launch helicopter.

Like the Sea Eagle, Sea Skua will be treated as a round of ammunition which can be rapidly loaded or unloaded—a particularly important point on the confined space of a small ship's flight deck or hangar. Although the exact rate of fire is still classified, it has been announced that ripple fire techniques can be used, thus allowing the engagement of the larger warships of destroyer size and above. In normal circumstances, one missile would be used against targets of less than 1,000 tonnes. Aboard ship, the missile is stored with its fins detached and a special trolley is used to support the missile during ground operations.

During the Falklands operations, it is reported that seven Sea Skua missiles were launched, causing the destruction of at least two Argentine patrol boats.

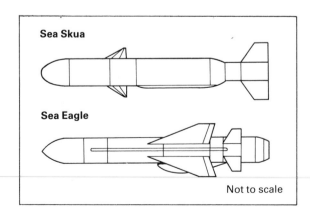

Sea Skua

Sea Eagle

Not to scale

Sea Eagle

Role ASM (Sea Harrier-launched); **Status** Under trials and evaluation; **Weight** Classified; **Length** Circa 2.5 m; **Body diameter** Circa 0.30 m; **Warhead charge** High lethality; **Velocity** Supersonic; **Rate of fire** Simultaneous; **Range** 100 km; **Manufacturer** BAe Dynamics; **Aircraft equipped** Sea Harrier FRS 1.

The Sea Eagle is a second-generation 'fire and forget' missile which will be used operational by the RN's Sea Harrier squadrons against warship targets. It has a stand-off capability using an onboard computer and an active radar homing head. In a typical attack, the target position would be fed in just prior to launch and after leaving the aircraft the missile will use this information to plan its own trajectory. The stand-off capability means that the launch position is well outside the target's missile engagement zone (MEZ) in normal circumstances. The missile flies like an aeroplane with cruciform wings mounted on the centre line and moving control fins aft.

The missile is powered by an air-breathing Microturbo TR160 turbine engine which gives it supersonic performance. This and the onboard computer to provide the guidance undoubtedly contribute to the missile's £350 million development costs. Micro-circuitry is used a great deal so as to keep down the size of this complex missile, which is similar in dimensions to the Sea Dart.

In Naval terms, it is designed as a replacement for the Anglo-French Martel missile over which it has a far better performance with good sea-skimming characteristics. It has a strong ECCM potential, being able to discriminate between multiple targets. It is designed as a round of ammunition, meaning that on-board test facilities should not be necessary and a round should stay operational for more than 15 months without need to test.

Installation aboard a Sea Harrier will need only a special pylon (the missile will take the inboard position), a simple control panel for the pilot and one 'black box' of tricks; normal complement will be two missiles.

Nord AS 11 (SS 11)

Role ASM (wire-guided); **Status** In service; **Weight** 29.9 kg; **Length** 1.2 m; **Body diameter** 0.16 m; **Warhead charge** HE or fragmentation; **Velocity** 160 m/sec; **Rate of fire** Single; **Range** 3,000 m; **Manufacturer Aérospatiale; Aircraft equipped** Wasp HAS 1; Wessex HU 5; Scout AH 1 (RM).

The first of the wire-guided, multi-purpose and lightweight missiles to be fitted to naval helicopters in the Fleet Air Arm, the system has been mainly used as part of the 'gun-ship' fit for Naval Air Commando Wessex HU 5 helicopters and originates from the French-designed SS 11 surface-to-surface missile. Three different warheads can be fitted to the missile before it is in turn fitted to the helicopter and these are for anti-tank, fragmentation or high explosive uses. With a flight time of only about 20–25 seconds, the firing helicopter has only a limited time out of cover whilst the missile is guided to its target by the aircrewman by means of a visual but stabilised sight. The actual guidance is provided by command signals being passed down the wire to the missile and all the operator has to do is maintain sight of the missile and in this he is aided by tracer sources on the missile body. The missile is really obsolescent in modern terms but may still be used for practice and for limited exercises.

Nord AS 12

Role ASM (wire-guided); **Status** In service; **Weight** 76 kg; **Length** 1.87 m; **Body diameter** Circa 0.18 m; **Warhead charge** See below; **Velocity** Circa 300 m/sec; **Rate of fire** Single; **Range** 8,000 m; **Manufacturer** Aérospatiale; **Aircraft equipped** Wasp HAS 1, Lynx HAS 2.

Used primarily in an anti-surface ship or anti-surfaced submarine role, this weapon is the successor to the AS 11 and is manufactured by the same French concern. Again it is classed as a lightweight weapon of multi-purpose design, being wire-guided and using an improved sight which allows the helicopter to move during the flight period. The variety of warheads used allows operations against land targets as well as maritime ones. All embarked Wasp flights are equipped to carry the missile and the time needed to mount the

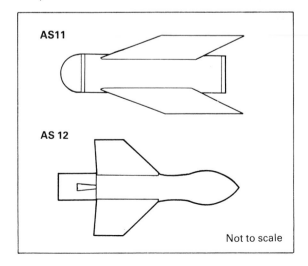

AS11

AS 12

Not to scale

Left *AS 12 on pylons for operations in Wasp helicopters.* **Below left** *The Sidewinder AIM-9L unit in place on a Sea Harrier.* **Bottom left** *Birmingham Flight's Lynx armed with Stingray lightweight torpedo* (Westland).

Right *A Lynx helicopter (702 NAS) demonstrates air-dropping a torpedo (Mk 46)* (Westland).

Below right *Mk 46 torpedo on its weapons carrier on a Wessex HAS 3.*

launcher an to accelerate to circle and choose the best possible angle of attack. It can almost 'sniff' the most vulnerable parts of a target, according to informed sources. It is versatile, being capable of shallow water running at about 18 m, or to attacking stick. The sight itself is a periscope-like device with a head in the helicopter's cabin roof. Tracking is by means of infra-red emission from the missile. This missile is thought to have severely damaged the Argentine submarine *Santa Fe* during the operations to re-take South Georgia; it is believed that Mk 11 depth charges were also used.

Sidewinder AIM-9L

Role Short/medium range AAM; **Status** In service; **Weight** 75 kg; **Length** 2.84 m; **Body diameter** 0.127 m; **Warhead charge** HE; **Velocity** Supersonic; **Rate of fire** Single or salvo; **Range** 1,100 m; **Manufacturer** Philco-Ford; **Aircraft equipped** Sea Harrier FRS 1.

The AIM-9L is produced under licence in Europe by a team from several countries led by British Aerospace Dynamics Group. Classified as an all-aspect AAM using infra-red homing, the missile has a dogfighting ability. It has been developed for many years and has seen action in Vietnam and during the Arab-Israeli conflicts in the Middle East. A possible

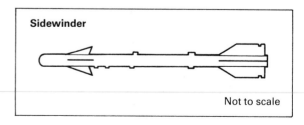

Sidewinder

Not to scale

replacement is the Advanced Short Range Air-to-Air Missile (ASRAAM) being developed by the European consortium. It was a most successful weapon in the dogfights against Argentine strike aircraft in the South Atlantic, equipping not only Sea Harriers, but Harriers, Vulcans and Nimrods of the Royal Air Force as well.

Torpedoes

The aircraft of the RN are also equipped with Lightweight Torpedoes for anti-submarine warfare.

Stingray
Role AS; **Status** In production; **Weight** Classified; **Length** Classified; **Body diameter** 0.324 m; **Warhead charge** Classified; **Velocity** Circa 50 knots; **Range** Classified; **Running** Classified; **Aircraft equipped** Lynx HAS 2; Sea King HAS 5.

This is an advanced design with the ability to acquire and destroy submarine targets using a fast underwater speed and on-board computer to enhance targetting data. It will be deployed in the very near future to Ships' Flights, especially aboard the destroyers and frigates which are equipped with the Westland Lynx HAS 2. It is possible that it will be deployed aboard Ikara- and STWS-equipped warships for launching via the Mk 32 tubes. It is powered by a small electric motor which is quiet and gives it the ability to stalk its prey, then to accelerate to circle and choose the best possible angle of attack. It can almost 'sniff' the most vulnerable parts of a target, according to informed sources. It is versatile, being capable of shallow water running at about 18 m, or to attacking deep running submarines at 300 m plus. It is equipped to overcome jamming devices.

Mark 44
Role AS; **Status** Still operational but obsolescent; **Weight** 223 kg; **Length** 2.56 m; **Body diameter**

0.32 m; **Warhead charge** HE 40 kg; **Velocity** Circa 30 knots; **Range** 2.7 nm (5 km); **Running** Down to 300 m;

The Mark 44 is an electric torpedo designed to be dropped by parachute from the weapons carrier of a helicopter. It has been largely replaced by the Mark 46. The warhead has proximity or contact fuzing.

Mark 46
Role AS; **Status** Operational with the Fleet Air Arm; **Weight** 230 kg; **Length** 2.56 m; **Body diameter** 0.32 m; **Warhead charge** Classified; **Velocity** 40 knots; **Range** 5.9 nm (11 km); **Running** Down to 300 m; **Aircraft equipped** Wasp HAS 1; Wessex HAS 3; Sea King HAS 2/5; Lynx HAS 2.

This is an electric-powered, active/passive homing torpedo which is dropped by parachute from an aerial vehicle, including helicopters and Ikara. The Stingray will replace this torpedo in service during the next few years.

Depth charges/bombs

The RN has a number of depth charge/bomb devices in both conventional and nuclear spheres. The conventional Mk 11 depth charge is of old design, but still useful for 'keeping the heads of enemy submariners down'. The nuclear depth bomb or Lulu is a high kill weapon which would only be

Above, below and below right *Sea Harrier ordnance—SNEB 68 mm rocket launcher; free-fall bomb (30 mm Aden cannon behind); and practice bombs.*

Above *The Mk 11 depth-bomb which is still used by most types of naval aircraft.*

used as a last resort weapon at some distance from the warship of the helicopter. It is interesting to note that the depth charge is the most dangerous device in the event of a flight deck fire, but that the nuclear depth bomb is considered one of the most safe devices to handle in normal conditions. No details of the nuclear weapon are available and the ships carrying it have not been disclosed. All FAA helicopters are nuclear-capable. (For further details on depth charge/bomb devices, see shipboard ordnance section.)

Sea Harrier

The British Aerospace Sea Harrier has its own suite of weapons: Aden 30 mm cannon; Cluster Bomb No 1 Mk 1; SNEB 68 mm rocket pod; AIM-9L Sidewinder (see above); P3T Sea Eagle (see above).

The Aden Mk 4 30 mm cannon has been in service for many years, and the fittings on the Sea Harrier are optional, being placed in fuselage belly strakes with about 100 rounds of 30 mm HE or solid

shell. The gun is designed as both a dogfight and strike weapon, being equipped with electrical cocking, camera-gun and other facilities.

The Cluster Bomb No 1 Mk 1 is designed as a battlefield support weapon and the normal payload of the Sea Harrier is five (two on each wing and one on the centre-line station). It is a low-level weapon, covering the target area with a pattern of small bombs. **Length** 2.436 m; **Weight** 272 kg; **Diameter** 0.419 m; **Span** 0.566 m.

The SNEB 68 mm rocket pod is of French design and has been developed for both air-to-ground and air-to-air operations, although only the former is envisaged for the Sea Harrier. The rockets are unguided but stabilised in flight by the use of folding fins. There are a number of warheads available, including Blast (AA role); Inert (practice); Hollow charge (air-to-ground) and Fragmentation (air-to-ground). Two launchers are in service, designated Matra M116 and Matra M155.

Other aircraft ordnance is standard Royal Air

Seaspray radar components for Lynx aircraft (Ferranti).

Force design and will be found in the companion *Encyclopaedia of the Modern Royal Air Force* currently under preparation.

Aircraft radar
Seaspray
This radar has been specially designed by Ferranti to operate in Westland Lynx HAS 2 helicopters for anti-surface vessel purposes. The aerial is a traditional 'scanner' shape which is fitted into the nose of the helicopter, but weighs less than 60 kg. The display and control unit is set in the cockpit, on the left-hand side, and is operated by the observer. It has two principal modes: search and track, and transponder. The former allows wide-angle or limited sector surveillance but both modes can detect potential targets. The system is linked to nose

and after fuselage ECM and ESM gear. Another major use of the system is the control of the Sea Skua anti-ship missile which is currently being introduced into service with 815 NAS which operates the Lynx from small ships, up to and including Type 42 destroyers. At long range it can pick up FPBs in very rough conditions and considered to be very good by squadron observers.

Blue Fox
This is modelled on the highly successful Seaspray and equips all the current Sea Harrier aircraft, plus two Hunter T 8M radar training aircraft which are flown by 899 NAS but maintained by Airwork Limited at FRADU. The Blue Fox is a frequency agile radar, lightweight and used for search and strike operations. It is linked to a complex computer system and is able to unclutter radar returns to present the single pilot with the correct data for air-

Blue Fox lightweight air intercept search and strike radar (Ferranti).

main rotor, is used as the primarily tactical control sensor for the ASW fight with the display being the main focus of all information. The range is thought to be in excess of 50 nm (92.6 km) and it has the capability of distinguishing between friendly aircraft with compatible transponders. It is thought that this system is being developed for the Sea King HAS 5 to have more definition, power, range and the ability to act as a mid-course guidance computer for surface-launched and air-launched missiles.

Other sensors
Dunking sonar
The main other type of sensor is the dunking sonar, known as Type 195, which equips Sea King and Wessex HAS 3 aircraft. This is the airborne version of the Plessey MS26/27, known as Type 195M, for surface ships, and described later. The transducer is lowered a maximum of about 55 m by a winch through the centre of the helicopter and is controlled by the aircrewman from this sonar position alongside the observer, in the rear cabin of the ASW helicopter. Its sonar has a range of about 7 nm (12.9 km) and has the advantage over hull-mounted sets of being easily and rapidly transported from 'jump' to 'jump' by the parent helicopter. In this way, it is unpredictable and can out-guess and usually out-run the enemy submarine.

The sonar operation is to give the aircrewman specific bearings and ranges to search on, based on other data from friendly sonars in the area or even the intuition of the aircrewman or the observer. Target information can be fed straight into the ARI 5955 display and the attack is conducted from there.

Sonobuoys
The 'spitting' of sonobuoys is relatively new to ASW, especially to the RN as the mini-Jezebel

to-air interception. It is the aiming device for the air-to-air Sidewinder AAM and for the surface attack payload.

The Sea Harrier's avionics fit has been enhanced by the microchip revolution and this has 'led to a software bonus for the hard working pilot'. Part of this is the Blue Fox with its link to the inertial navigation computer and HUD (head-up display) facility.

Blue Parrot
This is the name given to the former Buccaneer strike/attack radar fitted in a number of Canberra T 22s operated by FRADU. The radar training role for the Buccaneer ceased in 1979 with the disbandment of 809 NAS following the demise of *Ark Royal*, but the aircraft and, one suspects, the system, are retained for radar training with the Fleet.

ARI 5955
This system entered FAA service in 1978, equipping the Sea King HAS 1 (now out of service) and the Wessex HAS 3 helicopters originally. Today the system, manufactured by MEL, is fitted to Sea King HAS 2/5 and Wessex HAS 3 for ASV, SAR and ASW roles. The radar, housed in the dome aft of the

British-made sonobuoys on display.

system has only recently been adopted for selected Sea King aircraft. The air-dropped sonobuoy is deployed from a helicopter flying at between 45 m and 3,050 m, and 60 to 325 knots. On hitting the surface of the water it is used to detect and amplify the underwater noises in its operating area. The procedure is to sow a pattern of sonobuoys across the presumed track of an enemy submarine. Although the sowing of so many sonobuoys might seem wasteful, the results obtained are such that RN personnel believe they are most worthwhile and regret not having had them before. The operating time is 1.4 to 8 hours depending on the pre-setting of the equipment before it is put down the sonobuoy chute; it scuttles itself after completion of its mission; even so it must be a concern to Command that these sensitive pieces of kit are left floating around the ocean for an AGI (Soviet spy trawler) to scoop up. The Dowty Ultra Mini-Jezebel has the following characteristics: **Length** 0.305 m; **Diameter** 0.125 m; **Weight** 4.5 kg; **Power** seawater-activiated battery; **Transmission** VHF radio.

In addition, there are bathythermal buoys which can be dropped in the same way in order that sea temperature and salinity data can be collected. The Dowty Ultra bathythermal SSQ936 has the following characteristics: **Length** 0.305 m; **Diameter** 0.124 m; **Weight** 5 kg; **Operating depth** Up to 427 m.

MAD

During 1981 and 1982, the RN carried out trials with the ASQ-501 Magnetic Anomoly Detector 'bird' fitted to Lynx HAS 2 (815 NAS) and Sea King HAS 5 (826 NAS) helicopters from shore and afloat platforms. This device is designed to pick up and classify very small changes in the regular magnetic field of the Earth which may indicate the presence of a submarine (metal objects distort the magnetic

A Lynx HAS 2 (815 NAS) equipped with ASQ-501 MAD.

Sea King HAS 2 equipped with Type 195 dunking sonar.

field): an airborne metal detector. The bird is flown from the undercarriage oleo of the helicopter and towed about 1 km behind the aircraft in order that its own magnetic field does not influence the MAD bird. It is possible that this device will become standard in the FAA's two types of ASW helicopter of the late 1980s. In addition, the EH-101 (see Future ASW helicopter developments above) will be equipped with a MAD system according to current thought on the subject.

LAPADS

The new Sea King HAS 5 helicopter which carries the mini-sonobuoys is also equipped with the

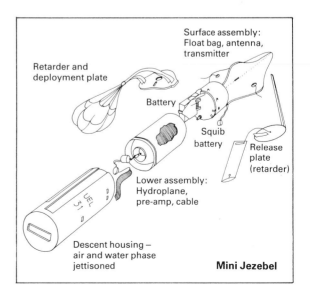

Sea King HAS 5 with LAPADS gear stowed in the rear fuselage (Westland).

AQS901 LAPADS system which processes the information returned from the sonobuoys. LAPADS stands for Lightweight Acoustic Processing and Display System and is a computer based declassifier of information and noise. It is operated in the after end of the helicopter's rear cabin by the aircrewman. If Lynx helicopters are fitted with LAPADS and sonobuoys, the ASW war will be very much different. The passive sonobuoys are known as Jezebel and Mini-Jezebel and are launched from the carrying aircraft through chutes.

Survival equipment

There are two types of survival equipment used by the RN (and RM): aircrew gear and sea-service gear. The aircrew equipment, looked after by the Survival Equipment Sections on Air Stations and in aircraft-carrying warships and RFAs, are: the Immersion Suit Mk 10; Aircrew Coverall Mk 14A; Quick-Don Immersion Coverall/Suit; Single-Seat Liferaft; Multi-Seat Liferaft; Aircrew Lifepreserver Mk 15; Aircrew Lifepreserver Mk 29.

The **Immersion Suit Mk 10** is worn when the sea temperature drops below 15°C and it is used by both fixed-wing and rotary-wing aircrew. For warmer weather there is the **Aircrew Coverall Mk 14A**, which is a one-piece flying suit, tailored and interlined for comfort. It has the normal map pockets and can be worn over anti-G suits. Passengers in fixed-wing and rotary-wing aircraft can be equipped with bright orange one-piece **Quick-Don Immersion Suits** to provide protection against exposure in the event of ditching. On ditching, there is the all enclosed **single-seat liferaft** for single-seat aircraft like the Hunter and Sea Harrier. **Multi-seat liferafts**, for Sea Heron, Jetstream and similar, are fitted with comprehensive ancillary equipment. There are two types of life preserver in use: **Mk 15** for helicopter and subsonic aircraft and the **Mk 29** for ejection modes. Both have various SAR assist items and are coloured orange on inflation.

Warships are equipped with various items of survival equipment including canistered multi-seat liferafts which are similar but larger than the aircraft type mentioned above. In addition, submarines are equipped with **Submarine Escape Suits** which enable personnel to escape from a stricken submarine and ascend to the surface to be rescued. There is even a lamp attachment. When working on deck or operating aircraft from the flight deck of a warship, crew members wear the **Naval Lifejacket Mk 3** which is designed for constant wear. It has a

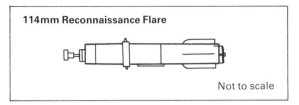

114mm Reconnaissance Flare

Not to scale

special hood/visor for extra protection. Royal Marines, especially assault troops, wear the **Assault Troop Lifejacket** specifically designed for amphibious operations so as not to restrict movement and yet inflate rapidly. All this equipment is produced by Beaufort.

Flares and illuminators

There are numerous flares and illumination devices which are used by the RN for ship and aircraft use: 114 mm reconnaissance flares; Very pistol and flares; Dial-a-Star; and smoke generators.

114 mm reconnaissance flares

These can be air dropped for battlefield and maritime reconnaissance, in the case of the latter for

Survival gear—groundcrew lifejacket and aircrew 'goon' suit and (over shoulder) aircrew lifejacket.

26-man aircraft/ship liferaft.

visual identification of fishing vessels, smugglers or other small craft. They are also used for search and rescue operations. The flare lasts 3/4 minutes and has an illumination output of 750,000 candle power. The flares are produced by the Royal Ordnance Factory.

Very pistol and flares

This is the age-old system of shooting up flares and stars to give illumination, SAR identification and tactical identification. The star cartridges available are red, green, yellow and white. The cartridge, fired from the hand-held Very pistol, reaches a height of 90 m and has a burning time of six seconds.

Dial-a-Star

This is the updated version of the Very pistol and cartridge because it is self-contained. It is officially known as the Cartridge Signal 17 mm and is described as a pyrotechnic signalling kit capable of firing eight flares of various colours which are visible for 2 nm (3.7 km) in daylight or 7 nm (13 km) in darkness. It saves the operator from having to reload with different colours, and allows Command to select continuously changing 'colours of the day' without the need to issue different cartridges. It weighs 250 g, is waterproof and is declared 97.5 per cent reliable.

Smoke generators

The FAA have smoke generators for towed targets (known as Generator Smoke Towed Target No 1 Mk 1 and GSTT A 21). They are designed for attachment to the Rushton aircraft towed target (see below) in order to indicate the position of the target to gunners and missile controllers under training during practice shoots. Both systems are fitted to the Canberra TT 18 of FRADU based at Yeovilton. GSTT No 1 Mk 1 produces smoke for 30 seconds and A 21 for 60 seconds. Their specifications are:

	No 1 Mk 1	A 21
Length	250 mm	510 mm
Diameter	45 mm	45 mm
Weight	800 g	1,300 g
Colour of smoke	Red	Red
Visible range	9,000 m	9,000 m

Towed aircraft targets

The FRADU, based at Yeovilton and flying Hunter and Canberra aircraft, uses four basic types of target for use by gunnery and missile firing warships' practice: Rushton; Low-Level Height-Keeping Rushton; Sleeve Towed Target; and Banner Towed Target. The only aircraft currently equipped to take the above targets are the Canberra TT 18 aircraft which can be readily identified by their grey top surfaces, black/yellow striped undersides and target positions under the wings.

Rushton

This is a torpedo-shaped target produced by Flight Refuelling for optical or radar tracking and as a normal gunnery target. The above-mentioned smoke generators can be used to identify the position of the target for a shoot and radar reflectors are also used to enhance the radar 'picture'.

A recent adaption of the standard Rushton is the T-tailed low-level height-keeping target which can be pre-set for an optimum height between 7.6 m and 76.2 m to simulate sea-skimming missile attacks on warships.

Rushton target on pylon; aircraft is a Canberra.

Gunnery targets

The sleeve and banner gunnery targets have been used by air forces, navies and armies for many years. The sleeve is the ship gunnery target, whilst the banner is used for air-to-air training. Today, there are still a number of 40 mm Bofors and there will soon be 30 mm and 76 mm guns which will need to have trained gun crews. The training vessels are therefore MCMVs, OPVs and certain frigates with close-support guns. With the introduction of the Sea Harrier, the RN had to re-equip with banner targets which are towed some three nautical miles (5.6 km) behind the Canberra for pilots to use either camera guns or 30 mm Aden cannon; near misses can be recorded electronically as well.

Ship-launched weapons

The 1970s and 1980s will go down in naval history as the age of the ship-borne missile system and, indeed, during this period the traditionally conservative Royal Navy introduced its first class of all-missile frigate, the Type 22. Ship-launched weapons are primarily missiles designed for ASVW, AAW and ASW. In addition, there are weapons which are guided by one means or another, but which do not rate the term 'missile' in the naval scene. Today, it is not possible to be too specific about a missile type because the first generation Seacat has a dual capability these days and many of the latest generation, like the Sea Dart, are designed to cover several roles. This is a field in which the Royal Navy has pioneered indigenous designs to suit the particular warships and the particular operational areas covered by the Service.

Missiles

Sea Dart (GWS 30)

Role Medium range SAM/SSM; **Status** In service; **Weight** 550 kg; **Length** 4.36 m; **Body diameter** 0.42 m; **Warhead charge** HE; **Velocity** Circa Mach 2.5; **Rate of fire** Classified; **Range** 30 km; **Manufacturer** BAe Dynamics; **Ships equipped** *Invincible*, *Sheffield* and *Bristol* Classes.

The Sea Dart is one of the world's most advanced missile system and is claimed to be the best area defence against guided weapons system afloat, although the success of Argentinian ASV missiles recently may cause this assessment to be modified. It provides medium-range defence against high and/or low-flying aircraft and missiles which pose a threat to the launch vessel. In the modern RN, the launch vehicle is primarily the large type of warship because the Sea Dart system is expensive. In fact, it is the sole ship-borne method of defence for *Invincible*. Not only does the system protect the carriers from aerial threats, but it also has an anti-surface role as well—providing, of course, that the single launcher remains operational. During its initial sea time there were faults in the magazine feed but these have now been cleared and the missile has carried out some astonishing feats during exhaustive trials, including the destruction of two silver-foil covered balloons—one at high level and one at sea level—after a simultaneous launch. The missile uses semi-active homing and it is powered by a Rolls Royce ramjet motor to give it a high sustained speed. In the Royal Navy, the system is classified as GWS30 (Guided Weapons System 30).

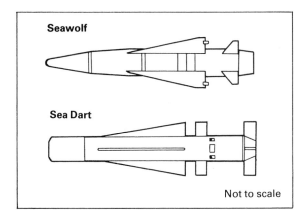

Seawolf (GWS 25)

Role Point defence SAM/SSM; **Status** In service; **Weight** Circa 80 kg; **Length** Circa 2.0 m; **Body diameter** Circa 0.175 m; **Warhead charge** HE; **Velocity** Circa Mach 2.0; **Rate of fire** Classified; **Range** Circa 10 km; **Manufacturer** BAe Dynamics; **Ships equipped** *Leander* and *Broadsword* Classes.

Another classic British design, the British Aerospace Dynamics Group Seawolf GWS 25 is capable of destroying both aircraft and missile targets in a point defence role. In other words, if a hostile penetrates the MEZ of the area defence Sea Dart, then the Sea Wolf has the job of destroying the missile before it reaches its target. The launcher, carried on the *Broadsword* Class and some of the *Leander* Class frigates, contains six individual missiles encased in their own containers which are reloaded from adjacent missile lifts from the ship's magazine where, unusually, the missile can be

stored vertically. The Seawolf is treated as a round of ammunition and has a service life of at least 15 months before it needs to be serviced. Vertical stowage does give the missile greater immunity from damage due to underwater explosions because, like all missiles, it is a highly complex piece of kit. The missile launcher is fully automatic and has a very rapid reaction time.

During trials in 1980/81, the GWS 25 successfully intercepted a great variety of targets including a standard 114 mm RN shell round in mid-flight! Sadly, the system is rather expensive and at the time of writing it was not envisaged that it would be fitted to other warships at present, even though the *Invincible* Class are particularly in need of a PDMS and events in the South Atlantic have demonstrated the RN's vulnerability to ASV missiles such as Exocet; it seems likely that the inevitable post mortem will produce a significant re-appraisal of the

Sea Dart missile launch from Type 42 (BAe).

Seawolf missile launch (BAe).

Left Battleaxe's *GWS 25 installation.*

Below *Possible installation of Seawolf in Type 21, made unlikely because of Defence Cuts, yet desirable from the RN's point of view and one of the points which will be discussed in the aftermath of the Falkland operations* (Vosper Thornycroft).

Below right *Seaslug, the beam-riding missile system on the stern of a* County Class DLG.

cost-effectiveness of systems like Seawolf and Sea Dart, especially in the lightweight form or containerised for merchant ships in a war zone.

Seaslug

Role Long range SAM; **Status** In service; **Weight** ? kg; **Length** 6 m; **Body diameter** 0.41 m; **Warhead charge** He/proximity/DA*; **Velocity** Transonic; **Rate of fire** N/A but reloads carried; **Range** 45 km plus; **Manufacturer** BAe Dynamics; **Ships equipped** *County* Class.

* Delayed action.

The beam-riding Seaslug missile system was designed as the primary weapon of the *County* Class DLG where it is carried in the stern position, abaft the flight deck. As the Class has two Batches, so the Seaslug has two marks corresponding with the respective sub-group. Although on the exterior there is no difference between the Mark 1 and the Mark 2, the latter is credited with a slightly enchanced range. The missile is also capable of an SSM role.

On launching, the missile is accelerated by four wrap-around solid fuel boosters which are ejected after several seconds leaving the solid fuel sustainer motor to continue the flight to the target. Guidance is provided by the Type 901 radar using beam-riding techniques for an incredible 45 km plus.

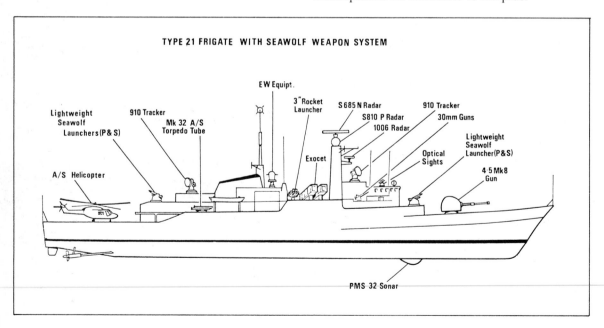

TYPE 21 FRIGATE WITH SEAWOLF WEAPON SYSTEM

Lightweight Seawolf Launchers (P & S) · 910 Tracker · Mk 32 A/S Torpedo Tube · EW Equipt. · 3" Rocket Launcher · S 685 N Radar · S810 P Radar · 1006 Radar · 910 Tracker · 30mm Guns · Lightweight Seawolf Launcher(P&S) · Exocet · Optical Sights · A/S Helicopter · 4·5 Mk8 Gun · PMS 32 Sonar

Aboard ship, the missile is automaticaly loaded and handled from the magazine with two missiles being presented to the launcher ready for action. The launcher trains to follow the contact until a launch position is reached. The target is destroyed by the high explosive warhead using either delayed-action, proximity or contact fuzes. The system will not remain in service after the demise of the *County* Class DLGs, probably in 1984/5.

Seacat
Role Close range SAM/SSM; **Status** In service; **Weight** 68 kg (launcher 4,700 kg); **Length** 2.0 m; **Body diameter** 0.60 m; **Warhead charge** HE; **Velocity** Subsonic; **Rate of fire** Single; **Range** 4.75 km; **Manufacturer** Short Bros & Harland;

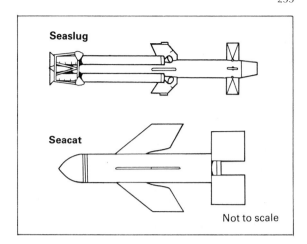

Seaslug

Seacat

Not to scale

A Leander Class frigate's Seacat launcher and guidance.

Ships equipped *Hermes*; *County*, *Leander*, *Amazon* and *Rothesay* Classes.

Seacat was introduced to service in 1962 and today is probably the world's most widely used naval guided weapon system. It is a first generation weapon, but it has, over the years, been continuously uprated to meet the needs of the modern RN; the latest development being the introduction of sea-skimming height control which prevents the missile from ditching.

The lightweight missile and launcher is reliable in the close-in (but not PD) environment, being equally effective against surface or aerial targets. The normal launcher complement is four missiles which have to be hand-loaded using special cradles.

The missile is powered by a boost charge which moves it away from the ship where a sustainer takes over to propel it to a target within 4.75 km. There is no pre-firing 'warm-up' period required and the missile is activated at launch. Line of sight, manual radar (dark fire) or radar tracking (blind fire) modes are possible as engagement techniques. The system is probably destined to continue in service with the RN until the demise of the *Amazon* Class at the end of the decade.

Sub-Harpoon

Role Submarine SSM; **Status** On order (Service entry 1982); **Weight** 900 kg; **Length** 0.80 m; **Body diameter** 0.30 m; **Warhead charge** Classified; **Velocity** Subsonic; **Rate of fire** Classified; **Range** Classified; **Manufacturer** McDonnell Douglas; **Ships equipped** To be announced, but probably all *Valiant*, *Swiftsure* and *Trafalgar* Classes.

The Sub-Harpoon programme began in 1972 when the US Navy became interested in a submarine-launched variant of the already successful air-launched Harpoon missile. The RN submarine *Churchill* carried an eight-month trials programme in American waters during 1979/80 to prove the missile's adaptability for use in the new generation of SSNs currently being built and for those which have already entered service. In the trials, the *Churchill* fired more than 120 capsules including six live firings of Sub-Harpoon against ship targets—all of which were successful.

This missile gives the RN an over the horizon capability for the first time and enhances the already formidable armament of the Tigerfish Mk 24 torpedo in SSNs. The missile is launched from standard tubes; on breaking the surface, a booster motor cuts in to provide the acceleration necessary to sustain flight. Guidance is pre-programmed, although there is mid-course guidance available and it is thought that Naval helicopters acting in a Task Force situation may be able to provide this facet of the flight envelope. Terminal guidance is thought to be by means of radar homing.

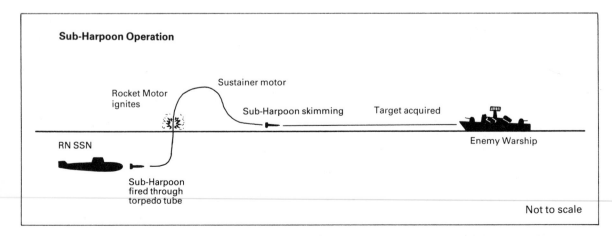

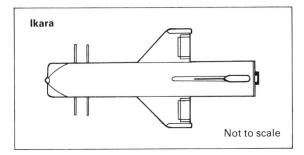

Ikara

Role Vehicle to deliver ASW weapon; **Status** In service; **Weight** Classified; **Length** 0.342 m; **Height** 0.157 m; **Span** 0.152 m; **Weapon** Mk 44 or Mk 46 torpedo; **Velocity** Subsonic; **Rate of fire** Classified; **Range** 24 km; **Manufacturer** BAe/ Australian government; **Ships equipped** *Leander*, *Bristol* and *Sheffield* Classes.

Although generally described as a missile, this Anglo-Australian product is really an ASW torpedo launch vehicle which takes a standard Mk 44 or Mk 46 torpedo to a target out of range of other ship-borne systems. The Ikara body is propelled by a solid fuel rocket and derives its targeting information from the mother ship or from ASW helicopters such as the Sea King or Wessex 3. Once in the target area the torpedo, which spent the flight semi-enclosed in the Ikara body, drops by parachute to the sea from where it becomes a conventional homing torpedo. The Ikara body clears the area and is lost.

The launching mode is from a special piece of equipment in the forward end of the warship which allows the Ikara to be ejected at 55°. The system is capable of operating in all weather conditions and is

An Ikara launch showing the guided weapon speeding skywards with a Mk 46 torpedo underslung (BAe).

In the Ikara preparation room where the body comes up from the ship's magazine and is fitted with finlets and prepared for flight. The scene is aboard Galatea *(RN).*

controlled by one man in the ship's operations room. Advantages of the system are rapid reaction, silent approach to the target and that it accepts data from multiple sources. The possible disadvantages are that the latest type of Soviet submarine is thought to be able to outrun the Ikara's operational pattern and this may account for the fact that only eight *Leander* Class frigates were modified to receive the system. Certainly the Mark 2 variant will not be developed for the RN.

Exocet MM38

Role SSM. (The RN does not possess the AM39 airborne variant used so destructively by Argentine Super Etendard aircraft); **Status** In service; **Weight** Classified; **Length** 5.20 m; **Body diameter** 0.348 m; **Warhead charge** HE 150–200 kg; **Velocity** Mach 1; **Rate of fire** Single or salvo; **Range** 38 km; **Manufacturer** Aérospatiale; **Ships equipped** *Amazon*, *Leander* and *County* (Batch 2) Classes.

The RN had to turn to France to purchase an 'off the shelf' missile for the ASV role enhancement required by the *Amazon* Class FFH and by the refitted *Leander* Class frigates. Both Classes of warship carry four non-reloadable Exocets forward of the bridge and in the case of the *Leanders* the launchers have replaced the twin 114 mm guns. In addition, it was decided to refit the last four *County* Class DLGs—the Batch 2 warships—with a battery of four launchers in place of 'B' turret.

The missile provides the Fleet with an updated, over the horizon, ASV capability, although the fact that the units cannot be reloaded from shipborne supplies must be a disadvantage. At the time of writing it was believed the missile was mainly useful against smaller warship targets, particularly FPBs and corvettes, and it was thought that against larger targets more than one Exocet would be fired in salvo; however, the missile's ability to cause fierce fires in lightly armour-clad vessels has now been sadly proven, so this assessment is another which will require revision.

Exocet is pre-programmed for the immediate post-launch phase of its flight with active homing on to the target at the end. It has a sea-skimming ability using a radio altimeter for height determination although it is considered a first generation weapon and may well be replaced in RN warships by Sea Eagle in 1985+.

Exocet launch: trials were conducted in Norfolk *during 1974* (RN).

Exocet—the refit equipment in Antrim, *a DLG.*

Polaris A3 RN

Role Submarine-launched Ballistic Missile (SLBM); **Status** In service but approaching obsolescence; **Weight** 16,257 kg (launch); **Length** 9.7 m; **Body diameter** 1.37 m; **Range** 2,500 nm (4,600 km); **Ships equipped** SSBNs.

The Polaris is an American-designed missile manufactured by over 800 sub-contractors in the UK and the USA. It is a two-stage missile with inertial guidance, deploying multiple re-entry vehicles (MRVs) of about 3×200 kilotons capacity. Each missile is housed in its own launch tube which is pressurised to slightly above the local sea water pressure prior to launch. High pressure gas is then squirted into the bottom end of the tube to launch the Polaris to the surface where the first-stage motor ignites. The only sensation experienced by SSBN crews during the launch of practice rounds has been a quiet hiss and a slight vibration. The first-

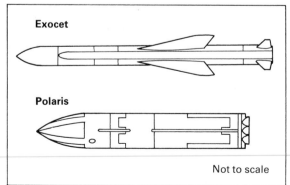

Exocet

Polaris

Not to scale

stage motor lasts for about one minute and is replaced by a second-stage unit after separation of the burnt-out motor. During powered flight, inertial guidance puts the missile on course, controlling yaw, pitch and roll. At a predetermined moment, the guidance system shuts off the rocket motor and would trigger separation of the re-entry module with the MRV warheads for ballistic trajectory to the target.

The missiles have a range of 2,500 nm and are equipped with British warheads which are loaded at Coulport within the Clyde Submarine complex. It should be noted that the furthest point from the sea is near Lake Baikal, USSR, which is 1,720 nm (3,185 km) inland.

The targeting of a Polaris missile is a political decision notified to the boat by special LF radio transmission or preprogrammed onboard. It takes a number of special checks to launch a Polaris missile and no error is allowed in the system.

The British Government has published the following figures for the balance of strategic forces:
SLBMs Warsaw Pact-950; NATO-700 (including French M20 SLBMs).

The RN feel that the present Polaris system, which is now approaching obsolescence in the RN and has been replaced by Poseidon and Trident in the US Navy, could be kept operational into the 1990s and fitted into new submarines. The present *R*-Class hulls are now approaching the time when replacement will be required.

The Polaris missiles would need new motors and much of the support equipment would have to be replaced. Certainly, the removal of the firing and support equipment from the existing boats into a new Class would not be easy and the cost saving would be marginal. As an interim plan the RN will be receiving Chevaline*—updated Polaris missiles in the near future. This system costs about £1,000 million and will entail a new warhead system which will allow manoeuvring in space, but will fall short of a true multiple independently targeted re-entry vehicle system (MIRV) as with the current US and Soviet systems. Chevaline would remain credible until the mid- to late 1990s, when the Trident force could be expected to come into service.

The debate about a replacement for the Polaris has been long and deep; many believe that there is no need for a replacement and that the RN (and therefore the UK) should not have a credible deterrent of nuclear strategic weapons, remaining under a US umbrella instead. Between 1982 and

* Chevaline is the code name for the updating project.

Right *British Polaris missile launching at the Cape Kennedy testing range* (Navy International).

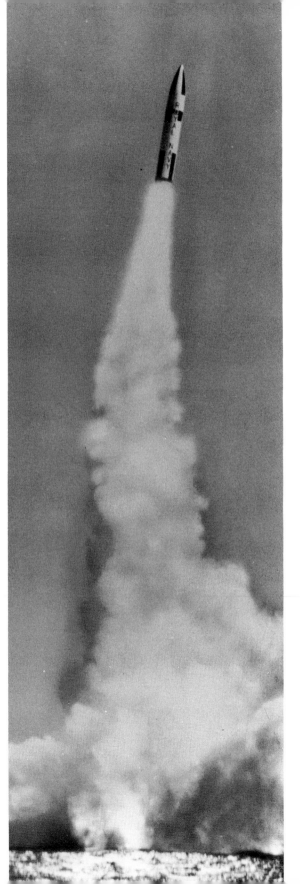

warheads). The main advantage of the Trident over the enhanced capability Polaris is that the former is expected to be able to survive in the Soviet Anti-Ballistic Missile (ABM) zone better because of updated avionics and the eight MIRVs carried. In addition, the submarines carrying the Trident would be able to hide in a greater sea area because of the latter's greater range—nearly twice that of Polaris. The House of Commons Select Committee on Defence announced in 1981 that they believed that no RN SSBN had ever been tracked or located by a potential enemy.

It is the policy of HM Government that no British strategic weapon would be used as a first strike weapon against any nation.

Ordnance

20 mm Single Oerlikon

Date* 1940s; **Status** In service; **Calibre** 20 mm; **Crew** 1–2; **Director** Local control; **Muzzle velocity** 835 m/sec; **Rate of fire** 800 rpm (60 rounds max burst); **Projectile weight** 0.40 kg; **Traverse arc** Unlimited; **Elevation** −15°–+80°; **Gun weight** Circa 250 kg; **Barrel length** 75 calibres (1.5 m); **Range** 2.2 nm (4 km); **Ammunition** HE;APSE; **Manufacturer** Oerlikon, Bührle and others; **Ships equipped** Most RN surface combat units and patrol vessels; some RFAs fitted for, but not with, 20 mm.

The ubiquitous Oerlikon 20 mm has been with the Fleet for local defence and AA duties for many years, but is due to be replaced in the near future. The design appears to have originated in Switzerland but has been used by many nations seeking a small, accurate and flexible gun for patrol/police work. The usual sighting uses ring and bead and the mounting can be operated by one man, or two if a loader is required. The usual mounting has a steel mini-shield.

20 mm Vulcan Phalanx CIWS

Date 1982; **Status** In service; **Calibre** 20 mm; **Crew** Automatic; **Director** Closed-loop spotting/tracking; **Muzzle velocity** Classified; **Rate of fire** 3,000 rpm; **Projectile weight** Classified; **Traverse arc** 360°; **Elevation** −35°-+90°; **Ammunition** Discarding-sabot; **Gun weight** Circa 1,000 kg; **Range** Circa 1 nm (1.85 km); **Barrel length** Classified; **Manufacturer** General Dynamics; **Ships equipped** *Illustrious* (others possible).

The second *Invincible* Class light aircraft carrier is the first warship in the Royal Navy to have been

The 20 mm Oerlikon mounting on a Leander.

1994, it is expected that the UK will spend £6,000 million on the development of a strategic deterrent force based on the Trident missile and a new Class of SSBN, perhaps similar to the USN's *Ohio* boats which are about to enter service. The *Ohios* themselves would, however, be too large for British installations to handle so a design between the existing *R* Class and the US boats is envisaged. The submarines themselves are reported to cost about £1,500 million for four hulls, with a further £600 million being spent on the purchase of the US Trident 2D5 units with British warheads costing £1,500 million, shore installations of £600 million and miscellaneous hardware for the submarines at £800 million. Shore installations are already under construction at the Clyde and will be finished in about 1989, three years after work will begin on the construction of the new hulls, probably at Vickers, Barrow-in-Furness.

Trident 2D5

Role SLBM; **Status** Under construction; RN order July 1980; **Weight** Circa 30,000 kg; **Length** 10.36 m; **Body diameter** Circa 2; **Range** 4,000 nm (7,408 km).

The Trident has a three-stage propulsion system but on different design to that of the Polaris, requiring only one nozzle per stage, instead of four with the latter. The propellant is solid fuel and the guidance inertial. It is designed to carry up to eight independently targetable warheads and the first missiles went to sea operationally with the US Navy in 1979.

The Trident 2D5 is a larger missile and would be deployed in perhaps 12 tubes per submarine (or 384

---

* Throughout this section, the date given is that of the system/equipment entering service.

fitted with a CIWS (Close-In Weapon System). Despite the arsenal of anti-aircraft missiles available to the Fleet, experience during the Falklands has shown that a 'last ditch' gun defence is vital, especially for large targets like a carrier. Apparently, in early 1982 (ie, before the Falklands), the RN had ordered a number of USN Mk 15 CIWS – the Vulcan Phalanx – for the larger units of the Fleet. The accelerated completion of *Illustrious* led to the fitting of the first two sets of CIWS aboard her: one right aft and the other for'ard. Basically, the system uses the American Vulcan 20 mm Gatling-gun cannon with a special tracking unit which brings the target (aircraft or missile) within the arc of fire. Many observers believe that this system would have saved warships in the Falklands.

It is understood that the RN will purchase the more advanced Swiss-made Seaguard system in due course.

30 mm Rarden LS Mounting

Date Under consideration; **Status** Under consideration; **Calibre** 30 mm; **Crew** Not yet known; **Director** Sea Archer (?); **Muzzle velocity** 1,070 m/sec; **Rate of fire** 90 rpm (6 round max burst); **Projectile weight** 0.35–0.90 kg; **Traverse arc** Unlimited; **Elevation** −20°–+70° (35°/sec); **Gun weight** 800 kg (with mounting); **Barrel length** 81 calibres (2.44 m); **Range** 2.2 nm (4 km); **Ammunition** HE; APSE; **Manufacturer** Royal Ordnance Factory; **Ships equipped** Under consideration.

The search for a new light gun for the RN includes the 30 mm Rarden cannon on a Laurence Scott mounting. It is seen here under test (Plessey).

All RNR tenders are armed with 40 mm Bofors guns (see next page) as seen here during a drill aboard Hubberston (RN).

The 30 mm Rarden with the Laurence Scott mounting was tested at Fraser Gunnery Ranges during 1980–81 as a replacement for the 20 mm and perhaps for the 40 mm mountings currently in service. Sea trials were carried out in *Londonderry* during the middle of 1981 and proved that the LS30R gun mounting is accurate in its intended patrol/police role from OPVs and similar. During tests, a small target (2 m²) was hit in poor visibility at 1,000–1,300 m for 80 per cent of the firing time. So far, three marks have been announced:

Mk 1 Locally controlled by a standing operator using line-of-sight tracking with binocular and image intensifier in low light.

Mk 2 As per Mk 1 but with remote control facility, capacity for dual role as optical director and optional clip-on magazine for 21 rounds total.

Mk 3 As per Mk 2, but with on-mount digital predictor with head-up-display (HUD) readings to operator using Ferranti F100-L microprocessor. With this Mark it is envisaged by *NAVY international* that first shot hits will be achieved.

40 mm Single Mounting Mk 7 and 9

Date 1946; **Status** In service; **Calibre** 40 mm; **Crew** 2–3; **Director** Visual or 1006 radar; **Muzzle velocity** 1,000 m/sec; **Rate of fire** 300 rpm; **Projectile weight** 2.4 kg; **Traverse arc** Unlimited; **Elevation** $-10°-+90°$ (45°/sec); **Gun weight** Circa 3 tons; **Barrel length** 60 or 70 calibres (2.4–2.8 m); **Range** 2.2 nm (4 km); **Ammunition** HE; **Manufacturer** Bofors, Sweden; **Ships equipped** *Leander*, Type 22, *Intrepid, Fearless, Ton, Castle, Hunt, Island* and *Ley* Classes.

The Bofors 40 mm has been a standard AA and general-purpose mounting, both single and twin, since the end of the war and at one time was the standard AA weapon of the Fleet. Today, it has a mainly police role especially in Fisheries' Protection and with the Hong Kong Squadron. The mountings in the RN are open and are usually powered to give rapid target training and following. Local gunnery control is usually practised with gyrostablised sights with speed rings. This weapon will probably be replaced by the 76 mm Oto Melara and the 30 mm Rarden guns currently under trials at the Fraser Gunnery Range.

76 mm Oto Melara

Date 1969; **Status** In service; **Calibre** 76 mm; **Crew** Fully automatic; **Director** Sea Archer; **Muzzle velocity** 925 m/sec; **Rate of fire** 85 rpm; **Projectile weight** 6.2 kg; **Traverse arc** Unlimited; **Elevation** $-15°-+85°$ (35°/sec); **Gun weight** 7.5 tons; **Barrel length** 62 calibres (4.71 m); **Range** 9 nm (16 km); **Ammunition** HE, star, etc; **Manufacturer** Oto Melara, Italy; **Ships equipped** *Peacock* Class (on completion).

This mounting, with its excellent depression, has been chosen for the *Peacock* Class of OPVs destined to serve with the Hong Kong Squadron in the 1983–1990 period. The mounting has a glass fibre turret and is fully automatic from the operations room, needing no crew closed-up in the turret during the action. Many think there is a need to fit such a mounting to the new *Castle* OPV2s as well. The gun is equally effective against surface or aerial targets.

Trials began at *Cambridge* Gunnery Range in late 1981 with the associated Sperry Sea Archer fire-control system also being utilised. One of the drawbacks with the system may be that the Type 1006 is the only fire control radar available to the *Peacock* Class.

Top left *The Vickers Mk 8 mounting for the 114 mm gun: Newcastle at sea.* **Centre left** *The Mk 6 mounting for the 114 mm gun in Achilles.* **Left** *The Corvus decoy launcher of a Leander Class frigate, starboard side.*

114 mm Twin Mounting Mk 6

Date 1946; **Status** In service; not in production; **Calibre** 114 mm; Crew 4 (also semi-automatic); **Director** MRS 3; **Muzzle velocity** 850 m/sec; **Rate of fire** 20 rpm/barrel; **Projectile weight** 25 kg; **Traverse arc** 180°; **Elevation** −10°−+70°; **Gun weight** 50 tons; **Barrel length** 50 claibres (5.70 m); **Range** 10 nm (19 km); **Ammunition** Full range; **Manufacturer** Vickers; **Ships equipped** *County*, *Leander* and *Rothesay* Classes.

The twin 4.5-in (114 mm) turret of the *County* Class and the older general-purpose/AS frigates was first introduced for the *Daring* Class in the immediate postwar years. It is in widespread service in the Commonwealth and other foreign navies, being relatively simple and hazardless. It is controlled by means of a joystick at local level but is normally electro-hydraulically remotely controlled from the operations room. Unlike the later Mk 8, the loading process is not fully automatic. It is envisaged that this system and mounting will remain in service until the mid-1980s when the last *Gun Leander* is paid off.

114 mm Single Mounting Mk 8

Date 1971; **Status** In service; **Calibre** 114 mm; **Crew** None closed-up (operations room); **Director** GWS 22; **Muzzle velocity** 850 m/sec; **Rate of fire** 20 rpm; **Projectile weight** 36.5 kg; **Traverse arc** 170° (40°/sec); **Elevation** −10°−+55° (40°/sec); **Gun weight** 25.75 tonnes; **Barrel length** 55 calibres (6.22 m); **Range** 12 nm (22 km); **Ammunition** New range for gun includes HE and star; **Manufacturer** Vickers; **Ships equipped** Types 21 and 42 and *Bristol* Class.

The Vickers Mk 8 mounting was trialed aboard *Bristol* and fitted to the Type 21 *Amazon* Class and to the Type 42 *Sheffield* Class in the early 1970s to 1980s. It has also been installed in several Classes of foreign warship. It is undoubtedly a superb mounting with no crew closed-up in the turret and control being performed from the ship's operations room. It is a multi-role concept which is able to engage surface and air targets. The gun has special effect against surface targets because of its accuracy, against land targets because of its range, against aerial targets because of its quick reaction time and for patrol/police duties because of its flexibility. The Mk 8 was designed with a special range of ordnance which consists of star-shells or proximity-fuzed HE rounds; they can be interchanged within seconds. The suite of rounds has a chaff item which is designed to produce false echoes on the enemy's search radar/fire control radar, thus causing confusion in a tactical situation.

Corvus Countermeasures Launcher

Date 1950s; **Status** In service; **Calibre** Various; **Crew** Automatic; **Director** Automatic; **Muzzle velocity** Inapplicable; **Rate of fire** Various; **Projectile weight** Various; **Traverse arc** Unlimited; **Elevation** Inapplicable; **Weight** Various; **Barrel length** Various; **Range** Various; **Ammunition** Various; **Manufacturer** Plessey; **Ships equipped** Most surface combat units.

Radar confusion is the main rationale behind the use of Corvus or Wallop launchers for Chaff. The system can also be used to launch infra-red sources away from a target and for illunination flares.

Chaff comes in several forms: Chem Chaff which is used in conjunction with active EW jammers and infra-red decoys as a defence against radar guidance systems for incoming weapons. The usual material is aluminium-coated glass filament to give fine dipoles which fall at a rate of 0.29 m^{-1}, or cut aluminium foil, silver-coated nylon filament and other reflective media. There is also a hand-held Chaff dispenser for ground environments which can be fitted with cartridges for survival and rescue operations. Plessey Aerospace produce a Broadband Chaff (BBC) Rocket Decoy System for use against the modern range of anti-ship missiles. These systems allow for seduction and distraction of weapons. Decoys are usually fired to operate at about 200 m and at ranges of 800–1,800 m from the launching ship.

Limbo Mk 10 AS Mortar

Date 1955; **Status** In service but obsolete; **Calibre** 305 mm; **Crew** 7; **Muzzle velocity** Inapplicable; **Rate of fire** 3 rounds per shoot; **Projectile weight** 200 kg; **Range** 1–2,000 m; **Ammunition** DA and hydrostatic fuze; **Manufacturer** MoD(N); **Ships equipped** *Leander* Class, Type 12 and older warships.

The Limbo is a trainable launcher for anti-submarine projectiles of delayed action and hydrostatic fuze types which are deployed in the older frigates and *Bristol* for point defence against submarines. It is acknowledged today that the Limbo is not an effective weapon for killing hostile submarines but it would 'put the enemy skipper off his aim'. The mortar is trained automatically via the operations room and hull-mounted sonar information and the firing sequence is also automatic; the mortar is stabilised for pitch and roll.

Depth charges

Although the AS Mk 10 Limbo system is still in service with the Royal Navy in limited units, the use of the depth charge from warships has been

overtaken by the AS torpedo. The depth charge associated with the Limbo has delayed action or hydrostatic fuze to explode in front of the target and thus cause damage to the pressure hull and fittings. It is unlikely that a single depth charge will critically damage a modern submarine but it could give the surface ship a chance to evade a submarine-launched torpedo and to manoeuvre into a better AS position. The depth charge was invented many years ago and introduced to the RN during World War 1. Basically, it remains the same today—134 kg of explosive with a depth limit of about 90 m.

In the 1950s, the US Navy introduced the nuclear depth charge or Lulu but it is not used in the conventional way by the RN because it requires a vehicle to take it away from the launching warship. It is posible that certain systems could be fitted with nuclear warheads, but this has never been acknowldeged by the RN. There are warheads for aerial torpedoes, however, although which ships' flights are equipped is classified for obvious reasons.

STWS

The Shipborne Torpedo Weapons System is fitted to *Leander*, *Amazon* and *Sheffield* Class warships for launching heavyweight torpedoes against sub-

marine targets. The main torpedo used is the Mk 46 and the more obsolescent Mk 44. The STWS is known to the RN as the AS Launcher Mk 32 and three tubes are usually situated amidships with gantry and hatch equipment for reloading. The calibre is 32 cm.

Torpedoes

The RN has an inventory of heavyweight (ship/submarine-launched) and lightweight torpedoes which are designated by Marks. The former free-running torpedoes have now been replaced by complex guided torpedoes which are, for all intents and purposes, underwater guided missiles.

The heavyweight torpedoes of the RN are described below; the lightweight torpedoes are described under the Air Launched Weapons heading earlier.

In addition to these offensive systems, the RN uses a special torpedo-like device as an ASW target. Called the Deep Mobile Target and produced by EMI Electronics, the DMT is capable of preprogrammed manoeuvres and of simulating the acoustic and automotive characteristics of conventional submarines. It can travel at speeds between eight and 22 knots and run to a depth of 1,200 ft (366 m). This system is used to supplement the use of training submarines of the *P* and *O* Classes for ASW exercises and trials. **Dimensions** 3.28 m × 0.32 m; **Weight** 236 kg. Compatible with submarine and surface ship torpedo tubes.

Mark 8

Purpose Anti-ship; **Status** In service but obsolete; **Length** 6.70 m; **Diameter** 0.533 m; **Weight** 1,535 kg; **Propulsion** Compressed air; **Range** Up to 2 nm (4.5 km); **Velocity** Circa 45 knots; **Running** Down to 18 m; **Ships equipped** Patrol Submarines.

The Mark 8 was developed for the inter-war classes of conventional submarine and is now being rapidly replaced by the Mark 24 Tigerfish in all RN SSKs. Despite its age and its outmoded free-running, pre-set depth and course criteria, the torpedo has proved to be a most useful training aid. It was formerly used by destroyers in the anti-ship role. This weapon, launched from a British SSN, sank the Argentine cruiser *Belgrano* in May 1982 off the Falklands.

Mark 20 (Improved)

Purpose Anti-submarine homing; **Status** In service but obsolescent; **Length** 4.11 m; **Diameter** 0.533 m; **Weight** 820 kg; **Propulsion** Electric; **Range** Up to 5.9 nm (11 km); **Velocity** 20 knots;

Left *The Limbo Mk 10 mortar of a Leander is fired at Chatham Navy Days.*

Right *The Mk 32 STWS tubes in Cleopatra, with a Corvus launcher to the left.*

Below right *Loading a Mk 24 Tigerfish torpedo aboard an SSK; note the torpedo lighter alongside* (HMS Dolphin).

Running Down to 244 m; **Ships equipped** Patrol Submarines.

The Mark 20 (Improved) is an acoustic homing torpedo now used for anti-submarine training only and build by Vickers with a warhead charge of 91 kg HE. It is designed to seek passively for a target submarine and is being superseded by the Mark 24 Tigerfish; the Mark 23 as described below is a development of this weapon.

Mark 23

Purpose Anti-submarine homing; **Status** In service but obsolescent; **Length** Circa 5.0 m; **Diameter** 0.533 m; **Weight** Circa 1,220 kg; **Propulsion** Electric; **Range** Up to 4.3 nm (8 km); **Velocity** Circa 20 knots; **Running** Down to 250 m; **Ships equipped** SSKs and SSNs.

Described now as a training torpedo, the Mark 23 was the first wire-guided torpedo to be placed in service with the RN, but retaining a passive acoustic homing head for the final tracking of the target.

Mark 24

Purpose Anti-ship and anti-submarine; **Status** Mk 24 Mod 0 in service 1974 and being replaced by Mod 1 from 1978; **Length** 6.46 m; **Diameter** 0.533 m; **Weight** 1,550 kg; **Propulsion** Electric; **Range** Circa 18.9 nm (35 km); **Velocity** Circa 45 knots; **Running** Down to Circa 300 m; **Ships equipped** SSKs, SSNs and SSBNs.

The Tigerfish took nearly 15 years to develop and the first Mod 0 torpedoes were not in service with the Fleet until 1974. Since the original design concept, the Soviet Navy has placed greater emphasis on the design and construction of fast, deep-running

submarines and this in turn has led to modifications to the Tigerfish and the development of NST 7525. The Tigerfish is carried in nearly all the RN's submarines and is guided by wire and an active/passive homing device for the final attack sequence. With impact and proximity fuzes, plus a two-speed attack pattern, the torpedo is able to cope with all but the newest submarine developments.

NST 7525

Purpose Advanced anti-ship and anti-submarine; **Status** Ordered into production in December 1981; **Length** Not known; **Diameter** 0.533 m; **Weight**

Not known; **Propulsion** Electric; **Range** Estimated 21.6 nm (40 km); **Velocity** Estimated 80 knots; **Running** Down to estimated 300 m; **Ships equipped** None as yet.

The Naval Staff Target 7525 torpedo has been developed by Marconi in the face of competition from the US. The torpedo is a development of the aerial-launched Stingray with wire-guidance, active and passive homing and the ability to attack the most vulnerable part of the target. It is thought that the torpedo has a quick dash ability to counter the high underwater speeds of the modern Soviet submarine. It is not expected that this weapon will be in service before 1985.

Mark 44

Purpose Anti-submarine (lightweight); **Status** In service but obsolescent; **Length** 2.56 m; **Diameter** 0.324 m; **Weight** 233 kg; **Propulsion** Electric; **Range** 2.7 nm (5 km); **Velocity** Circa 30 knots; **Running** Down to 300 m; **Ships equipped** STWS and Ikara equipped Classes.

The American-built Mark 44 is an active homing torpedo with wire-guided initial guidance from the Mk 32 STWS tube or from an air-dropped situation (aerial weapons are described separately). Today, it is mainly used for training and has been replaced by the Mark 46 and Stingray.

Mark 46

Purpose Anti-submarine; **Status** In service; **Length** 2.56 m; **Diameter** 0.324 m; **Weight** 230 kg;

A Mk 44 torpedo is fired from Mk 32 STWS—note wire-guide (Vosper Thornycroft).

Propulsion Liquid fuel; **Range** 5.9 nm (11 km); **Velocity** 40 knots; **Running** Down to 300 m; **Ships equipped** STWS and Ikara equipped Classes.

The American Mark 46 is used operational in the STWS and the Ikara launch vehicle systems, as well as being deployed from aircraft. The torpedo is guided by active and/or passive homing devices. Various modifications are in service, although the exact deployment is not known at present. These mods are in terms of propulsion: **Mod 0** (1965)—solid fuel monopropellant; **Mod 1** (1967)—liquid fuel monopropellant; and **Mod 2** (1972)—improved version of Mod 1.

Naval radars

Since the early days of the Second World War, the RN has been increasingly reliant on radars to observe, track, locate and designate the surface and air environment in which its ships sail. Although the radars of today are complex, highly technical and very reliable, the modern war scenario does envisage that warships, unless detected, will be on passage with the medium of active radar in operation. The look-out—the infamous Eye Ball Mk 1—is still important in the modern RN. There are currently a large number of radars at sea with the RN, but only the more important ones are described. The full list is given below, but its accuracy cannot be guaranteed because of the confidentiality aspects of radar.

Type	Purpose	Status
268	Surface search	Obsolete
278	Height finding	Obsolescent
901	Target tracking	Obsolescent
909	Target tracking	In service
910	Target tracking	In service
912	Fire control	In service
965	Air search	In service
967	Surveillance	In service
968	Surveillance	In service
975	Navigation	Obsolescent
975ZW	Minehunting	In service
978	Navigation	In service
992	Long range search	Obsolescent
992Q	AIO	In service
993	Tactical air search	In service
994	993 update equipment	In service
996	Long-range search	Development
1003	Navigation	In service
1006	Navigation	In service
1022	Search	In service

In addition, there is the GWS22/MRS3 fire control radar for Seacat SAM and gunfire. The

Naval equipment, weapons and sensors

Right *Glamorgan's Type 901 Seaslug radar.*

Below right *A view of Norfolk showing the Type 227/278 radar (nodding type) on the mainmast, below the Type 965, together with MRS3 fire control equipment abeam of the funnel.*

Bottom right Newcastle *at sea, showing, inter alia, two Type 909 radars in protective housings, fore and aft, plus Type 992Q on the mainmast.*

Sperry Sea Archer equipment is for fire control but usually relies on input from another radar; in the RN this is the Type 1006.

Type 268 A few older ships of the Fleet and the Reserve are equipped with this radar for surface search.

Type 278 This is the nodding height-finding radar used to support Wessex HAS 3 operations aboard the *County* Class DLGs. It is of open lattice design and will vanish from service with the demise of the last Batch 2 *Counties*, by 1985.

Type 901 Another *County* Class DLG set, this is used for target-tracking by the beam-riding Seaslug missile. It is found toward the stern of the DLG in the shape of a 'searchlight'. It will vanish from service with the demise of its host class.

Type 909 This is the target tracking radar for the Sea Dart system and is fitted to *Invincible, Sheffield* and *Bristol* Classes. It is often enclosed in a GRP dome to protect it from the harsh maritime environment. It is understood that ECCM systems are incorporated to counter enemy ECM. The antenna is Cassegrain type, with an IFF housing; the main dish has a diameter of 2.44 m. The set is manufactured by Marconi.

Type 910 This is the target tracking radar for GWS25/Seawolf and is fitted to the *Broadsword* Class and certain units of the *Leander* Class on refit. It operates in conjunction with the Type 967/968 radars. It is a complex antenna with one major and two minor dishes, as well as optronics gear for low-light and visual tracking. It is manufactured by Marconi.

Type 912 This is the commercial design by Selenia, known as the RTN-10X Orion fire control radar fitted to the Type 21 frigates. It has a range of

about 21.6 nm (40 km) and can be operated by one man. It is linked into the GWS24 system and can be used for low altitude search to augment the other tracking/search radars. Two sets are carried, one aft of the bridge and the other aft of the funnel on a small control structure.

Type 965 This is the ubiquitous long-range air search radar fitted to *County* Class, *Leander* Class, Type 42, *Hermes* and *Bristol*-type warships of the RN. It comes in two forms; the AKE-1 single bedstead and the AKE-2 double bedstead designs with associated IFF. It can also be used for target designation. Antenna height is 2.72 m with a length of 7.92 m; the double bedstead increases the height to 5.11 m. The double array weighs an incredible 2,490 kg and hence the replacement of this set with lighter units on more modern and refitted warships. The Batch 2 and 3 Type 42s will be equipped with Type 1022 as a replacement.

Type 967 This is the air search facet of the Seawolf system and is integral with the Type 968 to form a single radar system/array. It is to be found atop the foremast of the Type 22 frigates and on mast-tops of certain Batch 3 *Leanders*. Sea clutter and ECM elimination is thought to be part of the processing computer (Ferranti FM 1600 series).

Type 968 This is the surface surveillance facet of the GWS 25/Seawolf system.

Type 975 This is a lightweight high definition surface warning radar array for frigate-size warships down to inshore craft. It is now used for navigation in *Leanders*, *Rothesays* and the like. It is considered obsolescent. Range scales from 0.75 nm (1.4 km) to 48 nm (88.9 km) are fitted to the display and it is known that bearing and range are particularly accurate.

Type 975ZW This is the minehunting adaptation of the above mentioned navigation radar, which incorporates a true motion plot/display and the ability to mark on sonar targets from hull-mounted sets. The good distance accuracy and bearing information read-out is ideal for this type of work.

Type 978 This is the navigation radar which equips later frigates, such as the Type 21s. It is known as a 3 cm radar using a 'double-cheese' scanner. The picture is displayed on a PPI (plan position indicator) which shows true motion, rather than always correcting to north.

Type 992 A high-powered, long range air surveillance radar which was developed during the 1950s and is now considered to be obsolete.

Type 992Q A development of the above, used to provide raw data for the Action Information Organisation (AIO) systems aboard various destroyers and frigates. One of the most prominent fittings is to the mainmast of early Type 42s, also seen on top of the Type 21's foremast. Range scales are thought to be from 1.5 nm (2.78 km) to 144 nm (266.6 km). The AIO provides the Command with all the information necessary to assess a given situation and thus is a most important radar system.

Type 993 This is the characteristic 'cheese' tactical air search radar seen on the foremasts of *Leander* and *Rothesay* Class frigates. It is thought that *Fearless* and *Intrepid* are also thus equipped.

Type 994 This is an improved Type 994 set with uprated transmitter/receiver gear based on the Plessey AWS-2 which has been exported, but is not in RN service. Tactical air control, indication of targets and other associated functions are possible with this update. This is now considered to be a medium range system.

Type 996 New long-range radar to replace Type 992; details secret.

Type 1003 Little is known about this system, other than it is in service aboard SSKs and SSNs as a navigation and search radar. It is housed in a special

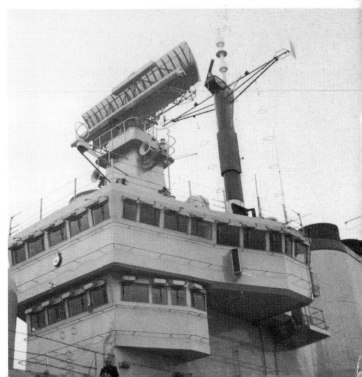

Left *DLGs like* Antrim *carry the Type 992 on the foremast top* (RN). **Above** *The foremast of a Type 12* Rothesay *Class shows the quarter-cheese Type 993 and the navigation Type 975.* **Top right** *A close-up of Type 992Q and its IFF aerial.* **Centre right** *A* Ton *Class craft with bridge-top Type 1006.* **Right** Invincible *carries Type 1022 radar above the bridge.*

conning tower-top compartment and can be raised or lowered as required.

Type 1006 This is the now ubiquitous Kelvin Hughes commercial and naval navigation radar which is fitted to a large number of warships of all sizes. In *Peacock* and *Castle* Class OPVs it will be used for fire control and gunnery radar. It has a range up to 65 nm (120 km) depending on height above the surface of the sea. It has a scanner of similar design to the Type 975 which it is due to replace.

Type 1022 This is the new long range search and surveillance radar for *Invincible* and Batch 2 and 3 Type 42 destroyers. Little has been released about the set, but it is known to be amongst the best in the world and carries IFF. It is a joint development with the Netherlands Navy.

Left *Seacat missile and GWS22 guidance—the ship is* Amazon.

Below left *ADAWS 5—*Cleopatra's *Ops Room in action with PWO (Principal Warfare Officer) manning the PPI (Plan Position Indicator)* (Ferranti).

Right Amazon's *operations room showing a section of Ferranti Computer System's CAAIS (Computer Assisted Action Information System) and WSA 4 (Weapon System Automation)* (Vosper Thornycroft).

GWS 22/MRS 3 This is a combined (or occasionally separate system) Seacat SAM and 114 mm gunnery control system, fitted to *Leander*, *Rothesay*, *County* and *Amazon* Classes of warship. The controller is positioned in the bridge-top compartment on most ships, from where he uses an optical sight to track the target. Marconi television guidance can also be mounted to the set but original development, begun in the 1950s, did not have this kind of sophistication. Target acquisition is via radar or visual sighting.

Action Data Automation Systems

As the kind of warfare in which modern warships would be involved has become steadily more complex and requiring rapid responses, the RN has developed Action Data Automation Systems* as part of a computer-based Action Information

* ADAWS 3 was originally developed for the subsequently cancelled *CAVA-01* aircraft carrier project.

Organisation (AIO), giving data to the Command. There are steadily progressing designs and five are covered below: ADAWS 1—*County* Class DLGs; ADAWS 2—*Bristol*; ADAWS 4—Type 42s; ADAWS 5—*Ikara Leanders*; CAAIS—Type 21s.

ADAWS 1 This is a shipborne automatic data-handling and display system which uses two Ferranti digital computers to give a picture of the air, surface and sub-surface situation, particularly in regard to potential threats. The sources of the information are the ships' radars and sonars, plus similar equipment operated by compatible warships and aircraft. Although the weapon systems do retain their individual fire control, the ADAWS 1 does provide data for the effective operation of Seaslug II SAM.

ADAWS 2 Using the Ferranti FM1600 series computer, the RN ordered the ADAWS 2 system for their Type 82 DLGs, of which only *Bristol* was built. This system provides the data and calculations for the integrated use of Sea Dart GWS and Ikara. It is a comprehensive system using several displays including Plessey plots and labelled plan displays to identify all the features of the possible battle.

ADAWS 4 Although using the same hardware as ADAWS 2, this system is designed for the different needs of the Type 42 destroyers, including a data link system for transferring in almost total security tactical information between similarly equipped vessels. The system also provides control for the Mk 8 114 mm gun and air control of fighter aircraft.

ADAWS 5 Again using the hardware of the ADAWS 2, the Mk 5 system is fitted to the Ikara-refitted *Leander* Class frigates engaged in sub-surface warfare.

CAAIS (Computer Assisted Action Information System): this is based on the Ferranti FM1600B microminiature computer which provides the

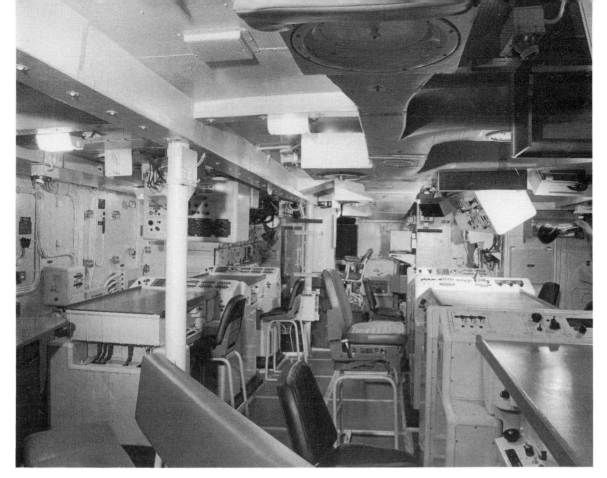

Command with a fully automated command and control system for fighting modern sea battles in Type 21 frigates. Automation is necessary because of the use of modern sensors with longe range facilities which enable decisions to be taken with the benefit of more knowledge than could have been possible even 25 years ago. In the Type 21, weapon control is provided by the WSA 4 (Weapon System Automation Mk 4) and the Type 912 radar. The Type 21's Operations Room has facilities for a dozen display operators which are linked to IFF, warning radars, navigation radars and EW sets to give a comprehensive picture.

Naval sonars

There are a large number of hull-mounted sonars in the RN and several remote vehicle types are also thought to exist. The information released about these sensors is strictly limited and therefore it is only possible to give a general picture of developments. These systems are listed below and described individually; it must be stressed, however, that this list may not be complete.

Type	Purpose	Status
177	ASW ships	Obsolescent
183	Submarines	In service
184	Large warships	Obsolescent
193/		
193M	Minehunters	In service
195M	Escort ships	In service
197	Submarines	In service
199	Surface ships	In service
2007	Submarines	In service
2016	Escort ships	In service
2093	Minehunters	Entering service

Type 177 Is a hull-mounted sonar which has been fitted to ASW escorts in the past and is now being replaced by the Type 2016.

Type 183 Is a hull-mounted sonar for submarines with long range detection and classification capabilities.

Type 184 This set is also used in ASW escorts and is due to be replaced by the Type 2016. Types with it at present are thought to include *Sheffield*, *Amazon* and *Invincible* Classes. It is produced by Graseby, has an arc of 360° and can be active or passive.

Variable Depth Sonar in a Tribal *Class frigate.*

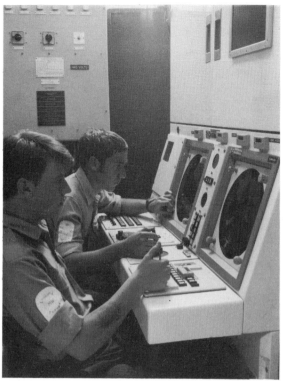

Plessey 2093 minehunting sonar installation in a Hunt *Class* (Plessey).

Type 193/193M The former is the forerunner of the latter, which was designed for operations aboard the new *Hunt* Class MCMVs and probably to refit the existing *Ton* Class MH force. It includes precise navigation and automated plotting facilities and can be interfaced with CAAIS and other AIO systems. The system is used to control automatic mine-disposal weapons such as the remote PAP104 device or manned Gemini dinghy assaults. When all the special equipment is fitted to the Type 193M, including Plessey Speedscan, it will be known as Type 2093.

Type 195M This is a hull-mounted sonar set for small escorts and goes by the commerical name of the Plessey MS26/27. It is used for general underwater surveillance up to 7,000 m (3.8 nm). The Type 195 is the helicopter 'dunking' sonar.

Type 197 This is another submarine hull-mounted sonar on which there is no information.

Type 199 This is a variable depth sonar (VDS) which is towed behind a *Leander* Class frigate in order that information from a Depressed Sound Channel at about 150 m depth may be obtained. Because the sea differs in temperature and salinity according to depth, it is important that an ASW escort captain is

given all the available data, because a hostile submarine may lurk under a layer. Transmissions from a hull-mounted sonar may bounce off the layer giving false readings or inaccurate information. The areas where the VDS is most useful are in the North Arabian Sea, Caribbean and Pacific coast of South America. In anything but the Depressed Sound Channel, the VDS does not necessarily improve upon the performance possible from the standard hull-mounted sonar. *Bristol* was built with Type 199.

Type 2007 This is most recent submarine sonar to be identified and it is thought that it is fitted to the *Swiftsure* and *Trafalgar* Classes, plus the four SSBNs. No further data is known.

Type 2016 Is probably the most advanced fleet escort hull-mounted sonar available in the world at present. It has an improved detection, classification (using a computer to identify what is making the noise), and tracking capabilities over previously existing sets, as well as having torpedo attack warning facilities. It is the first system to have a complex monitoring and automatic transfer system which can be linked to the AIO and CIC (Control Information Centre). The Type 22 frigates have been carrying out trials with these sets, built by

EW, IFF, ECM, ESM and ECCM are there somewhere!

Plessey Marine, and they have proved most successful. Like most hull-mounted sonars, the Type 2016 has a GRP dome in a fixed position.

Type 2020 New SSN sonar; details secret.

Type 2093 This is the fully fitted and equipped Type 193M destined for the *Hunt* Class and later for certain *Ton* Class MHs.

The modern RN is currently studying with great interest the new lightweight **towed arrays** which will probably put to sea in a refitted *Leander* Class frigate in 1983. It is thought that the main system is known as Type 165 and that it will be part of the sensor fit on the proposed Type 23 frigate which was announced by the RN in July 1982. The system is designed to scan the sea below any interfering bathythermal layers. It is still considered secret and very few details have emerged at the present time. Associated with this is the new **MCM deep sweep gear** which will be used in the new Class of coastal MCMV. It is not expected that this system will go to sea before 1986.

All major combat ships are equipped to tow bathythermal recording instruments to evaluate the salinity and water temperature of the sea area in which the warship is operating. In addition, all submarines are thought to have the device in their conning tower or fin. Most warships also carry the **towed torpedo decoy** which uses suitable acoustic transmissions to fool enemy torpedoes. These devices can be seen on the quarterdecks of most warships, painted yellow and lowered and recovered by means of a davit. One particular example is manufactured by Graseby Dynamics and is towed well astern of the ship; it is said to be extremely effective in decoying active and passive homing torpedoes. It can also interfere with an attacking submarine's sonar.

For minehunting, but not a sonar, is the **towed acoustic generator** which, linked to a towed acoustic monitor, can destroy enemy acoustic mines. It is not successful against moored mines (which still require to be swept) nor against magnetic mines (which require an influence sweep or clearance diving). Sperry manufacture the Osborn Sweep for this purpose in *Ton* Class CMSs. Associated with mines countermeasures are the **Hi-Fix** survey/navigation system and the Marconi **Hydronsearch sector scanning sonar**. The former is now advanced into the Mark 6 set whilst the latter is to be found in Survey vessels.

Electronics

The growth in the radio and electronics side of the RN is astounding. The large number and types of radios now carried, including deciphering telex machines, etc, is incredible. Direction finding by means of high and medium frequency (HF/DF and MF/DF) is still used to determine the exact position of radio source and the aerials can be seen on every modern RN vessel. In addition there is the SCOT system; electronic warfare (EW) equipment and IFF systems. Most of the gear is considered to be very secret, therefore it has only been possible to describe the mere basics below.

SCOT

SCOT stands for Shipborne COmmunications Terminal and was designed by Marconi to improve the standard of signalling at long range between the Fleet and the Command structure at Home. Communications, using a satellite link-up, as with SCOT, are unaffected by ionspheric interference and radio station jamming.

The terminals which contain aerials in plastic radomes, 1.07 m (SCOT 1) or 1.83 m (SCOT 2) in diameter, are mounted in an unobstructed position, either side of the ship's centre-line where they are made independent of the ship's motion by gyro stabilisation. The active communications equipment is not housed with the antennae but in a small,

Protective dome for the SCOT system in a DLG.

Improved SCOT

The improved SCOT system provides an interface with NATO and American Defence Satellite systems and the system can either be fitted to existing terminal equipment or by updating SCOT 1 and SCOT 2 equipment already at sea. The main advantages of the improved system are that it uses less power and that it has an improved reliability factor. Also built in are beacon receivers and independently tunable communications channels. The system is currently under examination and appraisal by the Royal Navy which hopes to have SCOT equipment in all large warships and RFAs by 1985.

Electronic Warfare (EW)

Unlike other systems, it is not possible to go into any detail in respect of EW gear, other than to give a general résumé of the current situation.

The RN is faced with a known Soviet threat of RECS (radio electronic combat support) against its command and control structure in time of war, but even in times of peace, the 'other side' are listening in to normal radio and radar traffic. There is therefore a pressing need for investment in new EW equipment in all spheres of Defence, but especially in connection with warships. Many more warships, especially the surface combat units, have EW aerials mounted in selected parts of the ship.

Current EW gear includes ECCM (electronic counter-counter measures) which helps prevent interference with friendly transmissions and these are supported by ESM (electronic support measures) which are used in the analysis of enemy traffic. In addition, there is ECM (electronic counter measures), both active and passive, which disrupt signals and can be used against electronic-based offensive or defensive weapons. In the latter class is the new Sea Gnat shipborne decoy system for use against anti-ship missiles, Corvus and special shells fired from standard gun mountings like the 114 mm Mk 8. New equipment plans also call for an improved series of jammers, threat alert receivers for monitoring hostile radar transmissions and devices for decoying attacking anti-ship torpedoes. Submarines, especially SSBNs, are thought to have even more specialist equipment. EW is a cost-effective way of contributing to the Fleet's future capability.

IFF systems

The system known as IFF—Identification, Friend or Foe—has been in operation in various forms since the Second World War. Today, there is considerable use made of IFF interrogation especially by the RN.

unmanned cabin on the upper deck and is connected to the terminal by a low loss waveguide. Control is maintained from the ship's Communications Office, situated within the citadel.

The terminals are slowly being fitted to warships of frigate size and above, and some RFAs. Initial trials were actually carried out aboard the *County* Class DLG *London* during the mid-1970s. Ships can communicate with other similarly fitted vessels at sea practically worldwide, or with any specially fitted ground station ashore. The type of system means that signals can pass freely and in a secure way.

The satellites themselves have until now been mainly American or the products of NATO co-operation after the decline of the Skynet system. Nuclear submarines, particularly the SSBNs, have need of an effective satellite back-up communications system and to this end the Ministry of Defence is currently studying proposals from BAe and Marconi; these could even have export potential to NATO as other powers wish to have independent systems.

The standard system is the Cossor IFF 800 series which can be found mounted above the antennae of Type 965 and other search radars. Very little information is available on IFF systems, but one can state that they are complex using the following items: an interrogator and a high power, long-range transmitter/receiver. The IFF850 has a 3.3 m-long aerial whilst the smaller antenna (for smaller radars) is only 1.6 m long. Aircraft are also fitted with IFF systems for ready identification by warships, airfields and troop concentrations. Anti-jamming devices are thought to exist and special coded transponders ensure that enemy aircraft cannot make use of the other side's codes.

Royal Marines equipment

Over the years, the RM has depended on the mainstream of British Army equipment for all but the most specialist roles. Today, the Royal Marines have been actively involved in Northern Ireland where they have made use of the existing IS (internal security) gear provided for the resident and visiting

The Browning SL pistol, holster, magazine and cleaning tool (MoD).

units. The RM are unique in the Armed Forces of the United Kingdom and therefore there are various elements of their equipment which have no place elsewhere.

The following section has been derived from several sources but with due regard to security.

It has not been possible to list all the types of vehicle employed by the Royal Marines for two reasons: one is that it is customary for the Corps to make use of considerable numbers of Army vehicles and, secondly, that not all RM-marked vehicles are driven or operated by members of the Corps. It has therefore been decided to restrict the coverage to those vehicles most commonly seen with the Corps. In addition, there has been some problem in deciding on the method of designation for vehicles—RN, Army or NATO—and on the designation of the personal weapons. Rather than use a standard designation, the commonplace usage has been adopted.

The UK designation system

All the British Services use a somewhat awkward, yet sensible system, for describing equipment in the field and battle categories considered below. Each item has a designation under the following headings:

Description: Characteristic: Model: Modification.

In the following description, L=Land Service (Army pattern).

Personal weapons

9 mm Pistol Automatic L9A1

Calibre 9 mm; **Length** 0.196 m; **Length of barrel** 0.112 m; **Weight empty** 0.88 kg; **Weight loaded** 1.01 kg; **Muzzle velocity** 354 m/s; **Magazine capacity** 13 rounds; **Rate of fire** Single-shot; **Maximum effective range** 40–50 m.

This is the officer and special duties pattern pistol which has been standard since the 1940s. It is also known as the Browning 9 mm. The pistol is worn on the hip in a canvas holster or in a shoulder holster for special duties. It has an unusually large magazine capacity and can be used accurately by relative newcomers because of the long grip which can help steady the user's aim. The butt is also a fine combat weapon in its own right.

Sub-Machine Gun 9 mm L2A3

Calibre 9 mm; **Length (butt folded)** 0.482 m; **Length (butt extended)** 0.69 m; **Length of barrel** 0.198 m; **Weight empty** 2.7 kg; **Weight loaded** 3.5 kg; **Muzzle velocity** 390 m/s; **Magazine capacity** 34 rounds; **Rate of fire (cyclic)** 550 rpm; **Rate**

and associated work. It is possible to fit a bayonet to the muzzle. In service, many users tape two magazines together for quick changes.

Rifle 7.62 mm Self loading (SLR) L1A2

Calibre 7.62 mm; **Length overall** 1.143 m; **Length of barrel** 0.5334 m; **Weight empty** 4.337 kg; **Weight loaded (20-round magazine)** 5.074 kg; **Muzzle velocity** 838 m/s; **Magazine capacity** 20 or 30 rounds; **Rate of fire** 40 rpm; **Maximum effective range** 600 m plus.

The NATO standard rifle, known as the FN, SLR or FA in various formations. The 7.62 mm is equipped to fire ball rounds (L2A2 or L11A1): it has fittings for a bayonet (L1A1 or L1A4); for 0.22-in conversion in order to facilitate indoor range work (L12A1); for a grenade launcher (L1A2) which is rarely used by the RM; for the Infantry Weapon Sight (IWS) type L1A1 or L1A2 and for the blank firing attachment L6A1 (with yellow cap on muzzle). The basic sight is most commonly used but in certain places the Sight Unit Infantry Trilux (SUIT or L1A1/L1A2) is fitted; this looks for all intents and purposes like the back half of a telescopic sight, as seen in American war films.

SUIT Specification: **Weight** 340 g; **Length** 188 mm; **Height** 69 mm; **Field of view** 8°; **Sight settings** 300 and 500 m; **Magnification** × 4. The SLR is now fitted with plastic furniture and the butt may be varied in length by using one of four different butt-plates, thus enabling the weapon to be adjusted to suit the stature of the individual firer.

Competition Rifle 7.62 mm L39A1

Calibre 7.62 mm; **Length** 1.18 m; **Length of barrel** 0.7 m; **Weight empty** 4.42 kg; **Weight loaded** Circa 5 kg; **Muzzle velocity** 841 m/s; **Magazine capacity** 10 rounds; **Rate of fire** Single shot only; **Maximum effective range** 1,000 m plus.

Used in place of the SLR for competition work, this is a bolt-action rifle using the green spot target ammunition (L2A2) for training and actual eventing. Bisley in Surrey is the main venue for such shoots.

Sniper Rifle 7.62 mm L42A1

Calibre 7.62 mm; **Length** 1.181 m; **Length of barrel** 0.699 m; **Weight empty** 4.43 kg; **Weight loaded** ? kg; **Muzzle velocity** 838 m/s; **Magazine capacity** 10 rounds; **Rate of fire** Single-shot only; **Maximum effective range** 1,200 m.

This is a classic sniper rifle which would be used in many battle areas to pick off special targets, such as enemy commanders. It is the result of re-barrelling the old Lee Enfield Service Rifle and is most

A special unit places demolition charges on a bridge; the personal weapons are 9 mm SMGs (RM).

of fire (practical) 102 rpm; **Rate of fire (single-shot)** 40 rpm; **Maximum effective range** 200 m.

This is the universally known Sterling SMG which is the replacement of the equally well known Sten gun of the Second World War. It is the third modification on the standard 1945 pattern Sterling and is used by support units and for house clearing

The SLR and its standard accessories (RM).

The AR-15 Armalite rifle and rounds; the bayonet is not commonly used (RM).

often seen with a telescopic sight, known as Sighting Telescope (L1A1). The sniping role is difficult and dangerous; various types of ammunition are used as well as several types of grip and sling.

Target Rifle No 8 Mark 1

Calibre 5.48 mm/.216 in (.22); **Length** 1.043 m; **Length of barrel** 0.956 m; **Weight empty (approx)** 4.025 kg; **Weight loaded (approx)** 4.025 kg; **Muzzle velocity** 320 m/s; **Magazine capacity** Single-shot only; **Rate of fire** Single-shot only; **Maximum effective range** 50 m.

This is similar to a commerical rifle and is used by units for training and recreational shooting only.

Rifle 5.56 mm M16

Calibre 5.56 mm; **Length** 0.99 m; **Length of barrel** 0.508 m; **Weight (gun alone)** 3.1 kg; **Weight loaded (20-round magazine)** 3.68 kg; **Weight loaded (30-round magazine)** 3.82 kg; **Muzzle velocity** 1,000 m/s; **Magazine capacity** 20 or 30 rounds; **Rate of fire (cyclic)** 700–950 rpm; **Rate of fire (practical)** 40–60 rpm; **Maximum effective range** 400 m.

The Armalite (or M16 or AR-15) is a small calibre assault rifle used in the British Armed Forces primarily for close-quarter and jungle warfare and it was in this role that the RM first became familiar with it. It is now used by the Corps for special operations (SBS) and by reconnaissance troops. It is well liked by those who operate it, although there is some conjecture about the light weight of the projectile as compared to the SLR. It is a good close-quarters weapon and has what will most probably be chosen as the calibre for future NATO personal weapons—5.56 mm.

7.62 mm Light Machine-Gun L4A4

Calibre 7.62 mm; **Length** 1.133 m; **Length of barrel** 0.536 m; **Weight empty** 9.96 kg; **Weight loaded** 10.68 kg; **Muzzle velocity** 869 m/s; **Magazine capacity** 30 rounds*; **Rate of fire (cyclic)** 500–575 rpm; **Rate of fire (practical)** 120 rpm; **Rate of fire (single-shot)** 40 rpm; **Maximum effective range** 800 m.

This is the Light Machine-Gun (LMG) which the Corps use mainly in the jungle and Arctic for light anti-aircraft and anti-personnel operations. It is basically a modified Bren Gun of Second World War vintage which was replaced at Section level by the GPMG in the 1960s.

7.62 mm General Purpose Machine-Gun (GPMG) L7A2

Calibre 7.62 mm; **Length as LMG** 1.232 m; **Length as HMG** 1.049 m; **Length of barrel** 0.679 m; **Weight empty (LMG role)** 10.9 kg; **Weight loaded (LMG role)** 13.85 kg; **Weight of tripod** 13.64 kg; **Muzzle velocity** 838 m/s; **Type of feed** 100-round belt; **Rate of fire (cyclic)** 750–1,000 rpm; **Rate of fire in LMG role** 100 rpm; **Rate of fire in HMG role** 200 rpm; **Maximum effective range (LMG)** 800 m; **Maximum effective range (HMG)** 1,800 m.

The L7A2 GPMG is based on the FN MAG and is used by the RM as a Section weapon in all areas of operation. It is particularly valuable as a sustained fire machine-gun (SFMG) when it is fitted with a tripod mount. It is fully automatic, belt-fed, gas-operated, air-cooled and can continue firing for considerable periods. The gun is fed from left to right using M13-type disintegrating linked belts. There is a gas regulator and a flash-hider attachment to aid concealment.

The GPMG SF is designed to give sustained fire for effective infantry cover and control, day or night, on a range of predetermined targets. The SF kit is

* In an emergency the 20-round magazine of the L1A1 Rifle can be used.

easily portable and can quickly be in action. It is normal to have at least two marines at the SF location—the aimer/firer and the loader; in addition, whenever possible, a third man acts as a gun controller. Spare barrels are necessary in this role.

SF kit specification: **Overall folded dimensions** 190 × 190 × 810 mm; **Weight** 13.4 kg; **Traverse** 360°; **Elevation** −11°–+22°; **Tripod type** L4A1; **Sight for SF role** Sight Unit C2; **Magnification** 1.7.

The L20A1/L7A2 GPMG mountings can be used on Scout helicopters of the 3rd Commando Brigade Air Squadron for anti-personnel operations, but this is not considered to be a standard fitting.

Future weapons

It is thought that the Corps will follow the example of the British Army and adapt the new NATO standard infantry weapon when this is agreed. At present, the RM have been involved in the Individual Weapon XL70E3 (formerly XL65E5) and Light Support Weapon XL73E2 (formerly XL65E4) programmes to a limited degree only. The calibre will be 5.56 mm and the weapons will be manufactured by the Royal Small Arms factory at Enfield Lock, Middlesex; the ammunition at Radway Green.

Ammunition

Below are listed the current ammunition types for the standard 7.62 mm NATO guns; all rounds are 51 mm in length:

Designation	Description
Round 7.62 mm Ball L2A2	Normal Service round for operational use
Round 7.62 mm Tracer L5A3	Tracer to 1,100 m; red colour
Round 7.62 mm Drill L1A2	Inert round for training purposes
Cartridge 7.62 mm Rifle Grenade L1A2	For projecting 'Super Energa' rifle grenade
Cartridge 7.62 mm Blank L13A1	Crimped blank for training use

Grenades

The grenades used by the RM are identical to the British Army pattern, and are covered in the companion volume, but are subject to review at

Top left *Marines from the RMR man a temporary GMPG position.* **Centre left** *The GPMG in the SF role with special sight and additional ammunition* (RM). **Left** *Grenades—HE type illustrated but smoke similar.*

1.5-in signal pistol and anti-riot cartridge (CoI).

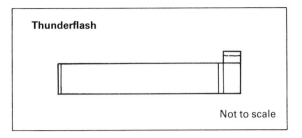

present. They can be divided into three types: HE (High Explosive); Smoke and Irritant.

Anti-personnel hand grenade (L2A1) This grenade can be used as a hand-thrown weapon with a range of 25 m or as a rifle projectile; the RM has chosen not to use it with the latter. It has the following specification: **weight of explosive** 170 g TNT; **length** 77.5 mm. It is based on the American M26 series and there are two training grenades available for inert practice—L3A1 and L4A1. This is the standard RM hand grenade.

Smoke generators and grenades

The RM's smoke grenades are due to change to the new XL6E1 and XL21E1 series currently under development during the next few years. These new designs will weight about 0.5 kg; stand 140 mm high and have a diameter of 63.5 mm. Until they are in service the following grenades will continue to be used:

Type	Colours available	Weight	Height	Diameter
No 80	Red, yellow, blue, green	0.55 kg	140 mm	63.5 mm
No 83	Red, yellow, blue, green	0.5 kg	140 mm	63.5 mm
No 8*	White	1.75 kg	100 mm	100.0 mm
No 28†	White	2.5 kg	205 mm	100.0 mm

* Used as a training aid.
† Used to mark landing grounds and burns for 5 minutes.

The 25 mm signal cartridge and the Very pistol are still used for dispensing smoke grenades for defence and rescue purposes. The cartridges are available in red, yellow, green and white single star and reach a height of 90 mm with a burning time of six secs. The pistol's designation is L4A2.

Thunderflash This is designed to give safe maximum simulation of battlefield conditions for training purposes.

Irritants

Although these have mainly been used in Northern Ireland, there are two irritant grenades available to the Corps for IS and training purposes, both containing CS gas, which has become infamous in Ulster and elsewhere for crowd control. The RM use CS for NBC simulation and training.

Cannister Irritants (L1A1/L2A1) are the major weapons, being only slightly different in their method of dispensing CS. The former (L1A1) is the older type which uses holes in the base and sides to emit gas, whereas the newer version has overcome the anti-cannister measures of rioters by exploding to emit CS. Both cannisters are 114 mm × 57 mm. Because they have proved ineffective they have been replaced by the **Hand Anti-Riot Irritant L13A1**. This is larger, 175 mm × 66 mm, weighs 0.55 kg and can be thrown about 25 m unaided.

Grenades—No 80 smoke grenade (left); L1A1 anti-riot grenade (centre); and No 83 smoke grenade (RM).

RM 81 mm mortar team in action on the slopes of Mount Kent, East Falkland (Popperfoto).

Northern Ireland theatre

As the RM operates in the Province as an Army battalion, it uses the standard Army anti-riot and IS equipment, including: Grenade discharger (L1A1); Anti-riot gas dischargers (L6A1, L9A1 and L11A1); 1.5 in Anti-riot cartridges (L3A1); and Baton rounds—plastic and rubber bullets. These items are described fully in *Encyclopaedia of the Modern British Army*.

Support weapons

Unlike the United States Marine Corps (USMC) or the British Army, the Corps goes into action with only the bare essentials. Support weapons can be carried as troop weapons up to the 84 mm Carl Gustav size. Mortars are operated by mortar troops within a Support Company of a Commando, but are transported in ½-ton Land Rovers or broken down into man-portable loads. The same applies to the Milan-equipped Anti-Tank Troop of each Support Company, but they are more mobile, using 1-tonne Land Rovers. All RM support weapons are air-portable for flexible deployment.

51 mm Light Mortar L3

Calibre 50.8 mm; **Length of barrel overall** 0.7 m; **Length of bore** 0.515 m; **Weight of barrel** 1.5 kg; **Weight of breech piece** 0.99 kg; **Weight of sight unit** 0.65 kg; **Weight of monopod** 0.48 kg; **Weight of base plate** 0.76 kg; **Weight complete in action** 4.6 kg; **Maximum range** 800 m; **Minimum range** 150 m; **Bomb weight (HE L1A1)** 0.68 kg; **Bomb weight (smoke L1A1)** 0.68 kg) **Bomb weight (illuminating L1A3)** 0.85 kg; **Rate of fire (maximum)** 8 rpm for 2 minutes; **Rate of fire (normal)** 3 rpm for 5 minutes.

This is a man-portable light mortar which is rapidly replacing the old 2-in muzzle-loading mortar at Troop level. The latter is still found in RMR use and at CTC, however, so a specification is given: **Calibre** 51.2 mm/2 in; **Length complete** 0.482 m; **Weight complete** 3.3 kg; **Maximum range** 500 m; **Bomb weight (smoke)** 0.909 kg; **Bomb weight (signal)** 0.511 kg.

The 51 mm is designed to: provide rapid and accurate smoke screen up to 750 m from the mortar; bring down quick, accurate and lethal neutralising or protective fire on the section front; provide target illumination for 'Charlie G', MAW and Milan AT systems; be capable of direct or indirect fire with only one man; and to overlap in range with the 81 mm mortar.

The 51 mm has increased range, lethality and accuracy over the old 2-in mortar, but the latter's ammunition can be used if required.

This mortar will fire high explosive, smoke and illuminating bombs which have an aluminium casing and are fitted with plastic rings to prevent damage to the barrel. There are also drill and practice rounds.

Round	Weight	Filling	Remarks
HE	1.025 kg	TNT	272 mm long with fragmentation effect
Smoke	0.95 kg	HCE	Time delay of six seconds, duration 120 seconds
Illumin- ating	0.825 kg	Various	Maximum range to light-up 750 m; burst height 250 m; duration 70 seconds

A rate of fire of three rounds per minute for five minutes (15 rounds) can be achieved, but it is more usual to require eight rounds per minute for two minutes in most tactical situations. The mortar is manufactured by the Royal Ordnance Factory.

Rocket 66 mm HEAT L1A1

Calibre 66 mm; **Length extended** 0.893 m; **Length closed** 0.655 m; **Length of rocket** 0.508 m; **Weight complete** 2.37 kg; **Weight of rocket** 1 kg; **Muzzle velocity** 145 m/s; **Maximum effective range** 300 m; **Armour penetration** Up to 300 mm steel plate.

This is the American M72 HEAT (High Explosive Anti-Tank) weapon to give anti-tank protection at Section level. Basically it is a man-portable, disposable system which can be used against most modern AFVs. This weapon is in service with Commandos and RMR units but may be replaced in 1983 by the MAW. It is essentially an extendable tube with primitive sight.

Medium Armour Weapon (MAW)

This is the replacement for the 66 mm and as a lighter AT weapon than the 'Charlie G' for section and troop use. It is intended to introduce the weapon into service during 1983, but at present information is very limited. It is thought that it will be 94 mm calibre with a telescopic launcher tube made from GRP. It will have an effective range of about 300 m.

84 mm Carl Gustav L14A1

Calibre 84 mm; **Length of barrel** 1.13 m; **Weight complete** 16 kg; **Muzzle velocity** 160 m/s; **Weight of HEAT round L40A4** 2.59 kg; **Weight of HEAT projectile** 1.7 kg; **Range, anti-tank (mobile)** 400 m; **Range, anti-tank (stationary)** 500 m; **Range, HE and smoke** 1,000 m; **Rate of fire** 6 rpm; **Armour penetration (HEAT at 60°)** 228 mm.

This is the Swedish-made 'Charlie G' which is the largest weapon at troop level. It may well be replaced after 1983 by the MAW. It is designed as an anti-tank weapon which is shoulder-held in action; it is recoilless and capable of knocking out any known tank. There is a kit available to convert it for training purposes to 6.5 mm; other rounds are HEAT (L40A4) (weight 2.59 kg) and Smoke.

The business end of a Carl Gustav demonstrated by RMs in winter clothing (RM).

An 81 mm mortar team wades ashore during a NATO exercise (RN).

81 mm Mortar L16A1

Calibre 81 mm; **Length of barrel overall** 1.27 m; **Weight of barrel** 12.27 kg; **Weight of mounting** 11.8 kg; **Weight of sight unit** 3.40 kg; **Weight of base plate** 11.6 kg; **Weight complete in action** 39.6 kg; **Muzzle velocity (maximum)** 255 m/s; **Maximum range** 5,660 m; **Maximum range (HE L31E3)** 5,800 m plus; **Minimum range** 180 m; **Elevation** 45° to 80°; **Traverse** 5° left/right at 45°; **Bomb weight (HE L15A3)** 4.47 kg; **Bomb weight (Smoke L19A4)** 4.49 kg; **Rate of fire** 12 rpm.

Although of medium calibre, this mortar is considered to be a lightweight type. It is accurate, portable and reliable with an extensive range of ammunition available. It is equivalent to a medium artillery piece in some roles using a bipod mount. There are usually six in a Mortar Troop.

The main feature of this weapon is its high accuracy, being 0.5 per cent in any range setting. It is broken down into a three-man load with the heaviest part, the barrel, weighing 12.28 kg. It is also capable of a high sustained rate of fire.

The ammunition is specially made and HE, WP and illumination rounds are available to match the mortar's own considerable characteristics. Three basic rounds are British-made—HE, WP and practice (the illumination round for the 81 mm is under development at present). HE round (L15A3): **Weight** 4.45 kg; **Filling** TNT/RDX; **Overall length** 0.472 m; **Range** 180-5,660 m. Smoke (L19A4); **Weight** 4.45 kg; **Filling** White phosphorus (willie peter); **Overall length** 0.46 m; **Range** As HE. Practice (L21): A re-usable round with a range of 25–75 m.

Milan

Weight of missile 6.65 kg; **Weight of missile and**

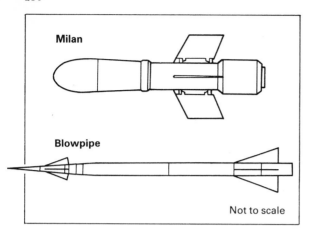

Milan

Blowpipe

Not to scale

and in the RM the weapon equips the Anti-Tank Troop of a Support Company within a Commando. The usual complement of a Troop is one officer, 48 Marines and 14 launchers, plus nine vehicles for transportation. The usefulness of Milan depends on how mobile the team is because, once spotted, the Milan emplacement or position is bound to come under attack, such is the effectiveness of the weapon. Armour penetration is 352 mm.

The system comprises a launcher on a tripod support with clip missiles in sealed containers. The missile is fin-stabilised and powered by a rocket motor which ignites away from the launcher. Milan has replaced the Wombat recoilless gun.

Blowpipe

Weight complete 19.39 kg; **Weight with IFF** 21.2 kg; **Length of missile** 1.349 m; **Body diameter** 76.2 mm; **Span** 0.274 m; **Maximum range** 3,000 m plus.

This is a lightweight anti-aircraft missile which equips the Air Defence Troop of a Commando Brigade Headquarters for immediate area defence against low-flying aircraft and assault helicopters. Normally about a dozen missile launchers are available. Like Milan, Blowpipe is supplied in a sealed container for fitting to the launcher tube. The missile is powered by two rocket motors and is aimed with a monocular sight. The warhead is fitted for proximity or impact detonation and an IFF unit can be used to establish whether an aircraft is hostile or not. In the field, there would not be time for visual identification of a small, fast moving and low flying

container 11.5 kg; **Weight of launch unit** 15.5 kg; **Length of missile** 0.769 m; **Body diameter (minimum)** 90 mm; **Span** 0.225 m; **Weight of warhead** 2.98 kg; **Weight of warhead charge** 1.45 kg; **Velocity** 75 to 200 m/s; **Maximum range** 2,000 m; **Minimum range** 25 m; **Rate of fire (maximum range)** 3–4 rpm; **Time of flight to 2,000 m** Up to 13 seconds; **Armour penetration** Up to 352 mm.

The Milan (*Missile d'Infantrie Leger Anti-Char*) is a second generation wire-guided ATM which replaced the Aérospatiale SS 11 in French Army service. It was ordered for the British Armed Forces in 1978 and is manufactured under licence by British Aerospace. The standard Milan team is one man with the support of one or two with extra missiles,

Milan ATM ready to fire—the operators are wearing protective clothing against both the arctic cold and possible blast (RM).

The Blowpipe shoulder-held AAM equips Air Defence Troop, RM (RM).

Using a mine detector on a roadway in northern Europe (Commando Forces News Team).

target. It is thought that the Blowpipe missile's radio guidance instructions cannot be jammed, because of the short range involved. The system proved to be very effective in bridgehead and landing ground defence during the Falklands campaign and it accounted for several enemy aircraft. The Royal Marines are thought to be studying a helicopter-mounted system for their gazelles to use in self-defence.

Heavy weapons

The Corps does not have its own heavy weapon support, but relies on 29 Commando Regiment, Royal Artillery, to provide batteries of the 105 mm Light Gun for service with the Corps at Commando Brigade level. The model used is the L118 which is air portable (1,862 kg) by Sea King HC 4 as a single load or in two loads by the Wessex HU 5. The normal towing vehicle is the 1-tonne Land Rover with gun crew, plus another Land Rover as ammunition carrier. Each Commando Regiment battery would have six 105 mm Light Guns in wartime; there is a TA battery (No 289) in addition.

Specialist equipment

Although the Mountain and Arctic Warfare (M&AW) cadres have special weapons for their environment, and it is presumed that the Special Boat Squadron (SBS) would be similarly equipped with whatever equipment was thought necessary, the RM has very little special equipment. The major exception to this is in Northern Ireland where the bulk used is of British Army origin: Nitesun illumination for use in Scout and Gazelle helicopters; Skyshout speakers for use in Gazelle helicopters; Pocketscope hand-held night vision aids (also found in Hong Kong); and Claribel 2B2981GS No 14 Mk 1) and Prowler surveillance radar. These items are described in the *Encyclopaedia of the Modern British Army*.

Several night vision aids are in more regular use, including the Individual Weapon Sight (IWS) L1A2 and the Telescope Straight II (L1E1); also known as 'Twiggy'. In Northern Ireland, it is usual for SLRs to be fitted with SUIT (*qv*) for clearer vision. RM Surveillance Troops are often equipped with the Night Observation Device (NOD). The IWS has a magnification of × 3.75, a 180-mil field of view and weighs 2.78 kg; 'Twiggy' a × 5.0 magnification, 129-mil field of view and weight of 11.0 kg. Details of the NOD are still classified.

Mines and detectors

There are a large number of mines available in the modern world and they have become a favourite weapon of terrorist groups, even though it is never possible to predict who will be killed or maimed as a result of detonation. More often than not in these cases it is the innocent civilian who is hurt. On the battlefield the mine can be used as an offensive or defensive weapon depending on tactics. It is not known whether mines are particularly effective in snow conditions.

Claymore Anti-Personnel Mine M18A1
Weight 1.58 kg; **Length** 0.216 m; **Height** 0.083 m; **Width** 0.035 m; **Weight of charge** 0.68 kg; **Range** 50 m (16 m rearwards).

This is an American-made device which is used to disrupt enemy patrols. It is a curved box with 700 'nasty' steel balls which are propelled by the explosive charge to a height of 1 m and a range of 50 m. Detonation is by remote control or trip wire. The device is carried in a bandolier.

Horizontal Action Anti-Tank Mine

Weight 12 kg; **Length** 0.26 m; **Diameter** 0.2 m; **Range** 80 m.

This French-made device is used against heavy vehicles such as armoured personnel carriers (APCs) and AFVs. It is located, in similar fashion to Claymore, at the side of a route used by vehicles and is exploded to cause as much damage to the tracks and softer parts as possible. The charge is propelled against the AFV/APC and can penetrate 70 mm of armour.

Anti-Tank Mine Mk 7

Weight 13.6 kg; **Diameter** 0.325 m; **Height** 0.13 m; **Weight of charge** 8.89 kg.

The old Anti-Tank Mine Mk 7 is occasionally used for the RM for setting defensive minefields; it is more commonly used by the Army and is being replaced by a new Bar Mine Layer which will not see RM service at present.

Mine Detector No 4C

Weight in use 9.15 kg; **Weight in transit box** 14.4 kg; **Search head length** 0.286 m; **Search head height** 0.108 m; **Search head width** 0.184 m; **Amplifier depth** 0.216 m; **Amplifier height** 0.108 m; **Amplifier width** 0.108 m; **Handle extended** 0.127 m; **Handle collapsed** 0.38 m;

Detection depth (soil) 0.51 m; **Detection depth (pavé)** 0.305 m.

This is the standard metal mine detector used by the RM for sweeping paths and other areas where enemy mines may be located, and has been in service since 1968.

It is possible to use this device whilst walking or, if in action, in the prone position, because the handle and search head are adjustable to the conditions. Various anti-sweep devices such as iron filings can be overcome using the special selector for pavé material. Like all detectors of this type, it works on the principle of electromagnetic induction when two coils are in balance; any metallic object coming into the field is usually strong enough to put the balance out and so register.

P6/2 Sweep Metal Detector

Weight complete 4.5 kg; **Length of long probe** 1.016 m; **Length of short probe** 0.4 m; **Length of open loop probe** 1.143 m; **Length of personnel probe** 0.4 m; **Dimensions of electronic unit** 0.25 × 0.08 × 0.25 m.

The P6/2 Sweep metal and mine detector is a militarised version of the Plessey P6 pulse indication metal detector. In military use the Sweep is issued with four different probes which can be used to fulfil almost any detection role from conventional mine detection to personnel body searches. The probes are an open loop probe for normal ground searches, a ferrite rod for searching foliage and water locations, a short probe and the personnel search probe. Using the ferrite probe an object the size of an automatic pistol can be detected up to 0.28 metres away.

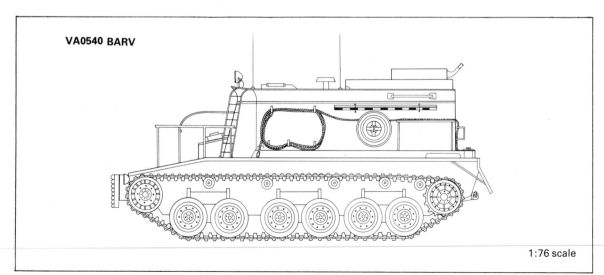

VA0540 BARV

1:76 scale

In the amphibious role, the RM use BARVs to bring their equipment ashore—here one hauls an LCVP (from Intrepid*) up a beach; in the background is an Army Mexeflote* (RM).

Royal Marines vehicles

As has been explained previously, it is not possible to list all the RM vehicles, but the following have been selected as the most commonly operated by uniformed RM personnel. The reference used is the NATO vehicle code and the titles are those used by the Royal Marines, rather than the British Army or the Royal Navy.

There are no fighting vehicles in the RM and only one armoured vehicle, because unlike the USMC, for example, the RM are highly mobile on foot, by skis or by helicopter. The Northern Flank does not lend itself to armoured operations in any case. Command Vehicles are usually Land Rovers and/or tents. In Cyprus, whilst on United Nations duties, the RM does have the use of British Army-supplied, UN-marked Ferret scout cars for secure transportation, but these are outside the scope of this book. The one exception to the armoured vehicle non-operation policy is the BARV:

VA0540* Beach Armoured Recovery Vehicle (BARV)

Armament 1 × 7.62 mm L4A4 Machine-Gun; **Crew** 4; **Weight in action** 40,643 kg; **Length** 8.076 m; **Height** 3.453 m; **Width** 3.402 m; **Track width** 0.61 m; **Ground clearance** 0.5 m;

* NATO parlance denotes VA as Vehicle Armoured and VB as Vehicle Second Line.

Maximum road speed 34.6 km/h; **Range (roads)** 64.5 km; **Engine type** Rolls-Royce Meteor Mark IVB; **Engine power** 650 bhp; **Engine capacity** 27 litres; **Fuel capacity** 550 litres; **Ammunition capacity** 7.62 mm—400 rounds.

The BARV is based on a Centurion MBT and was designed in the early 1960s to assist stranded vehicles during amphibious operations, being able to wade to a depth of 2.9 m. Most of the LPD/LSL vessels which provide amphibious lift for the RM have at least one BARV on their complement, but with the diminution of the Marine assault role and the experience that the BARV is not all it was designed to be, many of the vehicles have passed into Army hands for service with the British Army of the Rhine.

VB1620 ½-tonne Land Rover Truck Utility 4 × 4

Crew 1 + 2; **Weight loaded** 2,018 kg; **Length** 3.632 m; **Height** 1.95 m; **Width** 1.524 m; **Wheel track** 1.308 m; **Ground clearance** 0.21 m; **Maximum road speed** 105 km/h; **Range on roads** 560–600 km; **Engine type** Rover 4-cylinder OHV; **Engine power** 77 bhp; **Engine capacity** 2.286 litres; **Fuel capacity** 91 litres.

The ubiquitous Land Rover is used at all levels of the RM, including Headquarters, Mortar Troops and Signals Troops. The usual complement of this vehicle in a Commando is 48 with a similar number

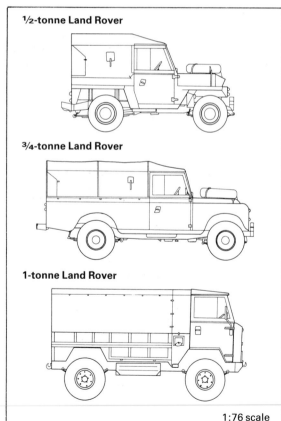

½-tonne Land Rover

¾-tonne Land Rover

1-tonne Land Rover

1:76 scale

Two air-portable ½-tonne Land Rovers at Yeovilton awaiting a 'lift'. The nearer vehicle is equipped with the now-replaced BAT Wombat. Note the lead counterweights on the bumper to balance the gun, also useful for push starting (R. L. Ward).

of ¾-tonne trailers. It is air-portable by Wessex HU 5 (when stripped to lighten the load), or with trailer by the new Sea King HC 4.

Deliveries began in 1968 and the vehicle is well liked for its good four-wheel drive performance and comfort. There are two variants, dependent on radio fit—12v and 24v. Other features include convoy lights and the ability to operate the 'Rover without any lights burning.

The normal paint scheme is drab dark green and black, but there are a number of RM vehicles in standard Navy blue with white 'ROYAL MARINES' legends on the side doors. Several vehicles have, over the years, been fitted with the 120 mm Wombat weapon but this system has now been replaced by Milan. Petrol-driven engines are commonly used for, despite fire risk when carried at sea, especially on the deck of an LPD or *Hermes*, they can be bump-started in the field. The reinforced bumpers assist with starting and pushing.

VB1720 ¾-tonne Land Rover Truck Utility FFR 4 × 4

Crew 1 + 2–8; **Weight loaded** 2,620 kg; **Length** 4.648 m; **Height** 2.057 m; **Width** 1.689 m; **Wheel track** 1.308 m; **Ground clearance** 0.228 m; **Maximum road speed** 88 kmh/h; **Range (roads)**

The 1-tonne Land Rover and trailer unit (RN/LA (Phot) Campbell).

450/500 km; **Engine type** Rover 4-cylinder OHV; **Engine power** 77 bhp; **Engine capacity** 2.286 litres; **Fuel capacity** 91 litres.

The long wheelbase Land Rover has been in production for many years and is a general carrier for the RM, but in much smaller scale use than the half-tonner because they are not so readily air portable. Generally, the ¾-tonne is used at RM barracks and for exercises. There are a number serving with the RMR as supply vehicles. They can be fitted with hard or soft tops, with or without radios, as plain troop transports or for more specialist work. They are not, however, as good as the ½-ton version in cross-country work, being heavier for the same power.

VB1054 Ambulance 4-Stretcher Medium Mobility 4 × 4

Crew 1–2; **Weight in action** 2,670 kg; **Length** 4.826 m; **Height** 2.146 m; **Width** 1.905 m; **Wheel track** 1.308 m; **Maximum road speed** 96 km/h; **Range (roads)** 450 km; **Engine type** Rover 2.5; **Engine power** 77 bhp; **Engine capacity** 2.286 litres; **Fuel capacity** 90.86 litres.

This is an ambulance conversion of the ¾-tonne Land Rover which has been developed by Marshall of Cambridge for use by the Army and RM. It has seen service in Northern Ireland and elsewhere, including the Northern Flank areas. Basically, the long wheelbase Land Rover has been fitted with a new aluminium body to take four Service stretchers and a sitting attendant. The stretchers can be folded away for the accommodation of sitting casualties. The vehicle is finished in olive drab or olive drab and black, with prominent red crosses.

VB1840 1-tonne Land Rover Truck SI Service 4 × 4

Crew 1 + 1–8; **Weight loaded** 3,120 kg; **Length** 4.127 m; **Height** 2.138 m; **Width** 1.842 m; **Wheel track (front)** 1.524 m; **Wheel track (rear)** 1.549 m; **Ground clearance** 0.254 m; **Maximum road speed** 120 kmh/h; **Range (roads)** 560 km; **Engine type** Rover V8; **Engine power** 128 bhp; **Engine capacity** 3.5 litres; **Fuel capacity** 109 litres.

The 1-tonne Land Rover was jointly developed by

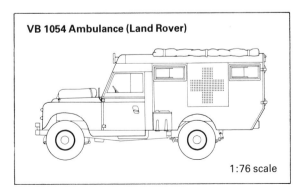

VB 1054 Ambulance (Land Rover)

1:76 scale

Left *Bedford 4-tonne truck for rough terrain work.*

Below *Bedford RL Cargo with 3-ton crane for lifting Rigid Raider craft at a training area* (RM).

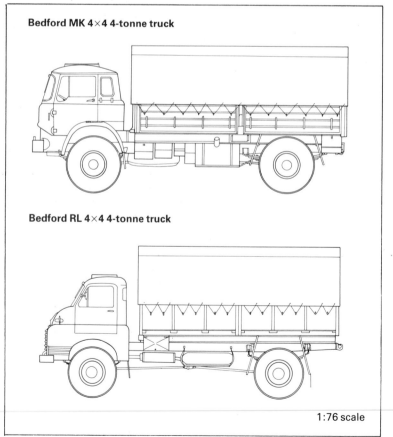

Bedford MK 4×4 4-tonne truck

Bedford RL 4×4 4-tonne truck

1:76 scale

British Leyland's Rover subsidiary and the Motor Vehicle Experimental Establishment for an Army and RM requirement. The vehicle is air-portable by Sea King HC 4 and is used in considerable numbers. It is found in service with Anti-Tank Troops and as a tug for the 105 mm Light Guns of 29 Commando Regiment. It can operate with 81 mm mortar teams and is fitted with a 12v electrical system.

VB2025 Bedford MK 4-Tonne Truck Cargo 4 × 4

Crew 1 + 2; **Weight loaded** 9,650 kg; **Length** 6.579 m; **Height (top of cab)** 2.501 m; **Height (tarpaulin)** 3.404 m; **Width** 2.489 m; **Wheel track (front)** 2.05 m; **Wheel track (rear)** 2.03 m; **Maximum road speed** 73 km/h; **Range (roads)** 560 km; **Engine type** Bedford 6-cylinder; **Engine power** 106 bhp; **Engine capacity** 5.42 litres; **Fuel capacity** 150 litres; **Load area** 4.28 × 2.01 m.

The highly successful Bedford MK 4-tonne truck has all but completely replaced the Bedford RL Truck which had been produced in large numbers

for all the British Armed Forces. It is seen in two main variants: the Bedford EJN which is a commercial transport for driver training at RM Poole and for limited roadwork; and the cross-country 4 × 4 MK with its characteristic drab paint finish. Actually, several MK models are painted Navy Blue with the 'ROYAL MARINES' legend for recruiting (with Recruit Company, RM Poole).

The basic role of the 4-tonner in RM service is as a Rifle Company transport and support vehicle with the B echelon (stores). A typical Commando will have between 15 and 20 Mks on strength. Other typical uses of the cargo, soft or hard top truck are to transport the Assault Engineer Troop and to provide mobility and transport to the Commando HQ.

There are three basic variants of the MK in service with the RM: VB2050 4-tonne truck with winch; VB2091 4-tonne truck with flat platform; and VB2204 4-tonne truck with bulk fuel. The flat bed truck can have a number of special containers fitted which include provision of a workshop for the RM's craftsmen. The bulk fuel adaption is widely used to support RN and RM helicopters in the field and during training sorties/exercises on such places as Salisbury Plain. These vehicles are often manned by RN personnel.

Bedford MK Crane and Flat

Crew 1 + 2; **Weight** 9,000 kg (approx); **Length** 6.36 m; **Height (top of cab)** 2.602 m; **Width** 2.39 m; **Wheel track** 1.854 m; **Maximum road speed** 72.4 km/h; **Range (roads)** 402.3 km; **Engine type** Bedford 6-cylinder; **Engine power** 130 bhp; **Engine capacity** 4.93 litres; **Load area** 4.27 × 2.18 m.

The Bedford Crane and Flat Bed truck is based on the standard 4 × 4 Bedford 4-tonne chassis and can be used to transport small craft, including Raiding Craft and Motor Dories, or Gemini.

Water Tankers

The RM, like all Services, needs water for everyday needs. Marines are particularly fussy about washing and cooking, maintaining that one can only fight well when completely fit, and this includes well fed and clean: 'why else are the Army's troops called Pongos? . . .'

The Corps has 1- and 3-tonne water carriers, both trailer-borne and self-propelled. One will be found with each Commando, probably at the Commando HQ.

Motor cycles

The RM still operates motor cycles as war machines and for convoy escort work. The current bikes are

cars used, the Ford Granada and Cortina as staff cars and the Ford Escort Estate and BL Mini for personnel transportation.

Recovery vehicles

There are a number of light and medium recovery vehicles operated by the RM in uniform, including the former Army FV13115 Recovery Vehicle Wheeled which uses a Bedford RL chassis. Many of these vehicles, although available to the Royal Marines, are operated by Army units and thus are outside the scope of this book.

Specialist vehicles

VC7765 Tractor, Wheeled, Fork Lift 4,000 lb—Rough Terrain

Crew 1; **Weight complete** 2,961 kg; **Weight air-portable** 2,560 kg; **Length** 5.461 m; **Height (fork raised to maximum)** 3,708 m; **Height (top of mast)** 2,388; **Height (airportable)** 1.829 m; **Width** 1.854 m; **Wheel track** 1.55 m; **Maximum road speed** 64 km/h; **Range (roads)** 644 km; **Range (cross-country)** 322 km; **Engine type** Perkins 4-236 diesel; **Engine power** 78 bhp; **Engine capacity** 3.8 litres; **Fuel capacity** Unknown; **Maximum lift** 1,814 kg.

One of the strangest specialist vehicles, used for amphibious operations and for general purpose duties at RM barracks, is the Eager Beaver wheeled fork lift. The vehicle can ford 0.76 m so can be used to transfer materials from a landing craft to the beach, or on river crossings. The fork lift part is adjustable and is laid back 60° for air transport in a C-130K Hercules C 1 or C 3 RAF transport aircraft,

the Canam Bombadier for combat and the Triumph Tiger with Polaris fairing for convoy work and driver training. The latter is carried out at RM Poole. Kawasaki 'scramblers' were also used during the drive on Port Stanley in May/June 1982.

Utility vehicles

As in any organisation which needs to be mobile and to carry personnel and light equipment around the countryside, the RM has a number of utility ('tilly') type vehicles which are usually found at RM centres and barracks. The Bedford Sherpa is extensively used, usually in an RM blue scheme with the Corps legend on the side. The RM also use Naval vehicles which are designated Car Utility Large 1144-4828. In addition, there are a large number of commercial

FV13115 Recovery vehicle

1:76 scale

Above left *Canam Bombadier motor cycles for combat duties.*

Above right *The Eager Beaver wheeled fork-lift with fuel/water 'Jerry' cans (Commando Forces).*

Right *Now used mainly by the RCT, the Tractor Wheeled Fork Lift Rough Terrain Waterproofed Medium—or the Michigan for short. Here it is fitted with Class 30 trackway and track dispenser (CGRM).*

Disembarking from an Army landing craft, a Bv202 and trailer also tows a 105 mm Light Gun of the RA Commando (45 Commando).

or underslung from a Sea King HC 4. In the Northern Flank operating areas, the Eager Beaver is fitted with a cab for driver protection.

The RM also make use of the Tractor Wheeled Fork Lift Rough Terrain Waterproofed Michigan. The RCT also use this vehicle for a similar purpose of laying Class 30 trackway.

VB1260 Carrier Full Tracked Arctic LHD
Armament 1 × 7.62 mm L7A2 Machine-Gun (if fitted); **Crew** 2 + 8–10; **Weight in action** 4,200 kg; **Length** 6.172 m; **Height** 2.21 m; **Width** 1.759 m; **Ground clearance** 0.3 m; **Maximum road speed** 39 km/h; **Range (roads)** 400 km; **Engine type** Volvo type B18 petrol; **Engine power** 91 bhp; **Engine capacity** 1.78 litres; **Fuel capacity** 156 litres.

The Volvo Bv202 Mk II is a Swedish-designed over-snow vehicle which has been adopted by the RM and the British Army since 1968. The vehicle can be used to draw the 105 mm Light Gun, an

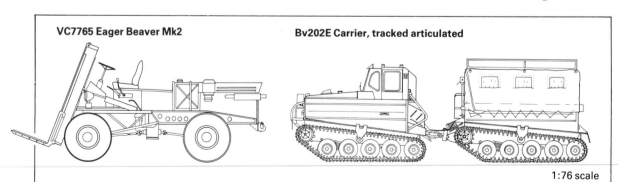

VC7765 Eager Beaver Mk2   Bv202E Carrier, tracked articulated

1:76 scale

The Aktiv Fischer ST4 can be either operated with canvas canopy (nearer) or without, as for the Wombat-carrying variant (3 Commando Brigade).

Articulated Passage Compartment or stores carriers, and is frequently seen with a section of ski-troops in tow. Because its use is restricted to Norway, except for a few training models, the Bv202 is left hand drive (LHD) and is used for cross-country work. If the Articulated Passage Compartment has a soft top, this can be opened to give a cargo area of 2.3 × 1.56 m. The Bv202 is air-portable under a Sea King HC 4. The general appearance of these vehicles is white with occasionally dark green/black camouflage patterns painted overall. The vehicle was used on East Falkland, especially around Goose Green and San Carlos.

Snow Cat AB Aktiv Fischer ST4

This vehicle resembles a rather small Bv202, which replaced it in general use, and is used by Surveillance Troop of 45 Commando and for training with Naval Air Squadrons at Yeovilton. It is tracked and can be fitted with a canvas cab cover or used without one, and was formerly used as such for BAT Wombat. The vehicle is of Swedish design and is classified as a Carrier Fully Tracked.

Vehicle summary

A typical Rifle Company of the Royal Marines will probably have the following vehicles on strength: 2 × ½-tonne Land Rovers and 1 × 4-tonne Bedford truck. A Mortar Troop, on the other hand, has a considerable amount of kit to move around and the following could be typical: 2 × ½-tonne Land Rovers and 7 × 1-tonne Land Rovers. A Commando Brigade could be considered fully equipped with 500 vehicles and 400 trailers.

Royal Marines aircraft

The RM maintains close link with the Army Air Corps for providing its helicopters and associated equipment. Currently there are three types of helicopter in service: the Gazelle AH 1 and the Lynx AH 1, which will replace the Scout AH 1 in the HQ element of 3 CBAS. It is envisaged that the Royal Marines Air Squadron will move into the vacant hangars of the RN's Lynx squadrons at Yeovilton in 1982/3.

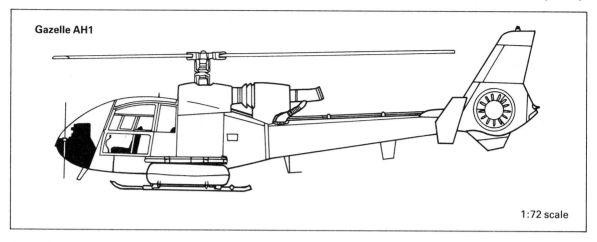

Gazelle AH1

1:72 scale

Gazelle AH 1

Manufacturer Westland; **Purpose** Commando utility; **Crew** 1/2 pilots; up to 3 passengers; **Squadrons** 3CBAS; **Range** 650 km; **Endurance** 2.46 hours; **Max speed** 265 km/h; **Cruise speed** 240 km/h; **Service ceiling** 4,549 m; **Rate of climb** 408 m/min; **Length** 9.52 m; 12.09 m (rotors); **Height** 3.02 m (to rotor hub); **Width** 2.0 m; **Rotor diameter** 10.5 m; **Weapons** Flares; 68 mm rocket pads; **Engine** 1 × Turbomeca/RR Astazou; **Fuel capacity** 445 litres; **All-up weight** 1,800 kg; **Embarked** *Hermes*; LPDs, LSLs, etc.

Conceived as a replacement for the Sud Aviation Alouette II, the SA341 Gazelle was eventually produced by Anglo-French arrangement under the aegis of Aérospatiale and Westland. The Gazelle AH 1 is the Army/Royal Marines variant, the first prototype of which flew on April 28 1970, at Yeovil.

Initially 29 were ordered and at any one time the Royal Marines have about 12 available, although they normally draw from Army stocks at Middle Wallop, where major servicing is carried out.

The Gazelle is a semi-rigid rotor type and is used at present by 3 CBAS at RM Bickleigh near Plymouth and at RM Condor. The RM flies the helicopter in a battlefield reconnaissance, observation, and QRF role, being very pleased with the type's quick response even in the severe conditions in northern Norway. RM aircrew, usually Sergeant Pilots or Lieutenants, have become very adept at landing the Gazelle in tight places and, even aboard large ships like *Hermes*, it is possible for the pilot to put the Gazelle down on a lift for immediate transfer below decks. When operating from ships, the Gazelles are equipped with special wheels to facilitate easy deck handling. In overwater

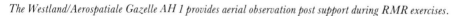

The Westland/Aérospatiale Gazelle AH 1 provides aerial observation post support during RMR exercises.

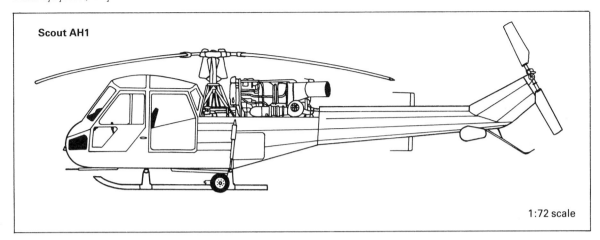

Scout AH1

1:72 scale

operations, flotation bags are worn on the skids to keep the helicopter upright or at least afloat in the event of a ditching. Most aircraft are fitted with radalts (radio altimeters) for operations over snow where it is possible for the pilot to misjudge the height of his 'cab' from the snow on the landing ground and, as a result, make a heavy landing. This would be particularly unfortunate if the Gazelle was in its casevac role. The helicopters are painted dark green/black (similar to Army machines) and carry white RM lettering, serials and codes (painted out in war).

Scout AH 1

Manufacturer Westland; **Purpose** Commando utility; **Crew** 1/2 pilots; up to 4 passengers; **Squadrons** 3CBAS; **Range** 507 km; **Endurance** Circa 2.5 hours; **Max speed** 210 km/h; **Cruise speed** 196 km/h; **Service ceiling** 3,810 m; **Rate of climb** 439 m/min; **Length** 9.34 m; 12.29 m (rotors); **Height** 2.72 m (to rotor hub); **Width** 1.65 m; **Rotor diameter** 9.83 m; **Weapons** GPMG; AS 11; Flares; **Engine** Rolls Royce Nimbus 105 rated at 710 shp; **Fuel capacity** 709 litres; **All-up weight** 2,404 kg; **Embarked** Usually shore-based but can be embarked in *Hermes*, LPDs, LSLs, etc.

The Westland Scout is the military version of the Navy's Wasp HAS 1 anti-submarine helicopter and is used by the Army and by the Royal Marines Commando Brigade Air Squadron. With the Lynx AH 1 entering service the Scout AH 1's days are numbered but it has provided a good utility and anti-tank vehicle for the Commando units in the field, especially with the use of Nord AS 11 ATM (in association with the AF120 sight mounted on the left-hand side of the front cabin). For service in the snow-covered areas of the Northern Flank, a radalt (radio altimeter) is fitted and the helicopters usually fly with Wasp-style flotation equipment above the

cabin. In Norway, the helicopters are sometimes white-washed over the green areas of their camouflage to give a black/white effect which is most useful in the mountain-side terrain of Norway. In peacetime the Union Flag is carried on the nose of 3CBAS aircraft, but this would be deleted in time of war or tension. The Scout also has a casevac role and totally enclosed stretcher cases may be carried on the skids, whilst others are accommodated in the rear cabin which has special extensions on the fuselage sides.

Lynx AH 1

Manufacturer Westland; **Purpose** Assault and utility; **Crew** 1 pilot; 1 aircrewman; up to 10 passengers; **Squadrons** 3CBAS; **Range** 650 km; **Endurance** 2.25 hours; **Max speed** 295 km/h plus;

Seen during a 'wash and rocket' is a Scout of the HQ Flight of 3rd Commando Brigade Air Squadron.

Cruise speed 275 km/h (250 km/h on 1 engine); **Service ceiling** Classified; **Rate of climb** 710 m/min; **Length** 13.17 m; 15.16 m (rotors); **Height** 3.51 m; **Width** 2.96 m; **Rotor diameter** 12.8 m; **Weapons** 6 × TOW; 2–4 × 7.62 mm L20A1 MG; Flares; **Engine** 2 × RR BS360 Gem turboshafts rated at 850 shp; **Fuel capacity** 909 litres; **All-up weight** 4,310 kg; **Embarked** Can be deployed afloat.

Although it first flew in 1973, the Westland-designed Lynx AH 1 only began operations with the Royal Marines' Commando Brigade Air Squadron in 1982/3. The helicopter, used by the British Army at home and in Germany, is probably the finest multi-role aircraft of its class in the Western world. Its performance is particularly good and the cockpit arrangement, including the TANS computer-assisted navigation system, reduces pilot workload enabling more effective tactical flying. The Lynx in RM service will be primarily an anti-tank weapon using the proved Hughes TOW system already in operation with the Army. As TOW is an optically tracked wire guided missile, the normal flying complement is a pilot (in the right-hand seat) and an Air Gunner/Observer, in a similar fashion to the AS 11-equipped Scouts, which it will replace. Most probably destined for the Northern Flank area in wartime, the Lynx could be used for quick reaction forces equipped with the Milan ATM and for utility tasks. The fact that it has two engines and very superior manoeuvrability will undoubtedly mean that it will be far more flexible in operation than the Scout or even the Gazelle. Besides TOW, 7.62 mm machine-guns can be fitted and various ancillary stores such as reconnaissance flares and Nitesun used. Another modern feature incorporated in the design is the BITE (built-in test equipment) which gives an immediate indication of a fault thus enhancing the serviceability of the helicopter in the field. TOW trials were carried out in northern Norway in the winter of 1981/1982, where the helicopter was shown to have good NoE (Nap of the Earth) tactical flying ability.

Air-launched missiles
BGM-71 TOW M151E2

Role Anti-tank; **Status** In service; **Weight** 24 kg; **Length** 1.168 m; **Body diameter** 0.152 m; **Warhead weight** 3.9 kg; **Velocity** Mach 1; **Rate of fire** Single or ripple; **Range** 65 m to 4 km; **Manufacturer** Hughes; **Aircraft equipped** Lynx AH 1.

Although the Hughes TOW (Tube-launched, Optically-tracked, Wire-guided) missile has been in

Seen during trials in Norway, Royal Marines Lynx fitted with TOW (Westland).

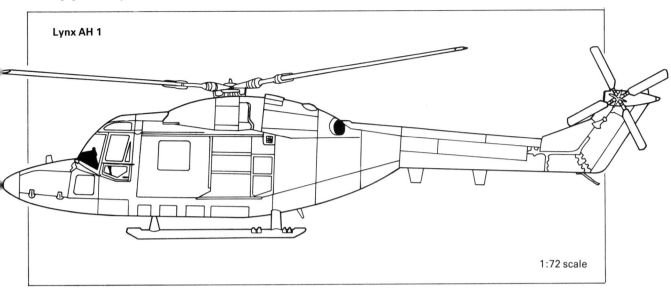

Lynx AH 1

1:72 scale

Army Air Corps service since 1980/1, it has only been introduced to RM service since 1982/early 1983, when the Lynx AH 1, its carrier, came into service also. TOW is a second generation anti-tank missile which is designed to penetrate the hulls of every known main battle tank (408 mm at 60°). The aiming sequence is relatively easy as the aimer (sitting in the left-hand seat of the front cockpit) just keeps the target in the sight cross-wires until impact at a range of up to 4 km. The Scout helicopters of the Commando Brigade Air Squadron are currently equipped with AS 11* and this will soldier on until 1984/5, but without doubt the Lynx and TOW combination is a versatile and potent anti-tank weapon. During trials on Salisbury Plain in 1980, AAC Lynx flown by Company test pilots achieved 100 per cent accuracy with the missiles. The normal complement is eight missile tubes, each 2.2 m long, four on either side of the main cabin, plus a further eight tubes available in the cabin for reload.

* The AS 11/SS 11 system is described in the RN air-launched weapons section of this Chapter.

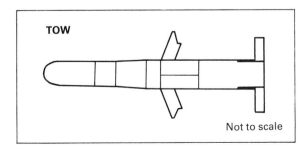

TOW

Not to scale

Royal Marines water craft

The Royal Marines is a water-borne force with salt water running through the veins of every Marine. Even though the amphibious role is no longer predominant, the Corps still maintains a pre-eminence in water craft under the guidance of Landing Craft Company based on the side of Poole Harbour, Dorset. Marines are trained to operate small boats and the larger landing craft at Poole as part of the specialist qualifications (SQ) system. Landing craft and small craft crews are known as LC1 (highest) to LC3 competence.

Water craft in the RM are: Landing Craft Utility (LCU); Landing Craft Vehicle & Personnel (LCVP); Rigid Raider Craft; Gemini; Avon Searider; and Klepper Canoe. In addition, 59 Independent Commando Squadron of the Royal Engineers operates the Mark 5 Assault Boat which weighs 181 kg and has the dimensions of 4.88 m × 1.68 m × 0.64 m. It can carry 1,043 kg or 12 fully-equipped troops. The type may be seen in operation with Marines as crew or complement in certain operations, especially in the Northern European Command (NEC) area.

Landing Craft Utility

Formerly known as the Landing Craft Mechanised, the main purpose of this craft is to land vehicles of the order of MBTs and trucks, for logistic re-supply and for the transportation of large groups of Marines. Four are carried in the well dock of each LPD—*Intrepid* and *Fearless*—from where they can load vehicles, supplies and personnel under cover.

Above *One of* Intrepid*'s LCUs landing Marines on the Dorset coast* (Commando Forces). **Below** *This LCU is manoeuvring out of* Fearless*'s well deck during landing operations—note the Wessex HU 5 and Scout AH 1 on the ship's flight deck* (Commando Forces).

They have a limited beach assault role in the modern context. During 1980–1 and 1982–2 winter seasons, the RM have experimented with an 'arcticised' LCU to prove that such craft can be operationally effective even in northern Norway. Previous LCU operations have been concentrated on and in LPDs with all their facilities. Part of the cargo deck has been covered by a GRP 'igloo' for living accommodation and the craft has been camouflaged drab and black: it is now named the 'Black Pig'. Its normal base is RM Poole.

Length 25.7 m; **Beam** 6.5 m; **Draught** 1.7 m; **Displacement** 76,272 kg up to 178,985 kg fully loaded; **Crew** Colour Sergeant + 6; **Capacity** 100 tonnes of cargo, vehicles or personnel; **Engines** 2 × Paxman diesels rated at 624 bhp; **Speed** 10 knots.

Numbers L700–L711 are operated at RM Poole, and four make up the complement of each active LPD. L3508 was built by Vospers after the war and is operated at Instow for trials. When operating from LPDs, the craft carry 'tactical pennant' numbers: *Intrepid* (T series); *Fearless* (F series). Training craft carry P. One of the LCUs at Poole has a Portakabin in the main cargo deck for use as a chart house for navigation training. The craft are fitted with navigation radar and an enclosed wheelhouse. At least one LCU was lost in San Carlos water in May 1982 as a result of Argentine air action; it was designated F4 from *Fearless*. Other LCUs were used as casualty ferries and as auxiliary fire-fighting craft during the conflict.

Landing Craft Vehicle & Personnel

Length 12.7 m; **Beam** 3.1 m; **Draught** 0.8 m; **Displacement** 8,644 kg up to 13,730 kg; **Crew** Corporal + 2; **Capacity** 35 Marines or 2 × ½-tonne Land Rovers (1 × Land Rover if launched from ship's davits); **Engines** 2 × Foden diesels rated at 200 bhp; **Speed** 10 knots.

These are small light landing craft which operate from davits in *Fearless*, *Intrepid* and *Hermes* for the transportation of 35 marines or two ½-tonne Land Rovers. Examples of these craft are either painted grey with black boot top and tactical number, or camouflaged drab green and black. The LCVPs aboard LPDs are LCVP(2) type for which the specification above is correct and they are numbered 142–149; in addition there are still a number of LCVP(1) craft in training and utility roles, numbered 102, 112, 118, 120, 123, 127–8, 134 and 136. LCVP(3)s, which have a length of 13.1 m and are powered by 130 bhp Foden diesels (8 knots) are numbered 150–158.

The Royal Corps of Transport operate a number

Paratroops pour ashore at San Carlos from LCVPs (Popperfoto).

of former RM landing craft for logistic re-supply; they are believed to be the LCVP(3) type.

There are a number of other landing craft in service with the RN in auxiliary or training roles, including two Landing Craft Mechanised (LCM(7)) types: dimensions 18.4 m × 4.9 m × 1.2 m, powered by 2 × Gray diesels rated at 290 bhp to give 10 knots. They are numbered 7037 and 7100. In addition, there are three LCP(L)3 type craft (Landing Craft Personnel) which are operated as RN utility craft and displace 10 tonnes loaded; their dimensions are 11.3 m × 3.4 m × 1.0 m and they have 2 × Paxman diesels rated at 225 bhp to give 12 knots.

All other Landing Craft are operated by the British Army's Royal Corps of Transport in UK and Hong Kong waters.

The RM are currently considering two new designs of Landing Craft for service in the middle to late 1980s, because not only does the withdrawal of the LPDs by 1985 and of *Hermes* the same year, render the amphibious capability seriously weakened, but the LCVP types are now long in the tooth. At the RM Amphibious Trials and Training Unit at Instow, Devon, the Corps is considering a new aluminium craft capable of longer-range work and of greater transit speeds, which could be as high as 20 knots. A larger craft which could be capable of carrying four trucks and a Commando Company with its equipment is also under consideration, but it has not gone beyond the model/planning stage at present. This craft would be in the order of 60 m long and displace 350 tonnes with a speed of 12–15 knots. It could be used for independent operations in the Northern Flank area as a Mobile Command Post, Communications Centre or Medical Evacuation craft. It would be equipped with self-defence weapons such as 20 mm Oerlikon guns and perhaps an anti-aircraft missile system. The Landing Craft organisation in the Royal Marines is therefore going to have a very important role in the future.

In Norwegian waters, an LSL unloads an LCVP with arctic canopy and (behind) a Rigid Raider (45 Commando).

A Rigid Raiding Squadron at speed (RM).

Rigid Raider

Length 5.2 m; **Beam** 2.2 m; **Height** 1.1 m; **Draught** 0.25 m; **Weight** 590 kg; **Engine** 1–2 Johnson outboards rated at 140 hp; **Speed** 35 knots plus.

The Dell Quay Rigid Raider is GRP-constructed, unsinkable and able to penetrate even high surf. It is modelled on the Dory 17 hull (also used by the RN). The normal complement is a coxswain, usually from one of the Raiding Squadrons (again trained at RM Poole), and there is room for nine marines. When the Illegal Immigrant (II) situation became particularly tricky in 1979, 3 Raiding Squadron, RM, was formed in Hong Kong with Rigid Raiders, but experience soon showed that the craft were easily damaged in brushes with the smugglers' snake boats, and although not sunk, the Raiding Craft are expensive. The Avon Searider was substituted. Raider hulls can be stacked three high and are fitted with inflatable bags for 'passenger' comfort. These craft are also used for guard boats and provided a valuable service keeping private yachts away from the Royal Fleet Review at Spithead in 1977.

Gemini

Type Avon; **Length** 4.72 m; **Beam** 1.9 m; **Weight** 144 kg; **Displacement (dry)** 2,500 kg; **Displacement (swamped)** 1,800 kg; **Max payload** 954 kg/10 persons; **Engine** 40 hp outboard to give 18 knots.

Type Dunlop; **Length** 4.6 m; **Beam** 1.9 m; **Weight** 137.4 kg; Other specifications as for Avon type.

The inflatable Gemini is a famous assault, patrol and supply craft which is manufactured to a Ministry of Defence specification by several subcontractors, including Dunlop and Avon. The Assault version is a 10-man craft (see RN Small Craft for details of the 6-man type). The craft has been in service for about 25 years, and the 2nd Raiding Squadron, RMR, based at London, uses the Gemini exclusively. They can be rolled up into maximum dimensions of 176 × 89 × 54 mm (including floorboards) for transportation in the cargo compartment of a 4-tonne truck. Alternatively, they may be kept inflated, thus saving 30 minutes.

Avon Searider SR5M

Length 5.43 m; **Beam** 2.03 m; **Weight** 300 kg; **Weight (operating)** 495 kg; **Displacement (dry)** 2,450 kg; **Displacement (swamped)** 1,545 kg; **Capacity** 750 kg or 10 persons; **Engine** 1 × Johnson outboard rated at 90 hp; **Speed** 40 knots.

The Searider is designed as a rigid-hull inflatable craft to give resilience and yet be portable. Many warships are now equipped with them and 3 RSRM in Hong Kong uses them in the anti-II role. In this role, they are crewed by a coxswain and an LEP (locally enlisted personnel) to operate in conjunction with RN hovercraft in the inlets and around the many harbours of the Colony. Although they have navigation lights as standard equipment, they are forced to operate without lights during the night-time patrols. A radar reflector is, however, used with which the radar-picket hovercraft can guide them against snake boats and sampans. Many successful chases and arrests have been made by the Squadron using the Searider. They operate as a

Three Avon Seariders at Hong Kong await a night-time anti-smuggler operation: note the radar reflector and furled Union Flag.

group of four or five, mutually assisting one another as required.

Although, the Searider's bow is double-skinned there is still a risk in travelling at maximum speed through Hong Kong harbour at night in pursuit of a suspected smuggler. The propellor is particularly vulnerable to the floating debris which abounds.

Klepper Canoe

Length 5.36 m; **Beam** 0.91 m; **Weight** 50.8 kg (dry).

This craft is used by the SBS and their swimmer-canoeist specialists for reconnaissance and clandestine assault and other unspecified tasks. The canoe can be towed behind a submerged SSK, launched from its deck or floated out of a landing craft. The canoe is a two-man kayak type with camouflaged pattern covering.

Uniforms and insignia

The Senior Service has always had the smartest uniform of any of the British Armed Forces, and for all intents and purposes, the RN and the WRNS dress alike. The RFA have a distinctive marine uniform dictated by their merchant status, whilst the RMAS wear a mixture of civilian work dress and marine reefer jacket. The RNXS wear quasi-naval dress not unlike that of the now disbanded Civil Defence war surplus kit. The Royal Marines have adapted British Army dress to suit.

Special Dress

In the late 1970s, Special Dress regulations were issued to cover the appointment of RN and RM officers to NATO, North American and hot climate

Arctic warfare calls for some interesting gun positions—note particuarly the ski-pole rest. The Marines illustrated are wearing NCB gear and full arctic protective clothing (RM).

appointments. The RN have noted this as No 1W White Full Dress whilst the RM call it No 4W Stone Coloured Service Dress; basically it is a cap or beret (RM) with stone-coloured tunic and trousers, tie, shirt and boots/shoes. RM officers wear Sam Brownes and could be required to wear the white helmet as well.

Mountain & Arctic Warfare

Today, most of the UK's Commando Forces are M&AW trained for operations in Norway and other regions with a similar climate. The Royal Marines have specialist dress for these operations which are not mirrored by the RN. Any RN officers or ratings who go to Norway, for example the Naval Air Commando Squadrons, wear RM issue clothing.

Naval officers attached to RM units will wear the RM dress for working with 'ROYAL NAVY COMMANDO' shoulder flashes and the naval crest in the beret, as opposed to the anodised or bronze Corps crest. Naval rank badges will also be worn on RM uniform as required. RM officers wear either cloth or bronze rank badges (Army pattern) as applicable to the style of dress. Some aircrew from the Commando Brigade Air Squadron will wear Army Air Corps pattern flying suits or camouflage (DMP) suits and Army pattern boots as required; Naval Air Commando aircrew also wear DPM suits in certain situations. The latter are more comfortable than certain of the Naval aircrew dress garments.

In hot climates, the RN and RM have adapted their dress accordingly. Both RN and RM officers wear white dress (No 2W) for mess functions as per No 2s. Whereas RN officers continue to wear white (including 'safari' jackets) with long or short trousers, the Corps have adopted stone-coloured bush jackets (No 5W)—equivalent to Nos 1, 4 and 5 Dress. The RN has a speciality in its No 10W Red Sea Rig which consists of white dress shirt, navy blue trousers, black (or FAA Squadron) cummerbund and shoes; this is worn in the evening for normal

No 1 Dress Uniform as worn by ratings of the RN; in front are two Petty Officers. This is a rehearsal for the Albert Hall Remembrance Service (HMS Excellent).

mess dress. The RM have a similar dress for hot climates which is made up of white tropical shirt, blue trousers, scarlet cummerbund and black shoes—this is known as No 10W as well.

In hot climates in action, the RM have No 11W Tropical Combat Dress which consists of beret, combat shirt, light-weight trousers, puttees, DMS boots and web belt; tropical DPM combat smocks may be worn if ordered. RN officers on bridge watchkeeping wear a form of rating action dress, and at sea in tropical climates, wear blue short-sleeved shirt and blue shorts with sandals.

In hot climates, Marines and ratings have special clothing including stone-coloured bush jackets (RN—No 2A/6/7; RM—No 5W) or shirt sleeve order (RN—No 7A/7N; RM—No 6W). Light-weight working dress (RN—No 8s; RM—No 8W) consists of shirt and trousers whilst there is seagoing tropical routine dress of shirt and shorts known to both Services as No 10s. in stone colour or No 10W in blue (eg, Hong Kong Squadron). Royal Marines

wear No 11W Tropical Combat Dress: this is in place of No 11 Combat dress.

No 8A Arctic Working Dress Winter hat; windproof jacket; lightweight trousers; combat shirt; jersey; ski march boots; snow gaiters; wool mittens and windproof outer gloves. In addition, arctic overalls are worn by technicians and thermal overboots are issued to ranks on static duty.

No 11A Arctic Combat Dress Winter hat; windproof jacket; windproof trousers; white camouflage suit; ski march boots; snow gaiters and mittens/gloves as required. Underneath combat shirt and Jersey Wool Heavy ('Woolie-Pullie') are worn. The same additions of overboots and overalls apply.

Rating Aircrew No 3A Aircrew blouse and trousers; red badges; shirt/tie or vest; heavy navy jersey; beret; and boots/shoes may be worn during working hours at sea, in harbour, on RNASs, but by aircrew only.

During the last few years, the old rough serge

Dress for officers

Royal Navy	Royal Marines	RN description	RM description	Occasion for wear
No 1 Full Dress Flag Officers	No 1 Full Dress General officers	Ceremonial Day coat; gold-laced trousers; sword; shoulder straps	Ceremonial tunic; sword and cap	Major ceremonial
	Band officers	Not applicable	Full dress tunic; white helmet	Ceremonial parades
Other officers	Other officers	Undress coat; blue trousers; sword; cap; black shoes	Blue RM tunic; white helmet; officer pattern boots (Captain and below), otherwise Wellington boots	Ceremonial parades and special duties
No 2 Ball Dress	No 2 Mess Dress	Mess jacket (Captain and above can wear undress tail coats and gold-laced trousers blue trousers) waistcoat; white shirt; sword; cap; shoes	Scarlet mess jacket; evening shirt; winged collar; Majors and above wear overalls and Wellington boots; other officers blue trousers and shoes	Official and public dinners and receptions
No 4 Blue Dress	No 4 Blue Service Dress	Undress coat; blue trousers; white shirt; cap; shoes; (this is the traditional wedding dress of RN officers)	RM blue tunic; Sam Browne; lanyard; (infantry sword worn on parade with troops carrying side arms at courts martial)	Inspections by Senior Officers; courts martial; funerals; minor ceremonial
No 5 Undress	No 5 Lovat Service Dress	Undress coat; waistcoat; blue trousers; white shirt; cap/beret; shoes/boots	Beret; Lovat tunic and trousers; shoes; cloth belt; Lovat socks	Minor parades; informal visits to HM ships and RM establishments
No 5J Day Undress Jersey	No 5J Lovat with Jersey Wool Heavy	Heavy wool jersey; blue trousers; white shirt; black day tie; cap/beret; shoes/boots	Beret; stone shirt; Lovat trousers; 'Woolie-Pullie'; shoes (boots worn on parade)	Routine duties
No 6 Mess Dress	None	Mess jacket; white waistcoat; blue mess trousers; evening shirt; cap; shoes	None	Civilian evening dress is equivalent; RN wear for dinner with Flag Officers
No 7 Mess Undress	No 7 Mess Undress	Mess jacket; blue trousers; evening shirt; cummerbund/waistcoat; cap; shoes; Captains and above may wear undress tail coat	Cap or side cap; scarlet mess jacket; blue mess waistcoat; blue trousers; evening shirt; shoes or Wellingtons	Mess dinners and evening wear ashore (dinner jacket is civilian equivalent)
No 8 Working Dress	No 8 Military Training Dress	Navy blouse; blue trousers; cap/beret; shoes; (Aircrew wear aircrew pattern blouse and trousers)	Beret; combat shirt; green trousers; jersey; puttees; DMS boots; Corps belt	Training dress (RM and Naval Commando instructors wear DPM jackets)
No 11 Action Dress	No 11 Combat Dress	Blue shirt; blue trousers; cap/beret; shoes/boots (heavy navy jersey may be worn)	Beret; combat jacket; shirt and trousers; puttees; DMS boots or Army pattern boots; (steel helmets)	Operational or training in temperate climates including armed landing parties
No 12 Shirt Sleeve Order	No 5S Lovat Shirt Sleeve Order	White shirt; tie; blue trousers; cap/beret; shoes	Beret; stone shirt; Lovat trousers; Corps belt; shoes	Routine duties in warm weather

Dress for Other Ranks and ratings

Royal Navy	Royal Marines	RN description	RM description	Occasion for wear
No 1s (hot climate equivalent is No 6)	No 1 Full Dress	Worsted surge suit; gold badges; black boots/shoes; Class II Seamen wear seaman's collar; lanyard; black scarf; cotton vest and boots	Cap; blue tunic and trousers; boots; white belt; gloves; (WOs and SNCOs also wear scarlet sash); Band Service wear blue berets or white helmets	Major ceremonial Going on leave or for inspections
No 1s/2s	No 4 Blue Dress	Worsted surge suit; heavy navy jersey; red badges; boots/shoes; Class II Seamen wear as above	Cap; blue tunic, trousers; boots; white belt; shoes if ordered; (WOs and SNCOs wear scarlet sash)	Ceremonial parades, Sundays at sea and in harbour; duty men on upper deck; duty boatcrews
No 2s (hot climate equivalent is No 7)	No 5 Lovat Dress	See text; there are various amendments for hot climates, etc: 2B and 2J	Beret; Lovat trousers and tunic; shoes/boots; stone shirt; white belt	Minor ceremonial; sentry and dutymen; courts martial
No 2N	No 5J Lovat Dress	Dress negative jacket or jumper; shirt; trousers; shoes; Class II wear cotton vest	Beret; stone shirt; jersey; Lovat/barrack dress trousers; shoes	Routine duties
No 2A/2N	No 5S Lovat Shirt Sleeve Order	Tropical shirt; trousers; waistbelt and shoes	Beret; stone shirt; Lovat/barrack trousers; Corps belt; shoes; Army/Naval pattern boots as required; (Band wear white belt)	Routine duties in warm weather
None	No 7 Mess Dress	None	Cap; scarlet mess jacket; blue trousers; scarlet cummerbund; shoes	WOs and SNCOs, Regimental dinners
No 8/9 (No 4 is any clean article of clothing other than No 8)	No 8 Military Work Dress	Blue action working dress shirt and trousers; windproof working jacket; (LC and ship Detachments RM also); Overalls by some trades; blue badges	Beret; combat shirt; trousers; jersey; DMS boots; puttees; (Corps belt as required); overalls for technicians	Working parties
No 9	None	Blue overall suit	None	Dirty jobs
No 10/10A	None	Hot climate vest/shirt; shorts; stockings; shoes; No 10A includes blue shorts	None	Hot climates as ordered
None	No 11 Combat Dress	None (Certain RN ratings may wear RN dress for associated Cdo operations)	Beret; DPM jacket and trousers; combat shirt; puttees and boots; (helmet) may also be worn); Instructors wear Denison smocks; combat clothing worn; denims for arduous training	As ordered by Senior Officer; operational wear (temperate)

items of clothing have been replaced by lightweight polyester materials. This gear is easier to wear, and stands up to washing in automatic laundrettes which now equip ships and establishments, replacing the Chinese laundry service of the old Fleet. Even so, there are still several contingents of Hong Kong Chinese serving in HM Ships, especially the larger ones.

From mid-1980, the familiar ratings' cap was altered to give the wearer better service: it is now two-piece consisting of a peak and frame with a detachable white top. The naval rating still wears 'Square Rig' on all semi-formal and formal occasions and this tradition is very unlikely to change, other than for convenience, the regulations about pressing them in the normal onshore fashion

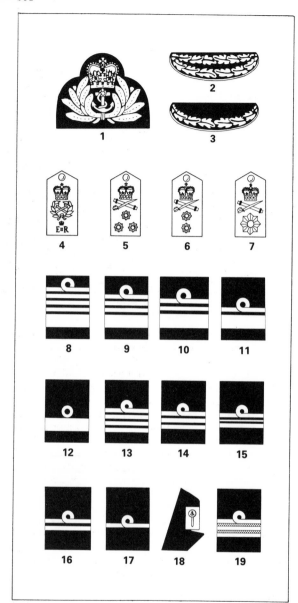

(rather than horizontal creases) being an example.

The 1970s saw the introduction of the Jersey Wool Heavy—the 'Woolie Pullie'—which has revolutionised naval and marine dress. Not only officers wear the garment with rank tabs on the shoulders, but ratings and other ranks now also wear them for routine dress and as part of combat clothing. The WRNS have a V-neck pattern jersey which has replaced the cardigan and lightweight jersey. Shoulder flashes are worn, including 'ROYAL NAVY COMMANDO', 'ROYAL NAVAL RESERVE' and 'ROYAL MARINES COMMANDO'. In 1979, it was announced that a Commando Skills badge would be introduced for ratings who are Commando-qualified, the design being a representation of the Commando fighting knife.

Naval Rank badges

The use of the nautical gold ring and curl is an ancient tradition in the RN, and today they are not only worn on the sleeve of the blue tunic/jacket but also as shoulder straps on Jersey, DPM jackets and flying suits.

Flag Officers

Admiral of the Fleet A broad gold ring with four quarter width rings above; on certain ceremonial dress, a crown over crossed batons within a wreath over the royal cypher is worn on a shoulder strap.

Admiral A broad gold ring with three quarter width rings above; on certain ceremonial dress, a crown over a crossed baton and sabre over three pips (triangular formation) is worn.

Vice Admiral A broad gold ring with two quarter width rings above; on certain ceremonial dress, a crown over a crossed baton and sabre and two pips worn on the shoulder.

Rear Admiral A broad gold ring with one quarter width ring above; on certain ceremonial dress, the shoulder badge is a crown over crossed baton and sabre, over a single pip.

Flag Officers' caps have the Naval cap badge (anchor surmounted by crown in wreath) with two rows of gold oakleaf embroidery to top and edge of naval cap with white cover. (The white cover on all naval caps is retained irrespective of location, climate or season.)

Naval Officers

Commodore A broad gold ring on sleeve or shoulder flash.

Captain Four gold rings on sleeve or shoulder flash.

Commander As for Captain RN, except that only three gold rings are worn. (Cap peaks: the above

1 RN Officers' cap badge, gold with silver anchor and red centre to crown. 2 Flag officers' cap peak, gold on black. 3 Commodore's, Captain's or Commander's cap peak, gold on black. 4–7 Admiral of the Fleet's, Admiral's, Vice Admiral's and Rear Admiral's shoulder boards, gold base, silver insignia, red centre to crown. 8–11 Admiral of the Fleet's, Admiral's, Vice Admiral's and Rear Admiral's sleeve lace, gold on Navy Blue. 12–17 Commodore's, Captain's, Commander's, Lieutenant Commander's, Lieutenant's and Sub-Lieutenant's sleeve lace (duplicated on shoulder boards), gold on Navy Blue. 18 Midshipman's lapel distinction, white with gold button. 19 Distinction cloth, see text: Medical Officers, scarlet; Medical Service Officers, pink; Dental Officers, orange; Instructors (now rarely worn) white.

At sea in the Tropics. The captain of Beachampton *wears Tropical Whites, the Midshipman under Training is in Action Dress and the ship's First Lieutenant still wears his life jacket after boarding a fishing boat.*

A Leading Naval Airman working on the cockpit of a Sea Harrier.

three have a single row of gold oakleaf embroidery to top and peak of the service cap; the badge is the same for all naval officers.)

Lieutenant Commander As for Captain RN except that rank is denoted by two gold rings with a single thin gold ring interposed.

Lieutenant As for Captain RN, except that only two gold rings are worn.

Sub-Lieutenant As for Lieutenant, except that only a single gold ring is worn.

Midshipman A white lapel flash with gold/brass/anodised naval button is worn.

Medical and dental officers

The medical and dental branches of the RN have corresponding ranks to their brother officers from Vice Admiral (Medical) and Rear Admiral (Dental) downwards. There is no equivalent to Commodore in the dental branch. All medical and dental officers have their ranks prefixed with 'Surgeon' and dental officers have (D) after their rank. There are rarely Surgeon Sub-Lieutenants in the active list and never Midshipmen in the medical and dental branches.

Examples of corresponding ranks are:

Medical and dental officers are recruited post-qualification, although they may be university cadets of the RN in the first place. Many use Service life as a unique place to obtain medical training before returning to the National Health Service much enriched for their experience.

The medical officers (including dental officers) of the RN are to be found in establishments and Dockyard sickbays, in Naval hospitals, aboard the larger ships, and attached to frigate and destroyer squadrons. Women are recruited directly into the dental branch of the RN and are not considered to be members of the WRNS. Medical research is carried out at INM Alverstoke where entrants to the branch are also sent after a course at BRNC Dartmouth. Medical and dental students are given the rank of Surgeon Sub-Lieutenant until pre-registration, when they become Acting Surgeon Lieutenants and, on registration, they are commissioned as Surgeon Lieutenants RN.

The RN medical and dental branches are also responsible for the health and general wellbeing of the RN, RM and the other branches. Several RN doctors and dentists are Commando-trained and serve with the RM and RMR.

Medical and dental uniforms are identical to those of the RN's other branches except that the gold rings have intermediate red (medical) and orange

General List RN	Medical officers	Dental officers
Rear Admiral	Surgeon Rear Admiral	Surgeon Rear Admiral (D)
Commander	Surgeon Commander	Surgeon Commander (D)

(dental); pink intermediate rings signify a Medical Service Officer.

Seaman Officers

The 'Fishheads' are perhaps the backbone of the RN at sea, in that they have several sub-specialisations which give variety to the branch's activities: aircraft control; aviation—pilot and observer; mine warfare and clearance diving (MCD); submarines; and hydrographic surveying. It is important to remember that only Seaman Officers are eligible for command at sea, but that the individual sub-specialisation does affect the selection process.

The Aircraft Controller is trained at Yeovilton and is responsible for the guidance and safety of the Fleet's aviation assets, either afloat or based at a Naval Air Station ashore. Pilots and Observers, however, have an intensive and costly (about £1.5 million) course which takes them from elementary flying with the RAF to the operational skills of a front-line helicopter or Sea Harrier unit (pilots only). Training would begin before the Seaman Officer's 23rd birthday. Supplementary List (SL) officers often join the Royal Navy to fly, but all Naval aircrew officers are Naval officers first, having spent time in the 'Grey Funnel Line' at sea. At some time in their careers, they will have undergone watchkeeping training.

Medically fit officers are able to train to become ship's divers and later, if selected, to go on to mine and explosive ordnance disposal courses and training mines countermeasures (MCM). Many such officers are selected to 'drive' the RN's MCMV flotilla units of *Hunt* and *Ton* Class vessels. Today, many officers are volunteering for the Submarine Service and the right to wear the coveted Double Dolphin badge. With the current trend to increase the sub-surface fleet at the expense of the surface combat units, there are openings on the initial training courses at Dolphin. The Submarine Command Course is often called the 'Perishers' Course'. The final sub-specialisation open to the Executive branch is that of hydrographic and oceanographic survey, but unlike others, this branch retains those who have trained throughout their post-Grey Funnel service careers. Many hydrographic officers are members of the Royal Institution of Chartered Surveyors, the world's leading professional body in this field.

The Chaplaincy

The RN is conscious of the needs of men and women for spiritual and community guidance. For many hundreds of years, ships at sea have borne 'men of the cloth' and the major warships of the RN still do. There are Chaplains in the RN and RM from the

Above *The Aircrewman of a Naval Wessex with full flying gear.*

Right 20–22 *Petty Officers' cap badges, gold with silver anchor and red centre to crown: Fleet CPO, Chief PO and PO.* **23** *Other ratings' cap badges (worn when not dressed as seamen), red.* **24** *Fleet CPO's rate badge, predominantly red, gold and blue with white unicorn.* **25** *CPO's gold cuff buttons.* **26** *PO's rate badge, gold with red centre to crown.* **27** *Leading Rate's badge, gold.* **28** *PO's armlet, blue/white/blue stripes, dark blue crown with red centre.* **29** *Naval Patrol armlet, colours as above.* **30** *Chaplain's cross with fouled anchor superimposed.* **31–44** *Specialist badges, normally gold on No 1s, blue on working and tropical dress and otherwise red.* **31** *Pilot's wings;* **32** *Parachutist (gold wings, white parachute);* **33** *Submariner (red centre to crown);* **34** *Observer;* **35** *Aircrew;* **36** *Aircraft controller;* **37** *Seacat aimer;* **38** *Airborne missile aimer;* **39** *Marksman;* **40** *Commando;* **41** *Navigator's Yeoman;* **42** *Volunteer bandman;* **43** *Subsunk parachute assistance group;* **44** *Seaman assigned to duties on the Royal Yacht* Britannia.

20

21

22

23

24

25

26

27

28

29

30

31

32

33

34

35

36

37

38

39

40

41

42

43

ROYAL YACHT

44

Church of England, Church of Scotland, the Free Churches and the Roman Catholic Church. They all wear the cross of their calling on a suit-like uniform jacket, or No 5J and the traditional 'dog collar'. Several RN Chaplains have successfully completed the Commando Training Course at RM Lympstone and are thus entitled to wear the Green Beret.

Chaplains are members of the Wardroom Mess with ranks for administrative purposes and thus considered officers; nevertheless, they are capable of reaching all ranks and their families.

Instructor Officers

The RN's 'Schoolies' are one of the four specialisations of the General List (GL). They are distinguished by the white intermediate rings of their rank insignia and are carried at sea and based ashore. They offer technical advice, meteorological

A seaman of the radar specialisation in action/working dress.

and oceanographical services to the Fleet as well as teaching the trainees of the RN and RM.

After initial training at Dartmouth, the Instructor Officer attends the RN School of Education and Training Technology at *Nelson*. At sea, the 'Schoolie' may well double up as a Flight Deck Officer (FDO) and those serving with the RM can take the Commando Course. Their rank is sometimes suffixed by (I) to indicate their branch.

Supply and Secretariat Officers

The 'Pussers' of the RN provide the support to the Fleet and the RN/RM in general. The Branch provides Supply Officers (SOs) afloat and ashore (Base Supply Officer—BSO) and also the Assistants and Secretaries to Captains and Admirals. Pussers also deal with legal, promotion and welfare matters. Aboard ship, the Pusser can be the Public Relations Officer and undertake secondary duties, such as FDO. Supply officers look after pay, wardroom staff, stores and catering. Like Instructor Officers, they are often trained for bridge watch-keeping and as Officers-of-the Day (OODs).

Examples of Supply and Secretariat specialisations:

Rear Admiral Director General Naval Manpower and Training; Area Flag Officer; Admiral President, RN College, Greenwich.

Commander Supply Officer, DLG; Naval Attaché; BSO Royal Yacht.

Lieutenant Captain's Secretary, Destroyer; Section Officer, Admiral's Staff; Flag Lieutenant to Admiral, General or Air Officer.

Engineering Officers

The RN today and tomorrow is a complex working place with many high technology systems which require competent engineering skills. The RN is lucky to have a university-equivalent training college at Manadon (*Thunderer*) at Plymouth in which to train Engineering Officers of the five sub-specialisations: Marine Engineering (Surface Ship)—both steam and diesel; Marine Engineering (Submarine)—both conventional and nuclear; Weapons Engineering (Surface Ship); Weapons Engineering (Submarine); Air Engineering—including Maintenance Test Pilots.

The Marine Engineering Officer (Surface Ship) is responsible for the hull and general structure of ships, their main propulsion, associated systems, power generation, ventilation and controls for all systems, including fuel and water. The MEO (Submarine) has similar duties aboard submarines which also include the reactors and specialist sub-surface systems. The Weapons Engineering Officer (Surface Ship) is primarily tasked with ensuring that

DPMs and warm jackets characterise this photo taken during winter training in the UK.

weapons are effective at all times. This includes computers, mountings, EW and sonar. The WEO (Submarine) has a similar function in the boats, but includes watchkeeping and Polaris missile systems within his tasks. Finally, the Air Engineering Officer (AEO) ensures that all aircraft perform as required, both fixed and rotary wing types. All avionics and weapons for aircraft come under the AEO's guise.

Royal Naval Reserve

In recognition of the way officers of the Reserve (then RNVR and RNR) answered their country's needs in World War 2, HM King George VI granted the right to wear the gold bands of the RN with the only distinctive mark being the tiny 'R' in the curl of the rings. This move, in 1951, abolished the use of 'Wavy Navy' stripes. Further integration took place in 1976 when the RNR and WRNR came under the command of CINCNAVHOME.

Ratings of the RNR wear the shoulder badge 'ROYAL NAVAL RESERVE' and personnel of the WRNR wear 'WOMEN'S ROYAL NAVAL RESERVE'. Officers of the WRNS wear WRNS

uniform with a tiny blue 'R' in the quadrangle of the rank rings. In all other respects, the badges and uniform of the RNR and WRNR are identical to the regular equivalent.

Special Duties List

SD officers have been commissioned from the ratings of the Fleet and are special in that they have a great wealth of technical expertise and experience of Service life. A large minority of Naval Officers are now commissioned this way. They attend Dartmouth but can only rise in normal events to Lieutenant Commander (SD) rank, many remaining at Lieutenant for up to a dozen years. They are found in specialist branches, such as Photography, Naval Provost and technical skills, such as Engineering. They cannot be distinguished from GL or SL officers on commissioning, except that their beards tend to be greyer.

Sea Cadet and CCF Officers

These gentlemen can be considered as part-time officers who carry out a special task with young men who wish to join the RN or who like the nautical life. They are invaluable to the RN of tomorrow. Their rank marks are illustrated below, being wavy rings from Sub-Lieutenant to Lieutenant Commander.

The Ship's Secretary, in his operational job of Flight Deck Officer, brings Antrim's *Wessex HAS 3 in over the starboard side.*

45–63 *Branch badges. Stars and crowns are added to denote appropriate standards of qualification.* **45** *Missile.* **46** *Sonar.* **47** *Radar.* **48** *Mine warfare.* **49** *Diving.* **50** *Surveying recorder.* **51** *Seaman.* **52** *Electronic warfare.* **53** *Coxswain.* **54** *Radio operator.* **55** *Communications (tactical).* **56** *Master-at-Arms.* **57** *Regulating.* **58** *Physical training.* **59** *Naval airman (*MET *= meteorological recorder). Other letters beneath the badge are:* AH *= aircraft handler,* P *= photographer and* SE *= survival equipment). The air engineering mechanic's badge is identical but carries different lettering:* M *= mechanical,* R *= radio/radar,* WL *= weapons electrical,* W *= weapons,* L *= electrical and* O *= ordnance.* **60** *Marine engineering mechanic; letters under are* M *= mechanical or* L *= electrical.* **61** *Weapons engineering mechanic; letters under are* O *= ordnance or* R *= radio.* **62** *Supply and Secretariat; in this case, letters are carried within the circle:* CA *= caterer,* C *= cook,* S *= steward,* SA *= stores accountant or* W *= writer.* **63** *Medical (red and white); letters under are:* N *= State Registered male nurse,* R *= radiographer,* P *= physiotherapist,* H *= health inspector,* L *= laboratory,* M *= mental nurse or* HP *= health physicist.* **64–66** *Good conduct badges—4, 8 and 12 years respectively.*

Other distinctions

Chaplains wear a gold cross of Christ with naval anchor (fouled) superimposed. Submarine officers and ratings are entitled to wear the Submarine Badge of two gold Dolphins, naval crown and anchor. Officers of the Fleet Air Arm wear either the double wings of the Naval pilot or the wings of the Observer. These awards are worn on the lower sleeve except on certain tropical dress and flying suits; the latter often have name/wings/squadron flashes on the left breast.

Naval ratings

Fleet Chief Petty Officers The Royal Crest of lion and unicorn is worn on the lower sleeve of cuffs on jacket, or on shoulder flash. The cap badge is the Naval crown with anchor surrounded by an oak wreath. FCPOs are technically holders of the Sovereign's warrant—Warrant Officers.

Chief Petty Officers Wear three gilt buttons on each cuff to denote rank. The cap badge is a more compact FCPO badge. Chief Regulating Officers are known in certain circumstances as Master-at-Arms, the senior rating in a ship very often. These much respected men (and women) are allowed to wear their anodised metal branch badges (a crown) on a white strap above the right cuff on the Jersey Wool Heavy.

Petty Officers Wear two crossed and fouled anchors below the Naval crown. The cap badge is a fouled anchor in a circle below a Naval crown.

Leading Rates Wear a fouled anchor on the left arm. Leading Rates and below, when not dressed as seamen, wear the fouled anchor with single circle and a simpler crown on caps and berets.

Good Conduct and Service

RN and RNR ratings are permitted to wear chevrons denoting good conduct, or undetected crime, with a single stripe for each four years', up to a maximum of three for 12 years.

RN ratings wear gold badges on No 1s, red badges on No 2s and blue badges on other dress.

Royal Marines' Rank badges

The Royal Marines, although very much a part of the Royal Navy, make use, where appropriate, of the British Army dress, badge and uniform system. RM officer rank badges are gold, grey or black, depending on circumstances.

General Officers

Lieutenant General A crown over crossed baton and sabre.

Major General A pip (four-pointed star) over a crossed baton and sabre.

Naval diving equipment.

(Cap badges: various forms of globe and laurel badge of the Corps.)

RM General Officers are usually mounted for the review and ceremonial inspection of Marines. There are no Brigadiers in the Corps of Royal Marines.

Field Officers

Colonel A crown over two pips all in line.

Lieutenant Colonel A crown over a pip.

Major A crown.

Junior Officers

Captain Three pips all in line.

Lieutenant Two pips in line.

Second Lieutenant One pip.

Officer Cadets A white stripe across shoulder or white patch with gold button.
Warrant Officers Royal Coat of Arms.

NCOs

Colour Sergeants A crown over three chevrons worn on the upper arm.
Sergeant Three chevrons.
Corporal Two chevrons.
Lance Corporal One chevron.
Colours are altered to suit dress; the Corps cap badge is also worn on the green beret (signifying Commando qualified) or blue new intake beret (also worn by Band Service) when badge is worn on red patch.

WRNS rank badges

The Women's Royal Naval Service have the same eight-button reefer jacket as their male counterparts, but rank is indicated for officers with cornflower blue rings around the cuff, surmounted with a similar blue square. The WRNS wear distinctive hats for officer, senior rates or rating/ Wren use with the Naval cap badge, with cornflower blue wreath.

Officers

All wear the rank indication similar to their male counterpart, but the square instead of the RN curl.
Chief Commandant (HRH the Princess Anne): Rear Admiral equivalent.
Commandant Commodore RN equivalent.
Superintendent Captain RN equivalent.
Chief Officer Commander RN equivalent.
First Officer Lieutenant Commander RN equivalent.
Second Officer Lieutenant RN equivalent.
Third Officer Sub-Lieutenant RN equivalent.
The Senior and Junior rate Wrens wear similar rank badges to their male counterparts, except that they are depicted in cornflower blue. Junior and Leading Wrens wear the Naval pattern cap. The WRNS' crest is a fouled anchor with Naval crown superimposed with 'WRNS' in a scroll at the base. A Wren (ornithological) is perched on the anchor; the whole thing is surrounded by 'naval' rope. WRNS buttons, badges, good conduct awards and marksman badges are the same as the corresponding RN pattern except for the colour.

Queen Alexandra's Royal Naval Nursing Service

Officers of the QARNNS wear a complex insignia of rank which is due to be reviewed in 1982/3; in early 1982 the following system was operating:

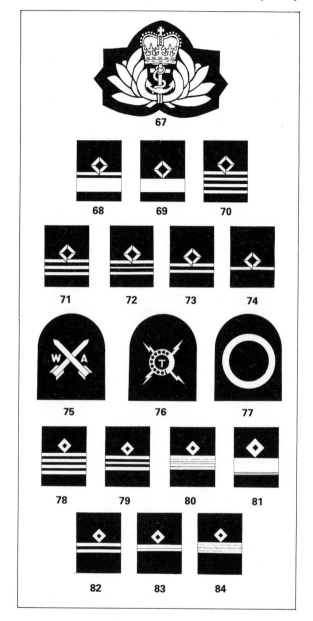

Matron-in-Chief A crown, over the QARNNS badge, over a gold-surrounded red cross on a white background, over the Sovereign's cypher, all on black surrounded by two gold lines. It is worn on the red cape of a senior QARNNS' officer which also has two gold lines around the blue insignia area.
Principal Matron As for Matron-in-Chief but with the Sovereign's cypher replaced by a gold horizontal bar and a thick gold line rather than two thin ones. The two gold cap lines are also not worn.

Left 67 *WRNS cap badge. Like most WRNS badges, identical to its RN counterpart but in blue instead of gold.* **68–74** *WRNS officers' cuff and shoulder board lace: Chief Commandant (only worn by HRH Princess Anne), Commandant, Superintendent, Chief Officer, First Officer, Second Officer and Third Officer.* **75–77** *WRNS category badges. Other than those illustrated, WRNS share the following badges, in blue instead of gold, with their male counterparts: marksman, regulating, radio operator, radar and physical training. They also share the air badge (59 above) with the following letters under: M, R, WL, P or MET; and the Supply and Secretariat badge with the letters C, S, SA and ST (writer, shorthand) or W (writer, pay and general).* **75** *Weapons analyst.* **76** *Telephonist.* **77** *Other categories: this badge may carry the following letters within the circle: DH = dental hygienist, DSA = dental surgery assistant, E = educational assistant, FS = family services, MT = motor transport driver, QA = quarters assistant or TSA = training support assistant.* **78–84** *RFA rank insignia: Master, First Officer, Ship's Surgeon, Commodore Chief Engineer, Second Officer, Assistant Purser and Senior Electrical Officer—all in gold with distinction cloth as described in text.* **Right** *Marines from 45 Commando wear special protective clothing during anti-terrorist operations in Northern Ireland* (RM).

Matron As for Principal Matron but without the gold bar.

Superintending Sister As for Matron but with a red surround to the rank badge.

Senior Sister The cap is blue with red badge area surround; the insignia is as for Superintending Sister but is rectangular and has no red surround. A red bar is also worn under the red cross badge.

Sister As for Senior Sister but without the red bar.

Head Naval Nurse, Assistant Head Naval Nurse and Senior Naval Nurse Wear grade badges on the cuff consisting of vertical red bars; three, two and one respectively. HNN (and Head CQA) and AHNN (and Assistant Head CQA) wear tie pins: the QARNNS' badge with a wreath and crown above, and the same without the wreath respectively.

Clerical and Quarters Officers Wear the same basic badge as Nursing Officers but without the red cross device.

Cap badges The hat badge is the traditional Naval pattern and similar to the WRNS' except that the wreath is red and the Naval crown is replaced by the baton/fouled anchor device of the QARNNS in red and gold. There is also a hat and beret badge of a crown surmounting a red and gold fouled anchor/baton device within a gold line.

Ratings badges QARNNS ratings wear the red batons outlined in gold; CQA ratings wear the WRNS pattern red circle with CQA inside, the 'C' above the QA.

Royal Fleet Auxiliary Service

Officers of the RFA are technically on contract to the Service, being merchant seamen. Their marks of distinction are shown below, and are worn on reefer jackets and jerseys, Naval pattern:

Commodore Master Broad gold ring with gold square of all officers (cf Commodore RN).

Commodore Chief Engineer As for Commodore Master but with purple ring below broad gold.

Master Four gold rings.

Chief Engineer Four gold rings with purple between.

Chief Officer Three gold rings.

Second Engineer Three gold rings with purple between.

Ship's Surgeon Three gold rings with red between.

First Officer Two gold rings with smaller one between (cf Lieutenant Commander RN).

Senior Radio Officer As for First Officer, but light green between.

Senior Electrical Officer As for First Officer, but dark green between (hence the term 'greenie' for this branch).

Senior Purser As for First Officer, but with white between.

Second Officer Two gold rings.

Third Engineer As for Second Officer, but with purple between.

Radio Officer (A) As for Second Officer, but with light green between.

Purser As for Second Officer, but with white between.

Uncertificated Second Officer Two thin gold rings.

First Electrical Officer As for Uncertificated Second Officer but with dark green between.

Uncertificated Third Engineer As above but with purple between.

Third Officer Single gold ring.

Fourth Engineer As for Third Officer but with purple ring below.

Radio Officer (B) As above but with light green below.

Assistant Purser As above but with white below.

Uncertificated Third Officer/Fourth Officer Single narrow gold ring.

Uncertificated Fourth Engineer/Junior Engineer As for Uncertificated Third Officer but with purple narrow ring below.

Second Electrical Engineer As above but with dark green narrow ring below.

NB Uncertificated Third Engineer's rank mark is also used for Senior Refrigeration Engineer; Uncertificated Fourth Engineer's marks for Junior Refrigeration Engineer.

Corresponding Ranks

Today, the RN and RM work closely with their colleagues from other Services and it is important for efficiency and for discipline that everyone knows exactly who is senior to whom. In addition, in bi-or or tri-Service situations, it is important for command to pass smoothly and to the next senior. From the Naval point of view, the controlling apparatus is the Naval Discipline Act 1957, to which all members of the RN, RM, WRNS, RNR and QARNNS are subject. Corresponding ranks are noted in Queen's Regulations and are précised below:

In tropical climates, lightweight combat kit is worn. This is a Lieutenant RM with 81 mm mortar (HMS Bulwark).

Naval	RM and Army	Royal Air Force
Admiral of the Fleet (AF)	Field Marshal*	Marshal of the Royal Air Force
Admiral	General*	Air Chief Marshal
Vice Admiral	Lieutenant General	Air Marshal
Rear Admiral	Major General	Air Vice Marshal
Commodore	Brigadier	Air Commodore
Captain	Colonel	Group Captain
Commander	Lieutenant Colonel	Wing Commander
Lieutenant Commander	Major	Squadron Leader
Lieutenant	Captain	Flight Lieutenant
Sub-Lieutenant/		
Acting Sub-Lieutenant†	Lieutenant	Flying Officer
Midshipman†	Second Lieutenant	Pilot Officer, Acting Pilot Officer

* No equivalent in the Royal Marines.
† Junior to military and RAF ranks on same level.

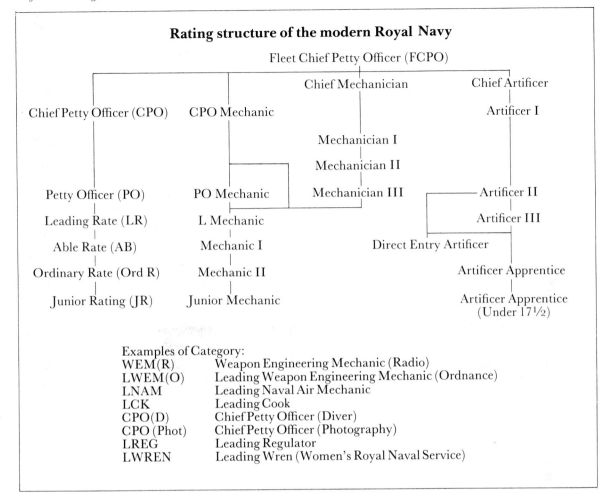

Rating structure of the modern Royal Navy

Fleet Chief Petty Officer (FCPO)

Chief Mechanician

Chief Artificer

Chief Petty Officer (CPO) — CPO Mechanic

Artificer I

Mechanician I

Mechanician II

Petty Officer (PO) — PO Mechanic — Mechanician III

Artificer II

Leading Rate (LR) — L Mechanic

Artificer III

Able Rate (AB) — Mechanic I — Direct Entry Artificer

Ordinary Rate (Ord R) — Mechanic II

Artificer Apprentice

Junior Rating (JR) — Junior Mechanic

Artificer Apprentice (Under 17½)

Examples of Category:

WEM(R)	Weapon Engineering Mechanic (Radio)
LWEM(O)	Leading Weapon Engineering Mechanic (Ordnance)
LNAM	Leading Naval Air Mechanic
LCK	Leading Cook
CPO(D)	Chief Petty Officer (Diver)
CPO (Phot)	Chief Petty Officer (Photography)
LREG	Leading Regulator
LWREN	Leading Wren (Women's Royal Naval Service)

When Royal Marines officers are carried on the 'books' of warships and RFAs, the rank system is altered slightly because the Corps is then considered to be subject to the Naval Discipline Act rather than the Army Act 1955. This also applies to RM officers attached to Naval establishments (see above).

WRNS & QARNNS

As with their male Naval counterparts, these two branches of the RN are subject to the Naval Discipline Act 1957. Because they use their own ranks it is necessary to draw up a table for corresponding ranks, and read in conjunction with the earlier rank tables (see overleaf).

Special clothing

The Royal Navy has developed clothing to suit its specific needs over the years, including the now familiar white hood and gloves of anti-flash gear, worn with action dress aboard ship. On the flight deck, there are various special dresses for fire fighters and other flight deck personnel, including heavy-weather jackets, protective caps with integral ear-defenders and life-jackets with face protection. In the engine room, machinery control room or boiler room, the Engineering Department usually wear as little as possible, usually just a white overall with cap. This can be considered to be their working rig, which is navy blue shirt and tough trousers elsewhere on the ship.

In Northern Ireland, the Royal Marines have adopted the standard British Army dress and equipment for specific operations and this is well illustrated in the companion *Encyclopaedia of the Modern British Army*.

Standard Temperate Combat Dress is made up of

Corresponding Ranks

RN	QARNNS	WRNS
Admiral of the Fleet	-	-
Admiral	-	-
Vice Admiral	-	-
Rear Admiral	-	-
Commodore	Matron-in-Chief	Commandant
Captain	Principal Matron	Superintendent
Commander	Matron	Chief Officer
Lieutenant Commander	Superintending Sister	First Officer
Lieutenant	Senior Nursing Sister	Second Officer
Sub-Lieutenant	Nursing Sister	Third Officer
Fleet Chief Petty Officer	-	Fleet Chief Wren
Chief Petty Officer	Head Naval Nurse	Chief Wren
Petty Officer	Assistant Head Naval Nurse	Petty Officer Wren
Leading Rating	Senior Naval Nurse	Leading Wren
Able Rating	Naval Nurse	Wren
(Ordinary Seaman)		
Junior Rating	-	Probationary Wren

85 86 87 88 89 90

91 92 93 94 95 96

97 98 99 100 101 102 103 104

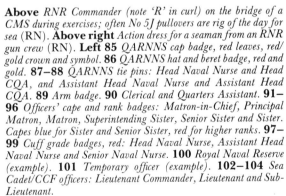

Above *RNR Commander (note 'R' in curl) on the bridge of a CMS during exercises; often No 5J pullovers are rig of the day for sea (RN).* **Above right** *Action dress for a seaman from an RNR gun crew (RN).* **Left 85** *QARNNS cap badge, red leaves, red/ gold crown and symbol.* **86** *QARNNS hat and beret badge, red and gold.* **87–88** *QARNNS tie pins: Head Naval Nurse and Head CQA, and Assistant Head Naval Nurse and Assistant Head CQA.* **89** *Arm badge.* **90** *Clerical and Quarters Assistant.* **91– 96** *Officers' cape and rank badges: Matron-in-Chief, Principal Matron, Matron, Superintending Sister, Senior Sister and Sister. Capes blue for Sister and Senior Sister, red for higher ranks.* **97– 99** *Cuff grade badges, red: Head Naval Nurse, Assistant Head Naval Nurse and Senior Naval Nurse.* **100** *Royal Naval Reserve (example).* **101** *Temporary officer (example).* **102–104** *Sea Cadet/CCF officers: Lieutenant Commander, Lieutenant and Sub- Lieutenant.*

jacket, trousers and occasionally hat made in DPM (disruptive patterned material) and worn with DMS boots (directly moulded soles). The Denison smock of the parachutists is also worn but this is no longer issued new. Tropical combat gear is more lightweight and suited to the climatic conditions near the equator, whilst Cold Weather Clothing is equally as complete for operation in Norway.

The former standard helmet is now being replaced by a glass reinforced plastic variant for the Royal Marines, whilst the RN still wears the

American-style curved and round helmet for action duties, including missile crews (such as the Seacat aimer, who also wears a special badge to display his skill). More often than not, both RN and RM action dress head gear is the beret.

NBC clothing

Nuclear, Biological and Chemical warfare is not new to the Royal Navy nor the Royal Marines, but today's methods of protecting personnel are based on high technology and experience. It is not possible to give more than an indication of the current clothing available to the Royal Marines and Naval ratings ashore as a Naval party, but the reader will gain an insight to the real world of NBC.

Basically, a two-piece suit is used and the current system is Suits Protective NBC No 1 Mark 3 manufactured by Remploy Limited of London. The smock has two layers of materials: the inner, anti- gas, and the outer nylon layer, complete with integral hood which fits in with the standard Service (S6) Respirator. A detector plate is carried to give warning of the hazard being experienced. Quick adjustments to the wrists, neck, etc, are important. The trousers also have two layers of material and there are gloves and special overboots to complete the 'noddy suit'. NBC No 1 Mark 2 is the Naval equivalent of the RM suit. Weight: smock 0.8 kg; trousers 0.66 kg.

Aircrew have the benefit of a special inner NBC Mark 1 Undercoverall Flyers NBC which is designed as an inner garment to be worn under a flying suit, on top of 'long johns'. A special hood is also issued and there are socks available. The hood is worn over the standard Type 'G' Aircrew helmet and can be used with the AR5 Respirator. Weight: inner coverall 0.6 kg; hood 0.12 kg; socks 0.09 kg.

The standard non-aircrew respirator is the Haversack Respirator (Anti-Gas) S6 Mark 2 which is carried in a haversack 26 × 21 × 13 cm and weighs 0.4 kg. Casualties are cared for with Casualty Bags, either Whole or Half.

Flags and Pennants

The White Ensign—the red cross of St George with the Union Flag in the top left-hand corner, against the host—is carried by all vessels of the Royal Navy, including the Avon Seariders operated by the Royal Marines in Hong Kong waters. In harbour or at anchor it is customary for the Ensign to be worn at the Ensign Staff on the quarterdeck, but at sea it is more usual to see a warship with the Ensign at the gaff (from the fore- or mainmast). In the morning and at sunset, the 'colours' are hoisted and struck respectively, whether the 'vessel' is a ship or a shore establishment. The Alert is sounded by pipe or bugle (larger ships only) and all officers and men on deck face aft and stand at the salute until the 'carry on' is sounded. In establishments, the officers and men in the open stand at the salute facing the Ensign. One warship will also salute another when passing at sea or on entering/leaving harbour. The rules are a little complex, and are considered outside the scope of this book.

Flags

Royal Standard This is the personal flag of the Sovereign, the Lord High Admiral, and is only hoisted when the Sovereign is actually present; it is struck when the Sovereign departs. HMY *Britannia* wears the Royal Standard at sea and in harbour whenever the Sovereign is aboard.

White Ensign As described above; came into full and complete use in 1864.

Union Flag The flag of the United Kingdom of Great Britain and Northern Ireland is worn at the jackstaff (bow) of all RN vessels at anchor or alongside, unless escorting the Royal Yacht or another vessel in which the Sovereign is present. It is

also the flag of an Admiral of the Fleet. This flag is only called the 'Union Jack' when used as a jack from the jackstaff

Admiral's flag A red cross of St George against a white background; like all flags is worn at the mainmast or foremast, or from the establishment flagstaff.

Vice Admiral's flag As for Admiral but with a red ball in the upper left corner next to the hoist.

Rear Admiral's flag As for Admiral but with two red balls next to the hoist.

Pennants

Commodore's pennant A red cross of St George against a white background with a red ball next to the hoist.

Senior Officer's pennant A white/green/white/ green/white pennant worn at the yardarm of the ship bearing the most senior officer when warships are in harbour.

Commissioning pennant Worn from the day a ship commissions until she is de-commissioned. It is not struck until that day, unless temporarily replaced by a Royal Standard or appropriate flag.

Paying-off pennant When a ship is nearing de-commissioning, she wears a paying-off pennant—a red cross of St George against a white background— which is proportional to the length of the commission. It is apparently a custom rather than a requirement in the RN. It is only worn when entering or leaving harbour, and on Sundays, during this time.

Pennant number This is the group of letter(s) and number(s) worn on the hull and stern of British warships and auxiliaries being made up of a 'flag superior' letter denoting type and the hull number. They are carried in black with a white outline, or white on black hulls. Certain vessels, including submarines and survey ships, do not carry them.

A   Auxiliary (also Y, which is not carried)
C   Helicopter cruisers
D   Destroyers
F   Frigates
K   Helicopter support ship/diving vessel
L   Assault vessels
M   Mines counter measures vessels
N   Netlayers/MCMV support ships
P   Patrol vessels
R   Carriers
S   Submarines

Some landing craft carry what appear to be pennant numbers but which denote their parent ship (eg, T4 is an LCU from *Intrepid*).

Glossary and index

The following index combines a glossary of abbreviations. Where an abbreviation is common, eg, RN, it is not indexed as it would be of no value as a reference. Entries in italics are ships' names, numerals in italics refer to illustrations. (Index compiled by Lyn Greenwood.)

The classic role of the Royal Maritime Auxiliary Service has always been to serve the Royal Navy—here the tug Dalmatian *and a sister-ship manoeuvre* Hermes (RN).